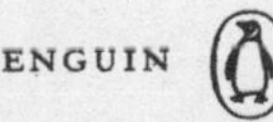

# LIFE OF ST COLUMBA

St Adomnán was born in Ireland *circa* 628, a descendant of St Columba's grandfather. In 679 he became the ninth abbot of Iona. After a mission to Northumbria on behalf of Irish captives there, and a later visit to the monasteries of Wearmouth and Jarrow, he rejected the Celtic customs relative to the date of Easter and other matters. He later played an important role in persuading the northern Irish churches to adopt the Catholic date for Easter, but he was unable to persuade his own monks in Iona. At Birr in Offaly in 697 he was instrumental in the enacting of 'Adomnán's Law' for the protection of women, children and clergy, especially during warfare. He was a peace-loving man, a voice of moderation in the Irish church and a notable biblical scholar. He wrote *On the Holy Places*, the text of which still exists, but his most famous work is the *Life of St Columba*, written at Iona, where he died in 704.

Richard Sharpe is Professor of Diplomatic in the Faculty of Modern History and a fellow of Wadham College, Oxford. His publications include *Raasay: A Study in Island History* (1977–8; 2nd edn, 1982), *A Bibliography of Celtic Latin Literature 400–1200* (with Michael Lapidge, 1985), *Medieval Irish Saints' Lives* (1991), and *A Handlist of the Latin Writers of Great Britain and Ireland before 1540* (1997).

Adomnán of Iona

# LIFE OF ST COLUMBA

*Translated by* RICHARD SHARPE

*Et dixi, Quis dabit mihi pennas sicut Columbae: & uolabo, & requiescam?* Ps. 54:7

PENGUIN BOOKS

PENGUIN BOOKS

Published by the Penguin Group
Penguin Books Ltd, 80 Strand, London WC2R 0RL, England
Penguin Putnam Inc., 375 Hudson Street, New York, New York 10014, USA
Penguin Books Australia Ltd, 250 Camberwell Road, Camberwell, Victoria 3124, Australia
Penguin Books Canada Ltd, 10 Alcorn Avenue, Toronto, Ontario, Canada M4V 3B2
Penguin Books India (P) Ltd, 11 Community Centre, Panchsheel Park, New Delhi – 110 017, India
Penguin Books (NZ) Ltd, Cnr Rosedale and Airborne Roads, Albany, Auckland, New Zealand
Penguin Books (South Africa) (Pty) Ltd, 24 Sturdee Avenue, Rosebank 21 6, South Africa

Penguin Books Ltd, Registered Offices: 80 Strand, London WC2R 0RL, England

www.penguin.com

First published 1995

035



Maps drawn by Nigel Andrews

The tailpieces throughout this volume depict some of the eighty early medieval crosses from the site of the Columban monastery in Iona. These stones, mostly grave-markers, are described in the Royal Commission on the Ancient and Historical Monuments of Scotland's inventory, *Argyll IV: Iona* (Edinburgh 1982), pp. 179–92, from where these drawings are reproduced by permission. The stones depicted are No. 6, 16 (below, p. 99), 19 (p. 106), 22 (p. 108), 44 (p. 153), 60 (St Columba's pillow, p. 205 and n. 411), 37 (p. 234), 53 (p. 369). Crown copyright.

Set in 11/13 pt Monophoto Garamond
Set by Datix International Limited, Bungay, Suffolk
Printed and bound in Great Britain by Clays Ltd, Elcograf S.p.A.



ISBN-13: 978–0–140–44462–9

www.greenpenguin.co.uk

Penguin Books is committed to a sustainable future for our business, our readers and our planet. This book is made from Forest Stewardship Council™ certified paper.

# Contents

# Preface

A source of the first importance for the early history of Ireland and Scotland, Adomnán's Life of St Columba is also the most engaging of the Lives of Celtic saints. It conveys a vivid sense of the holy man among the brethren of his community, often sitting in his little hut in Iona at the centre of the lives of all his monks. Adomnán wrote a century after Columba's death, drawing on the collective memory of the community, on public declarations made in the presence of the abbot and elders over the years, and on stories recorded in writing. Most of his stories are told with circumstantial detail and most have a miracle as their point. Some are biblical miracles in which Columba imitates Christ; others are more like folk tales, occasionally quite out of keeping with a monastic context; and many are everyday miracles – events and impressions interpreted after the event as signs of Columba's sanctity. External reality, superstition, and a theological understanding of the holy man in his relationship to God are so mixed that the Life has appealed to readers across the spectrum of Christian belief and outside it.

The text survives in a manuscript copied at Iona, probably while the author was still alive. The saint himself is presented as someone devoted to the copying of sacred books, and Adomnán gives instructions that each copy made of his work should be carefully compared with its exemplar. In this translation I tried to take such care, though I have been more concerned to express his meaning in English than to replicate his words or his sometimes contrived style. The Introduction sets the scene for Columba, for Adomnán and for the early monastery in Iona. The notes, more extensive than in previous translations, aim chiefly to explain to modern readers what Adomnán's original audience knew, but I have not always resisted the temptation to add stories from later traditions at Derry and Iona.

The translation was based on the Latin text published in 1961 by Alan Orr Anderson and Marjorie Ogilvie Anderson. In 1989 Dr Marjorie Anderson very kindly read over my draft translation and notes, while I read in typescript the introduction to her second edition, published in 1991. I am most grateful to her for this friendly sharing of our independent work and for the improvements she contributed to this book. Other friends and colleagues read the whole book at a later stage, and I am grateful again to Professor Robert Bartlett, Dr Clare Stancliffe, Dr Alan Thacker, and Professor Charles Thomas, for their advice and comments. Help in other ways was given by Noreen Gypson, Professor Pádraig Ó Riain, Dr Paul Russell, Cornelia Starks and the Ven. Yeshe Zangmo, and for this I thank them all.

Columba, Adomnán, and his Life are all rooted in the island of Iona, and I too have returned to stay there several times during the course of my work. Anyone who has looked over the Sound from Iona to Fionnphort will call the view to mind when reading Adomnán's stories about visitors who shouted to attract the attention of the ferryman. Little has changed in that scene of sea and sky. Although we cannot now recover the appearance of the early monastery, Iona has a powerful sense of place, which permeates much of Adomnán's Life; while through the Life one can recapture the atmosphere of Adomnán's and Columba's Iona.

23 September 1994

# MAPS

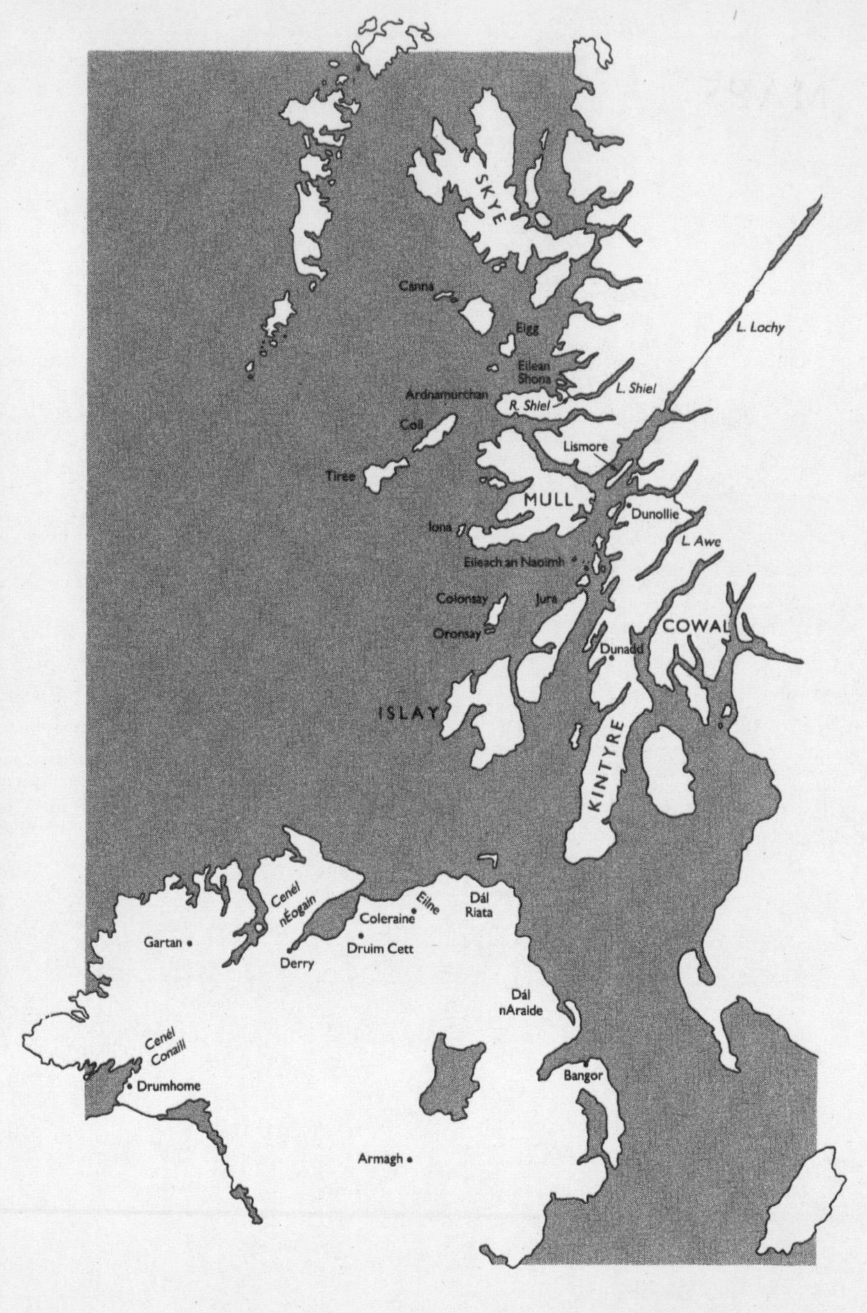

SKYE
Canna
Eigg
Eilean Shona
Ardnamurchan
R. Shiel
L. Shiel
L. Lochy
Coll
Tiree
Lismore
MULL
Dunollie
Iona
L. Awe
Eileach an Naoimh
Colonsay
Jura
Oronsay
COWAL
Dunadd
ISLAY
KINTYRE
Cenél nÉogain
Eilne
Dál Riata
Coleraine
Gartan
Druim Cett
Derry
Dál nAraide
Cenél Conaill
Drumhome
Bangor
Armagh

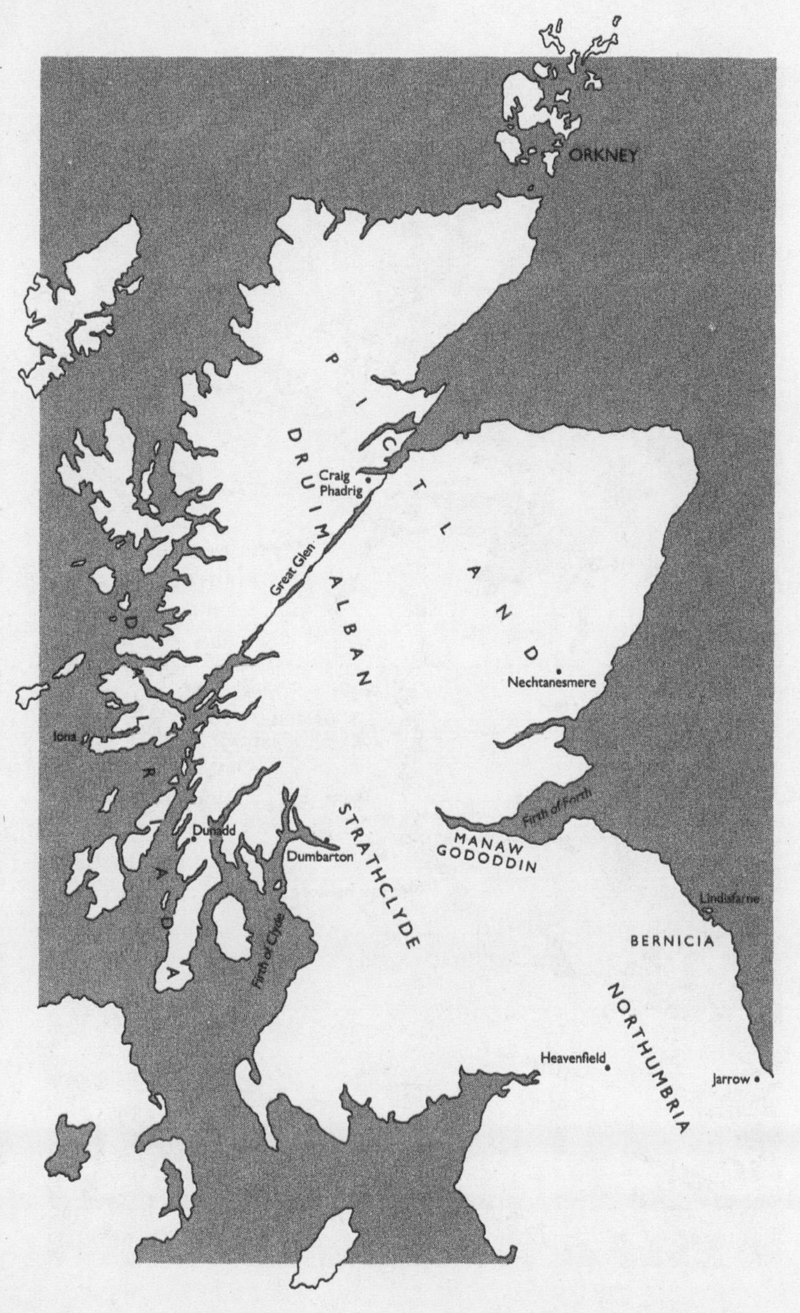
ORKNEY
PICTLAND
DRUIM ALBAN
Craig Phadrig
Great Glen
Nechtanesmere
Iona
DAL RIADA
Dunadd
Dumbarton
STRATHCLYDE
Firth of Forth
MANAW GODODDIN
Firth of Clyde
Lindisfarne
BERNICIA
NORTHUMBRIA
Heavenfield
Jarrow

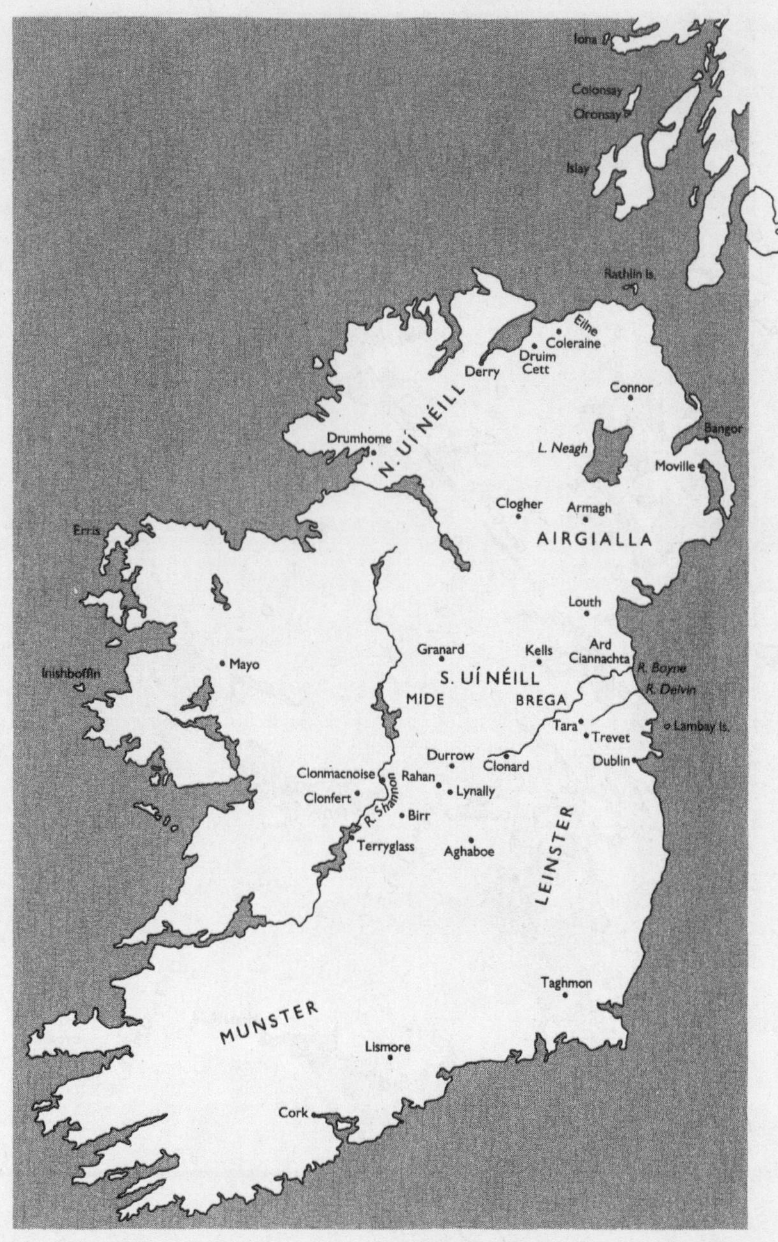
Iona
Colonsay
Oronsay
Islay
Rathlin Is.
Eilne
Coleraine
Druim
Cett
Derry
Connor
N. UÍ NÉILL
Bangor
Drumhome
L. Neagh
Moville
Clogher
Armagh
AIRGIALLA
Erris
Louth
Granard
Kells
Ard
Ciannachta
Mayo
Inishboffin
S. UÍ NÉILL
R. Boyne
R. Delvin
MIDE
BREGA
Tara
Lambay Is.
Trevet
Durrow
Clonard
Dublin
Clonmacnoise
Rahan
Lynally
Clonfert
R. Shannon
Birr
Terryglass
Aghaboe
LEINSTER
Taghmon
MUNSTER
Lismore
Cork

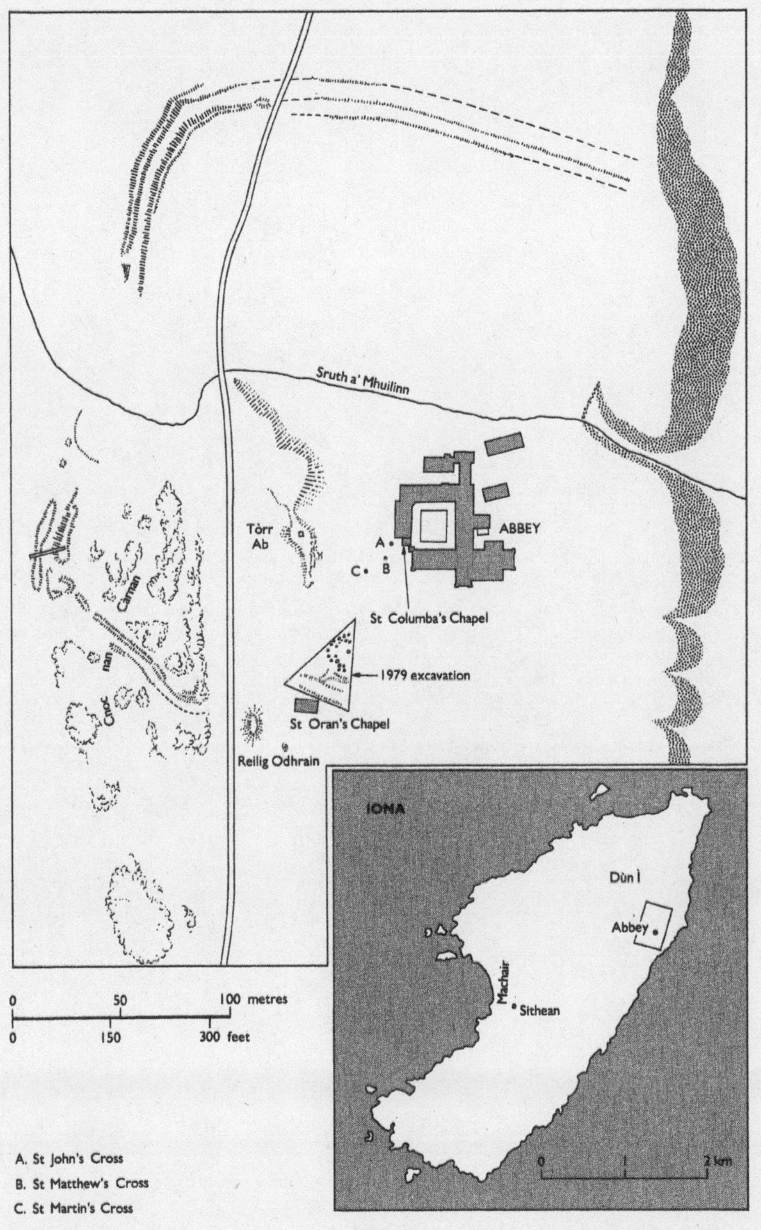

Sruth a' Mhuilinn
Tòrr Ab
ABBEY
A
B
C
St Columba's Chapel
1979 excavation
St Oran's Chapel
Reilig Odhrain
Cnoc nan Carnan
0 50 100 metres
0 150 300 feet
IONA
Dùn Ì
Abbey
Machair
Sithean
0 1 2 km
A. St John's Cross
B. St Matthew's Cross
C. St Martin's Cross

# GENEALOGICAL TABLES

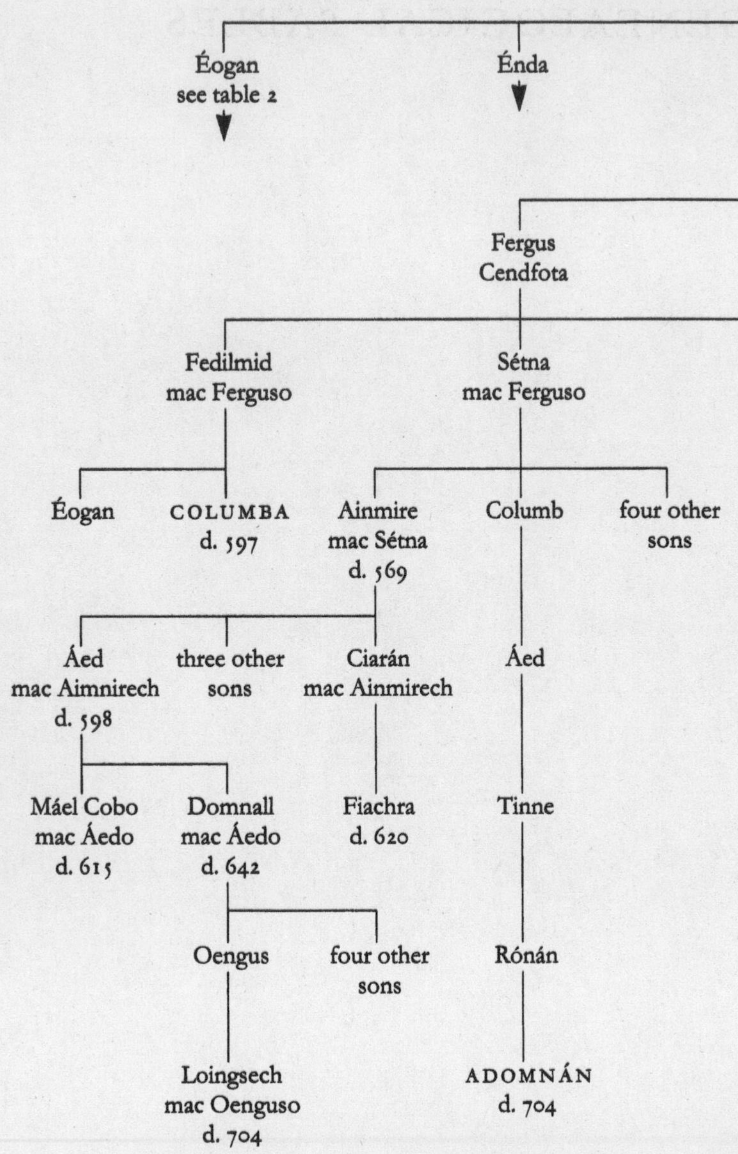


Abbots of Iona in CAPITALS

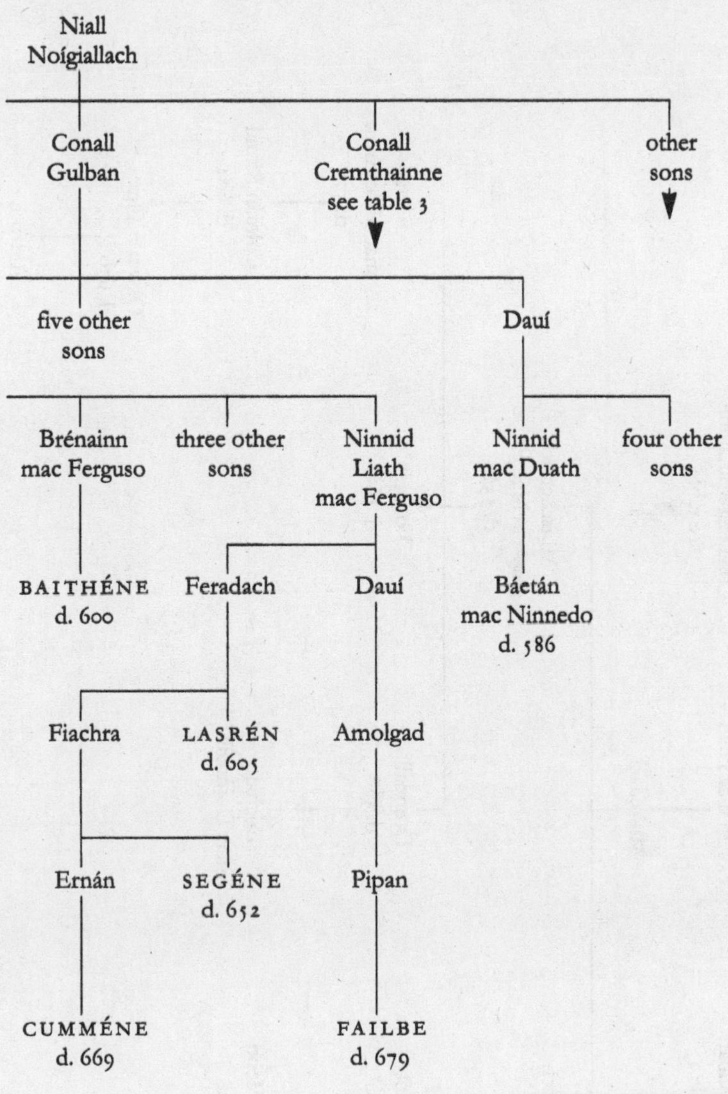


Table 1. *The Northern Uí Néill: Cenél Conaill*

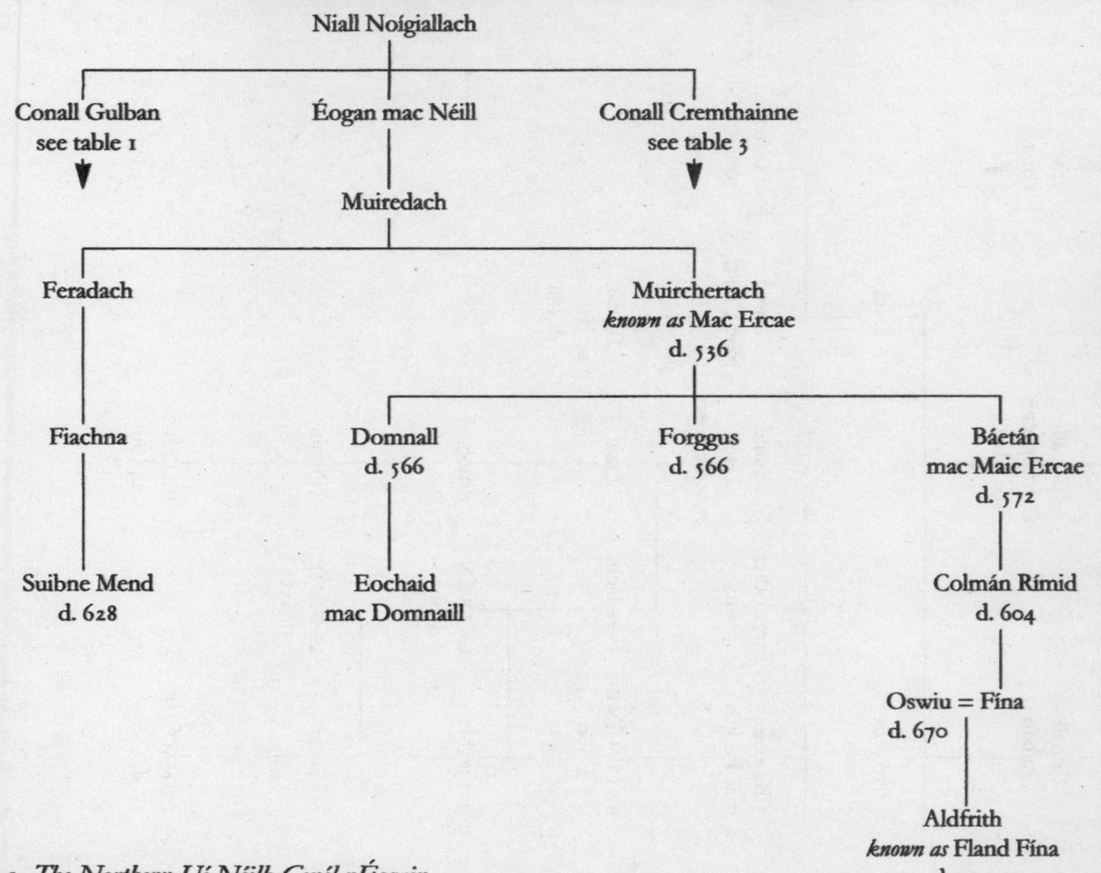


Table 2. *The Northern Uí Néill: Cenél nÉogain*

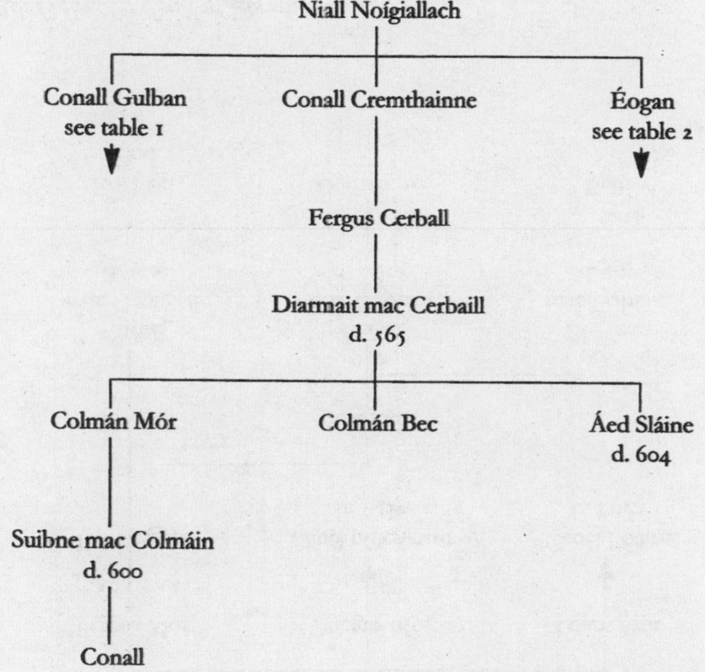


Table 3. *The Southern Uí Néill*

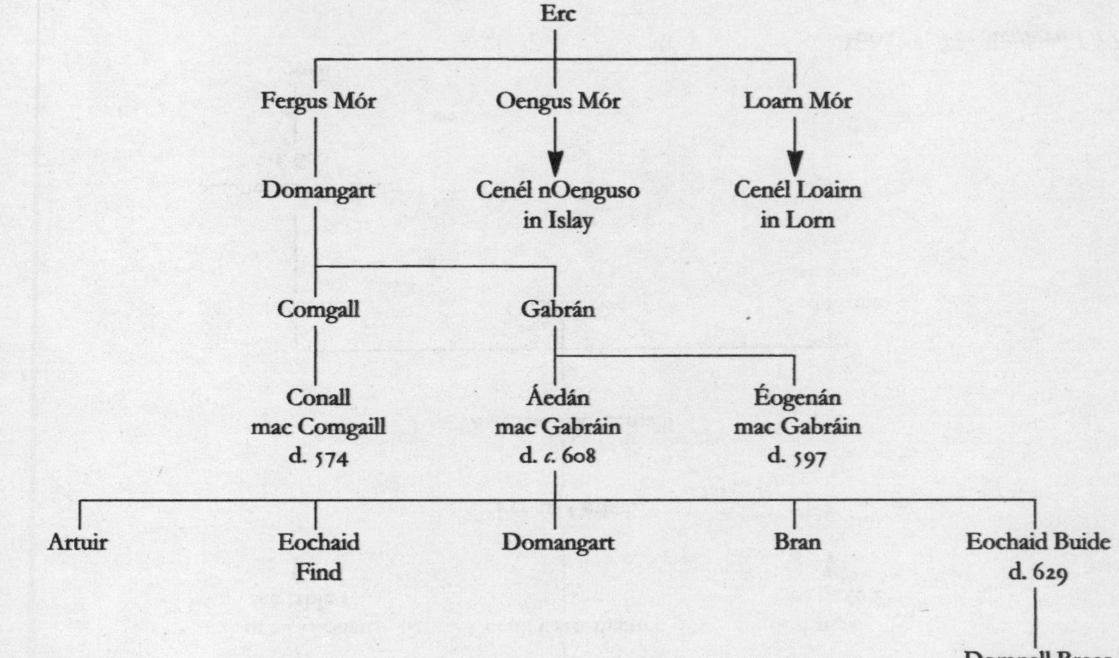


Table 4. *Kings of Scottish Dalriada: Cenél nGabráin*

# Introduction

Columba died on Sunday, 9 June 597. We are told by Adomnán, the author of his Life, that the saint's death occurred in front of the altar of his church at Iona. During his life he had been involved in the most important political events of his time in the north of Ireland and in the west and north of Scotland. Sometimes he appears almost at the centre of these events, but always as a man of religion, a priest and a monk. Columba was born perhaps three generations after the arrival of Christianity in Ireland, and in his time he saw a considerable expansion of the faith both in Ireland and Scotland. It was a period, particularly in Ireland, when the monastic ideal caught the imagination of the recently converted population and drew large numbers of people into the religious life. The founders of religious houses – men and women – were revered for their example, their teaching, their saintliness. St Columba had founded several monasteries, and enjoyed a reputation for holiness that was known through much of Ireland and Scotland, and perhaps further afield.

Columba's lifetime thus coincides with the period in the history of western Britain and Ireland that has become known as the Age of Saints. After so many centuries, it is impossible now to understand what any reasonable person in the sixth century may have thought of the foundation of monasteries and the enthusiasm for the religious life. This may have affected only a relatively small part of the population. Indeed, it is probable that at the time of Columba's death many of the Irish people and most of the inhabitants of Scotland were still pagan. To those involved in the monastic movement, however, it was something of tremendous importance. These were the people who have left a record of the period, and it is through their eyes and those of their successors that historians are likely to view the subject. An early monastic founder of importance was St Ciarán of Clonmacnoise, who died about 549, when Columba was a young man. St Uinniau, mentioned several times in the *Life of St Columba*, was also a generation older than Columba, and predeceased him by twenty years or more. So Columba did not belong to the first generation of saintly monastic founders. Others had died before him, and had become patron saints to the communities they founded, while Columba was still alive.

It is likely that, as soon as it was apparent that his monastic foundations would flourish and continue, Columba's future sainthood was expected by his monks and pupils. It was probably even anticipated in his lifetime. The personal qualities that had drawn Columba into the monastic life and made him a founder of monasteries combined with the expectation of his monks, at a time when men in his position were regularly regarded as saints, to ensure that his life could not disappoint. In a faith that knew and experienced a role continuing beyond the grave, his death was a crowning event that set the seal on his sainthood. The pattern of sanctity was already established while he still lived.

For those of us now attempting to understand his life, these facts have two significant implications. First, it is likely that stories about Columba's sayings and doings would be remembered and retold while he lived, and would continue to be told after his death. Any event, however trivial, that could be seen as revealing the holy man's prophetic or miraculous powers would be picked out and the story shaped to focus on these signs of his sanctity. These stories would later provide material for the written account of his life. Second, it is also likely that his monastic role as founder and saint-to-be largely determined the character of those stories both before and after his death. When it was later decided that such stories should be collected into a book, the nature of the stories and the general interpretation of Columba's life were probably determined by this role. These stories might not represent the whole truth in factual terms – they were from the start devotional truth.

The earliest account of St Columba's life of which we know anything at all was written by Cumméne, a monk of Iona, who was abbot from 657 to 669, the seventh abbot since the foundation. His work, probably written in the 630s or 640s, is only known from a short extract inserted into one copy of the later *Life of St Columba* by Adomnán. Cumméne's book is not referred to as a Life but as 'the book which he wrote on the miraculous powers of St Columba' (*360*).* The later *Life*, written by Adomnán, ninth abbot of Iona (AD 679–704), is made up almost entirely of miracle stories. Most are about powers that Columba was said to enjoy while he lived, and a few relate to other people's experiences after his death.

Many modern readers find such stories of miracles difficult to accept or believe. The eighth duke of Argyll, who was responsible for the restoration of the medieval abbey church at Iona, found many of Adomnán's tales wholly unacceptable. Complaining about 'the atmosphere of miracle in which the whole is presented to us', he even questioned whether Adomnán believed them or whether he resorted to 'deliberate invention'. The duke did not dismiss the work completely; for him, however, 'the imperishable interest of Adomnán's book lies in the vivid though incidental touches of life and manners which he gives us in the telling of his tales.' Yet much of the substance of the book, the argument for

*Italic numbers in brackets refer to the Notes.

Columba's sanctity, he rejected as 'childish and utterly incredible'. This attitude springs from his distaste for Adomnán's cast of mind, which reverenced holiness displayed in miracles. In his own day and with the life of a saint as his subject, Adomnán could hardly have written a book that was not full of miracle stories, for prophecy and miraculous powers were among the gifts of the Spirit (1 Cor. 12:10). These were the proofs that Columba was a saint, so this was the heart of the *Life*. Whether or not one wishes to believe that the events happened as told, they are true to the image of saint that was familiar throughout the seventh century. None the less, in the nature of the case, there is a major problem of historical credibility. Even if one accepts that the legend of St Columba had already begun to take shape at the time of his death, we have no substantial version of that legend until something like a century later.

They were years that witnessed immense changes in Irish society and in the Irish church. In particular, some early saints disappear from view as their churches were eclipsed by those of other saints. For example, a letter written in the 630s to Ségéne, fifth abbot of Iona, mentions a group of leading church founders; the list includes St Nessan, who fades from view before anything was recorded of him. Rahan, Co. Offaly, was regarded as the church of St Camelacus in the early seventh century, but a hundred years later his place had been reassigned to St Mochutu. Even St Patrick's cult seems to have moved in the early seventh century from an obscure church in south-east Ulster to Armagh, previously a major pagan site but by the 630s a church rising fast in importance. Among such changes in the saintly landscape Adomnán stands for us on the horizon: much of what he says ties in with what we learn from other sources of the late seventh and eighth centuries, but from time to time he shows us how things were at the beginning of the seventh century. St Uinniau, of whom more later, is a case in point: Adomnán's references to him are important evidence in getting behind the role given to this sixth-century teacher by eighth-century writers. Although what we know of the career of Columba arouses no strong suspicions that his past was remade in the late seventh century, the changes going on elsewhere should not be overlooked.

What Adomnán wrote about his patron, Columba, stands at the end of three generations of tradition. It was further shaped by Adomnán's personal understanding of the saint and what his life was to represent, and by Adomnán's reading of the Lives of other saints, especially those of St Martin of Tours, St Antony and St Benedict. We have no way of knowing whether Adomnán thought it necessary to distinguish between the outward facts of daily life when Columba was alive and those of his own time, up to a century later. Even the details of monastic life at Iona may have more to do with Adomnán's time than with Columba's. Although a Life written in the late seventh century may apparently promise an authentic account of a saint from the late sixth century, it cannot be trusted as a historical narrative. The Life of a saint was the subject of legend from the start. As circumstances changed, new interests could reshape the perception of the past. In the hands of an author such as Adomnán, the *Life* may be used to serve ends quite unknown or irrelevant to the saint himself.

Further, though Adomnán's *Life* is for us the first major instalment of the legend of St Columba, the story continued to grow and change. St Columba appears in the Lives of other saints written in Ireland during the eighth century and later. Other stories about him are known from Middle Irish texts of the tenth and eleventh centuries. Many more are known from Middle Irish notes, or scholia, written in the church schools as commentaries on older texts. Verses in both Latin and Irish written long after the saint's death were fathered on him, perhaps from as early as the seventh century, and in quantity during the eleventh and twelfth centuries.

About 1160 a new version of his Life was written in Irish: this text became widely but incorrectly known as the 'Old Irish Life', thanks to a translation by W. M. Hennessy published in 1876. It is a Life cast in the form of a homily or sermon, but it belongs to the period of late Middle Irish, not Old Irish. I shall refer to it as the Middle Irish homily on St Columba. Still later, in 1532, a long *Life of St Columba* was assembled in Early Modern Irish by Manus O'Donnell, a scholar-prince who was to become the ruler of Donegal. Even more recently stories and verses from popular tradition in Gaelic have enriched the legend of St Columba.

When legend has been handed down over such a long period, both losses and accretions are inevitable. Stories may take on different forms or be given a different emphasis according to the interests of those who retell them. In one respect, however, the legend of St Columba differs from that of all other saints of Ireland or Britain: it became the subject of more or less learned discourse in the late eighteenth century, since when older and younger traditions have been combined and reinterpreted in new ways.

It may in one sense be compared with the legend of St Patrick, which experienced a similar development in Ireland in the nineteenth century and after. The materials, however, on which the Patrick legend was based were less diverse than the materials of St Columba's legend, the rational and the devotional approaches were further apart, and it has been possible to see the St Patrick of history emerge from the St Patrick of legend. A hundred years ago churchmen of different persuasions, and their divided flocks, manipulated the Patrick legend to present two distinct versions – catholic and protestant – but in this century a liberal rational version of the legend by J. B. Bury was long accepted as history. This has now given way to a more limited account, based on St Patrick's own writings. Perhaps because the legendary version of St Columba never acquired the academic authority of

Professor Bury's St Patrick, there has been less effort to strip away accretions. Moreover, there is no firm foundation on bedrock to which one can return as one can to St Patrick's own writings. Adomnán is the fullest early source, but how far can he be trusted for historical information? Only perhaps where he can be tested against other sources.

Two such sources are most prominent. First, the texts that I refer to as the Irish annals are a series of different annal collections, of various dates, which for this period ultimately depend on year-by-year notes begun in Iona – perhaps in St Columba's time, but if not, then probably no later than the 630s, though entries become more numerous after about 660. The most important of these annal collections, incorporating the records from Iona but continued at different places down the years to the early sixteenth century, is referred to as the Annals of Ulster. Second, there are the chapters on St Columba and on Adomnán himself in Bede's *Ecclesiastical History of the English People*, written a generation later in 731. Bede is rightly respected for his authority as a source for Anglo-Saxon history, although any serious reading must also take account of the limitations both of his information and his interpretation. What he knew about St Columba and Iona was not firsthand and often has to be regarded as unreliable.

In the remainder of this Introduction I shall discuss what can be reliably known about St Columba and his age, and of Iona from then to the time of Adomnán and some way beyond. Where I refer to elements of the story known only from later legend, I shall try to distinguish these as clearly as possible. Thereafter I aim to show how the early and medieval legends have fed the imagination of modern writers to produce the modern legend of St Columba. By presenting the *Life* by Adomnán in a fresh English translation, I hope both to serve the needs of those who wish to understand the history of the early Church in Ireland and Scotland, and to provide a sound starting-point for those who wish still to take St Columba into their imagination.

### *St Columba, his early life*

Although Adomnán's *Life* will always be regarded as the principal source of information about St Columba's work, it is unhappily the case that Adomnán is very sparing of facts in the form of dates or significant events. It was not his intention to provide a biography as a historical record, and what he does say is not always in agreement with the evidence of the Irish annals or of Bede. First, therefore, I shall outline Columba's career.

His parents are named by Adomnán as Fedelmid mac Ferguso and Eithne. Fergus, Columba's paternal grandfather, was the son of Conall Gulban, the ancestor of the famous lineage of Cenél Conaill ('the kindred of Conall', from whom the district of Tyrconnel is also named). In the sixth and seventh centuries the Cenél Conaill was one of several lineages, occupying lands in the area of what is now Donegal and Tyrone, who expressed their relationship in terms of descent from a common ancestor. That ancestor, Niall Noígiallach ('Niall of Nine Hostages'), was supposedly the father of the ancestors from whom these lineages took their names. Thus Conall, progenitor of Cenél Conaill, and Énda and Éogan, progenitors of Cenél nÉnda and Cenél nÉogain (the latter give their name to Tyrone), were supposed to be brothers, the sons of Niall, and their lineages were collectively termed Uí Néill ('descendants of Niall'). A number of other lineages living in central and eastern Ireland also regarded themselves as descendants of Niall, through other sons, and it is now conventional to distinguish the lineages of Donegal and Tyrone as the Northern Uí Néill from the other lines of descent, the Southern Uí Néill. Most of these Uí Néill lineages were the ruling family in the territory they occupied, and the head of these would have called himself 'king' within that territory. Through the sixth and seventh centuries the kings of Cenél Conaill vied with those of Cenél nÉogain for a position of superiority over the other dynasties of the Northern Uí Néill; the successful 'overking' could take hostages from the other kings of the region. In the course of time the different Uí Néill lineages came to recognize a supreme overlord, called the king of Tara or the high king. On his father's side, therefore, Columba was born into a powerful, ruling family. Of his mother's lineage little can be said (*16*).

The date of Columba's birth is uncertain, but may be estimated from the date of his death. According to the Irish annals, he was seventy-five at that time; according to Bede, seventy-seven. Subtracting these figures from the known date of Columba's death, we may compute that he was born around 520–22. Later evidence favours 521 and makes Columba's age seventy-six at the time of his death. The village of Gartan in Co. Donegal is celebrated as the place of his birth, but this depends on a tradition that cannot be traced earlier than the Middle Irish homily in the twelfth century. The story may perhaps be doubted, since Gartan lies outside the territory ruled directly by Cenél Conaill. It probably reflects an interest of the author of the homiletic Life, who lived at Derry.

Adomnán leads one to believe that Columba was from boyhood – indeed, from before his birth – meant for the church. In the timeless perspective of theology this was so, as Adomnán would have understood from Romans 8:27–30. Within the framework of history, however, it is surprising. Of all the sixth-century monastic founders Columba is the only one to have been closely connected to a royal lineage of considerable power. His family's attitude to his choice of a religious life can hardly be imagined at this remove. By the time Columba died, the Uí Néill dynasties were more or less Christian in their observances, and some of his close kinsmen were monks. In Columba's boyhood, however, the most powerful Uí Néill rulers continued the pagan practice of royal inauguration, *Feis Temro* 'the Feast of Tara' (*157*). Active hostility to the church continued in some quarters right through Columba's life, as Adomnán was ready to admit.

It is possible – but only at the level of conjecture – that Adomnán has chosen to suppress the fact that Columba was born into a pagan family, perhaps with the given name of Crimthann, which much later tradition attributes to him. In this early phase of Christianity it is possible that a convert would assume a new name on baptism. Such a change of name, in this context, might account for the emphasis that Adomnán in his preface puts on the Christian connotations of the name Columb or, in Latin, Columba. It may seem odd to the modern mind that Adomnán preferred to depict Columba as Christian from birth rather than as one who rejected his pagan environment and chose baptism – like so many saints in the last centuries of the Roman Empire – but such a preference can be paralleled in the Life of St Brigit, written in Adomnán's time. Here too the author, Cogitosus, omitted all the information that the other Lives have about his subject's pagan parents, a slave-girl and a nobleman; instead, he simply quotes from St Paul, Romans 8:29, adding that Brigit was born into a noble, Christian family. The two Lives have in common the view that the holy person's sanctity is unaffected by time: they were as holy at birth as at death. As a result, both texts pay scant attention to straightforward chronological narrative.

We have to pick our way through Adomnán's book to discover the saint's career. If his childhood was in reality spent in a pagan environment, Adomnán says nothing of that. He tells us how the boy was brought up by a foster-father, according to the custom of his time and country; in Columba's case he was fostered with a priest called Cruithnechán (III 2). Columba's religious studies began at this stage, and later, as a young deacon, he is said to have studied divine wisdom in Leinster, where an older man called Gemmán was his master (II 25). In the first half of the sixth century Leinster may have had the best-established church schools. Columba's contemporary Columbanus was another future saint who studied in Leinster. Adomnán also mentions on more than one occasion that Columba, still a deacon, studied sacred scripture with a bishop called Finnbarr or Finnio or Uinniau (II 1). The variation in the name used by Adomnán for this bishop is a minor source of confusion; worse is the fact that Irish records treat as distinct individuals three men of this name, Finnbarr or Finnian, associating them with different places and different families, and assigning them different dates of death (*210*). Professor Pádraig Ó Riain has suggested that these three identities amount to no more than the attempts of different churches to claim Finnbarr or Uinniau as their own, a suggestion that derives support from the fluidity of Adomnán's use of the name. Whether or not this suggestion is accepted, there is clear and independent evidence that a holy man named Uinniau was influential as a monastic teacher in Ireland about the middle of the sixth century. The name Uinniau is British in form, not Irish; he probably came originally from western Britain, but his career was spent mainly in Ireland, where the name came to be pronounced Finnio. He wrote a little book on the penances for different sins, which still survives. According to a statement of Columbanus, Uinniau sought advice on matters of monastic discipline from a leading British teacher called Gildas; it is possible that passages attributed to Gildas in a seventh-century religious handbook came from his reply to Uinniau. At any rate, one can be reasonably confident that this Uinniau, whatever the connection between him and the Finnians of later Irish sources, was active and influential in the monastic movement in Ireland. He would be an elder contemporary of Columba, and a very plausible teacher for the young saint.

With the exception of the passages in which Adomnán mentions these teachers, no authority exists for any statement relating to the first forty or so years of Columba's life. There are other stories in the *Life* that may fit into these years, but of this there can be no certainty and little confidence. We do not know how long Columba spent in study, nor what he did between the completion of his studies and his departure from Ireland in 563.

The great turning point in Columba's career, the central event that most determines his historical significance, was his leaving Ireland to found the monastery at Iona. The circumstances of his departure, and the reasons for it, have been much discussed. If we had only the testimony of Adomnán, there would be little room for discussion, since he says merely that Columba 'sailed away from Ireland to Britain choosing to be a pilgrim for Christ'. Pilgrimage outside one's native district had a strong devotional attraction in the Ireland of St Columba, and pilgrimage overseas was regarded as a sign of greater dedication and devotion than pilgrimage within Ireland (*122*, *310*). Many other pilgrims subsequently visited Columba in Iona, and some sought to stay there as his monks. In this context the contemporary Irish reader of Adomnán – and to a large extent any audience in England and on the Continent – would seek no further to understand Columba's reasons.

Other evidence, however, makes the picture more complicated: to pursue the question thoroughly would not be profitable, but it is desirable to explain some of the theories that have gained widespread currency. First, Adomnán on two occasions (in the second preface and in I 7) dates Columba's pilgrimage about two years after the battle of Cúl Drebene. He makes no explicit connection between the two events, and the unprejudiced reader may assume that it was a convenient fixed point, widely understood, from which to date the saint's voyage. The Annals of Ulster, however, say that the battle was won by his Northern Uí Néill kinsmen 'through the prayers of St Columba'. The Annals of Tigernach give a more developed account, perhaps dating from the tenth century, saying that Columba's prayers drove away a mist conjured by pagan priests to conceal the opposing army of King Diarmait mac Cerbaill, high king and Southern Uí Néill overlord. By the eleventh century the story had grown up that Columba's involvement in the battle was the reason for his pilgrimage to Britain – whether as his chosen penance or as an exile imposed by others. A later medieval Life of St Molaisse has it that St Columba consulted Molaisse as a confessor and was advised to go into perpetual exile from Ireland to expiate the sin of having caused so many men to die in the battle. Still later versions, given at length by Manus O'Donnell, provide a story of how and why Columba caused the battle, and so on. It is extremely dangerous to accept any link between the battle and Columba's leaving of Ireland, but it is possible – on the evidence of the annals – that Columba actively supported his own king against the high king.

Second, it has also often been suggested that Columba's pilgrimage was imposed on him by the decision of the Synod of Teltown to which Adomnán refers (III 3). Adomnán says that Columba was excommunicated by the synod for some trivial offences, and that this was later held to have been a miscarriage of justice. The synod has even been dated to 562, between the battle and Columba's departure on pilgrimage. There is no foundation at all for any link between the synod and the battle; the association between the synod and Columba's pilgrimage depends on Adomnán's comment, apparently to be read at the end of his account of the synod, that 'during this period St Columba crossed to Britain' (*356*).

Dr Máire Herbert has put forward a persuasive suggestion to rationalize the supposed link between the battle, the synod and Columba's decision to enter his pilgrimage. In 561 Columba could not dissociate himself from the political and military concerns of his kin, and he prayed for their success, presumably in a public manner. His kin were successful and the high king was defeated. Teltown, where the synod met, was the scene of an annual fair, a coming together of people from all the territories of the Southern Uí Néill. The defeated king was their overlord, and he may have used his influence to persuade the clergy to act against Columba. Since King Diarmait was apparently a pagan, one must wonder whether it can be believed that the clergy would act for him in this way; but there is no getting away from the location of the synod at Teltown in his territory. Again, Dr Herbert suggests, Columba's role as a man of religion was compromised because he could not escape association with his family's political interests or hostility from their enemies. Wearied by these events, she proposes, he may have chosen to leave Ireland in the hope of releasing his religious commitment from the entanglement of Irish dynastic politics.

This interpretation of the circumstances makes perfectly good sense and explains, first, the connection assumed to underlie Adomnán's dating of Columba's departure by reference to the battle; second, the mention of Columba's prayers in the annal entry for the battle; and third, the inferred connection between Columba's excommunication and his supposed penitential exile. To attempt interpretation on top of so much inference – inference that may have been guided by later and more fanciful legends – seems unnecessary. It presupposes that Adomnán has suppressed unpalatable truth. Dr Alfred Smyth goes so far as to read the *Life* as a *roman-à-clef*, to which the key is the suppressed fact that Columba had actually fought in the battle of Cúl Drebene: to this is attributed his scar, mentioned in III 5; his excommunication by the synod; his penitential exile; even the story of Áed Dub (I 36) finds its place as Adomnán's attempt to recover the favour of the descendants of Diarmait mac Cerbaill, who was defeated in the battle. I cannot see any indication that Adomnán had the need to suppress anything: whatever the reason for Columba's excommunication, it did not lead to long exile or ostracism by the church, for we know that Columba remained a respected figure in Ireland. His praying for the Northern Uí Néill army before Cúl Drebene need not have been suppressed deliberately, since Adomnán, after all, does not suppress but emphasizes Columba's posthumous role in the downfall of King Cadwallon and Oswald's victory in I 1; he calls it a 'special privilege'. There is no serious reason for thinking that Columba's pilgrimage was undertaken in expiation of blood-guilt. The fact that men stained in this way came to Iona and had penitential exile imposed on them by St Columba (II 39) shows that the elements of the later story are plausible. It does not show that there was any truth in it.

### *St Columba, 'an island soldier'*

There is a picturesque story that St Columba left Ireland vowing never to look on that land again; that he sailed north-east and landed first on Oronsay, the small island connected to Colonsay, but finding that Ireland could still be seen from the higher ground, he continued further until he landed at St Columba's Bay in Iona; having climbed the hill above this bay and found no view of Ireland, he raised a pile of stones there, *Carn Cúil ri Érenn* 'the cairn of Back towards Ireland'. The story is not recorded until a very late date; it is first related by Dr Garnett, who would have heard it when he visited Iona in 1798. Medieval Irish poetry used *Cúl ri Érenn* as a nickname for Columba the exile, so the name of the hill means 'Columba's Cairn'. The story, however, obviously belongs to the Hebrides; it is a folk-tale intended to explain the name of the hill after the saint's nickname had been forgotten. The story has no value as evidence for the sixth century.

The notion that Columba sailed away from Ireland into the void, not knowing where he was going, ties in with the voyage-tales, a type of story known already in the time of Adomnán (*327*). It is not by any means clear that Columba's case fell into this category. The Hebrides were not unknown territory, for there was constant contact established long before the sixth century between northern Ireland and western Scotland. It is quite possible that Columba was already acquainted with Conall mac Comgaill, who was king of Dál Riata in Ireland and Scotland from about 559.

In this connection the question of where St Columba first landed in Britain is tied up with that of who granted to him the site of Iona. The early witnesses again differ. Adomnán says that, two years after the battle of Cúl Drebene, that is, 'when the holy man first set sail from Ireland to be a pilgrim', St Columba clairvoyantly described a battle in Ireland to King Conall mac Comgaill in Britain (I 7). This gives the clear impression that the saint's first destination was the king's stronghold, thought to have been at Dunadd (*136*). King Conall died in 574, and in his obituary notice the annals say that he had given Iona 'as an offering', that is, to God and St Columba. The simplest conjecture, therefore, is to suppose that when Columba arrived in Britain as an unprotected exile, he sought out the protection of the local king – himself an Irishman well connected in northern Ireland – and obtained from him a site where he could settle and build a monastery. This view was rejected by Dr and Mrs Anderson in their edition of the *Life* on the grounds that in the 560s Iona lay in Pictish territory, so that it was outside the power of King Conall to grant the island to Columba. The annal referring to his offering is attributed to a later date, 'long after Iona had passed from the Pictish to the Irish dominion'. Their case rests on the testimony of Bede.

Before looking into the details of the two views, we must pause to consider the political map of western Scotland at this date. Much the greater part of Scotland north of the River Forth was occupied by the Picts, of whom more will be said later in this Introduction (see p. 30). In the south-west of this area, what is now the county of Argyll, such Pictish population as there had been was overtaken, if not actually supplanted, by settlement from northern Ireland. The Irish rulers of this area came from the small territory of Dál Riata, and from them the Irish-occupied area of Argyll is known as Scottish Dál Riata, now conventionally written Dalriada. Connections between Irish and Scottish Dál Riata were quite close, and there may have been Pictish contacts across the channel between Kintyre and the Irish coast at an earlier date. The question here at issue is this: in the 560s did the rulers of Scottish Dalriada control north Argyll, including Mull, Iona and other islands, or was this Pictish territory? There is no evidence bearing on the question outside our three principal authorities, Adomnán, the Irish annals and Bede.

Bede always associates St Columba and Iona with the Picts. He thought that St Columba 'came from Ireland to Britain to preach the word of God in the provinces of the northern Picts'. He supposed that the mission was quickly successful, saying that on arrival in Britain (dated by him to 565) Columba converted the king of the Picts and received from his people the island where he founded his monastery. It is special pleading on the part of the Andersons to argue that 'the Picts who inhabit those parts of Britain', who, Bede says, gave the island to Columba, could be 'the inhabitants of the shores near Iona, to whom Columba would already have taught the Christian faith', rather than the inhabitants of north Britain as a whole. If Bede had meant only some local group of Picts, he could have said so clearly, but his connection between the arrival of St Columba and the conversion of the northern Picts overrides this interpretation. In any case, if it were those Picts local to Iona who gave the island to St Columba after their conversion by him, surely this supposes that they were converted from Iona and that it was already St Columba's base. The argument does not do justice to Bede's meaning, which is simply that Columba had gone to the Pictish king, converted him and his people, and been granted a site. The fact that this site is not close to any Pictish centre, but far to the west in what would shortly be, if it was not already, Dalriadic territory, must cast doubt on Bede's version. More than a century and a half after Columba's arrival Bede is giving us a Pictish version of how they, as a people, were converted.

A quite different view of Columba's first years in the islands has been offered by Dr Smyth in his book *Warlords and Holy Men*. He supposes that Columba may not have settled at Iona until ten years after he came to Britain:

Early Irish tradition – and the *Old Irish Life of St Columba* in particular – have reinforced the popular assumption that Columba founded Iona as soon as he reached Scotland in 563. It is just possible to infer from Adomnán, however, that while Iona did eventually become the headquarters of Columba's mission, it may have been a relatively late foundation, begun as late as 573. A close reading of Adomnán suggests that Columba's earliest base in Scotland was on the unidentified island of Hinba and that he moved from there at the beginning of the reign of Áedán mac Gabráin to take up permanent residence in Iona in 574. (p. 100)

Dr Smyth is right to say that it is a matter of assumption that Columba founded Iona in 563: Adomnán does not say so, the annals do not, and we have already cast doubt on Bede's account. But I challenge Dr Smyth's reading of Adomnán, especially of III 5. According to the story here, while Columba was living on the island of *Hinba*, he was bidden by an angel to ordain Áedán as king; Áedán had already gone to Iona, where the ordination took place in due course. Dr

Smyth's close reading interprets Adomnán's references to 'when the saint was living' in *Hinba* (*194*) as markers designating the earlier years of his mission. He dates the move to Iona from this passage, for Áedán succeeded to the kingship in 574. But the annals have told us that Iona was given to Columba by Áedán's predecessor, Conall mac Comgaill. It makes no sense to suppose that Columba should have delayed taking up the gift until Áedán preceded him to Iona for ordination, nor that the ordination should take place at an undeveloped site. On the contrary, if we accept what Adomnán says, this passage demonstrates that in 574 Iona was already Columba's principal church, where Áedán expected to find him and where he was to be ordained. *Hinba* was an outlying house where Columba stayed from time to time (*194*). Thus, when Adomnán tells us that the saint was in Iona, he locates an incident at the main church; when the saint was at *Hinba*, he was visiting one of his smaller foundations. There is no distinction here between early and later events. In I 21, when the saint came to *Hinba*, he was presumably coming from Iona. The case for a foundation in another place before Columba settled in Iona is insubstantial, and there is no reason to discard the assumption that Iona, his principal foundation in Britain, was also his first.

According to a short text, translated below (*356*), which is probably as old as Adomnán's *Life*, St Columba first sailed to Britain with twelve companions. This apostolic number may arouse suspicions as to the genuineness of the list, but it must be remembered that St Columba as well as Adomnán knew the gospels; he may have set out deliberately with that number of companions to establish his church in Britain. Assuming as we do that this was at Iona, nothing can be said about the initial foundation. It is not even known whether the island was already inhabited at that time, although there is archaeological evidence for some prehistoric occupation. The fact that Adomnán indicates that the machair was cultivated by the monks suggests that there were no laymen living or working on the island alongside the community. This seems to be confirmed when, at the time of Columba's funeral, bad weather prevented anyone from coming to the island, so that there were only members of the community present.

Stories of 'druids' on the island before his arrival emerge only in eighteenth-century accounts. Druids had a fascination for eighteenth-century antiquaries, who misinterpreted the evidence accordingly. That evidence was ultimately the Middle Irish homily, which has no authority for sixth-century circumstances. It refers to Irish pagan priests (*druí*, plural *druíd*); the passage was repeated by Manus O'Donnell, and, when his book was put into Latin by Fr John Colgan in the seventeenth century, Irish *druí* was translated as *druida*. This was inevitably read as evidence for 'druids' in Iona, and Fraser in 1693 is the first author to mention 'a societie of Druids when Columbus came there'. Eighteenth-century visitors misinterpreted visible antiquities. Thus Bishop Pococke in 1760 started the notion that the medieval structure surviving at Cladh an Dìsirt was 'the remains of a Druid Temple'. An abandoned burial ground, Cladh nan Druineach, near Martyrs' Bay, became 'Druids' burial place' on Douglas's plan of 1769. *Druineach* means 'craftsman', not druid, and the site is referred to only by sources from the period of the druid craze. This misleading story, therefore, should be laid to rest for good.

We may wonder how Columba and his companions were supplied with food or with building materials during their first season on Iona. It appears from III 22–3 that Columba began his pilgrimage in Britain in early June (*395*). Even if he came to Iona after only a short stay with King Conall, there can have been no time to clear ground and plant and harvest a crop before the winter. The new foundation must have depended on outside help for more than a year. The first monks of Iona were not, like the Pilgrim Fathers of 1620, cut off from willing sources of supply. Yet once established, the church at Iona must have grown rapidly both in reputation and in the number of its monks. The growing community attracted monks from different parts of Ireland and from other nations. We learn that the first of the community to die in Iona was a Briton; two of Columba's monks, Pilu and Genereus, are said to have been Englishmen; and we hear too of a Pictish monk, apparently also from Iona, travelling in Ireland. In Columba's lifetime, then, all four nations who lived in what is now Scotland were represented at Iona.

By the year 574 Iona appears to be an established centre with at least one dependency, *Hinba*. At different stages two of Columba's original twelve companions served as prior of *Hinba*, his cousin Baithéne and his uncle Ernán. Other daughter houses were also founded in the Hebrides, of which the most important was at Mag Luinge in the island of Tiree. It is possible that this house was established to take advantage of Tiree's fertile soils to supply the monks of the community in Iona and elsewhere. Nothing, however, is known about the foundation of the monastery at Mag Luinge. The fact that Columba appointed a prior in both these houses, as he did in his Irish foundation of Durrow, shows that these dependencies were linked to Iona under an organized structure of authority.

The *Life* mentions other daughter houses of Iona, including one on the island of *Elen*, not certainly identified, and another on the mainland near Loch Awe. Adomnán also shows that Columba and other members of the community travelled widely round the west coast of Scotland, visiting Eigg, and Skye to the north and other islands and coasts in the Firth of Lorn and southwards. One such visit, to Ardnamurchan, seems to be datable to 572 (*89*). What Adomnán does not make clear is the relationship between Columba, his churches and the local population. On one occasion we find Columba performing a baptism in Ardnamurchan, and there is a prevailing sense that the people living within reach looked to Iona for a ministry. We are left to guess at the extent to which the monks were also priests, involved in pastoral work, perhaps even missionary work, or whether some foundations were devoted strictly to the monastic life. Adomnán does not suggest anywhere that the people of Dalriada were pagans; he treats them as Christians who loyally regarded Columba as a local holy man, to whom they showed considerable devotion. Occasional references to evil men who did not live by any Christian morality do not imply that paganism in the western highlands and islands was any more prevalent than in Ireland. In general, however, the *Life* gives very little information about the kind of society in these areas, and without it it is very difficult to form conjectures about the church's role.

Adomnán implies that the Irish were settled as far north as Ardnamurchan. There are enough references to agriculture or stock-raising for us to accept that the coastal areas were well settled. One story shows a poor, apparently landless family living by hunting and fishing in the wilds; the obvious implication is that no cultivable land was left unsettled. Indeed, the scatter of forts and dùns from the Iron Age suggests that all or most of the usable land had been occupied for generations. What is missing, however, is any indication of the social structure of Dalriada. There are no references to local chiefs or lords, and very few to members of the ruling dynasties apart from the actual rulers. The rich man Feradach, who lived in Islay and acted as host to an exiled Pict (II 23), was presumably a landowner and stock-raiser with tenants under him, but we do not know whether he enjoyed aristocratic status. Adomnán would probably have specified if Feradach had belonged to the royal lineage, as he does in the case of the turbulent sons of Conall mac Domnaill (II 22, 24).

One point that emerges quite clearly is this: however thinly scattered the settlements of the west coast may have been, communications were good. Columba himself was at the centre of a network of communications, involving travel by land and sea; he was in contact with many places in Dalriada, with his own churches in Ireland, and with Irish leaders and people in many other places; he was sufficiently familiar with the king of the Strathclyde Britons to regard him as a friend; he was able to visit Pictland, and presumably to retain contact with the churches that we are told he founded among the Picts. It is a mistake to imagine that Iona was remote and isolated from contacts with Ireland and Britain. The time taken in travelling from Iona to the Columban church at Derry was doubtless less than that taken to reach Derry from Durrow. In neither case is the distance a problem; the Irish of the seventh century were quite accustomed to travelling considerable distances over land or by water. Most of Dalriada was easily accessible by boat, and from Cowal or Kintyre it was even easier to cross the Firth of Clyde to Dumbarton and the British kingdom of Strathclyde. From here the Clyde–Forth route led to the east and south, into an area where in Columba's lifetime the Britons of Gododdin were losing ground to the English as the kingdom of Bernicia came into existence. From Dalriada the Great Glen provided an accessible route to northern Pictland, while the Clyde–Forth line gave access to Fife and the south of Pictland as well as to Northumbria. Such isolation as Iona suffered was due to periods of bad weather, when the sea was too dangerous to travel, and not to any supposed remoteness. Adomnán gives the impression that this was from time to time a temporary inconvenience, but the men of the community were experienced seamen, with boats suited to their needs; the sea was much more an aid to communication than an obstacle.

The organization of the network of Columba's monasteries, not to mention any political or other contacts and interests, demanded regular communication through the islands and into both Ireland and mainland Scotland. We learn that Columba used to send envoys on the business of the monastery.

One such envoy, Luigbe moccu Min (*133*), was sent to Dunadd on one occasion and to Dumbarton on another; Luguid Látair was sent to Ireland as envoy, but members of the community seem also to have changed their place of residence between Durrow, Derry, Iona and other houses. Conversely, Columba was constantly receiving visitors from Ireland and elsewhere. On some occasions Adomnán specifically mentions their bringing news of this or that event.

These visitors were sometimes local people, from Mull or Cenél Loairn, visiting their local holy man. Some of the visitors were penitents, seeking amendment of life on pilgrimage outside Ireland. Some became monks and lived out their days in the community. Other visitors were long-term exiles from troubles at home, hoping to find refuge for a time under Columba's protection. These stories are told with local detail and carry considerable conviction.

Doubts creep in where the visitors are saints from other parts of Ireland. For example, can one really credit the gathering of SS Comgall, Cainnech, Brendan and Cormac sailing from Ireland together and finding St Columba in *Hinba*? In stories of this sort Adomnán is writing within a hagiographical tradition in which saints recognize and support one another. Unlike the authors of some Lives of Irish saints, Adomnán does not introduce dramatic anachronisms. The contacts described could have taken place: St Cainnech, for example, enjoyed some cult in Scotland, and his own Life, written probably in the eighth century, made use of Adomnán's work; St Brendan, according to the author of his Life, was said to have founded a monastery at *Ailech* in the Hebrides, which has sometimes been identified with Eileach an Naoimh. It is not possible, however, to be confident in trusting these stories of saintly visitors. One feature of them is their strongly Irish slant. Two saints, Mauchteus and Uinniau, are mentioned in ways that do make sense in a sixth-century context but which are problematical at a later date;

the other saints were all famous in Ireland in the late seventh and eighth centuries. Yet the *Life* makes no mention of St Donnan (d. 617), the patron of Eigg (an island visited by Baithéne), nor of St Moluag, according to later legend a pupil of St Comgall at Bangor and founder of the church at Lismore in the Firth of Lorn. Dedications of churches to both these saints suggest that they enjoyed a widespread cult in the Hebrides. Where Adomnán quotes Columba's words to Baithéne prophesying the coming of St Fintan, he speaks of Baithéne's 'not wishing to keep this man in our islands' (I 2). While there were Columban churches on several of the islands, there were other churches among the islands that were not associated with Iona. The *Life* makes little reference to these. We learn merely that other monasteries in Tiree suffered during the plague, while Columba's was spared (III 8).

Iona lay at the heart of a network of Hebridean and mainland churches in Argyll, yet we should not think it was the sole luminary of this area. Iona achieved the greatest importance, and it was able to produce and preserve records of its greatness in the *Life of St Columba*, in the Iona annals and in those manuscripts which for centuries were preserved as relics in Ireland. The survival of such books may have been achieved only because Iona remained permanently integrated into the church in Ireland itself. (As Dr Aidan Macdonald has pointed out, the minor churches mentioned by Adomnán in Ireland can still mostly be identified; those in Scotland sank into obscurity too early for information to have survived.) Because Iona was the mother house of Irish foundations, because of St Columba's personal greatness, and because of the important family connections and personal achievements of his successors, Iona was not marginalized. St Moluag may have retained links with his mother house of Bangor, but his foundations in the islands were daughter houses, which later became cut off. Iona did not become cut off from its Irish dependencies, but was able, when the time demanded, to transfer its leadership to a more secure location at Kells. Without these strong ties between Iona and Ireland, we should know much less than we do about Iona, Dalriada and all Scotland in the early Middle Ages.

### *St Columba and the Irish*

Setting aside the unknown quantity of Columba's role in the battle of Cúl Drebene and the events that followed, he plays no known part in Irish history until after he left Ireland and established his monastery at Iona. I have suggested that he was already able to approach King Conall mac Comgaill directly, and that Iona was founded with the cooperation of the king. This is plausible in view of Columba's close family relationship with the Northern Uí Néill overlord, Ainmire mac Sétna. Within a little more than ten years after his arrival in Dalriada, however, Columba is portrayed at the centre of a very significant event.

In 574, following the death of King Conall, the king's cousin and successor, Áedán mac Gabráin, is said to have come to Columba to be consecrated as king of Dalriada – the first occasion in the history of Europe when elements of the ritual of priestly ordination were used as part of the process of royal inauguration. The significance of this event in the history of Christian kingship has been much debated (*358*), though it is unsafe to presume that it took place as described. Locally, it suggests that a special relationship existed between Columba and the ruling dynasty of Dalriada, Cenél nGabráin. That relationship continued to be prominent. Cumméne's book attributed to St Columba a prophecy that, as long as Áedán's descendants did right by the saint, they should continue as kings of Dalriada (III 5). Adomnán tells another story, closely modelled on the biblical story of how the future King David was anointed by the prophet Samuel, about how

Columba prophesied that Eochaid Buide mac Áedáin would succeed to the kingdom, and his sons after him (I 9). Columba was treated, Adomnán seems to say, as the spiritual leader of their territory by the kings of Dalriada. His monastery at Iona served as the spiritual centre of the kingdom, where the king received his Christian consecration and where, in the course of time, successive kings of Dalriada were brought for burial.

On the other hand, Columba himself was closely related to the kings of Cenél Conaill, leaders of the Northern Uí Néill; during his lifetime more than one of his close kin became the supreme Uí Néill overlord, the king of Tara. Moreover, many of his successors as abbot also belonged to the lineage of Cenél Conaill, suggesting that for at least a century after Columba's death Iona remained securely linked to this branch of the Northern Uí Néill. Is it possible that Iona was a principal church for both Dalriada and the Northern Uí Néill?

Towards the end of the century – I have suggested a date around 590 rather than the year 575 given by the annals (*204*) – the king of Dalriada, Áedán mac Gabráin, and the Northern Uí Néill overlord, Áed mac Ainmirech, met at Druim Cett, a hill outside Derry. Columba himself was the third participant of importance and it seems likely that it was through his close connections with both rulers that the meeting was arranged. An incidental event at this meeting was the blessing of Áed's son, Domnall mac Áedo, when Columba prophesied his future succession to the Uí Néill kingship (I 10). Adomnán organized stories in groups linked by subject-matter, but it may be more than a literary device that two such prophecies of succession – for Eochaid Buide in Dalriada and Domnall mac Áedo of the Uí Néill – follow one after the other. In his narrative Adomnán makes Eochaid's story the first of a series of prophecies about kings (I 9). The reason for this may have been one of association: the prophecy concerning Eochaid happened shortly before his brothers were killed in the battle with the

Miathi, which had been mentioned in the previous chapter; or it may have been a more deliberate desire to give precedence to the Dalriadic succession over that of the Uí Néill. It has been argued that Adomnán was trying to support a shift in allegiance on the part of the community from the Uí Néill, who had supplied seven of the first nine abbots, to the Cenél nGabráin. The possibility of such a change between Columba's time and Adomnán's will be considered later in this Introduction (see p. 63), when I examine Adomnán's purposes. Meanwhile my primary concern is to establish Columba's personal role in the relations between the northern Irish and the Dalriadic dynasties.

There is no way of knowing how often Columba himself visited Ireland after the founding of Iona. Adomnán appears to refer to two separate visits: one when the saint attended the meeting of the kings at Druim Cett, and the other when he stayed for some time 'in the midland part of Ireland', that is, in *Mide*. The dating of these visits is unclear. For the one it obviously depends on how one dates the meeting of the kings. Adomnán makes it clear that the other visit was when the monastery of Durrow was founded (I 3), and on this basis we may guess at a date in the late 580s (*59*). Three stories are told about incidents when Columba was near Lough Key in Co. Roscommon, but it is not possible to tell whether these were during the visit to *Mide* or another occasion altogether (*184*). It is not a matter of great importance to know how often Columba returned to Ireland.

It is of a piece with Adomnán's silence about the founding of Iona that he tells us so little concerning the establishment of the Columban churches in Ireland. By the tenth century, when Iona was on the margins of the Irish Columban community, it was thought that Derry had been the saint's first church, that he founded many others in Ireland, including Durrow, and that Iona was the late foundation of his exile. I have referred to the indications that Durrow was actually founded more than twenty years after Iona, and I think it probable that Derry too was begun after Columba had settled outside Ireland (*54*). We may speculate that the reason for the founding of a church at Derry was as a port for communications between Iona, the lands of the Northern Uí Néill and what may have been a growing number of associated churches in Ireland.

It appears from the *Life* that Columba took a close interest in the progress of Durrow; Adomnán tells stories about the building work going on under the direction of Lasrén as prior (I 29, III 15). It is also evident that monks from both Derry and Durrow were in communication with Iona and the elders of the *familia*. Individual monks are named as moving between Durrow and Iona, so that there was some degree of integration between the scattered Columban monasteries. The only other church mentioned by Adomnán as housing 'the monks of St Columba' is Druim Tuamma, now Drumhome, in the district of Cenél Conaill (III 23 p. 231), but this reference does not make it clear that there was a Columban church here in the saint's lifetime. Nor does Adomnán say that Cell Mór Díthruib was a Columban church, though other evidence may suggest that it was (*209*). By collecting references from sources of all dates and by using place-name evidence William Reeves, in his edition of the *Life* was able to give a list of nearly forty churches in Ireland belonging to the community, but this list is no guide to how many churches were founded by Columba. This list is likely to reflect the extension of the community under his successors; it may include churches associated with his kindred that were not necessarily integrated into the Columban *familia*.

Columba may or may not have been constant in his travels around Scottish Dalriada. He is mentioned as visiting *Hinba* and Ardnamurchan, both more than once, and on at least one occasion he visited Skye. The *Life*, however, makes no mention of any personal visit to Mag Luinge in Tiree, although we should perhaps assume that Columba did visit his local monasteries from time to time, at least until he was too old for travelling. It is certainly not possible to say that Columba was more involved in the life and society of the communities of Scottish Dalriada than he was in the affairs of Ireland. It is too narrow to regard him as a Scottish saint, for he certainly enjoyed as great a reputation in Ireland as in Dalriada, and his monastic legacy in Ireland lasted much longer than in Scotland.

### *St Columba and the Picts*

The role in which St Columba seems particularly a Scottish saint is as the missionary who converted the Picts north of the mountains. This is the part that Bede gave him:

> A priest and abbot named Columba, distinguished by his monastic habit and life, came from Ireland to Britain to preach the word of God in the provinces of the northern Picts, which are separated from those of the southern Picts by a range of steep and desolate mountains. ... Columba arrived in Britain in the ninth year of the reign of the powerful Pictish king, Bridei f. Meilochon; he converted that people to the faith of Christ by his preaching and example, and received from them the island of Iona on which to found a monastery. (Bede, III 4)

Bede's history of the English church draws several times on information from his contacts in Pictland. Here Bede's knowledge of Bridei's regnal year probably indicates a Pictish source. It is possible that Bede had firsthand information from Pictish informants in 710, when Naiton, the king of the Picts, sent envoys bearing a letter to Bede's own abbot, Ceolfrith. The king had been contemplating the arguments of churchmen over the method of calculating Easter, a subject in which Adomnán himself was much involved. According to

Bede, the Picts had until this point used an erroneous method, by which he means the Irish method favoured by the Columban churches throughout their country. Naiton renounced this and, encouraged and instructed by Ceolfrith, he used his royal authority to command the use of catholic Easter-tables and the destruction of those based on the Irish method. Bede does not add that Columban monks were expelled from Pictland by the king in 717; we learn this from the Irish annals.

It can scarcely be denied that up to this point the monks and priests of Iona must have played a large role in the conversion of Pictland. What is debatable is whether this was already under way in Columba's lifetime. Perhaps the best evidence for Columba's missionary work in Pictland comes from the poem *Amrae Coluimb Chille*, composed soon after the saint's death. Here it is said (if the line is correctly interpreted) that 'he preached to the tribes of Tay'. Adomnán's *Life* tells how the saint travelled to the fort of King Bridei and engaged in conflict with the king's pagan wizards. The episode is a folk-tale form of a conversion miracle, the contest between the powers of light and dark for the king's favour. St Columba wins the contest but at no stage is it made clear that the king was converted and baptized.

One may well wonder what was the reason behind Columba's visit or visits to Pictland. Adomnán tells several stories, some of them about 'when St Columba stayed for some days in the province of the Picts' and others 'when St Columba was journeying at the other side of Druim Alban'. It is uncertain, however, whether the saint visited once only or on a number of occasions (*283*, *300*). Several stories have a local setting along the route from the Firth of Lorn through the Great Glen to King Bridei's fortress above the River Ness; one should not for this reason link them with Columba's visit to the king, since he would probably use this route as often as he travelled to Pictland. While in Pictland Columba converted individual families on two occasions, but for the most part Adomnán makes no attempt to describe the work of missionary preaching. On the one hand, this may merely reflect a lack of interest on the author's part in Columba's missionary role; if the Picts were securely Christian and adherents of the customs of Iona when he was writing, Adomnán may not have considered the period of their conversion. On the other hand, there are two references to Columba's preaching the gospel through an interpreter to Pictish converts (I 33, II 32). Adomnán does not really help either to confirm or refute Bede's depiction of Columba as a missionary to Pictland. It would seem, however, that, more than a century after his death, this was the role for which Columba was remembered by the Picts who were Bede's informants.

The principal reason in Adomnán's mind for Columba's visit to King Bridei may have been more political than anything else. Bridei was a powerful king, who appears to have become ruler of all the Picts about 558. His authority would have extended over all the north-west from Moidart northwards as well as over all the eastern side of the country. Adomnán mentions a sub-king of Orkney, from whom King Bridei had taken hostages to insure his political submission. It is possible that Columba's reason for visiting the king was primarily to ask for the king's goodwill in permitting Irish monks and pilgrims to establish themselves on the western fringes of his territories. We are specifically told that he asked King Bridei to ensure that Cormac Ua Liatháin came to no harm from the sub-king of Orkney. Twenty years after Columba's death the martyrdom of St Donnan in Eigg (*388*) by seaborne Pictish forces shows that matters did not always work out safely.

The unfortunate truth is that the *Life* tells us too little to begin to understand Columba's dealings with King Bridei or his people. We can, however, say that the anonymous monks of Iona who decided what to enter in their annals maintained a continuous, though sketchy, interest in Pictish events; and that little more than one hundred years after Columba's death dependencies of Iona formed a major part of the church in Pictland.

The evidence for Irish cultural influence in Pictland is divided. Pictish sculptured monuments of the late seventh and eighth centuries exhibit an easy familiarity with the decorative techniques of Hiberno-Saxon manuscript art. There are some signs of Pictish artistic influence in Irish manuscripts: for example, the moulding of the muscles on the calf, symbol for the evangelist Luke, in the gospel-book of Durrow has been seen as recalling the style of Pictish animal-sculpture. The *Life of St Columba* mentions a Pict in Ireland with a book written by Columba (II 9); one may guess that he had at some stage been a monk of Iona. The great imponderable is whether the Picts adopted the writing of Latin in their homeland, a question that exercised Dr Kathleen Hughes: if the Picts were producing books at all, can we sufficiently explain why nothing has survived, neither Pictish-made copies of the standard biblical and liturgical texts nor any native written works? The only evidence we have is that King Naiton, according to Bede, had made a careful study of ecclesiastical writings concerning the date of Easter. The Columban monks in Pictland must have had and used, and almost certainly made, books of their own.

Although the Columban legacy in Pictland is difficult to assess, its existence cannot be denied. Both Adomnán and Bede believed that this influence began with Columba himself. How rapidly progress was made we cannot know, but by the beginning of the eighth century the Columban churches must have been of considerable significance. The Picts attributed the conversion of their nation to St Columba, a view that was communicated to Bede, and yet, during the period when Bede was most aware of events to the north, the Pictish king expelled the Columban monks from his territory. In some way, it seems, their position in Pictland had become a challenge to the ruler.

### *St Columba's death, and his successors*

For at least the last thirty-four years of his life Columba had lived as a holy man. In the nature of our historical evidence it is not possible to measure the extent and importance of his reputation in Ireland and in Britain at that date. I do not doubt, however, that for those Christian people who knew Columba, or who knew of him, his sanctity was assured. From the moment of his death he was believed to have been carried to heaven. Columba had become St Columba.

Adomnán's moving account of the holy man's last days provides an intimate view of how the ideal abbot prepared his community for his going. His death was marked by angelic visitations, and these were witnessed far afield. Columba had also been the centre of devoted attention in all the provinces round about; many lay men and women would want to attend his funeral. This was miraculously prevented by bad weather, so that the three days of his funeral ceremonies were conducted by the monks of his own community alone. The few words Adomnán gives about his funeral are more than we learn elsewhere about the burial rites of any Irish holy man. He was buried, it seems, without a coffin in an earth grave. Although heavenly lights and angelic visitors identified this as a very special grave, there is no suggestion that the body had been elevated and enshrined when Adomnán wrote. At the end of the sixth century the beginning of a saint's cult did not require any ritual translation.

Nor was his passing marked only in a Christian manner. The Irish poet Dallán Forgaill, according to later tradition, composed a eulogy of Columba as he might have done for a dead king. The poem, *Amrae Coluimb Chille*, survives, one of the oldest texts in the Irish language. Columba's grave, his books, even the white tunic in which he died, were the tangible remembrances of his mortal life, kept by his monks and successors. The anniversary of his death was commemorated, and stories about him were told and retold within the community. So the cult of the saint evolved, and the material that Adomnán used in his *Life* began to take shape.

Columba was succeeded as abbot by Baithéne (*55*), his cousin, who had been with him throughout his pilgrimage in Britain. Baithéne, it appears, was abbot for three years, dying in 600. He was commemorated, as Adomnán tells us (II 45), on the same day as St Columba. The third abbot was Lasrén mac Feradaig (*91*), the son of another cousin of the saint; he too led the community for only a few years. Both men are mentioned more than once in the *Life*, and while Columba was still alive both shared in the administration of his monasteries, Baithéne at *Hinba* and later at Mag Luinge in Tiree, and Lasrén at Durrow.

Only with the fourth abbot, Fergnae (*389*), does it become clear that the community is in the hands of a new generation. Unlike both his predecessors and his successor, he was not a blood relation of the founder, and he seems to have had some British blood. He is mentioned in the *Life* only as a youth who was an unauthorized witness of heavenly light in the saint's lodging (III 22). By the time Fergnae became abbot, it is likely that King Áedán mac Gabráin was dead, as were Columba's saintly colleagues in Ireland, Cainnech and Comgall. We begin, however, to be aware of the stages by which stories were transmitted. Fergnae's experience of the saint's heavenly light was reported to his nephew, a priest called Commán, and it was he who bore witness to the facts in the presence of Adomnán himself (*391*).

When Fergnae died in 623, he was succeeded as abbot by Ségéne, the nephew of Lasrén mac Feradaig. Ségéne was abbot for nearly thirty years. In his time we see Iona once again take a close interest in the political affairs of Ireland, when for the first time in thirty years one of the saint's kinsmen was high king. In 628 Domnall mac Áedo, king of Cenél Conaill, became supreme Uí Néill overlord (*86*). He was the son of Áed mac Ainmirech, one of the kings at Druim Cett, and at that meeting – so the story goes – Domnall was himself blessed by St Columba (I 10). This story suggests that the monks of Iona had an interest in his career, and this is also reflected in the annals, which regularly chronicle his doings. The annal entry for his death calls him 'king of Ireland', apparently the earliest use of this title. Ségéne, and the traditions about St Columba represented by the writings of Cumméne and Adomnán, seem to have sought to link Domnall's achievements with the saint's blessing of the boy.

In the early years of Ségéne's abbacy 'the great dispute' broke out 'among the churches of Ireland concerning differences in the date of Easter', as St Columba had predicted (I 3). The date of Easter depends on the date of Pesach, the Jewish Passover, which is determined by the lunar calendar. Christian churches used various calculations to harmonize the lunar calendar with the solar calendar in order to establish which was the Paschal moon. Easter was celebrated on the Sunday following the full moon. In the sixth century the Latin church as a whole more than once changed the system in use, at one stage adopting a system that was arithmetically worse than what had gone before. Scholars in Ireland detected these shortcomings and adhered to an older system. But a habit of conservatism persisted even when the Roman church had moved on to a better system. Until the 620s all the churches in Ireland, Scotland and Wales were still using Easter-tables based on an older method of calculating the date of Easter. The rest of Western Europe used a different system, which in certain years gave a different moon. There were also differences about what to do when the full moon fell on a Sunday. As a result, there could be one week's or four weeks' difference between the dates. Wherever adherents of the Celtic practice came into contact with followers of the Roman practice, there could be argument. In time some Irish churchmen began to advocate the adoption of the Roman practice at home; synods were called, technical questions were aired and there was much argument about diversity or unity.

One of the earliest known cases of this conflict involved Columbanus, an Irish abbot in Burgundy, around 600, and letters from him to two popes survive, in which he defends the Irish method but expresses tolerance for variation. Further clashes occurred following the arrival of the Italian Augustine to convert the pagan English to Christianity. Lawrence, another Italian, who succeeded Augustine as archbishop of Canterbury, was snubbed by a visiting Irish bishop called Dagán, about 610, and wrote to the Irish bishops and abbots, urging conformity with Rome.

The first we know of Ségéne's involvement is a letter addressed to him and a hermit called Béccán strongly advocating the Roman practice. The author, an Irishman called Cummian, gives some account of the synods at home and of how he and others had gone to Rome for guidance. On their return in 632 the argument was just as fierce, and Ségéne, it seems, was among the conservatives. Why exactly the letter was addressed to him we do not know: Cummian may have regarded him as an influential figure who might be amenable to argument or he may have been addressing himself to the leaders of the conservatives. Ségéne was not persuaded by Cummian nor by the similar arguments expressed in a letter to the Irish clergy by Pope Honorius I in 634. He was one of the leading Irish churchmen who put their names to a letter addressed to Pope Severinus about 638. Bede has preserved part of the reply from his successor, Pope John IV, written late in 640, to various Irish bishops, abbots and teachers. The pope argued strongly against the Celtic position. During this period of intensive debate, with synods at home and at least four communications between Ireland and Rome, many churches in southern Ireland adopted the Roman practice, but the northern churches, including St Columba's foundations, did not.

While the Roman mission in England began to suffer setbacks in the 620s, more than one Irish missionary began to set up churches among the English. In Northumbria King Edwin and his Kentish queen had brought the Italian Paulinus to set up a church in his kingdom, but on the king's defeat and death in 633 a pagan reaction set in and Paulinus went back to Kent. At this point Oswald returned from exile to take the crown. Some of his exile had been spent in Iona, where he was baptized (*41*). Very soon after his success in becoming king, he sent a messenger to Iona, according to Bede, asking the abbot 'to send him a bishop by whose teaching and ministry the English people whom he ruled might receive the blessings of the Christian faith'. Ségéne's first nominee was too stern to win converts and gave up the task, but the next man sent, Áedán, established a daughter house of Iona at Lindisfarne. The name by which he is known in England, Aidan, preserves the contemporary Irish spelling of his name. At some point, presumably as soon as he was secure in the kingdom, Oswald himself returned to Iona, where, according to Adomnán, he told Ségéne of St Columba's miraculous support for his cause.

Over and above these ecclesiastical connections, Bede indicates that Oswald was able to establish some political hegemony over the kings of Dalriada and of Pictland, circumstances that Adomnán seems to recognize in his description of Oswald as 'emperor of all Britain'. This overlordship, however remote it may have been in practice, continued from the 630s until the crushing defeat of the Northumbrian King Ecgfrith in 685.

In 634, the same year that Oswald asked Ségéne for a bishop, Pope Honorius wrote to the Irish clergy about the

Easter question and sent the papal stole, or pallium, to a new archbishop of Canterbury. It is possible that Ségéne, a defender of the conservative practice, might have seen the Northumbrian mission as a way of spreading the influence not only of the Columban community but also that of what he regarded as the correct calculation of Easter. For almost thirty years the Columban church was to flourish in Northumbria, while the Easter question lay dormant. 'During Aidan's lifetime', Bede writes, 'these differences of Easter observance were patiently tolerated by everyone, for it was realized that, although he was by loyalty bound to retain the customs of those who sent him, he nevertheless laboured diligently to cultivate the faith, piety, and love that marks out God's saints.'

It is only thanks to Bede that we know so much about the beginnings of Iona's mission to Northumbria. Without any comparable informant from Ireland or Scotland, we cannot know whether this was unique or whether Ségéne presided over a community expanding in these areas also. While Adomnán may give the impression that Columba left a widespread legacy in both countries, the truth may be that expansion took much longer; Ségéne's abbacy may have seen much of that growth. Yet we have specific knowledge of only one new foundation in Ireland, on Lambay Island off the coast north of Dublin (*71*).

Almost every abbot of Iona had come from Columba's kindred, and this may suggest that sons of the family regularly joined the community. If Ségéne became a monk in his youth, it is possible that he had some memory of the founder. But anyone who had been more than a youth when Columba died was by now an old man. If memories of the saint were to be preserved, there was no time to be lost. Three times in the *Life* Adomnán mentions Ségéne in relation to the transmission of stories about St Columba. On two occasions persons who had felt the saint's miraculous powers related their experiences to him. One of these was King Oswald (I 1), whose experience happened in 634. The other, a monk called Ernéne (I 3), had been a boy when he encountered the saint at Clonmacnoise, about the time of the foundation of Durrow. This was apparently in the 580s, and Ernéne died in 635. Among the others present on both occasions was Failbe, later abbot himself, who related the stories to Adomnán. In the third instance the monk Silnán, who was the intermediary for Columba's healing grace, 'gave testimony . . . in the presence of Abbot Ségéne and other elders' (II 4). The language here is distinctly legalistic, as if this was a formal deposition made in front of witnesses. From such phrasing, here and elsewhere in the *Life*, and from the particulars of names and circumstances that Adomnán was able to include in his stories about events within the community, Dr Máire Herbert has argued for two important conclusions: first, that Ségéne made an effort to collect attested stories about St Columba, apparently in the 630s, and second, that the preservation of detail suggests that these were written down at the time (*15*). The implication is that Adomnán was using a source of great authority. It is a matter of speculation whether this written record was 'the book on the miraculous powers of St Columba' by Ségéne's nephew, Cumméne, himself a future abbot, but the suggestion is very plausible.

It is evident that Ségéne provided strong leadership within the community and that he played a prominent part in the events of his time. It would seem that he was a stout traditionalist, a conservative holding fast to the views handed down within the community from the founder.

Bishop Aidan died on 31 August 651, and his successor, Fínán, was sent from Iona to continue the work at Lindisfarne. Within a year Ségéne himself died, on 12 August 652. His immediate successor, Suibne moccu Urthrí, is an obscure figure, but we gather from Bede that he continued the mission in England. In 653 the young Peada, sub-king of the

Middle Angles and son of King Penda of Mercia, came to Northumbria asking to marry King Oswiu's daughter. There, at Oswiu's estate on Hadrian's Wall, Bishop Fínán baptized Peada and provided him with priests both English and Irish to convert his peoples. The first two bishops in Mercia, Diuma and his successor, Cellach, were Irish; this Cellach, says Bede, 'relinquished the see after a short time and returned to the isle of Iona, the chief and mother house of many Irish monasteries'. Suibne died on 11 January 657, and it seems likely that Cellach was received in Iona by the new abbot, Cumméne, who kept up the close links with Northumbria.

Cumméne was a nephew of Abbot Ségéne and a great-nephew of Abbot Lasrén; with him the abbacy returned to the founder's kin. To this period may perhaps be assigned the first tangible evidence of the richness of monastic culture in the Columban community, the Book of Durrow, earliest of the great Irish gospel-books. This contains the four gospels in Latin, written in a large formal script with the most important initials elaborately decorated and with eleven whole-page pictures. Some of these depict the gospel writers, while six are 'carpet pages' of interlace and geometrical patterns. Experts used to date this manuscript to the eighth century; some would now place it much earlier; but there is some consensus on the third quarter of the seventh century. We are certain that the book belonged to Durrow when it was enshrined by the Southern Uí Néill overking Flann Sinna (d. 916). The style of writing and decoration have led to associations with Northumbria and even Pictland. The book could have been made at Iona, but the Vulgate affinities of its Latin text may perhaps rather indicate a Columban house nearer to the south of Ireland, very likely Durrow itself, where it was probably used only for ceremonial purposes at the altar. Its early date means that Adomnán himself may have seen and handled it. Every major Columban church probably had such a gospel-book, and there survive in Durham fragments from an earlier book which Aidan might have taken with him to Lindisfarne.

In Cumméne's time, too, Iona suffered what may be seen as its major setback. The Easter argument had again broken out, in Northumbria. King Oswiu had fostered the Columban clergy in his kingdom; he had himself in his youth spent sixteen years in exile among the Irish, one of his sons had an Irish mother and may have gone to study in Ireland, and for more than twenty years Oswiu had been well served by Irish monks. In Bede's words, 'Oswiu thought nothing could be better than Irish teaching, having been instructed and baptized by the Irish and having a complete grasp of their language' (Bede, III 25). The trouble had begun between Bishop Fínán, a hot-tempered fellow, and another Irishman, Rónán, 'who had been instructed in Gaul and Italy in the authentic practice of the church'. The king observed the Irish Easter, but the queen, who was brought up in Kent, kept the Roman one. In 664, at a synod held at Whitby, the queen brought the English abbot Wilfrid and the Frankish bishop Agilbert, who had spent many years in study among those Irish that kept the Roman Easter; they disputed with Fínán's successor, Bishop Colmán, and convinced the king that St Peter's authority was greater than St Columba's. Colmán, and the others who remained conservative, left Northumbria and returned to Iona, bringing with him some relics of St Aidan. Colmán's place was taken by an Englishman, Tuda, who had been trained and consecrated as bishop in the southern part of Ireland. Meanwhile, Cumméne received Colmán back in Iona, but Colmán chose not to stay and set off for Ireland, where he founded monasteries, first at Inishboffin and then at Mayo.

In the same year the churches of Ireland began to suffer badly from a recurrence of plague that was to continue until about 668 (*346*); Iona was unaffected, says Adomnán, but the Irish churches were not spared.

Cumméne is the first abbot of Iona of whom the annals record that he visited Ireland, in 661. This has been understood as meaning that he made a visitation of the Irish monasteries of his community, though we know very little of how the constitutional links between his churches worked. Previous abbots would presumably have done this; the fact that Cumméne's is the first such visit to be recorded probably reflects the increasing detail of the annals after about 660. Cumméne died on 24 February 669, and his successor was Failbe, his third cousin. We may assume that, like others of the founder's kin, Failbe joined the community as a youth, for Adomnán mentions that he was in Iona when King Oswald visited in the 630s. He is the only early abbot of whom the annals record that he spent a long period in Ireland: his sailing to Ireland is recorded in 673 and his return in 676. Of his abbacy there is little to say. The annals report that in 672 'the Hebrides were devastated', but we do not know what the entry may signify. The following year they mention that there was a fire at Mag Luinge, and we may presume that this was Iona's dependency in Tiree. Such accidents were not uncommon in early medieval Ireland, and the wooden buildings could easily be replaced. Failbe died on 22 March 679.

## *Adomnán of Iona, abbot and statesman*

St Columba's ninth successor, Adomnán, the author of his *Life*, is one of the most interesting figures in early Irish history. Unlike other Irishmen of his century, whether kings, poets or churchmen, he is known to us by enough tangible evidence to be properly a figure of history. It would be too much to say that we can approach his personality, but we know enough of his abilities, his concerns and his career to discuss his influence on events and the reasons that lie behind his doings and writings. Even so, the amount of hard factual information is quite small, and much of his biography must be based on inference.

He died in 704, and his death was commemorated on 23 September. According to the annals, he was in his seventy-seventh year, which, if correct, means that he was born between 24 September 627 and 23 September 628. This inferred date depends on our trusting that the annalist who entered the obituary, presumably at Iona, had an accurate knowledge of Adomnán's age. There is, however, also an annal entry at 624 for his birth, but, like other entries for births, this is probably less reliable than the information in the obituary. His kinship with Columba and succeeding abbots of Iona is attested by the genealogies, though in Adomnán's case the relationship is not close. He was descended from Colmán mac Sétna, a younger son of the saint's uncle; the descendants of Sétna's eldest son, Ainmire, were kings of Cenél Conaill. Nothing is known about Adomnán's father, Rónán mac Tinne, nor about anyone of his branch of the family. Adomnán's mother, Ronnat, came from another Northern Uí Néill lineage, Cenél nÉnda.

In the conclusion to the *Life* Adomnán makes it clear that he was born 'in our own Ireland', presumably in the territory of Cenél Conaill in the south-west of Co. Donegal. He mentions hearing, as a young man, a report about a miracle from Ernéne, 'who is buried in the burial ground of the monks of St Columba at Druim Tuamma' (*416*). This church lies in the heartland of Cenél Conaill; it is possible that Adomnán is recalling the story from his childhood before he left home, but another possibility is that Adomnán began his religious life as a youth at Druim Tuamma, a Columban house close to home.

We know nothing for certain about Adomnán's early career. He makes no mention of personal contact with any abbot earlier than Failbe (669–79), and the inference has often been drawn from this silence that he did not come to Iona until after 669. Yet it hardly seems possible that Adomnán did not meet earlier abbots. He must have spent years in the study of Latin texts and was almost certainly a churchman from his youth; it is most unlikely that he became a monk anywhere but in the Columban *familia*; and whether he joined the community at Druim Tuamma or Derry or elsewhere, it is equally unlikely that a monk with his family connections and personal talents could have avoided meeting the head of the community until he was over forty. Adomnán's silence, therefore, cannot bear the inference put upon it.

It is most probable that Adomnán joined the Columban community as a youth at a time when Ségéne was abbot of Iona and coarb ('heir') of Columba. As royal kin and founder's kin every opportunity to cultivate his talents was open to him, and he may well have spent time in more than one of the major churches of the *familia*. His middle years were spent studying the Bible and the Fathers in the first flowering of Irish ecclesiastical scholarship. It was a period when students from other countries travelled to Ireland in pursuit of religious studies, among them Agilbert, a future bishop of Paris, who went to Ireland 'for the sake of studying the scriptures' and who later defended the Roman position in the synod at Whitby. Aldhelm and Bede both comment on the strength of Irish biblical studies, and the names and works of several exegetes are preserved. The learning of Adomnán's surviving works is sufficient proof that much of his career had been spent in scholarship, and there is every likelihood that he was a teacher as well as a student.

Arguments have been advanced by Dr Smyth for supposing that until about 670 Adomnán's career was spent studying and teaching at Durrow, but they are not decisive. When Adomnán wrote the *Life*, he would have been familiar with Durrow, whether or not he had spent long there. His references to particular buildings and to a fruit tree nearby are therefore of no special significance, and, in any case, neither a fruit tree nor wooden buildings from the 580s would be likely to have lasted until the 640s or 650s. Adomnán's mention of listening to a story from Fínán, who 'lived for many years an irreproachable life as an anchorite beside the monastery of Durrow' (I 49), may well indicate that they met when he was staying at Durrow. But the broad interpretation of the evidence is preferable to the narrow. From perhaps as early as 640 Adomnán was a member of the *familia* of Columba. He became a monk and a priest, but much of his time was devoted to academic work. During thirty years or more in the community he may have spent time in all of its major churches, and there is nothing to prove that more of his time was spent at Durrow than at Iona or that Durrow rather than Iona served as the community's centre for advanced studies.

In later centuries, when Irish churches were often treated as family possessions and most of the community were laymen, it was still held that the coarb should be chosen for his learning from among the founder's kin. Adomnán's scholarship may have been one of the reasons why in 679 he was chosen to be the ninth abbot of Iona and coarb of Columba. He gives a sense of how he viewed this appointment, referring to an earlier abbot, Fergnae, 'who by the will of God later was the head of this church which I too, though unworthy, serve' (III 19). In the *Life* Adomnán twice mentions that Abbot Failbe communicated to him stories of St Columba that he had heard from Abbot Ségéne, and this may suggest that Failbe already saw Adomnán as a possible successor or at least a trusted bearer of Columban tradition. It would soon be seen that he had qualities that gave him far wider influence.

It may have been fortuitous circumstances that brought the abbot on to the public stage. He mentions in the *Life* that he visited his friend King Aldfrith of Northumbria 'after Ecgfrith's battle' (II 46), and from the annals we learn that in 686 'Adomnán brought back to Ireland sixty prisoners'. These had been captured in an attack on Brega by a Northumbrian commander in 684 (*350*). The defeat and death of King Ecgfrith in 685 opened the door to negotiations, and his successor, his half-brother, Aldfrith, was already a friend of the abbot of Iona. Indeed, it is possible that they had known one another for many years (*349*). Who better, therefore, than Adomnán to act as the envoy of the king of Brega, Fínnechta Fledach? In the year when the captives had been taken Aldfrith was staying in Iona, as we learn from a conversation between his sister and St Cuthbert, reported in the anonymous *Life of St Cuthbert*. Against this background the choice of Aldfrith as king of Northumbria may be seen as changing the course of Adomnán's life.

We know little enough about this diplomatic mission to Northumbria in 685–6, but it is probably fair to guess that there would have been no great difficulty in persuading the Northumbrians to release the captives, whom Adomnán accompanied back to Ireland. More than a year later he visited Northumbria a second time. On one of these visits – it is impossible to decide which – Adomnán took with him as a present for Aldfrith a copy of his book *The Holy Places*, discussed on pp. 54–5. In the book Adomnán mentions that he wrote it while 'daily beset by laborious and almost insupportable ecclesiastical business' (*424*). If this is more than conventional protestation, it suggests that the abbacy was itself already onerous without diplomatic business on top. Bede says that Aldfrith was well pleased with the book, adding that 'the writer was sent back to his own land richer by many gifts', a further insight into the relationship between the abbot and the king.

It is from Adomnán's own words that we know there were two visits – Bede conflates them and the annals make no mention of the second one. He gives no specific reasons for the second visit, but this is more likely the occasion when, as Bede says, he stayed for some time. Now that his friend

Aldfrith, a man of strong Irish sympathies, was king of Northumbria, Adomnán may have hoped that links could be re-established between Iona, Lindisfarne and the other churches associated with the mission of Aidan and his successors. Little more than twenty years had passed since Bishop Colmán's withdrawal in 664, and there were many living who remembered the work of the *familia* of Columba in England. Some of the monks who had withdrawn with Colmán were perhaps still alive at Inishboffin or Mayo. Whatever opinions Aldfrith himself held on the questions about the date of Easter and the form of the tonsure that had caused the disruption, he appears to have had no difficulty in living with both sides. In Iona before his accession he would have kept the Celtic Easter; having returned to Northumbria he observed the Roman Easter. The arguments rehearsed at the synod in Whitby must have been as familiar to him as to Adomnán, for the churches of Ireland had been divided over the issues since the late 620s. The two of them may even have discussed the subject at length, long before Aldfrith became king.

Bede, who is our principal source here, was not as impartial as Aldfrith. He tells how Adomnán remained in Northumbria for some time, 'where he observed the rites of the church canonically performed'. Since the question at issue was the date of Easter, this may imply that Adomnán kept this feast at Jarrow in 688. Bede goes on:

> He was earnestly advised by many who were more learned than himself not to presume to act contrary to the universal customs of the church, whether in the keeping of Easter or in any other observances, seeing that his following was very small and situated in a remote corner of the world. As a result he changed his opinions and readily adopted what he saw and heard in the churches of the English in place of the customs of his own people. . . . On his return home, he tried to lead his own people in Iona and those

under the jurisdiction of that monastery into the correct ways that he had himself learned and wholeheartedly accepted, but in this he failed. Then he sailed over to preach in Ireland and by his simple teaching showed its people the proper time of Easter. He corrected their ancient error and restored nearly all who were not under the jurisdiction of Iona to catholic unity, teaching them to observe Easter at the proper time. Having observed the canonical Easter in Ireland, he returned to his own island, where he vigorously pressed his own monastery to conform to the catholic observance of Easter, but he had no success in his attempts. Before the close of the year he departed this life. (Bede, V 15)

In the *Life* Adomnán alludes only once, and briefly, to 'the great dispute that arose among the churches of Ireland concerning differences in the date of Easter' (I 3). He must have been fully aware of the split between the churches in the south and those like Iona in the north; at Durrow one could not have been far from churches that in some years kept Easter on different dates. We must presume that Adomnán had previously accepted the rightness of the conservative arguments for the Celtic observance, but now his time in Northumbria and his discussion with Abbot Ceolfrith at Jarrow began a change of heart.

The implications of this are not as obvious as historians have sometimes thought. Bede's story is very clear-cut: Adomnán returned to Iona fully persuaded of the catholic view; he was unable to persuade his community to change and so, alienated from his own monks, he preached to other churches in Ireland and successfully won them over; he died soon after, in Iona, but still at odds with his own *familia*. It is easy to read this as meaning that Adomnán lived barely two years after his discussion with Ceolfrith, but Bede has telescoped a period of some sixteen years between Adomnán's second visit to England in 687–8 and his death in 704. He has also emphasized Adomnán's loss of authority over his own community.

The implied conflict between the abbot and his monks has led modern historians to give a pregnant meaning to those annals that record Adomnán's visits to Ireland: in 692 'Adomnán went to Ireland fourteen years after the death of Failbe'; and in 697 'Adomnán went to Ireland and gave the Law of Innocents to the peoples.' It has been thought that the abbot stayed in Ireland for most of the time between 692 and 697, and again from 697 to the last year of his life, when, Bede says, he returned to Iona. The only foundation for these long periods away lies in Bede's telescoped story. This view necessarily implies too that in Ireland Adomnán avoided the churches of his own community which were at one with the monks in Iona. Such an interpretation seems to be contradicted by Adomnán in the *Life*, where he writes of returning to Iona in June after he had been 'to the meeting of the Irish synod' (II 45), almost certainly a reference to the synod at Birr in 697, which adopted the Law of Innocents. The annals, however, mention only his going to Ireland, though his return to Iona is implicit: he could not have gone to Ireland in 686, 692 and 697 without returning between those dates. The meaning of the annalist is surely that in 692 and 697 Adomnán visited Ireland. The seemingly irrelevant comment 'fourteen years after the death of Failbe' may be an allusive way of saying that his first formal visitation as abbot of his Irish monasteries had been unusually delayed. We know that he had been in Ireland in 686 with the captives, but this too was a visit, after which he returned to Iona. On each occasion the annalist has indicated the reason for the visit, and I suggest that there are no grounds for conjecturing long absences from Iona or hostile estrangement between Adomnán and his community. Bede wanted his readers to understand that Abbot Ceolfrith had persuaded Adomnán to adopt the canonical view and that Adomnán's preaching, in turn, persuaded the churches of northern Ireland. Likewise, Bede emphasizes that it was Ecgberht, an English exile in Ireland, who finally convinced the Columban clergy in 716. His message is that the English were the bringers of Roman unity to the Irish. The reality may have been different. Prompted by discussions with Ceolfrith, Adomnán may have begun to reconsider where he stood on the Easter question, though not, it seems, on the tonsure. Whenever he finally made up his mind, his community held out in favour of the older practice. In Ireland he was more successful, but it is by no means clear when he won over the northern churches. To suppose that he first kept the Roman Easter with them in 704 may put too much trust in Bede's compressed chronology.

We have only Bede's word for it that Adomnán's views had changed during the preceding sixteen years, yet those are the years that Bede's version leaves out, going straight from Adomnán's meeting with Ceolfrith to the year before his death. In that period the annal for 697 records Adomnán's most notable personal achievement, the Law of Innocents. Before long this enactment came to be known as *Cáin Adomnáin* 'the Law of Adomnán', as further *cána* associated with other churches were enacted. Adomnán's is the first example of a new form of law, enacted by the church but enforced over both church and laity. Its purpose was to protect churches, women, and children from combat, and a similar concern may lie behind Adomnán's story of the divine retribution suffered by a 'slaughterer of innocents' who murdered a girl in front of St Columba and his teacher (II 25). The impact of this law may be seen reflected in a nearly contemporary tract on the Irish law of status, *Críth Gablach*; this mentions three types of enactment 'which it is proper for a king to bind on his peoples by pledge', among them 'a law of religion that inspires, such as the Law of Adomnán'.

What we know of Adomnán's Law depends on an Irish text of it, not as he wrote it but a composite of several layers, no older than the ninth century. This text, however, includes a list of guarantors supporting the enactment, which appears to be genuine except for the later titles added after some of the names. This list reveals the circumstances in which Adomnán 'gave the Law of Innocents to the peoples'. A great assembly was held at Birr, about twenty-five miles south-west of Durrow, in the spring of 697. Here Adomnán put forward his proposals and successfully persuaded the leading men in church and state to support his law. Assemblies were not unusual in seventh-century Ireland, but in other cases we have no comparable detail about who attended. What is particularly remarkable is the presence on the list of churchmen and kings from every part of Ireland and beyond, not only the king of Scottish Dalriada but also the king of the Picts. So far as we are able to tell, Iona was the only real connection between Ireland and Pictland, and this supports the inference that it was Adomnán himself who brought together this international assembly. If it is doubted whether all the guarantors actually attended the meeting at Birr, the alternative is that Adomnán took his Law around Ireland and Scotland collecting their support.

Of these guarantors, the first forty named are clerics, and they are followed by some fifty kings, great and small. We have no means of knowing how effectively the Law was enforced or what role the guarantors played in its implementation. On the one hand, the clerical guarantors included some undoubted conservatives on the Easter question, among them Bishop Ceti from Iona; on the other hand, there were many from churches that had adopted the Roman Easter and the Roman tonsure in the 620s and 630s. Wherever Adomnán stood on these matters in 697, it seems that he was not prevented from working with both sides.

Before we leave this subject, we should consider a little more closely the implications of Bede's words that Adomnán 'observed the canonical Easter in Ireland', returned home to argue the question again in Iona, and died within the year. Such a sequence of events is too memorable to be confused.

Bede's telescoping probably amounts simply to his ignoring the years since the conversations with Ceolfrith in order to emphasize the causal connection. Yet it is impossible to put a date on Adomnán's successful preaching of the Roman cause in northern Ireland. We should also be chary of interpreting Bede as necessarily meaning that 704 was the first time Adomnán had ever observed the Roman Easter rather than the Irish one in a year when they differed. Even so, they did differ in that year: Easter fell on 30 March by the Roman calculation and on 20 April by the Irish, and this must have focused attention on the problem in the last year of Adomnán's life.

He died on 23 September 704. Writing to the Pictish king, Naiton, in 710, Ceolfrith described his meeting with Adomnán, 'a renowned priest and abbot of the Columban community, who, when he was sent on an embassy from his nation to King Aldfrith and chose to visit our monastery, displayed remarkable wisdom, humility, and devotion in his ways and conversation'. Bede called him 'a good and wise man with an excellent knowledge of the scriptures'. He was no doubt aware that in 705 Easter would again be celebrated on two different dates in Ireland, and he comments on Adomnán's death: 'God in his goodness decreed that so great a champion of peace and unity should be received into everlasting life before he should be obliged, when Eastertide returned once more, to enter upon more serious controversy with those who refused to follow him in the truth.'

### *Adomnán and the writing of the* Life

Biblical studies and a concern for peace and unity are shown in Adomnán's two surviving books, his short treatise on *The Holy Places* and his *Life of St Columba*. Both were written on Iona, but we know rather more of the circumstances in which he wrote *The Holy Places*.

Adomnán, of course, knew what the Bible said about Jerusalem and the other holy places in Judaea, and he had studied Jerome's treatise on the Hebrew place-names mentioned in the Bible. When he met the Frankish bishop Arculf, who had spent nine months in the Holy Land and had also visited Alexandria, Constantinople and Rome, he seized the opportunity to learn what he could about the holy places, listening to Arculf, questioning him and noting down what he said. He wrote up these notes, in his somewhat mannered style, for the benefit of other Western students of the Bible, for whom such detailed eyewitness information was a novelty. In writing up what he learnt from Arculf, he sometimes compared this information with what he had learnt from books, including the works of Jerome and the Latin version of Josephus that goes under the name of Hegesippus.

What Adomnán does not tell us is how he came to meet Bishop Arculf and spend a considerable time in conversation with him at a time when, as abbot, he was 'daily beset by laborious and almost insupportable business from every quarter'. He took a copy of his book on the holy places with him to King Aldfrith, who encouraged its circulation in Northumbria. Bede – a theologian and biblical commentator himself – thought well of the book, though he is equivocal about its 'intricate' style; he quotes from it with praise in his *Ecclesiastical History*, and he even rewrote it in his own simpler style, helping to give the information supplied by Arculf a wider readership. Now, it is Bede who tells us that Arculf, returning by sea, 'was brought by contrary wind after many changes of course to our island, that is to Britain, and at length after not a few dangers he came to Adomnán . . .'. This surely raises more problems: why, in particular, should someone sailing from Sicily to France come to Iona? Bede, I suspect, has simply sketched a conjectural answer to our question. We do not know what brought Arculf to Iona, nor can we be sure when he visited, though such evidence as there is suggests a date between about 683 and 688.

The *Life of St Columba* was not written until several years later. Some idea of the date of writing can be got from stories about Adomnán's own experience of St Columba's miraculous powers. In one of these he implies that he had been abbot for at least seventeen years, which would make the date of writing no earlier than 696. In another he says that the saint had intervened three times to change a contrary wind to a favourable one, most recently in June 697, when the abbot was returning to Iona after the synod in Ireland (*341*). This does not make it clear exactly when the *Life* was written: Adomnán may have begun it before 697; he worked on it for some time, revising the text in places, and he was obviously still writing after that date. But the story mentioning St Columba's feast in the year of the Irish synod may give us a hint as to what prompted him to write: he was hurrying home to keep the one hundredth anniversary of the saint's death.

The community wanted a Life of their patron, and Adomnán (in a conventional phrase) mentions that he wrote 'in response to the entreaties of the brethren'. If we are fully to understand the Life he wrote for them, we need to ask what sources of information were available to Adomnán and what determined how he used them in presenting his own picture of St Columba.

Adomnán was concerned to make it clear that what he wrote could be relied upon, because he used only the best sources. In his second preface he says:

No one should think that I would write anything false about this remarkable man, nor even anything doubtful or uncertain. Let it be understood that I shall tell only what I learnt from the account handed down by our elders, men both reliable and informed, and that I shall write without equivocation what I have learnt by diligent inquiry either from what I could find already in writing or from what I heard recounted without a trace of doubt by informed and reliable old men.

In addition to this general statement about the quality of his sources, many times in the *Life* he mentions how he came by his information (*15*). Sometimes this is mentioned in general terms, from 'informed people' or 'learned men'; sometimes he makes clear what is the authority of his witness. This concern with the veracity of his account is unique among the Lives of Irish saints, and rare anywhere. No fewer than ten times Adomnán even says how the information was handed down from the saint's time to him. For example, the morning after Columba's death a monk called Lugaid described the vision he had experienced during the night at Cluain Finchoil to a fellow-monk, Fergnae. This Fergnae later joined the community at *Hinba*; there he lived for many years, often telling the story to the monks who stayed on the island. In his later years, Fergnae became a hermit nearby, but his story was known to many members of the community, and some of them lived long enough to tell Adomnán. But Adomnán had also found the story 'recorded in writing'. Stories about St Columba, then, were kept alive within the community, but they had also been committed to writing.

The only written material that we know about is Cumméne's book on St Columba's miraculous powers, but Adomnán never mentions it. Our knowledge of it depends entirely on the fact that an early copyist included a passage from that work as he was copying the *Life* (*360*). It is, therefore, only a matter of presumption that it was the chief of the writings to which Adomnán refers, and that he used it extensively as a source. The fact that Adomnán does not bother to explain this or say anything about the character of Cumméne's book asks for some explanation. Irish law favoured eyewitness testimony over documents, so that Adomnán's use of the

Latin language of testimony and his naming of informants may be seen as repeatedly underlining the credibility of what he writes, and doing so more effectively than citing the earlier book. If Dr Herbert is right in seeing Cumméne's book as a collection of written testimonies, Adomnán's was meant to be more than that, and it was surely his intention that Cumméne's work should be superseded by his own.

Adomnán was not only concerned with his credibility. He was anxious to present St Columba to his readers as the equal of those continental saints whose Lives were widely read. His knowledge of such Lives had an influence on the structure of the book; it also coloured the language and in some instances it may have shaped the way individual stories are told. Two Lives contributed most to the way in which Adomnán chose to write the *Life of St Columba*.

The more significant of the two was the *Life of St Martin* written by Sulpicius Severus at Tours in France at the end of the fourth century. Sulpicius arranged his work in three sections, describing in turn the events of Martin's life until he became a bishop, his miracles and the spiritual example of his way of living. Adomnán similarly writes in three books. In the first book he presents St Columba as a man whose vision was not limited by time and space, for he could see events far away or in the future. His prophecies are not like those of the Old Testament prophets but they show him as a man joined to the Lord in spirit (I 1 p. 112). Adomnán explains this cosmic vision (I 43), citing St Paul, but he has silently adapted a passage from another model, Gregory the Great's Dialogues (*189*). In so doing he places St Columba in the same contemplative tradition as Gregory's subject, St Benedict. In Book Two Adomnán goes on to deal with St Columba's miracles, beginning with one that parallels Christ's first miracle at Cana (II 1). At one stage, having told how the saint restored a dead child to life, Adomnán breaks into a homiletic style, expounding how this miracle proves that St Columba shared the same grace as the prophets and apostles (II 32). Prophecy and the working of miracles are gifts of the Spirit, but the third book is devoted to 'angelic apparitions and certain phenomena of heavenly light seen above the man of God' (second preface). Throughout the Bible God sends angels to those he has chosen, but in the *Life* these angels are not mere bearers of messages – St Columba shares in their society, proving even during his earthly life that his place is in the heavenly kingdom. While borrowing the basic shape of the *Life of St Martin*, Adomnán has set out his own argument, organizing his book around three proofs that St Columba was a man of God.

The part of the work in which the most detailed use is made of Sulpicius's book is in the two prefaces, where phrases are quoted almost verbatim. Indeed, the idea of having two prefaces was taken from Sulpicius, who had himself adopted it from the *Life of St Antony* (*6*). St Antony's *Life* was originally written in Greek by Athanasius, but it became widely known in the West through the Latin translation by Evagrius; the two prefaces in this case are those by the author and the translator. Evagrius's work is the other principal influence on the *Life of St Columba*. Adomnán quotes from Evagrius in both prefaces (*4*, *21*) and again elsewhere in the *Life* (*259*), but he uses this text chiefly in his account of Columba's last days. Seven or eight quotations, however, form but a very small element in the narrative; it can hardly be claimed that the description of how St Columba approached death is modelled on St Antony. We can, however, expect that many of Adomnán's readers would recognize the quotations and call to mind the implied comparison.

There is other evidence hinting that these two texts, Evagrius's *Life of St Antony* and Sulpicius's *Life of St Martin*, were the best known Lives of saints among the Columban churches. A monk of Lindisfarne wrote the *Life of St Cuthbert* at almost exactly the time when Adomnán was working on his book, though neither saw the other's work. The anonymous work also has two prefaces, in this case composed entirely of quotations from Evagrius, Sulpicius and two other works, one of which was also quoted by Adomnán (*18*). This marked degree of influence is not reflected in other Lives of saints written in Ireland or England. Looking for an explanation as to why only these two texts should share these models, we may perhaps conjecture that they were already studied with particular attention in Columban houses when Lindisfarne was closely linked with Iona.

Besides the two texts that most influenced how Adomnán approached the writing of St Columba's *Life*, other books provided him with phrases or ideas here and there. These are identified in the notes on the translation. The most commonly cited of these books is Gregory's Dialogues, which includes a Life of St Benedict as well as stories of other Italian saints. Adomnán's use of this text at one point raises an insoluble problem: in II 44 Adomnán tells how he and the elders in Iona decided to take the saint's tunic and books out into the fields in the hope of inducing rain, yet the story seems to be modelled on one related by Gregory (*331*). Did it happen, is it a literary fiction, or was the act itself influenced by Gregory's book? More often the influence of such sources is no more than to provide phrases that help Adomnán to say what he wants to say while reinforcing his words with echoes of more famous saints.

Principally, then, Adomnán's *Life* retells the stories of St Columba that were handed down, by word of mouth and in writing, within his own community. There are a few such stories set in Ireland, but most of them relate to Iona and places not far away. Literary influences helped Adomnán to organize and present this material in such a way as to make it clear that St Columba was a man of God in a mould that was both biblical and universal. But there is an element in the *Life* that cannot be explained in this way. At times Adomnán tells stories that seem to come from a popular tradition outside the monastic community. The story of the sorcerer who drew milk from a bull, for example, shows St Columba as a hero of folk-tale rather than as the model of a monastic leader. The accounts of St Columba and the king of the Picts lack the kind of circumstantial detail of the stories with a monastic setting, and may have derived from an oral source outside the community. There are stories of this kind set in Ireland as well as in Scotland, and they must reflect Adomnán's awareness of wider oral traditions about the saint. It is, however, the minor portion of the text that is of this character; the greater part belongs very much to the monastic milieu of Iona and the other churches of the Columban community.

In portraying St Columba as he did, with so little regard for the major events in the saint's career, Adomnán's approach is timeless. He was writing in and for an established monastic community. The brethren wanted to know about their founder but they were not concerned with when or how their monastery was founded. This indifference to time makes the *Life* a work that is thoroughly unhistorical in its approach, however much the writer was concerned with the veracity of his sources. This mattered to him, but not in the way it matters to a historian: the naming of informants reflects Adomnán's desire to attest the miraculous element of his story rather than any real concern to make historical sense of the saint's life.

On a great many points Adomnán was either indifferent to sixth-century reality or perhaps chose to ignore it. He most likely knew, for example, that Uí Néill tradition made Diarmait mac Cerbaill the last high king to celebrate the Feast of Tara; he may or may not have wondered whether there really was a high king as long ago as the 560s; but he chose to described Diarmait as 'ordained by God's will as king of all Ireland' (I 36). The expression resembles what he says of the Christian king, Oswald, 'afterwards ordained by God as emperor of all Britain'. Diarmait was probably neither Christian nor in any sense king of all Ireland, but his successors, the Uí Néill high kings of Adomnán's time, may have thought in these terms. From the time of Domnall mac Áedo the Uí Néill dynasties cultivated the idea that their supreme overlord was king of Ireland (*86*), and by the end of the century this idea was projected backwards in time. 'King of the Irish' is the phrase used in Muirchú's *Life of St Patrick*, written in the 690s, to describe a fifth-century Uí Néill king. Adomnán belonged to the Uí Néill; when he was writing, his kinsman Loingsech mac Oengusa, king of Cenél Conaill, was high king and had led the kings at the Synod of Birr; it is not surprising that Adomnán should view the past through this present perspective.

What is striking about Adomnán's references to kings has nothing to do with simple political affiliations. It is his perception that kings, like abbots, hold office by divine providence. Adomnán gives a very prominent place to stories about kings, from King Oswald's battle (I 1 p. 110) through a whole series of 'prophecies about battles and about kings' (I 7–15). The tone in which he comments on the killing of Diarmait mac Cerbaill suggests that he regarded the king of Ireland, 'ordained by God's will', as different from other kings. Dr Michael Enright has argued persuasively that the difference lies in an Old Testament perception of kingship. The first kings of Israel were chosen by God and anointed by the prophet Samuel; only God could remove such a king. The language of ordination is used in the Irish canon collection to refer to Samuel's anointing of Saul, and Adomnán has used the same words in describing how God commanded Columba to ordain his choice as king of Dalriada, Áedán mac Gabráin, when Columba favoured Áedán's brother Éogenán (III 5). Again, Adomnán uses Samuel as a model in describing how, while Áedán was still alive, Columba chose Eochaid Buide as Áedán's heir, kissing and blessing him (I 9). Whether anointing actually figured in the king-making rituals of Adomnán's time, we cannot know. I think it is unlikely, and it is still less likely that Columba ever anointed a king of Dalriada. But Adomnán's biblical sources are clear, and there can be no doubt that he is concerned to present a biblical view of kings, chosen by God and instituted by his prophet. Columba is presented as the prophet, not in the mould of Isaiah and Jeremiah but of Samuel. There are two points here: Adomnán's ideas about kingship have been strongly influenced by the Old Testament, and, more locally, he is arguing that Columba and his successors have a special role in mediating God's assistance to kings, a point made explicit at the start of the book (I 1 p. 110). This help is available to all kings who show due reverence to Columba, and there is no narrow political message. Oswald as 'emperor of all Britain' is given pride of place; two Uí Néill overlords, Diarmait mac Cerbaill and Domnall mac Áedo, are given the title 'king of Ireland'; Áedán mac Gabráin of Dalriada figures prominently; but Columba's support extended to minor kings such as Oengus Bronbachal (I 13). The emphasis given to Columba's part in the meeting of Áed mac Ainmirech and Áedán mac Gabráin at Druim Cett may indeed suggest that the Columban tradition tried to be evenhanded between the Northern Uí Néill and Dalriada, but other kings were not overlooked. This remarkable emphasis on the relationship between kings and the successors of Columba surely reflects the thinking of Adomnán, a biblical scholar himself, but also related to kings, the friend of kings, a negotiator with kings. He recognized not merely that the support of kings would benefit the church he headed; he is concerned also with the larger issue, that in creating a Christian society the church had to persuade kings that they depended for their position on God's providence mediated through his Church.

Some historians have analysed Adomnán's purposes in writing in a much narrower sense. He has been seen as seeking the special favour of the kings of Dalriada, on the supposition that Iona was in his day losing the support of the Uí Néill to St Patrick's principal church at Armagh. Yet at precisely the time when Adomnán was writing, he and the Uí Néill high king had cooperated to achieve the enactment of the Law of Innocents. The bishop of Armagh was the first of the ecclesiastical guarantors, and almost the last was Muirchú, author of the most recent Life of St Patrick. There is really no basis for suggesting that Iona had lost the allegiance of the Uí Néill, even though it is clear that Armagh too enjoyed their support. The claims put forward by Armagh to primacy in the Irish church were not necessarily acceptable to Adomnán, but they were still only claims. It is certainly probable that he meant to present a portrait of St Columba that could stand alongside that of St Patrick. The seventh-century Lives of St Patrick made extravagant claims for his power, his property and his jurisdiction, which Adomnán did not confront or challenge. His approach is less arrogant, more subtle. He is without question more spiritual in his biblical and his monastic understanding of the saint, and he is more international in his approach to depicting Columba as a saint in the mould of St Martin, St Antony and St Benedict.

Against this background one must ask for whom Adomnán wrote. He did not imagine that his principal readers were kings or the heads of rival churches, but he surely did expect the *Life of St Columba* to be read in Irish churches outside the Columban community, just as the Lives of St Martin and other saints were read. He was teaching his fellow religious about St Columba, about monastic devotion and about the dependence of kings on the church. The cult of St Columba was spread through much of Ireland, attracting devotion comparable to that to the other 'national' saints, St Patrick and St Brigit.

There is every chance that he also expected a wider audience. As Dr Picard has pointed out, the arguments in Northumbria about the date of Easter had involved attacks on the saintly authority of St Columba. Although we depend on Bede for the statement of his case, Wilfrid at Whitby had sought to undermine St Columba's standing as the patron of those arguing for the Celtic method of calculation. Adomnán may have been aware that the holy Cuthbert (d. 687), bishop of Lindisfarne, was becoming the subject of a saint's cult in the 690s; he may have wanted the monks of Northumbria to be able to read about St Columba, their former patron. Whether he expected a wider, Continental audience is debatable, and most of his allusions to the Continental diffusion of the saint's cult are imitative of Evagrius's *Life of St Antony*.

Much the greater part of the book, however, is rooted in the community of Iona. To a very considerable extent Adomnán was writing for his own monks. This explains not only the focus of what he wrote but also what he does not say. There is no account of the foundation of the saint's churches because that was taken for granted. The saint's missionary work among the Picts is not included because Adomnán was not writing for a Pictish audience nor, apparently, to explain the position of the Columban churches in Pictland. There are no political set-piece narratives, such as he might have written to describe the meeting at Druim Cett or the ordination of King Áedán, because he was not making a political point. The dominant interest throughout the *Life* is domestic, the focus is on St Columba as a man of God among his monks. He represents the ideal saintly abbot, and many episodes depict the proper concerns of an abbot for the brethren of his community. Communal activities provide the context for many of the stories. The sense of community is even carried forward from the saint's time to the time of writing by the mention of Columba's successors Baithéne, Lasrén, Fergnae, Ségéne and, more recently, Failbe and Adomnán himself, who had personal experience of the saint's continuing power. The memory of the saint was handed down within the community in which he had lived, and many named members of the community are involved in that transmission. The interpretation of Columba's sanctity is informed by Adomnán's reading in other saints' Lives as well as in the Bible, but the sphere in which it is most fully revealed is as the father of his own monks. Adomnán was able to understand Columba through his perception of his own role as abbot of Iona.

*The island and monastery of Iona*

Adomnán several times speaks of Iona as 'our island' and once as 'this our principal island' (I 1). It is clear that in his own day, when the saint was invoked to bring an end to the drought (II 44), the cultivation of the island was in the hands of the monastery. His stories of the monks' working in the fields at the machair suggest that he believed this was so in Columba's time. The monastery itself was situated on the east side of the island, looking out across the Sound to the Ross of Mull. There is no doubt that it was on the raised beach of cultivable land where the abbey stands today. In the seventeenth and eighteenth centuries some visitors seem to have imagined that the ruined abbey they saw was the monastery of St Columba, but in time it was generally understood that all the remaining buildings dated from the later Middle Ages. Even the paved road, the Street of the Dead, uncovered in 1962, is late medieval. There is simply not enough left of the early monastery to show us what it looked like in the days of Columba or Adomnán. Successive rebuildings of the church and conventual buildings have probably destroyed the evidence underground of the original structures. Burials in the Reilig Odrain may have been continuous since the early Middle Ages; later burials will have done away with older ones. In any case major excavation is impractical underneath the abbey, and in the Reilig Odrain it is prevented by the more recent use of the graveyard. Inevitably, therefore, the monastery of Iona presents great problems to the archaeologist.

One major feature still partly visible that goes back to the seventh century is the vallum, the boundary bank surrounding the monastic enclosure, first remarked upon by Thomas Pennant in 1772 (*281*). The line of this vallum can be traced in a great arc north, west and south of the abbey; to the east there was no bank, but the enclosure fell away gradually to the shore. Much of this can no longer be easily seen, and south of the abbey it is divided into several lines, suggesting alterations to the outline of the enclosure and perhaps divisions within it. Adomnán refers to this boundary bank in the *Life* (II 29), but we cannot be sure of its size or its full course in his time.

The site enclosed by the vallum covers some twenty acres, and we may be sure that the early church did not fill the entire space within. The ancient crosses still standing in front of the abbey date from the mid-eighth century, a generation or more after Adomnán's time, but they provide a good guide that the main church stood on the same line as the medieval abbey.

Almost opposite the front of the abbey there is a small rocky knoll, Tòrr Ab, where, Reeves reports, 'the socket of a cross is said to have been observed'. This name is first recorded by Pennant as 'the abbot's mount', but the same knoll appears to be what Martin Martin had called *Dùn nam Manach* 'the monks' fort'. Here excavations in 1956 and 1957 revealed something of the structure of the cross-base in several layers; the use of mortar in its construction implies a date in the later Middle Ages or after, but the base partly overlay the site of a small stone building just to the south. This was much older; it had at some point been abandoned and its site levelled to give a small cobbled platform. The archaeologists who dug the site have been keen to identify this as the remnant of the hut where Columba used to write and receive visitors. There are problems in the interpretation of Adomnán's description of this hut (*127*), but one thing is clear: it was a wooden structure. If this was the site of Columba's hut – and that is beyond proof – the stone structure was later than his time.

This is all that can be seen on the ground to help call to mind a picture of the early monastery. From the *Life of St Columba* we learn something of the buildings but nothing of their layout. There was the church, mentioned several times, with at least one side-chapel (III 19). There was Columba's hut, already mentioned, and a separate building that served as his lodging, where he slept on the bare rock. There was a large domestic building, rebuilt while Adomnán was abbot (II 45), providing communal facilities and almost certainly housing the majority of the monks (*377*). Here we see Columba sitting by the fire and Luigbe reading a book (I 24). There was a guest-house, where visitors could stay for some time. Other small buildings may be assumed, such as a kitchen, separate because of the danger from its large fire, and store-houses. There was also an open area, possibly with some form of paving (III 6), and there were crosses set up at various places about the monastery. A monk is described as the gardener (I 18), so there must have been a garden for the growing of medicinal herbs (*132*). A cemetery must have existed from an early date, and Adomnán mentions the burial of laymen at the monastery as well as of Columba and his monks. By the time Adomnán wrote the *Life* the bodies of kings were brought to Iona for burial, and it is possible that there were two burial grounds, one for the community and one for laity. Adomnán also mentions buildings associated with the agricultural life of the monastery, a shed, where the ears of corn were dried, and a barn, where grain was stored. He tells us that beams were needed for the larger buildings, and that these were towed in by sea from Loch Moidart (II 45). The church, like St Aidan's church at Lindisfarne, was probably built of timber planks set vertically, but other buildings were more likely constructed of wattles supported by posts. The withies from which the wattles were made seem to have been brought from not far away (II 3).

It is possible that more information may yet be provided by archaeological work. There is little prospect of our learning much about what occupied the sites of the medieval abbey or the Reilig Odrain, but elsewhere within the area enclosed by the vallum excavation has been possible and more may yet be contemplated. A programme of archaeological exploration was begun by Charles Thomas in 1956; this was continued by Richard Reece from 1964 to 1974. Since then there have been several shorter projects, of which the most revealing was the excavation carried out by John Barber in 1979. The resulting information is inevitably fragmentary, deriving from individual trenches in different spots; not all of the results have yet been published; and even where there is a report, it is sometimes difficult to disentangle what was found from the excavator's interpretations. Only in Ian Fisher's work for the Royal Commission on the Ancient and Historical Monuments of Scotland is there an attempt, very concisely, to draw together the results of these excavations.

Ample traces of early medieval occupation have been found close to the abbey on the west and south sides, but the findings add up to rather less than one might have hoped for from so much work on a site such as this. John Barber's excavation in 1979 revealed the most information about the early monastic site. An area of ground north of the Reilig Odrain, between the Street of the Dead and the field-wall to the east, was thoroughly investigated before it became a modern extension of the burial ground. At the south edge of this site and extending into the area of the Reilig Odrain, a stretch of the vallum was uncovered. Any trace of a banking had long since gone, but a major ditch was discovered, some nineteen feet wide and nearly nine and a half feet deep. A sixty-five-foot length of the ditch was excavated. At the western end the ditch came to a stop where a roadway had entered across the vallum; in its earliest phase a narrow cutting joined the ditch at either side of this entrance, and the roadway had been carried on planking; later the roadway was widened and the cutting filled in. The build-up of peat in the ditch indicated that the bottom had always been filled with water, so some steps must have been taken to help drainage when the planking was taken away and the cutting filled in. This ditch had evidently been used as a dump, since from it there came not only animal bones, presumably kitchen waste, but also quantities of worked leather, turned wood and similar detritus from the workshops of the monastery. These materials had been preserved by waterlogging and were used to obtain radiocarbon dates for this section of the vallum. It was dug in the early part of the seventh century and began to accumulate debris from the start. The craft waste seems to have stopped at much the same time that the entrance was altered, later in the seventh century, evidence that the workshops were moved to another part of the site.

Immediately to the north of this there was another ditch, following a rather wavy course even in the short length that was excavated. This northern ditch was much smaller and had been cut through by the vallum, suggesting that it was older. Radiocarbon dates obtained for charcoal from the smaller ditch confirmed that it was older, probably from the earliest phase of the Columban monastery, and it was clear that it had been filled in when the vallum was dug in the early seventh century.

The curve in this older ditch led the excavator, Mr Barber, to infer that it was part of the northern boundary of the earliest monastic site, which he conjectured lay in the area of the Reilig Odrain. He thought that the same was the case with the larger ditch that formed part of the vallum, and he suggested that the monastic site was extended northwards in the mid-seventh century, perhaps under Abbot Ségéne. The Royal Commission rejected this conjecture, which is not compatible with the evidence for the course of the vallum as a whole. If Mr Barber were correct, it would mean the church had been resited in this extension; between the dates from the vallum and the erection of the surviving crosses, this would have had to have happened in the late seventh or early eighth century, which is most unlikely; the church almost certainly continued on the same site from the sixth century. Further, Mr Barber's excavations revealed the post-holes of a large circular building to the north of the two ditches. This building belonged to the later seventh century and may have been one of the principal domestic buildings (*377*).

Rather than conjecturing that the church has changed its location, it is much easier to accept that the area of the Reilig Odrain lay outside the early line of the vallum. The Royal Commission's geophysical survey showed features that might mean that the vallum was extended to include the land where the St Columba Hotel now stands, though that is far from certain. It is possible that the Reilig Odrain does not date back to the earliest period of the monastery, but it is no less possible that it was in origin a burial place for the laity, not at first within the vallum.

From an archaeological point of view the Reilig Odrain has been disturbed not only by centuries of continuing burials but also by two hundred years of antiquarian interest. In the late eighteenth and early nineteenth centuries efforts were made to expose as many as possible of the medieval gravestones that had become partially buried over the years; these were later rearranged in two rows, which were enclosed with iron railings in 1868. They were then taken away in 1975 and the medieval carved stones were gathered into a museum behind the abbey. During this long period many stones from the early Middle Ages were found, and these were kept in St Oran's Church and in the abbey until they too were placed in the museum. Unfortunately, as a result of all this we have no means of knowing exactly where these stones came from. Among them there is much of interest.

The inventory compiled by the Royal Commission includes nearly eighty early medieval cross-marked stones. Some of these have simple incised crosses, others have the cross outlined and, in a few cases, recessed; nearly half of the stones have the outline of a ringed cross such as became very popular with the 'Celtic' revival in the nineteenth century. There are a small number with expansional crosses in interlace of an Irish style, which may be dated to the tenth or even eleventh century. A few stones have the usual Irish gravestone inscription, *Oráit do* . . . 'A prayer for . . .', with the name of the person. The individuals named in these inscriptions – Fergus, Éogan, Flann, Loingsechán – cannot be identified, but the form of lettering allows us to date them to the eighth and ninth centuries. The simple crosses are extremely difficult to date, and in many cases it is difficult even to tell whether the stone was meant to lie flat or stand upright; some recumbent crosses seem to have been altered and reused as upright stones. What all these stones show us is that through the eighth, ninth, tenth centuries and beyond the Reilig Odrain was used for burials and that some graves were marked with a stone. It is probable that most of these were the graves of laymen rather than monks. Some of the simple incised crosses may date from the seventh century, and there is one inscribed stone that very likely dates back to the seventh or early eighth century. It stands a foot high and its front surface is covered with a chi-rho cross. On the top edge an inscription reads *lapis Echodi* 'the stone of Echodius'; this is the same early spelling used by Adomnán for the common Old Irish name Eochaid. Unfortunately, it is not possible to identify the person with anyone mentioned in the *Life* or in other sources.

The main life of the community, however, is not revealed by the archaeological evidence. At the centre of the monastery's activities was the daily round of worship in the church, to which the brethren were summoned by a handbell. Most of the canonical hours of the office are mentioned by Adomnán, but he reveals very little of the actual liturgy, mentioning only 'a book of the week's hymns' (*231*). On Sundays and feast days the Eucharist was celebrated at the midday service (*344*), and on major feasts the brethren wore white for this service. Prayers in the church are mentioned at various times, and on occasions the saint orders the bell to be sounded to summon the brethren to church for a special reason. Fasting, too, was a part of the religious observance. The monks would fast on Wednesdays (I 26) as well as Fridays, though the fast could be relaxed in special circumstances (*130*). A special meal was eaten on Sundays and feast days, and this too might be ordered by the saint when it was appropriate (III 12).

Work was also a part of the daily routine except on Sundays and feast days. Some of this would include the copying of service-books and, presumably, of other manuscripts (*125*), but necessary agricultural and domestic demands would make for continuous work in a community that is represented by Adomnán as largely self-sufficient. Baithéne is mentioned once as being in charge of works at harvest-time, and this may have been an official role (*162*). Some occasional activities also come into Adomnán's narrative, including walling the fields at the machair, repairing the guest-house, towing logs at sea and rebuilding the 'great house', the main monastic building. The monks kept cattle for milk and for meat, there was a member of the community who did the necessary blacksmith's work, and references to a wooden pail, carts, a horse, shoes and a leather vessel, a millstone and so on all imply a range of other crafts and activities. The detritus of wood- and leather-working was found in plenty by Mr Barber's excavations in the ditch of the vallum. Other tasks must have included the preparation of writing materials such as parchment, ink and pigments.

The monastery also had its harbour. We do not know where this was, but the place-name *Port na Muintir* 'harbour of the community' is suggestive. This is the inlet nearest to the abbey, but others include *Port a'Chrossain* 'harbour of the cross', and *Port Rónain* 'St Rónan's harbour' between the modern jetty and the old landing place, *An Carraig fada* 'the long rock', just to the north. These names are not recorded until the last century and may tell us nothing. We learn from Adomnán that the community built its own boats, and manned and supplied them. These boats included both wooden vessels and skin-covered currachs. Members of the community were often at sea, moving about the west coast or crossing to Ireland. They were doubtless competent seamen, but, then as now, a seafaring community suffered its tragedies from time to time: in 641 the annals record 'the shipwreck of a boat of the community of Iona', on 16 September 691 'a gale caused some six men of the community of Iona to drown', and in 749 'the drowning of the community of Iona'. A special need was the maintenance of a ferry-service, since visitors without boats seem regularly to have arrived across Mull; the community's boat was summoned by shouting across the Sound.

Activities that Adomnán scarcely mentions are teaching and study. Once we hear of a young layman who studied with Columba (III 21) as the saint's foster-son before returning home to a worldly career. In another story a young monk was studying a book while Columba sat by the fireside in the monastic building (I 24). The essentials of literacy in Latin are assumed throughout and it is once suggested that Baithéne, had he been present, might have written down Columba's exposition of the Bible. Although books are treated as important, we might infer that the stories available to Adomnán did not include anything about the scholarly pursuits of the monks. It is possible that study was not a major element in the early days of the monastery but became more important later in the seventh century.

Adomnán names some twenty monks at Iona in the lifetime of St Columba; to this number we may add the names of some of his companions not mentioned in the *Life* but in the list included in some copies of the text. Yet we are still in no position to form a realistic estimate of the size of the monastery, still less of the community at its several sites. Adomnán's stories about work on rebuilding the great house show that there had been rebuilding over the years since the founder's time. We might guess that there was considerable change, and it is possible that in Adomnán's time there were many more monks in Iona than a hundred years before. We know from excavation and survey that the vallum was altered more than once in the seventh century, and it has been inferred by John Barber that the workshops were relocated during this period. How much other rebuilding had changed the appearance of the place between Columba's day and Adomnán's is unknown, but it must be borne in mind. Any picture of the monastery and its life, whether founded on Adomnán or on archaeological work, is more than likely to be in some ways a hybrid, for we simply do not know enough to say how much the place changed over its first one hundred and fifty years.

### *The Columban community after Adomnán*

In the twenty years after Adomnán's death, so historians have often asserted, the community in Iona was divided. It has been thought that there were two parties, those who supported Adomnán over the date of Easter and those who opposed change, or those who favoured the Cenél Loairn or the Cenél nGabráin as the ruling family of Dalriada. Historians have been unable to agree as to the nature of the split, perhaps because there is no evidence actually to tell us that there was a split at all. These theories arise from problems in understanding references in the annals to different people apparently holding high office in the community at the same time.

Adomnán's successor, Conamail, died in 710, but we learn that Dunchad had already become abbot in 707 and continued until his death in 717. In 713 Dorbbéne 'obtained the chair of Iona and, after five months in the primacy, died on Saturday, 28 October'. Next, in 716, Fáelchú 'received the chair of Columba at the age of seventy-three on Saturday, 29 August'; he died as abbot in 724. Before that date, in 722, the annals record that Fedlimid became abbot, but his death is not entered. It would seem, therefore, that between 707 and 710 both Conamail and Dunchad were abbots; during Dunchad's abbacy Dorbbéne held office for a short period; three years later Fáelchú was similarly installed alongside Dunchad and appears to have continued in office after Dunchad's death. It has been thought that Fedlimid was an assistant abbot to take care of business because of Fáelchú's great age. Another list, preserved in Salzburg from the eighth century, simply names the abbots in order: Conamail, Dunchad, Dorbbéne, Fáelchú. Conamail appears not to have belonged to the Cenél Conaill, but the other three all appear in a genealogical list of the early abbots. Dunchad was closely related to the ruling lineage, Dorbbéne was a distant relation, and Fáelchú belonged only to a remote branch of the Cenél Conaill. If the situation here were one of different parties recognizing different abbots, it is hard to understand why the annals should enter all of them impartially and without explanation. The detail of the dates given for Dorbbéne and Fáelchú show that these were contemporary entries, and there is nothing to suggest that the other annal entries were derived from a different source. Rather than conjecture a schism, we should admit that it is impossible to interpret how the abbacy was occupied during this period.

During this time we learn of some significant events. In 716 the annals concisely record that 'Easter was changed in the monastery of Iona'. Bede devotes a whole chapter to describing how 'the monks of the Irish nation who lived in the island of Iona, together with the monasteries under their jurisdiction, were led by God's providence to adopt the canonical rite of Easter and style of tonsure' (Bede, v 22). The aged Ecgberht, an Englishman who had lived most of his life in Ireland, came to Iona and persuaded the community to make the change they had so long resisted. Bede saw in this a completion of the circle: that Iona had brought the Faith to Northumbria and now Northumbria brought Iona into unity with Christendom. He knew that the abbot at the time was Dunchad, and he knew too that Ecgberht continued to live in Iona until his death on Easter Day, 24 April 729. Bede's *History* was finished in 731, so clearly he must have had recent information from Iona. We may presume too that the annal entry for Ecgberht's death 'on Easter day' derives from the Iona annals.

In 716 Easter fell on 19 April. In September of that year Fáelchú was installed alongside Dunchad, who died on 25 May 717. Later that year the annals record 'the expulsion of the community of Iona across Druim Alban by King Naiton'. The significance of this is very obscure. Some years earlier, around 710, King Naiton had supported the adoption of the Roman Easter in Pictland. In Bede's words, the king declared: 'I publicly proclaim in the presence of you all that I intend to observe this time of Easter with all my people for ever. And I decree that all the clergy of my kingdom shall adopt the tonsure of which we have now heard the full explanation' (Bede, v 21). At that date the Columban clergy in Pictland must have found themselves on the wrong side, but it seems hard to imagine that the king waited until Iona had come round to the Roman method before expelling them. It seems to me more likely that his reasons were secular. Perhaps some refusal on the part of the Columban clergy to accept the king's command made him aware that here in his kingdom were people owing allegiance to an authority outside his control. It may have been a political act to expel the Columban clergy, if that is really what happened. Bede's silence on such a major move is surprising. Perhaps the annal signifies that the authority of Iona over her churches in Pictland was ended; if it meant that a great proportion of the clergy were sent away, this would presumably have involved some corresponding recruitment of priests, perhaps from Northumbria, which Bede would surely have mentioned.

From the 720s the annals present a simpler picture. Cilléne Fota was abbot from 724 to 726, when he seems to have been succeeded by Cilléne Droichtech. The latter continued in office until 752, and his successor, Slébíne, was abbot from 752 to 767. From this period of about forty years there is ample evidence that Iona enjoyed something of a golden age.

In the year after Cilléne Droichtech became abbot the annals inform us that 'the relics of Adomnán are taken to Ireland and the Law is renewed'; another entry reports that in October 730 the relics of Adomnán returned from Ireland. This suggests that the abbot revived the seventh-century practice of an Irish visitation. Whether it was the corporeal relics of Adomnán that were taken we cannot be sure. Slébíne became abbot in 752 and in 754 he went to Ireland. He died in 767, but in 766 his successor, Suibne, is recorded as visiting Ireland, perhaps a sign that he was already abbot-designate. Suibne died in 772, and the next abbot, Bresal, visited Ireland in 778.

During the greater part of this period the Columban community also enjoyed the support of successive high kings. Concerning Cilléne's visit in 727, it is said in a twelfth-century note on a poem about the relics collected by Adomnán that Cilléne took these to Ireland to make peace between the Cenél Conaill and the other Northern Uí Néill lineage, Cenél nÉogain, whose battle is recorded in the annals. A few years later, in 733, these two kingdoms were again at war and a fleet was sent from Dalriada to support the Cenél Conaill, while the Cenél nÉogain were probably responsible for an attack on the Columban church on Tory Island to the north of Ireland. Then in 734 the defeated high king from the lineage of Cenél Conaill gave way to his rival from Cenél nÉogain, Áed Allán, who was high king until 743. During these nine years Iona may not have enjoyed royal support. Áed's successor, Domnall Midi, belonged to the lineage of Clann Cholmáin, the leading family of the Southern Uí Néill. Abbot Cilléne belonged to another southern lineage, a connection that may have helped the community. In 753 the annals mention that King Domnall proclaimed 'the Law of Columb Cille' in the year before the new abbot's visitation, and in 757 Slébíne renewed this law. We have no information on its terms, but this is clear evidence that the king favoured the community. A late and unreliable annal-collection even says that he was buried at Durrow. Domnall died in 763. His successor as high king, Niall Frossach, seems also to have supported the community, even though he belonged to the Cenél nÉogain; after seven years, he retired to live out his days at Iona, where he died in 778. His successor, Donnchad Midi, was Domnall's son, who ruled as high king from 770 to 797. He joined with Abbot Bresal in proclaiming the Law of Columb Cille in Ireland again in 778.

Under a succession of abbots, then, the community enjoyed a high prestige. The links between Iona and the Irish monasteries of the community seem to have remained strong, and successive impositions of the Laws of Adomnán and Columb Cille are thought to have brought in a considerable income in penalties. Iona, as the centre of the community, had long been an important cultural crossroads between Ireland, Pictland, and Northumbria. Greater wealth and security in the mid-eighth century may have been factors lying behind a series of major works of religious art at Iona.

The greatest and the most famous is the gospel-book now

known as the Book of Kells. Like the Book of Durrow, this contains the four gospels, but the book is much bigger because its script is larger and there is much more decorative detail. The text of the gospels in this manuscript is more characteristically Irish than that of Durrow, being of a 'mixed' type, reflecting both the Vulgate and the Old Latin texts of the Bible. The full-page pictures and carpet pages are astonishingly elaborate, and some text pages have developed into decorative pages, so that the letters are almost lost in the ornament. Scholars have long argued about its date, and it would not be right to say that there is now universal agreement. The most persuasive view is that the book was written and illuminated at an Irish centre open to the artistic influence of both Northumbria and Pictland in the middle years of the eighth century. Iona is very much the most probable place, from where at a later date, almost certainly some time in the ninth century, the book was taken to the Columban church at Kells. The hypothesis that the Book of Kells was written and decorated at Iona is supported by certain similarities with the art of the Iona crosses. These too show the artistic influence of Northumbrian sculpture and Anglo-Saxon metalwork, but there are specific details that make the parallels more exact.

The crosses that stand immediately in front of the abbey are St John's Cross, with its massive arms, and the taller, ring-headed St Martin's Cross. Only the latter is original; St John's Cross lies in fragments, and a concrete replica has taken its place. The stump of St Matthew's Cross remains nearby, but this is later in date. The earliest of the Iona crosses, however, is now known as St Oran's Cross, since its fragments were first recorded in St Oran's Chapel in the last century; it is now kept in store. These crosses have been discussed in detail by many art-historians, but the analysis by Ian Fisher, supported by the technical resources of the Royal Commission, is the most revealing. St Oran's is a wide-armed cross, made in three pieces from the local schist, which is liable to break. St John's Cross, made of more suitable stone from the mainland, is similarly a wide-armed cross, but recent discoveries show that this was altered by the addition of a ring. St Martin's Cross, with its integral ring, is the latest. The ring represents a solution to the technical problem of supporting wide arms on a free-standing high cross, leading to Mr Fisher's conclusion that they are 'an early and experimental group'. All three crosses are richly decorated. Both spiral ornament and elaborate bosses on parts of St Oran's and St John's crosses are very similar to spiral designs and roundels found among the decorative features in the Book of Kells.

More striking still is the iconographic parallel between the scene of the Virgin and Child flanked by angels on St Oran's Cross and a full-page picture in the Book of Kells. This scene is further paralleled on Kildalton Cross in Argyll, which is closely related to both St Oran's and St John's crosses. Devotion to the Virgin Mary is extremely rare at this date. One of the earliest Irish examples is an elaborate poem in Latin by Cú Chuimne of Iona (d. 747), *Cantemus in omni die*. The conjunction of this poem from Iona in the early eighth century and the scene on the Iona and Kildalton crosses with the illustration in the Book of Kells has been seen as supporting a mid-eighth-century date for the crosses and an Iona origin for the manuscript.

The technical experimentation implied by the work on the crosses suggests a workshop with a good deal of experience and craft skill, while the artistic accomplishment of the sculpture confirms that Iona must have had some exceptional stone-carvers. If, as seems likely, the Book of Kells was also written and decorated here, then Iona was also the most brilliant centre of manuscript art in this period. The pursuit of artistic achievement on this scale must represent a substantial investment in beautifying the rituals of the church, and we may guess that similar resources were devoted to the metalwork crosses, chalices and other altar plate of the monastery. In the same period it seems probable that the relics of St Columba were enshrined in the precious metal reliquary, which, we later learn, was hidden from the vikings in 825. We cannot quantify this investment, but a sidelight may be had from the fact that the Book of Kells is written on 170 animal skins. It cannot be doubted that Iona was a rich church by the middle of the eighth century,

By the time we reach the late eighth century, the character of many great Irish churches seems to have changed. Adomnán portrays Iona and Durrow as monastic communities, living by rule, singing the liturgy as a community, and supporting themselves by manual labour. Less than a hundred years later there is evidence to suggest that Durrow had become much larger and that many of its people were no longer monks but were lay people, men and women, living ordinary secular lives under the rule of the abbots. In 764, so the annals tell, two hundred members of the *familia* of Durrow were killed in battle against the monastery of Clonmacnoise. Clonmacnoise was victorious, nor was this its first battle to be chronicled. Twelve years later, in 776, the *familia* of Durrow supported King Donnchad in battle against the men of Munster, only two years before he joined with Abbot Bresal in reimposing the Law of Columb Cille in Ireland. Durrow must have had a considerable population, and it seems that its military forces could be called upon by the Southern Uí Néill overlord.

In Ireland as in England during the seventh and eighth centuries many places that had begun as religious communities grew into centres of population. Not all religious communities had devoted themselves to liturgy, study and contemplation. Many had been concerned primarily with the pastoral needs of the surrounding population. But in Ireland, where people clustered around a church, the emerging town came under the jurisdiction of the head of that church. Heads of religious communities, therefore, were more and more likely to be secular leaders, not necessarily in religious orders at all. Within the larger population of such a 'church', there remained a community of religious, living more or less as secular canons serving the needs of the church.

There is no evidence to suggest that Iona had changed to this extent, but clearly Durrow had. And it is against this background that we should consider the viking attacks that began towards the end of the eighth century. In the early ninth century such ecclesiastical towns were favourite targets, as centres of population, trade and wealth. But the first attacks affected the island monasteries. In 794 'the heathens' laid waste to 'all the islands of Britain', in 795 the Columban church on Lambay Island was attacked, in 798 Inis Pátraic. The vikings not only destroyed the shrine of St Do Chonna at Connor but also 'made great incursions in Ireland and Scotland' and seized tribute in the form of cattle. Iona was burned in 802, and in 806 the island was attacked again. This time sixty-eight members of the community were killed. In the very next year the annals record 'the building of the new monastery of Columb Cille at Kells'. Seven years later, in 814, we read: 'Cellach, abbot of Iona, resigned the abbacy when the building of the church of Kells was finished, and Diarmait was appointed in his place.' The following year Cellach died in retirement.

We have to rely on surmise as to what these entries signify. It is easy to suggest that because Iona had been attacked, Kells was built as a place of safety to which the community could retreat: it is less easy to see how this could have worked. The new site would itself have been threatened, and it is impossible to imagine how the community could have transferred its personnel and possessions from Iona to Kells when an attack seemed imminent. It may well be that the foundation of Kells had more to do with the community's relations with the Southern Uí Néill kings of that area than with the sea-borne attacks of the heathens. There is nothing to suggest that Iona was abandoned at this stage, nor that this was ever intended, though by the end of the ninth century it is evident that the leadership of the community had changed dramatically. Between 891 and 927 the headship of the *familia* of Columba was – remarkably – always combined with high office in another Irish church, and by the tenth century, the coarb of Columba and Adomnán was based at Kells.

## *The later history of Iona*

As the focus of the community's interests had shifted from the north to midland Ireland, so too in Scotland in the early ninth century the kings of Dalriada had successfully taken over the Pictish kingdom in eastern Scotland. Between the first viking attacks and the late ninth century Iona became to a considerable degree marginalized from both an Irish and a Scottish perspective.

In 825 the annals record 'the martyrdom of Blathmac mac Flainn by the heathens in Iona', and a Latin poem written at St Gallen in Switzerland by Walahfrid Strabo tells how he was killed for refusing to disclose where the precious reliquary of St Columba had been concealed. Over the next fifty years we hear much about the movements of relics of Columba, to Ireland in 831 and 849, and to Dunkeld in Scotland in 849. These relics would no doubt have included, for example, the saint's books and other possessions as well as his body. Finally, in 878, the Irish annals report: 'The shrine of Columb Cille and his other relics came to Ireland to escape the vikings.'

In the course of the ninth century and after, parts of the Hebrides were settled by Scandinavians, who have left their mark indelibly on the place-names of the west coast. Iona was now the crossroads of three cultures. Scottish kings were still brought for burial to Iona, which had not severed its links with Ireland; and in 980 we learn for the first time that a Norse king of Dublin visited as a pilgrim. Most of the Scandinavians settled on the west coast were probably still heathens, for in 986 it is recorded that the abbot and fifteen clergy in Iona were killed on Christmas eve. Converted to Christianity, the Scandinavians came to Iona. Among the stones from the Reilig Odrain is one of the tenth or more likely eleventh century with an interlace cross in the Irish style and an Old Norse inscription cut in runes: 'Kali the son of Ólvir laid this stone over his brother Fugl.' This and other memorial stones from the Reilig Odrain bear witness to the continuing importance of Iona as a church for burial. In the late eleventh century, as our sources become richer again, we hear once more of royal interests. Queen Margaret of Scotland is said to have rebuilt the monastic buildings and to have provided the clergy with new endowments, and in 1098 King Magnus Barelegs of Norway, on expedition in the Hebrides, visited 'St Columb Cille's little church'. It is thought that this refers to the small church, now rebuilt as St Columba's Chapel, which stands just to the north of the west door of the abbey, behind St John's Cross (*411*).

In the mid-twelfth century the position of Iona seems to have improved. Somerled defeated the Norse king of the Isles, creating a new Gaelic lordship in the southern Hebrides in 1156. St Oran's Chapel dates from about this period, and we find too that Iona again appears in the Irish annals. In 1164, at the instigation of Somerled and the men of Argyll and the Hebrides, a deputation from Iona visited Derry to ask Flaithbertach, the coarb of Columb Cille, to return with them as abbot of Iona. This deputation comprised the leaders of the community, including the arch-priest Augustine, the lector Dubside, the hermit Mac Gilla Duib, and Mac Forchellaig 'head of the *céli Dé*'. They failed, because the chiefs of northern Ireland and the clergy of the other churches were opposed to anything that might have restored Iona's leadership over Columba's Irish churches. Over the next forty years, when the annals seem to have been kept at Derry, they mention Irish visitors to Iona in 1174, 1188 and 1200. In 1203 Somerled's son, Ragnall, together with Cellach, the head of the religious community in Iona, refounded the community as a Benedictine abbey. Cellach secured a papal privilege for the new abbey, which is dated 9 December 1203. Then in 1204 there was a remarkable incident, described by the annalist at Derry:

A monastery was built by Cellach in the centre of the enclosure of Iona, without any right, in dishonour of the community of Iona, so that he wrecked the place greatly. A hosting however was made by the clergy of Ireland, namely by Florence Ua Cerballáin, bishop of Tír Eogain, and by Máel Ísu Ua Dorig, bishop of Tír Conaill, and by the abbot of the monastery of SS. Peter and Paul in Armagh, and by Amalgaid Ua Fergail, abbot of the monastery of Derry, and a large number of the clergy of the north, so that they razed the monastery, according to the law of the church. Then Amalgaid aforesaid took the abbacy of Iona by the choice of Norse and Gaels.

The bishops of Tír Eogain and Tír Conaill, from Derry and Raphoe, together with the abbot of Derry, were the leaders of the Columban community in Ireland. Notwithstanding the annalist's perception of their success, this appears to be a final attempt, which, in reality, failed to preserve Derry's influence over Iona. The new buildings of the early thirteenth century replaced almost all that remained of the early medieval monastery, and from 1204 Iona abbey was no longer a part of the Irish church.

The detailed history of Iona abbey, the contemporary nunnery, and their relationship with the lords of the Isles has been ably summarized by both Ian Fisher and Alan Macquarrie. Successive alterations to the buildings have been described and documented by Mr Fisher for the Royal Commission on the Ancient and Historic Monuments of Scotland. How much the monks and nuns clung to memories of the site's ancient glories we cannot tell, though surviving crosses about the abbey must have served as reminders. The late medieval monumental stones, carved by craftsmen of the Iona workshops, bear the emblems and effigies of the chief families of the Isles in the fifteenth and sixteenth centuries. Cultural ties between the Hebrides and northern Ireland remained strong until the sixteenth century, as the bards who composed praise-poems for the Gaelic chiefs moved freely between Irish and Hebridean patrons. Before the end of the sixteenth century, however, their world had gone.

The lords of the Isles suffered forfeiture to the crown of Scotland in 1493; in 1499 their abbey lost its independence from episcopal control, and its resources were handed over to the bishop of the Isles. The reformation in the Scottish church brought no instant destruction to the abbey, which remained the seat of the bishop. But decay affected the buildings none the less. Between 1631 and 1638, with the support of King Charles I, an attempt was made to restore the east end of the abbey for use as a cathedral. Then in 1638 the Scottish bishops were deposed by the General Assembly. After a meeting of the synod of Argyll in Iona in 1642, the earl of Argyll is said to have destroyed 'some of the finest monuments of the monastery, and the altars'. More than fifty years later the episode is alluded to in a letter by John Fraser of Tiree to Robert Wodrow in Edinburgh: 'Their buriall stones was carved with curious artificial knots, more noteably those at Icolumkill, where there was such a number of curious crosses that one sederunt of the clergy meeting there in the beginning of the Reformation caused destroy eighteen score of crosses.' Fraser regretted that he had lost a collection of transcripts made of the inscriptions in the 1650s, and for the next hundred years the story is one of decay.

But already, from a different source, interest in St Columba was beginning to revive. The first printed edition of Adomnán's *Life of St Columba* was published, in a shortened form, in 1604 at a catholic university in Germany by Henry Canisius, and the first English version by the Irish Franciscan Robert Richford at Saint-Omer in 1625. By this date the Irish Franciscans had launched a mission to the Hebrides, and there survive some reports of this mission from the 1620s and 1630s. Fr Cornelius Ward was conscious that he and his fellow friars were following in the footsteps of St Columba, St Baithéne and their eleven companions, as the story of the saint's life again exerted its influence.

### *The medieval legend of St Columba*

Thus far I have tried to concentrate on the data provided by historical and archaeological sources to reconstruct something of the career of Columba, the life and works of Adomnán, and the history of Iona and the Columban community. Occasionally I have referred to later stories in such works as the Middle Irish homily on St Columba. The image of the saint is a many-sided one because in different ages he was seen as representing different ideals. These varying perceptions of the saint depend in part on the attitudes and interests of the authors, in part on the range and quality of the information available at the time, and in part on the approach to collecting or selecting from what is available. Some writers were unconcerned with what had preceded them, others have preferred to fuse together everything from the past that they could find. The apogee of this latter approach was reached in the sixteenth century in the *Life of St Columb Cille* sponsored by Manus O'Donnell.

The medieval legend of St Columba can be seen developing from the sixth to the sixteenth century, but it is important to observe the difference between several traditions. These traditions can continue separate over long periods and then meet and interact. There is, for example, a strong tradition of saints' Lives in Latin, in which Adomnán has a very important place. Fifty or sixty years earlier Cumméne's book was almost certainly influenced by the pattern of sanctity familiar to him from the Lives of early saints. When Adomnán gave a polished shape to the *Life of St Columba*, he combined the stories handed down to him within the monastic community with ideas derived from the Lives of St Martin, St Antony and others, but his work was also affected by other concerns that had more to do with the context in which he wrote than with the subject of his book. The Life that he produced was widely read, and it has left a varied legacy.

Although only one early manuscript survives, copied by Dorbbéne, who 'held the chair of Iona' briefly in 713, we can tell from quotations in Lives of other Irish saints written in the eighth century that it circulated in Ireland. Later manuscripts show two separate traditions. The later medieval copies that form what is known as the B text all descend from an early copy more or less contemporary with Dorbbéne's A text but including some revisions by the author. These manuscripts represent the handing down of Adomnán's text in Scotland and northern England. Dorbbéne's copy was taken to the monastery of Reichenau in southern Germany, a popular destination with Irish scholars in the eighth century. It is probably from this focus that there issued a shortened and revised version of the *Life*, based on the A text. This shortened text circulated widely in Austria and Bavaria. A copy of the full text reached Lorraine, where we have one complete copy and several copies of another abridgement; these texts have in common a confusion of the name of St Columba with that of St Columbanus. A third abridgement was in circulation in Flanders and north-eastern France in the twelfth and thirteenth centuries, deriving very largely from the last book of Adomnán's *Life*. This abridgement was printed in the seventeenth century, when its editor conjectured that it was the 'lost' work of Cumméne; his guess has been proved wrong, and this abridgment is now known as Pseudo-Cumméne. Adomnán's *Life*, then, was the foundation of all knowledge of St Columba on the Continent.

This Latin tradition in Britain and on the Continent, though changing in its own way to meet the literary tastes of its readers, was completely cut off from the native Irish traditions of the saint, which continued to expand. A copy of the common shorter text of Adomnán did come back to Ireland and was copied, and in the thirteenth and fourteenth centuries we also find other rewritten Lives largely based on his work. These derivative Lives, in a Latin tradition, had a limited circulation among religious houses in the English-influenced areas of eastern Ireland. There are traces, none the less, showing that they were affected here and there by stories derived from native traditions in the Irish language, but in general these texts are of no historical interest.

In the early Middle Ages the Irish vernacular legend of St Columba did not take the form of a regular saint's Life. Many stories were known, and it is very likely that, especially among the Northern Uí Néill, there was some sense of how they fitted into an outline of the saint's life-story. The written texts that have survived are poems and little stories, sometimes themselves associated with poems. There are two narrative themes underlying this material: first, that Columba was in a special sense the patron saint of the poets and, second, that he was more than anything else an exile from his Irish homeland.

The oldest of these poetic texts is the *Amrae Coluimb Chille* 'Praise of Columb Cille', attributed to Dallán Forgaill, chief of the poets during the saint's lifetime, who is said to have sung this eulogy soon after Columba's death. The Irish text is extremely difficult; it was the subject of study in church schools by the tenth century, and the surviving copies present the text divided into short phrases and surrounded by explanatory notes. The preface to the *Amrae*, written in the year

1007, associates the poem's composition with a tradition that one of the achievements of the meeting at Druim Cett had been to save the poets of Ireland from expulsion. Poems of praise were much desired by the rulers of Ireland, and, as a consequence, the poets had come to make exorbitant demands in return for their work; so great had their demands become that the high king ordered their expulsion, but Columba intervened to protect the poets, and for ever after they regarded the saint as their own special patron.

Already the writer of the preface to the *Amrae* was able to quote passages of verse relating to episodes associated with the saint's role at Druim Cett. He also relates the tradition that, on leaving Ireland, Columba promised that he should never see it again, quoting the verses:

> There is a gray eye that looks back at Ireland:
> it will never hereafter see the men of Ireland nor their women.

We are taken into a substantial corpus of poetry in which the writers, from the ninth, tenth and eleventh centuries, imagine themselves composing verse in the persona of Columba himself. Some take the form of monologues in the saint's mouth, others are dialogues with one or other of his contemporaries, but all presuppose that the outlines of St Columba's life were familiar. Very little of this poetry is accessible in English translation, and a large proportion remains unpublished in any language. Some poems survive because they were quoted here or there, like the verses in the preface to the *Amrae*; some survive only in very late copies such as 'Columb Cille's address to Ireland', a composite of verses from different poems, copied by Br Michael O'Clery in the seventeenth century, translated by Eugene O'Curry for Reeves, and given wide circulation in the literary writings of Douglas Hyde. The majority of these poems, however, came down to us only because a scholar working with Manus O'Donnell collected them into a scrapbook, which has remained in the Bodleian Library since the seventeenth century. James Kenney observed of this literature: 'It presents the saint as he appealed to the imagination of his countrymen some five centuries after his death – particularly as the exile extolling the charms of his native land. It is the earliest corpus of formally nationalist propaganda' (p. 441).

The theme of Columba as exile was clearly prevalent when, around 1160, a new Life was written in Irish, in the form of a homily on the biblical text, 'Get thee out of thy country and from thy kindred and from thy father's house unto a land that I will shew thee' (Gen. 12:1). This Middle Irish homily on St Columba was written at Derry at a time when it had recently become the leading church in the community. Unlike the Life by Adomnán, this has a basic biographical framework, from Columba's birth at Gartan, through his training and his early career in Ireland. The saint is credited with the founding of many churches in various parts of Ireland, until, at the age of forty-two, 'he determined to go across the sea to teach the word of God to Scots and Britons and Saxons' (§ 50). The writer then quotes a quatrain, also quoted earlier in the *Amrae* preface, about the number of clergy who accompanied Columba into exile at Iona. A few stories in this homily are evidently taken from Adomnán's *Life*, but much of the material reflects rather the traditions in northern Ireland in the tenth to twelfth centuries.

This homily was copied in a number of places during the later Middle Ages, and some copyists augmented it by inserting stories from the *Amrae* preface; but the next instalment of the medieval legend was a work of a quite different character.

Manus O'Donnell was a sixteenth-century descendant of Columba's lineage, son and heir of the prince of Tyrconnel, and something of a scholar. He found the legend of St Columba in what he considered a disjointed state. He knew Adomnán's work, but only in the shorter recension (probably in one of the late medieval Latin collections of Irish saints' Lives). He found another part of the legend in 'very hard Irish'; this was the Middle Irish homily. And he also knew a scatter of stories in different places and from different parts of Ireland. He commissioned someone to translate Adomnán into Irish and 'to make easy the part that was hard Irish'. He himself collected what was scattered, organized the material in one sequence and so in 1532 produced the fullest of all the Lives of St Columba. O'Donnell's approach ignored the different status of Adomnán's book and the later developments of the legend; but it is easy for the reader to differentiate between what he derived from his two main sources and that which he collected, whether as written or oral stories. Some of the poems gathered together for O'Donnell are also quoted in the Life, so that in the one book one can see the three different branches of the medieval legend. O'Donnell's style is brisk, almost racy, though the English translation uses too much outdated language for the modern taste. Provided that one reads it for what it is – not as evidence for the sixth-century saint but as a learned compilation of the sixteenth century – O'Donnell's Life is a good read.

### *The modern legend of St Columba*

Although this considerable quantity of written material has survived, for centuries it was very little known. Manus O'Donnell's researchers drew together a high proportion of the evidence, but O'Donnell's book did not circulate widely and the sources he used were otherwise almost wholly unknown in the sixteenth century. Roderick MacLean, bishop of the Isles, had access to the full text of Adomnán's *Life of St Columba*, which had escaped O'Donnell, and in 1549 he published at Rome a paraphrase of the first two books in Latin verse. There is no evidence that anyone else read the full text until Dorbbéne's copy was rediscovered by Stephen White in 1621. Even when it was published by John Colgan in 1647, knowledge of the early text was confined to those few Latin scholars with an interest in Irish saints.

Devotion to St Columba continued at many places in medieval Ireland and even here and there in Reformation Scotland. Oral traditions survived in Iona, some of which are clearly derived from the same tradition as the Irish Lives. I have recounted the descent of two such stories, how Iona got its name (*56*) and how St Odran was sacrificed at the first founding of the monastery (*365*). The very few accounts of Iona from the late seventeenth century show little interest in the saint, though St Columba's Chapel was identified as the site of his grave and the small room in the fifteenth-century north-west turret of the abbey was thought to have been his cell. Only rarely do we hear a reference to a Life of the saint: Fraser, writing in 1693, knew of a copy, translated from Latin into Irish by 'Caal O horan', and Martin Martin in 1703 mentions Irish copies in Barra and Benbecula; none of these is known to survive.

Even in the late eighteenth century, when well-read visitors such as Thomas Pennant and Samuel Johnson came to Iona, they knew nothing of Adomnán's *Life*. Only John Walker, who toured the Hebrides in 1764, had read it. Although he had used only the shorter text as printed by Canisius, he formed a good opinion of Adomnán's work: 'Wherever he is led to mention the topography of Icolumbkil, or that of the adjacent islands, he speaks with the accuracy of a person who had lived in it.' Walker also mentions that in Iona 'every person has the traditional history of Columba, with numberless legends, which must have been handed down from his monkish seminary'. Some of the stories told seem to have been late- or even post-medieval: the Clann an Oistir, for example, were probably hereditary doorkeepers at the late medieval abbey, but their legend had them descend from the days of St Columba. Several clearly go back before 1700, though that is not to say they are ancient. While eighteenth-century visitors retell some of these stories, some of them even mistake the saint's name and call him Columbus.

The first really scholarly work since Colgan's edition was that of the Scottish catholic, Fr Thomas Innes, writing in the 1720s, who used editions of both the longer and shorter texts of the *Life of St Columba*, and even cites a manuscript copy; Innes's studies, however, seem to have had little or no influence. The first author to show a knowledge of both the Latin texts on St Columba and of the local Gaelic stories from Iona was the Revd John Smith, minister of Campbeltown, who wrote the first Life of the saint in English in 1798, which came to be widely known in Scotland. Smith depended very largely on Colgan, using his edition of Adomnán's *Life* and his translation of O'Donnell's work, with little discrimination.

Smith was writing about St Columba at a time when the broader picture of the ecclesiastical context was dominated by the idea that the early clergy of Scotland were 'culdees', a dimly understood expression, later described by Reeves as 'the most abused term in Scotic church history'. The origin of the term is in the Irish *céli Dé* 'clients of God', a group of religious who sought a more devout life within or apart from the large monastic centres in ninth-century Ireland. By the eleventh century it means nothing more than a canon associated with a collegiate church such as St Andrews or Armagh, but in the eighteenth century it acquired a peculiar gloss. At one level this arose from a body of protestant scholarship, going back to Archbishop James Ussher but manipulated by church-historians less familiar with the evidence; this tradition saw the ancient church of Ireland and Scotland as in some sense the natural forerunner of the national, episcopalian churches such as the Church of England. Culdees were religious but were not bound by the Roman Catholic monastic rules. Thus the Scottish poet Thomas Campbell could compose a poem in 1824 about Reullura, wife of Aodh, the last culdee of Iona, 'Long ere her churchmen by bigotry / Were barred from holy wedlock's tie'. A great deal of church history was, perhaps inevitably, distorted between a protestant desire to claim the ancient past and a catholic response. The history of St Columba, belonging alike to Presbyterian Scotland and Roman Catholic Ireland, was peculiarly subject to pressures in both directions. While John Lanigan in the 1820s was writing a learned work of Irish catholic history, the protestant tradition was dominant in Great Britain.

The late eighteenth century also saw the rise of a Romantic view of all things Celtic. In the years following the visits of Pennant in 1772 and Johnson in 1773 Iona became a popular destination for adventurous travellers, who came to be moved by the ruins and graves of antiquity, and to marvel at the wonders of nature on Staffa, where, in 1772, Joseph Banks had 'discovered' the magnificent basalt rock-formations. The cave here acquired the name Fingal's Cave from a leading figure in the poems of Ossian, a Romantic fabrication by James Macpherson. These very local subjects of Romantic interest blended with a growing tendency in the early nineteenth century to see the Celtic peoples as in a peculiar sense individualistic, inspired, visionary. It was a view largely founded on those literary works available in English translation and would not have survived any general knowledge of a wider range of Irish, Welsh or Gaelic sources. Against this background it is not surprising that in the early nineteenth century there was little study of the early Scottish church that has any value.

In 1857 the publication of Reeves's remarkable edition of Adomnán's *Life of St Columba* did a great service, placing a huge wealth of information at the disposal of the learned public. Reeves was an Irishman, an Anglican, and a man not misled by attitudes pretending that the ancient church was not as Roman as it was catholic. Although he was not entirely free from the desire to supplement early sources from later evidence, Reeves to a considerable degree succeeded in presenting a picture of the church in Iona founded on reliable information. With these riches now available to him, a French Roman Catholic controversialist, the Comte de Montalembert, used Columba as the paradigm of an austere personal monastic devotion with a great Romantic appeal.

In the same period, the protestant reading of the past derived a major boost from the increased attention to Bede's *Ecclesiastical History of the English People*. This came about through a Victorian interest in the history of the Anglican church. Bede's great theme was how the English were converted to Christianity through different traditions, particularly the Roman and the Irish, with a smaller part played by Frankish influence. The diversity of Easter practice was abhorrent to the rigidly orthodox monk of Jarrow, and he made the debate between the Irish and the Roman practice the centrepiece of his history, giving this debate a dramatic setting at a synod at Whitby. Thereafter the trend of his history is towards orthodoxy and the expansion of the English church into the Low Countries and Germany. Bede does not disguise the fact that many of the Irish churches were as Roman and orthodox as he himself. Yet read in the light of anti-Roman prejudice, his *History* was seen as justifying a stark difference between a Roman tradition, centralized, institutional and authoritarian, and a 'Celtic' tradition, personal, devotional, biblical and enlivened by saints such as Aidan and Columba. It has become a common misconception in Great Britain that the Synod of Whitby in 664 meant the end of 'the Celtic church', an idea which is meaningless to anyone better versed in the Irish sources. Columba, Iona and its Northumbrian offshoot at Lindisfarne were given special prominence in Bede's work. The 'Celtic' bishop Colmán, who left Lindisfarne after the synod at Whitby, is hardly a household name, but this approach to Bede has completely ignored the fact that one of his principal opponents, Bishop Agilbert, had studied among the Irish and that his Roman successor at Lindisfarne was another bishop trained in Ireland, Tuda. There were many Irishmen who followed the Roman rather than the 'Celtic' practice, but this did not suit the protestant reading, which derived from Bede's *History* a Celtic church characterized by its independence from Rome.

The contrast in terms of both churchmanship and Romanticism is succinctly expressed by Thomas M'Lauchlan in his book, *The Early Scottish Church* (1865). He contrasts Columba with the Roman missionaries in England, St Augustine and his companions: 'Thus did these men represent the ambitious, grasping spirit of their system, covetous of place and power; while the humble missionaries of Iona and Lindisfarne represented the spirit of their own system, covetous of exalting Christ, but crucifying self.'

M'Lauchlan was a member of the Free Church, but his admiration of the early Celtic church was shared by Montalembert, whose writings on St Columba were translated into English and published at Edinburgh in 1866. Presbyterian Scots, Irish catholics, and Episcopalians in Scotland, Ireland and England all found their own roots in Celtic Christianity as they imagined it was lived out in the Iona of St Columba, and from 1860 onwards writers of each denomination produced edificatory books that presented Columba and his church in their own idealized image. As one might expect, history guided by such nineteenth-century churchmanship misinterprets or misrepresents the past in many ways. Such common core as there is at times runs contrary to all expectations: the eighth duke of Argyll, whose words were quoted in the opening pages of this introduction, retained an admiration for Columba while rejecting almost every attribute that for Adomnán proved his holiness. What Adomnán wrote about his patron saint has a Christian appeal that clearly transcends sectarian divisions, though many modern accounts of the man and his religious foundations have been coloured by different modern views concerning the structure, discipline, and doctrine of the Christian church. In recent years, as the Eastern Orthodox churches have won an increasing number of western adherents, they too have found a special interest in the early church of Iona as a western opponent to Roman ways.

The appeal of St Columba goes beyond conventional Christianity. It is almost paradoxical that a Christian saint should be treated as the hero of religious teaching that rejects Christian doctrine, but in the early twentieth century this happened to St Columba. The humanist V. V. Branford in 1908 used Columba and Iona to illustrate the importance of pilgrimage in personal development and in what he called 'social inheritance'. Eleanor Merry, a Theosophist, made St Columba a central figure in a play, published in 1928, about spiritual forces older than Christianity. Odran too had an important significance for her, which she discussed in an unusual book on 'the mission of the Celtic folk-soul by means of myths and legends'.

In this age of secularism and reaction against it, Gaelic folk tradition, largely as it was documented by Alexander Carmichael and others around the turn of the century, has been absorbed into the modern legend of 'Celtic' Christianity. From William Sharp, writing under the pseudonym 'Fiona Macleod' about the fairy spirituality of the Celts, to modern booklets on St Columba, which superimpose contemporary responses to nineteenth-century folk piety on to the historic saint, there is a timeless sentimentality about too much of the recent devotional writing about the saint of Iona. Even books founded on wide reading in the learned literature are liable to offer something far removed from what the early sources provide, for too few writers have recognized the influence of older churchmanship on the history widely accepted as the authorized version.

The power of St Columba still to excite the imagination of those who visit or read about his church at Iona has produced a remarkable literature. Too much of it takes its departure from misconceptions dating back to the nineteenth or even the eighteenth century, and too much of it fails to recognize the important difference between that which bears witness to the Columban church in Iona in its first centuries and that which derives from later Irish legends. Nothing, however, can detract from Adomnán's vivid depiction of the abbot among his own monks, written on the spot by the saint's successor, one hundred years after Columba's death. Here, as in no other text, it is possible to see an early Irish monastery at work and prayer.

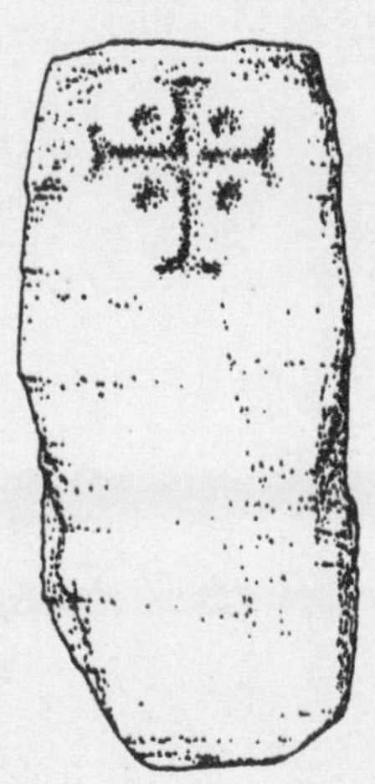

# THE LIFE OF ST COLUMBA

# In Jesus Christ's name the preface begins

Our blessed patron's life I shall now, with Christ's help, describe in response to the entreaties of the brethren. First, I am minded to warn all who read it that they should put their faith in accounts which are attested, and give more thought to my subject than to my words which I consider rough and of little worth. They should remember that the Kingdom of God stands not on the flow of eloquence but in the flowering of faith.[1] There are words here in the poor Irish language, strange names of men and peoples and places, names which I think are crude in comparison with the different tongues of foreign races.[2] But let no one think this a reason to despise the proclamation of profitable deeds, which were not achieved without the help of God.

The reader should also be reminded of this, that many things worth recording about the man of blessed memory are left out here for the sake of brevity, and only a few things out of many are written down so as not to try the patience of those who will read them.[3] But even in comparison with the little we now propose to write, popular report has spread almost nothing of the very great things[4] that can be told about the blessed man.[5]

Now after this little foreword, with God's help I shall begin the second preface with the name of our abbot.

# In Jesus Christ's name The second preface[6]

There was a man of venerable life and blessed memory, the father and founder of monasteries, whose name was the same as the prophet Jonah's. For though the sound is different in three different languages, in Hebrew *Jona*, in Greek *Peristera*, in Latin *Columba*, the meaning is the same, 'dove'. So great a name cannot have been given to the man of God but by divine providence.[7] For it is shown by the Gospels that the Holy Spirit descended upon the only begotten Son of the everlasting Father in the form of that little bird. For this reason, in the Scriptures the dove is generally taken allegorically to represent the Holy Spirit.[8] Likewise, the Saviour himself in the Gospel told his disciples that they should have the simplicity of the dove in a pure heart.[9] For the dove is indeed a simple and innocent bird, and it was fitting that a simple and innocent man should have this for his name, who through his dove-like life offered in himself a dwelling for the Holy Spirit. What it says in Proverbs is appropriate here: 'A good name is rather to be chosen than great riches.'[10] From the days of his infancy, our abbot was enriched with this appropriate name by God's gift.

Earlier still, many years before the time of his birth, by revelation of the Holy Spirit to a soldier of Christ, he was marked out as a son of promise[11] in a marvellous prophecy. A certain pilgrim from Britain, named Mochta, a holy disciple of the holy bishop Patrick, made this prophecy about our patron, which has been passed down by those who learnt it of old and held to be genuine:[12]

'In the last days of the world, a son will be born whose name Columba will become famous through all the provinces of the ocean's islands, and he will be a bright light in the last days of the world. The fields of our two monasteries, mine and his, will be separated by only a little hedge. A man very dear to God and of great merit in his sight.'

In describing the life and character of our Columba, I shall begin as briefly as I can with a summary which will set before the reader his holy way of life and also offer, as a foretaste to be savoured, some samples of his miracles, which will be unfolded more fully below in three books. Of these, the first will contain prophetic revelations, the second divine miracles worked through him, and the third angelic apparitions and certain phenomena of heavenly light seen above the man of God.[13]

No one should think that I would write anything false about this remarkable man, nor even anything doubtful or uncertain.[14] Let it be understood that I shall tell only what I learnt from the account handed down by our elders, men both reliable and informed, and that I shall write without equivocation what I have learnt by diligent inquiry either from what I could find already in writing or from what I heard recounted without a trace of doubt by informed and reliable old men.[15]

Saint Columba was born of a noble lineage. His father was Fedelmid mac Ferguso, his mother was called Eithne and her father Mac Naue which means 'son of a ship'.[16] In the second year following the battle of *Cúl Drebene*, when he was forty-one, Columba sailed away from Ireland to Britain, choosing to be a pilgrim for Christ.[17]

Since boyhood he had devoted himself to training in the Christian life, and to the study of wisdom; with God's help, he had kept his body chaste and his mind pure and shown himself, though placed on earth, fit for the life of heaven. He was an angel in demeanour, blameless in what he said, godly in what he did, brilliant in intellect and great in counsel.[18] He spent thirty-four years as an island soldier,[19] and could not let even an hour pass without giving himself to praying or reading or writing or some other task.[20] Fasts and vigils he performed day and night with tireless labour and no rest, to such a degree that the burden of even one seemed beyond human endurance. At the same time he was loving to all people, and his face showed a holy gladness[21] because his heart was full of the joy of the Holy Spirit.

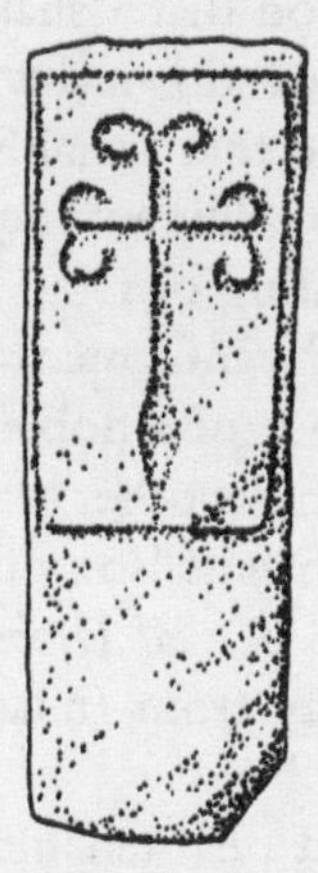

# Now the chapter headings of the first book begin[22]

[1] Summary of the miracles of power
[2] Of St Fintan mac Tulcháin, how St Columba prophesied concerning him
[3] Of Ernéne mac Craséni, his prophecy
[4] Of Cainnech's arrival, how he foretold
[5] Of the peril of St Colmán moccu Sailni, revealed to St Columba
[6] Of Cormac Ua Liatháin
[7–8] Prophecies about battles
[9–15] and about kings
[16] Of two boys, one of whom died at the end of a week, according to his word
[17] Of Colgu mac Áedo Draigniche, and of his mother's secret sin; and of a portent of his death
[18] St Columba's prophecy about Lasrén the gardener
[19] Of a great whale, how he prophesied
[20] Of Baithéne, who with others rowed to a desert in the sea
[21] Of Neman, a pretended penitent who afterwards, according to the saint's word, ate the flesh of a stolen mare
[22] Of the wretch who sinned with his mother
[23] Of the vowel I which alone was missing from the psalter
[24] Of the book falling into the water-jar
[25] Of the little ink-horn upset

[26] Of the arrival of Áedán, who relaxed the fast
[27] Of a wretch about to die who shouted over the Sound
[28] Of the Italian city on which fire from heaven fell
[29] Of Lasrén mac Feradaig, how he tried the monks with labour
[30] Of Little Fiachnae[23]
[31] Of Cailtan the monk
[32] Of two pilgrims
[33] Of Artbranan, an old man whom he baptized on Skye
[34] Of the removal of a boat on Loch Lochy
[35] Of Gallán mac Fachtnai, whom demons seized
[36]
[37]
[38] Of Lugaid the cripple
[39] Of Enan mac Gruthriche[24]
[40] Of the priest who was at Trevet
[41] Of Erc the thief
[42] Of Crónán the poet
[43] Of Rónán mac Áedo mac Colcen and of Colmán Cú mac Aleni, the saint's prophecy
[44–50]

# The text of Book One begins, concerning prophetic revelations

[I 1] *Summary of the miracles of power*

What proofs of his powers the venerable man gave must be briefly set out at the beginning of this book in accordance with our little promise already given.

By the power of prayer in the name of our Lord Jesus Christ he healed those who suffered attacks of various diseases.

When countless hosts of horrible devils were making war against him, visible to his bodily eyes, and beginning to inflict deadly diseases on his monastic community, he, one man alone, with God's help repelled them and drove them out of this our principal island.[25] With Christ's help, he curbed the raging fury of wild beasts sometimes by killing them and sometimes by driving them away.[26]

Once in a great storm the swelling waves that rose up like mountains were at his bidding quickly calmed and brought low, and the ship in which he was sailing was brought to its destination at the same time as the storm was stilled.[27] When he had been in the region of the Picts for some days and was returning, he hoisted his sail in a head wind to confound the wizards and his boat sailed off, making as swift a journey as if it had a following wind.[28] On other occasions, at his prayer, winds set against those at sea were changed into following winds.[29]

In the region just mentioned he took a white stone from a river and blessed it so that it would work as a cure. This stone when dropped in water floated like an apple in defiance of the natural order. This miracle of God happened in the sight of King Bridei and his household.[30]

Again, in the same province, he brought to life the dead son of a Christian layman and restored him alive and well to his father and mother – a very great miracle.[31]

Another time, when he was a young deacon living with the holy bishop Uinniau, there was no wine for the sacred mysteries but by the power of prayer he changed pure water into true wine.[32]

A great heavenly light was seen to shine above him by several of the brethren on separate occasions, both at night and in broad daylight. He also enjoyed the sweet and most delightful company of holy angels shining with light.[33]

By the revelation of the Holy Spirit he used often to see the souls of the just carried to the heights of heaven by angels.[34] But he saw too those of the wicked taken to hell by devils.[35] He used often to foretell the future rewards of many people while they still lived in mortal flesh – happy for some, miserable for others.

Some kings were conquered in the terrifying crash of battle and others emerged victorious according to what Columba asked of God by the power of prayer.[36] God who honours all saints gave this special privilege to him as to a mighty and triumphant champion, and it remained as true after he quit the flesh as it had been in this present life.[37]

We shall provide one example of this special honour granted by the Almighty from heaven to the honourable man. This was revealed to the English King Oswald on the day before his battle against Cadwallon, the most powerful king of the Britons.[38] While this King Oswald was camped ready for battle, he was asleep on a pillow in his tent one day when he had a vision of St Columba. His appearance shone with angelic beauty, and he seemed so tall that his head touched the clouds and, as he stood in the middle of the camp, he covered all of it except one far corner with his shining robe.

The blessed man revealed his name to the king and gave him these words of encouragement, the same the Lord spoke to Joshua, saying, 'Be strong and act manfully. Behold, I will be with thee.'[39] In the king's vision Columba said this, adding:

'This coming night go out from your camp into battle, for the Lord has granted me that at this time your foes shall be put to flight and Cadwallon your enemy shall be delivered into your hands and you shall return victorious after battle and reign happily.'

Hearing these words, the king awoke[40] and described his vision to the assembled council. All were strengthened by this, and the whole people promised that after their return from battle they would accept the faith and receive baptism. For up to that time the whole of England was darkened by the shadow of heathendom and ignorance, except for King Oswald himself and twelve men who had been baptized with him in exile among the Irish.[41] Why say more? That same night, just as he had been told in the vision, he marched out from the camp into battle with a modest force against many thousands. A happy and easy victory was given him by the Lord according to his promise. King Cadwallon was killed, Oswald returned as victor after battle and was afterwards ordained by God as emperor of all Britain.[42]

My predecessor, our Abbot Failbe, related all this to me, Adomnán, without question. He swore that he had heard the story of the vision from the lips of King Oswald himself as he was relating it to Abbot Ségéne.[43]

This too is not to be passed over:[44] certain men, wicked and bloodstained from a life as brigands,[45] were protected by songs that they sang in Irish in praise of St Columba and by the commemoration of his name.[46] For on the night they sang these songs, they were delivered from the hands of their enemies, who had surrounded the house of the singers, and escaped unhurt through flames and swords and spears. But a few of them made little of the holy man's commemoration and would not sing these songs. Miraculously, these alone perished in the enemies' attack. It would be possible to produce not just two or three witnesses of this event, enough to satisfy the law, but a hundred or more.[47] For the same occurrence did not just happen at one place or time, but it can be clearly shown to have happened at different places and times in Ireland and Britain,[48] and in the same way with the same reason for the deliverance. We have learnt of it with no room for doubt from informed people in each area where the same miracle took place.

But to return to the subject, besides these miracles, which by God's gift the man of the Lord worked while he lived in mortal flesh, he began as a young man to enjoy also the spirit of prophecy, to predict the future and to tell those with him about things happening elsewhere. He could see what was done afar off, because he was there in the spirit though not in the body.[49] For as St Paul says, 'He that is joined unto the Lord is one spirit.'[50] One time when a few of the brethren pressed him about this, the man of the Lord, St Columba, did not deny that by divine grace he had several times experienced a miraculous enlarging of the grasp of the mind so that he seemed to look at the whole world caught in one ray of sunlight.[51]

These stories about the miraculous powers of the holy man have been mentioned here in brief so that the reader, having a foretaste of a sweeter feast, may be more eager for what will be told more fully, with the Lord's help, in the three books to follow. Now it seems to me fitting to relate, though out of their proper order, the prophecies that the blessed man spoke at various times about some holy and famous men.[52]

### [I 2] *Of the abbot St Fintan mac Tulcháin*[53]

St Fintan, by God's help, kept himself chaste in body and soul from his boyhood and devoted himself to the pursuit of godly wisdom, and in due course he came to enjoy renown among all the churches of Ireland. But while he was still a young man he had in his heart this wish, to leave Ireland behind him and to join St Columba in his life of pilgrimage. On fire with this desire, he approached a wise and venerable priest, a man of his own people and a personal friend, called Columb Crag, and asked his advice. Having told him what was in his mind, he got this answer:

'Your desire, I think, is devout and inspired by God. Who can stop you or say you should not sail away to St Columba?'

That very hour it happened that two of St Columba's monks arrived, who, when asked about their journey, replied:

'We rowed across from Britain not long ago, and today have come from Derry.'[54]

'And is your holy father Columba in good health?' asked Columb Crag.

'Truly,' they said, with tears and great sorrow, 'our patron is in the best of health since only a few days ago he departed to Christ.'

Hearing this, Fintan and Columb and everyone present looked down at the ground and wept bitterly. In a little while, Fintan continued, asking:

'Whom has he left to succeed him?'

'Baithéne,' they said, 'his disciple.'[55]

And all cried out, 'It is meet and right.'

Columb said to Fintan:

'What will you do now, Fintan?'

'If the Lord will permit me,' he answered, 'I shall sail away to Baithéne, who is a holy and a wise man. If he will receive me, he shall be my abbot.'

Then he kissed Columb and took his leave, preparing to sail without delay to Iona.[56] At that time his name was not known here so that when he arrived, he was received as a stranger and guest. Next day he sent a message to Baithéne, requesting to talk to him face to face. Baithéne, who was an easy man to talk to and friendly towards strangers, said to bring Fintan to him. As soon as he was brought, Fintan threw himself to the ground on bended knee, as was proper. Being told to rise by the holy elder, he was given a seat and asked by Baithéne about his still unascertained people and province, his name, his manner of life and for what reason he had undertaken the effort of the journey. He answered every question as it was put, and begged to be received. Hearing what the guest said and recognizing him as someone of whom St Columba had once prophesied, Baithéne said:

'I should indeed give thanks to God on your arrival. But on this point, make no mistake. You shall not be our monk.'

Fintan was sorely disappointed, saying:

'Perhaps I am not worthy to become your monk.'

The elder man said:

'I have not refused you because you are not worthy, as you say. On the contrary. I had rather kept you with me, but I cannot profane the injunction of St Columba, my predecessor, through whom the Holy Spirit prophesied about you. For one day I was alone with him and he spoke with prophetic lips, saying among other things, "Baithéne, you must listen closely to my words. Soon after I have gone from this world to Christ, for which I wait and long, a brother will come to you from Ireland, called Fintan mac Tulcháin of the line of moccu Moie. At present he is still a youth, spending his time in the pursuit of good and the study of the Scriptures. He will beg you to receive him as one of your monks. But God knows this is not what is predestined for him, that he should be an abbot's monk. No, he has been chosen by God to be an abbot of monks himself, and one who leads souls to the kingdom of heaven. So you will not wish to keep this man in our islands, for that might seem to oppose the will of God. Instead, reveal to him what I have said and send him back in peace to Ireland, to Leinster, not far from the sea, where he may build a monastery, there feeding Christ's sheep and bringing countless souls to their heavenly home.

Hearing these words, the younger man shed his tears and gave his thanks to Christ, saying:

'May it happen to me as St Columba has foreknown and foretold.'

In the next few days, in obedience to the words of the saints, he received Baithéne's blessing and sailed to Ireland in peace.

This story was told me by a religious old man, a priest and soldier of Christ, called Oisséne mac Ernáin, from the line of moccu Néth Corb.[57] I am in no doubt as to its truth. He had heard the story from Fintan mac Tulcháin himself, whose monk he was.

### [I 3] *St Columba's prophecy concerning Ernéne mac Craséni*[58]

Once the saint stayed for some months in the midland region of Ireland, and during this period by God's direction he founded the monastery of Durrow.[59] At that time it pleased him to visit the brethren of St Ciarán in the monastery of Clonmacnoise.[60]

Hearing of his approach, the monks[61] who were in the fields around the monastery came from all sides, assembling with those who were inside, and all eagerly followed their abbot Ailither out past the boundary bank of the monastery[62] and went with one mind to meet St Columba as if he were an angelic messenger of the Lord. On seeing him, they bowed their heads and each kissed him reverently, and to the accompaniment of hymns and praises they brought him with honour to the church. So that the saint should not be troubled by the pressing crowd of brethren, four men kept pace with him, holding about him a square frame of branches tied together.[63]

Meanwhile, a boy belonging to the community approached from behind, hiding himself as much as possible. He was generally much looked down on for his outward expression and his attitude, and was not well thought of by the seniors. This boy hoped that he might secretly touch the hem of the cloak that the saint was wearing, if possible without St Columba's feeling or knowing it.[64] But it did not escape the saint's notice, for what he could not see behind him with his bodily eyes, he saw with the eyes of the spirit. At once he stopped and reached behind him, and taking hold of the boy by the neck, he brought him forward to face him. Everyone standing nearby said:

'Send him away. Send him away. Why do you hold on to this unfortunate and mischievous boy?'

In reply, the saint delivered from his pure heart this prophetic answer:

'Hush, brethren, let be.'

And to the boy, who was shivering apprehensively, he said:

'My son, open your mouth and put out your tongue.'

In terror the boy opened his mouth as he was told and put out his tongue. The saint reached forward and blessed it, speaking this prophecy:

'Although this boy may seem to you now worthless and to be scorned, do not let that make you despise him. For from this hour he will cease to displease you; indeed, he will please you greatly, and grow little by little day by day in goodness of life and greatness of spirit. Wisdom and judgement will increase in him from today and he will be an outstanding figure in your community. God will endow his tongue with eloquence to teach the doctrine of salvation.'[65]

This was Ernéne mac Craséni, a man who was later famous through all the churches of Ireland and very highly regarded. He himself gave this account of the prophecy about him to Abbot Ségéne. My predecessor Failbe was present with Ségéne at the time and listened attentively, and from his account I in turn learnt what I have recounted.[66]

During the time that St Columba stayed as a guest at Clonmacnoise he prophesied many things by the revelation of the Holy Spirit. Among them was the great dispute that arose years later among the churches of Ireland concerning differences in the date of Easter.[67] Also certain angelic visitations were made visible to him, in which he saw that places within the monastic enclosure were at that time visited by angels.

[I 4] *Of the arrival of St Cainnech the abbot,[68] which St Columba had prophetically announced*

Once, in Iona, one day of crashing storm and exceptionally high waves, the saint was at home when he announced these instructions to the brethren:

'Prepare the guest-house straightaway and draw water to wash the guests' feet.'[69]

One of the brethren then said:

'Who can make even the short crossing of the Sound on a day as windy as this? It is too dangerous.'

To which the saint answered;

'There is one, a chosen saint, to whom the Almighty has granted calm in the midst of storm so that he may reach us in time for vespers.'

On the same day – look! – the boat for which the brethren were waiting arrived as the saint foretold. In it was St Cainnech, whom St Columba and the brethren met and welcomed as an honoured guest. The sailors who had been on board with St Cainnech were asked by the brethren what kind of voyage they had had, and their answer agreed entirely with what the saint foretold of storm and calm together in the same sea at the same time, but by God's gift a marvellous line kept them apart, so that they had not felt the storm though, they said, they could see it afar off.

### [I 5] *Of the peril of the holy bishop Colmán moccu Sailni*[70] *in the sea near Rathlin Island*[71]

Likewise, another day, while St Columba was in his mother church, he suddenly smiled and called out:

'Colmán mac Beognai has set sail to come here, and is now in great danger in the surging tides of the whirlpool of Corryvreckan.[72] Sitting in the prow, he lifts up his hands to heaven and blesses the turbulent, terrible sea. Yet the Lord terrifies him in this way, not so that the ship in which he sits should be overwhelmed and wrecked by the waves, but rather to rouse him to pray more fervently that he may sail through the peril and reach us here.'[73]

### [I 6] *Of Cormac*

Once St Columba prophesied about Cormac Ua Liatháin, a truly holy man who no fewer than three times laboured on the ocean in search of a place of retreat yet found none:[74]

'Today again Cormac has set sail from the district of Erris, beyond the River Moy, desiring to find a place of retreat.[75] But again he will not find what he seeks. It is not for any fault of his, but because he has taken with him the monk of a religious abbot who is going away without his abbot's consent, and it is not right.'[76]

### [I 7] *A prophecy of the saint about the crash of battles far away*

Two years after the battle of Cúl Drebene, when the holy man first set sail from Ireland to be a pilgrim,[77] it happened one day that, at the very hour when the battle of Móin Daire Lothair[78] was fought in Ireland, the saint gave a full account of it in Britain, in the presence of King Conall mac Comgaill.[79] He described the battle and named the kings to whom the Lord gave victory, Ainmire mac Sétna and the two sons of Mac Ercae, Domnall and Forgus. Likewise he prophesied of a king of the Cruithin called Eochaid Laib, who was defeated but escaped in a chariot.[80]

### [I 8] *Of the battle with the Miathi*[81]

Once, many years later, when the saint was in Iona, he suddenly said to his servant Diarmait:

'Strike the bell.'

Summoned by this sound, the brethren ran quickly to the church, with the saint going on ahead.[82] Kneeling down before them, he spoke:

'Let us now pray fervently to the Lord for this people and for King Áedán, for even now they are going into battle.'

A little while later, he went outside and looking at the sky said:

'Now the barbarians are turned in flight and victory is granted to Áedán, though it is not a happy one.'

From Áedán's army, three hundred and three were killed as the saint had also prophesied.

### [I 9] *St Columba's prophecy about King Áedán's sons*[83]

Once, before the battle we have just mentioned, the saint questioned King Áedán about a successor to the kingdom.[84] The king answered that he did not know which of his three sons would be king, Artuir, Eochaid Find or Domangart. The saint then spoke to him thus:

'None of these three will be king. They will all be slaughtered by enemies and fall in battle. But if you have other, younger sons, let them now come to me. The one whom the Lord has chosen will run directly to my arms.'[85]

They were called, as the saint instructed, and Eochaid Buide went as soon as he entered and leant on the saint's bosom. The saint kissed and blessed him, and said to the father:

'This one will survive to be king after you, and his sons will be kings after him.'

Afterwards, all these things were wholly fulfilled. Artuir and Eochaid Find were killed soon afterwards in the battle with the Miathi we have mentioned. Domangart fell slaughtered in battle in England. But Eochaid Buide succeeded his father as king.

### [I 10] *Of Domnall mac Áedo*[86]

Domnall mac Áedo while still a boy was brought by his foster-parents to St Columba at Druim Cett.[87] The saint looked at the boy for a while and said:

'Whose son is this boy you have brought?'

'This is Domnall son of Áed. We have brought him to you so that he may be endowed with your blessing.'

As soon as he had blessed the boy, the saint said:

'This boy will outlive all his brothers and be a famous king. He will never be handed over to his enemies but will die at home in his bed, in a peaceful old age, in the friendly presence of his household.'

All this was fulfilled as the saint had prophesied.

### [I 11] *Of Scandlán mac Colmáin*

At the same time and in the same place, the saint desired to visit Scandlán mac Colmáin, who was held in irons by King Áed.[88] He went to him, blessed him and comforted him, saying:

'My son, do not be sad; rather be happy and of good comfort. For King Áed by whom you are held in irons will die before you, and though you spend some time in exile, you will afterwards be king over your own people for thirty years. Then you will again be a fugitive from your kingdom and for some days live in exile. Afterwards, your people will recall you, and you will be king once more for three short seasons.'

All these things were fulfilled in accordance with the saint's prediction. For after thirty years as king, he was driven out and spent some time in exile. Afterwards he was recalled by his people, and was again king, not for three years, as he imagined, but for three months, at the end of which he died.

### [I 12] *Of two other kings, descendants of Muiredach, namely Báetán mac Maic Ercae and Eochaid mac Domnaill*[89]

Once, when he was travelling through the rough and rocky district of Ardnamurchan,[90] St Columba heard his companion Lasrén mac Feradaig[91] and his servant Diarmait[92] talking on the way about these two kings, and he came out with these words:

'My dear sons, why do you gossip idly about these kings? For both of those you mention were recently killed by their enemies, and their heads cut off. Sailors will arrive today from Ireland and tell you this.'

On the same day voyagers from Ireland landed at a place called Paradise Bay[93] and they confirmed to the men sailing in

St Columba's boat that the saint's prophecy about the dead kings was fulfilled.

### [I 13] *The saint's prophecy about Óengus mac Áedo Commain*[94]

This man was driven out of his own country along with two of his brothers, and came as an exile to the saint living in pilgrimage in Britain. St Columba blessed him and spoke from his holy heart these words of prophecy:

'This young man will remain alive when his brothers are dead, and for a long time will be king in his country. His enemies will fall before him, and he will never be delivered into their hands. He will die in peace, an old man, with his friends around him.'

All this was fulfilled as the saint had said. This was Óengus nicknamed *Bronbachal*.

### [I 14] *The blessed man's prophecy about King Diarmait's son, called in Irish Áed Sláine*[95]

Once when the blessed man was staying in Ireland for a time, this Áed came to him and the saint spoke prophetically to him:

'You should take care, my son, for though God has predestined for you the prerogative of the kingship of all Ireland, you may lose it by the sin of a family murder.[96] If ever you commit that sin, you will not be king over all the peoples your father ruled, but only over your own people and that for but a little time.'

The saint's words were fulfilled according to his prophecy, for after Áed killed Suibne mac Colmáin by trickery, he held power over only the part of the kingdom granted him, and for no more than four years and three months.

### [I 15] *The blessed man's prophecy about Rhydderch ap Tudwal, King of Dumbarton*[97]

Once, this king – a friend of the saint – sent Luigbe moccu Min[98] to him with a secret mission, for he wanted to learn whether he should be slaughtered by his enemies or not. But the saint questioned Luigbe about the king and the kingdom and his people, and Luigbe answered him as if in pity, saying:

'Why do you put questions about the unhappy man, who cannot know at what hour he may be killed by his enemies?'

Then the saint said:

'He will never be delivered into enemies' hands but he will die at home on his own pillow.'

The saint's prediction about King Rhydderch was wholly fulfilled, for he died peacefully in his own home, in accordance with the saint's words.

### [I 16] *The saint's prophecy about two boys, one of whom died a week later, as the saint foretold*

Once, two laymen came to the saint when he was living in Iona.[99] One of them, called Meldán, asked the saint what lay in store for his son, who was present at the time. This is what the saint told him:

'Surely today is Saturday? At the end of seven days, on Friday, your son will die, and one week today, on the Saturday, he will be buried in this place.'[100]

Then the other layman, named Glasderc, likewise asked the saint about his son who was there with him, and he had this for answer:

'Your son Ernán will live to see his grandsons, and after a long life he will be buried in this island.'

Both of these prophecies about the boys were fulfilled, each in its appointed time, as the saint had foretold.

[I 17] *The saint's prophecy about Colgu mac Áedo Draigniche, from Uí Fiachrach, and about a hidden sin of his mother*[101]

Once, when this Colgu was staying with him in Iona, the saint asked him whether his mother was a religious woman or not. Colgu answered him:

'I know my mother to be a woman of good life and good repute.'

Then the saint spoke clairvoyantly:

'Soon, God willing, you must set out for Ireland and ask your mother about a secret sin of a very serious nature that she is unwilling to admit to anyone.'

Hearing this, Colgu followed the saint's advice and set sail for Ireland. He questioned his mother intently, while she at first denied and later admitted her sin. In accordance with the saint's directions she did penance and was healed,[102] marvelling greatly at what the saint could disclose about her.

Colgu returned to St Columba and stayed a while with him, when he asked about his own fate. He had this answer from the saint:

'In your own dear country you will for many years be the head of a church.[103] If at any time you see your butler enjoying himself at dinner with friends and swinging the serving-jug[104] round in a circle by its neck, know then that you are soon to die.'

Why say more? The saint's prophecy revealed to Colgu was fulfilled in every detail.

## [I 18] *Of Lasrén, a gardener and a holy man*

The blessed man one day sent one of his monks, a man called Trénán, whose people were the moccu Runtir, as a messenger to Ireland.[105] Following the saint's command, Trénán quickly made ready to sail, but he complained to the saint that his crew was one man short. The saint answered him from his holy heart with these words:

'You tell me one sailor has not yet approached you, but I am not able at present to find him. Go in peace. You will have a fair following wind until you reach Ireland. As you approach you will see a man running to meet you and he, ahead of anyone else, will be the first to take hold of the prow of your boat. This man will accompany you for the few days you are travelling in Ireland, and when you return to us here, he will come with you. God has chosen him, and he will live out life here in my monastery.'

Why say more? Trénán was blessed by the saint and crossed the sea to Ireland with the wind in his sails. As the ship drew near the harbour, Lasrén moccu Moie[106] ran ahead of the others and took hold of the prow. Those in the boat realized he was the man of whom the saint had foretold.

## [I 19] *How the saint spoke with foresight about a great whale*

One day, while the blessed man was living in Iona, a brother called Berach, who was on the point of sailing for Tiree, came to St Columba in the morning for a blessing.[107] The saint looked at him closely and said:

'My son, you must be very careful today. Do not try to go directly across the open sea to Tiree, but instead take the roundabout route by the Treshnish Islands. Otherwise you may be terrified by a monster of the deep and find yourself scarcely able to escape.'

With the saint's blessing he set off and boarded his boat, but he went against the saint's advice as though he thought little of it. While crossing the open sea between Iona and Tiree he and those with him in the boat saw – look! – a whale of extraordinary size, which rose up like a mountain above the water, its jaws open to show an array of teeth. At once the men dropped the sail and took to the oars, turning back in terror, but they only just managed to avoid the wash caused by the whale's motion. Remembering what the saint had foretold, they were filled with awe.

That same morning Baithéne was also going to sail to Tiree. The saint said to him:

'In the middle of last night, a great whale rose up from the depths of the sea, and today it will heave itself up on the surface of the sea between Iona and Tiree.'

Baithéne answered him:

'That beast and I are both in God's power.'

'Go in peace,' said the saint. 'Your faith in Christ will shield you from this danger.'

Baithéne was blessed by the saint and set sail from the harbour. They had already crossed a considerable stretch of sea when Baithéne and those with him saw the whale. While all his companions were terrified, Baithéne without a tremor of fear raised his hands and blessed the sea and the whale. Immediately, the great creature plunged under the waves and was not seen again.

[I 20] *The saint's prophecy about a man named Báetán, who with others had set sail in search of a place of retreat out at sea*

Once, a man called Báetán, by race a descendant of Nia Taloirc,[108] came for the saint's blessing before setting out with others to seek a place of retreat in the sea.[109] As he said farewell to him, the saint spoke this prophecy:

'This man who goes in search of a retreat in the ocean will not be laid to rest in such a place but will be buried where a woman will drive her flock over his grave.'

This Báetán, though he sailed many miles over the windy seas, was unable to find a place of retreat. So he returned to his own country where he lived for many years in charge of a little church called *Láithrech Finden.*[110] When he eventually died, he was buried at Derry.[111] Soon afterwards there was a hostile attack and the lay population round about, including woman and children, took refuge in the church there.[112] Hence it happened that one day a woman was noticed driving her sheep over the place where Báetán had only recently been buried. One of those who saw this, a holy priest, commented:

'Now the prophecy of St Columba is fulfilled which was reported many years ago.'

This same priest, a soldier of Christ called Máel Odrain moccu Cuirin, reported the story to me.[113]

[I 21] *The saint's prophecy about Neman, who pretended to do penance*

Once the saint came to the island of *Hinba*,[114] and the same day he granted a relaxation of the rules about diet even for those living in penance.[115] Among these penitents was a man called Neman mac Cathir, who disobeyed the saint and refused the little indulgence offered him.[116] The saint berated him with these words:

'Neman, Baithéne and I[117] have allowed a relaxation in the diet, and you refuse it. But the time will come when in the company of thieves in the forest you will eat the flesh of a stolen mare.'[118]

Later, when this man had given up the penitent life and returned to the world, he was found with thieves, as the saint had said, eating just such meat taken from a wooden griddle.

### [I 22] *About an ill-starred man who slept with his own mother*[119]

Once, at dead of night, the saint roused the brethren and called them into church, where he said this:

'Let us now pray earnestly to the Lord for this very hour a sin is committed unheard of in the world, for which the penalty judgement imposes will be truly fearsome.'

Next day, some of the brethren pressed him about the nature of the sin, and the saint answered:

'In a few months, Lugaid[120] will return to Iona, and this ill-starred fellow will come with him, though Lugaid will be unaware of his secret.'

So one day, months later, St Columba spoke to Diarmait with these instructions:

'Come on, quickly. Look, Lugaid is nearly here. Go and tell him that he must put the wretched fellow with him ashore on Mull, for he must not set foot on this island.'

Diarmait did as he was told. As he reached the shore, Lugaid was just arriving and he passed on to him all the saint had said about the ill-starred man. The man himself, hearing what was said, swore that he would take food from no one until he had first seen and spoken with St Columba.[121]

Diarmait went back to the saint and reported the man's words. Hearing them, the saint set off to the harbour. Baithéne suggested to him that the penance of the wretch should be accepted, quoting the evidence of Holy Scripture, but Columba answered:

'Baithéne,' he said, 'this man has acted like Cain and killed his brother, and he has debauched his own mother.'

At the shore, the miserable fellow fell on his knees and promised that he would do whatever the saint judged to satisfy the laws of penance. St Columba said:

'If you spend twelve years among the British,[122] repenting with tears of remorse, and never return to Ireland as long as you live, God may perhaps pardon your sin.'

Having spoken, the saint turned to his own people, saying:

'This man is a son of perdition, who will never perform the penance he has promised. Instead, he will shortly go back to Ireland, where before long he will die at the hands of enemies.'

All this took place as the saint foretold. In the next few days the wretch returned to Ireland and in the district of Fir Lí he fell into the hands of enemies and was murdered. He belonged to the Uí Thuirtri.[123]

### [I 23] *Of the letter I*[124]

One day Baithéne came to St Columba and said:

'I need one of the brethren to help me go through the text of the psalter I have copied and correct any mistakes.'[125]

The saint said to him:

'Why do you bring this trouble on us when there is no need? For in your copy of the psalter there is no mistake – neither one letter too many nor one too few – except that in one place the letter *I* is missing.'

So it was. Having gone through the whole psalter, it was found to be exactly as the saint predicted.

### [I 24] *About a book which fell into a water-butt as the saint had foretold*

Likewise, one day, St Columba was sitting by the fire in the monastery when he saw Luigbe moccu Min not far away reading a book.

'Take care, my son,' he said, 'take care. For I think that the book you are studying is going to fall into a vessel full of water.'

Before long it happened. The young man got up to do some chore in the monastery and forgot what the blessed man had said. He casually tucked the book under his arm, but it slipped and fell into a butt full of water.

### [I 25] *About a little ink-horn foolishly tipped over*

One day, shouting was heard from the other side of the Sound of Iona.[126] The saint was sitting in his raised wooden hut[127] and heard this, saying:

'The man who is shouting across the Sound is too careless to watch what he is doing. Today he will tip over my little horn and spill the ink.'[128]

His servant Diarmait heard him say this and for a while stood by the door waiting for the clumsy guest to arrive so that he could keep him away from the ink-horn. But soon he moved away for some other purpose, and then the troublesome visitor arrived. As he went forward to kiss the saint, he upset the horn with the edge of his garment and spilt the ink.

### [I 26] *How the saint foretold the arrival of another visitor*

Likewise, on another occasion, the saint said to the brethren one Tuesday:

'Tomorrow is a Wednesday, when we usually keep a fast.[129] However, we shall be disturbed by a visitor and our normal fast will be relaxed.'[130]

What had been revealed in advance to the saint happened, for in the morning, on Wednesday, a new arrival shouted across the Sound. It was Áedán mac Fergnai, a truly religious man, of whom it is said that he attended St Brendan moccu Altae for twelve years.[131] When he arrived, he relaxed the day's fast as the saint predicted.

### [I 27] *About a pitiable man who shouted across the Sound*

Again, one day, the saint heard someone shouting at the other side of the Sound.

'That man,' he said, 'shouting across the Sound, is much to be pitied. He has come to us to ask for medicines to heal the body but it would be better today for him to do penance for his sins,[132] because at the end of this week he will die.'

Those who were with the saint broke this news to the unfortunate man when he arrived, but he thought little of it. Having got what he asked for, he went away again at once. But, as the saint had prophesied, before the end of the week he was dead.

### [I 28] *The saint's prophecy about an Italian city consumed by sulphurous fire from heaven*

Once, Luigbe moccu Min (whom we have already mentioned)[133] came to St Columba, one day at the end of the threshing, but he could not bear to look at the saint's face, which was flushed red to an extraordinary degree. He became very frightened and hastened away. But the saint clapped his hands to call Luigbe back. When he came, St Columba asked why he had run away so quickly, and Luigbe answered:

'I fled because I was so frightened.'

But in a few minutes, his confidence had returned and he questioned the saint, saying:

'Surely it must be some vision revealed to you in the last hour that is so terrible?'

The saint gave him this answer:

'A very terrible vengeance has now been taken in a far off part of the world.'

'What kind of vengeance,' asked the young man, 'and in what part of the world?'

'In the past hour fire of sulphur has poured out of heaven on a city under Roman jurisdiction within the borders of Italy, and nigh on three thousand men have perished, not to mention women and children.[134] Before this year ends you will hear news of this from Gallic sailors arriving here from Gaul.'[135]

Months later these words were proved true. For Luigbe accompanied the saint to the capital of the country.[136] There he questioned the master and crew of a ship that arrived, and they told him everything the saint had clairvoyantly described about the city and its people.

### [I 29] *The blessed man's vision of Lasrén mac Feradaig*[137]

One very cold winter's day St Columba was troubled with great sorrow and wept. His servant Diarmait asked him what had caused this grief, and was told:

'Not without reason, my dear child, am I so sad at this hour. For I see my monks worn out with heavy labour, yet still Lasrén puts pressure on them in building a great house.[138] This makes me very unhappy.'

Strange to tell, in the monastery of Durrow, it was at that selfsame moment that Lasrén, prompted by some compulsion like a fire kindled within him, ordered the monks to stop work and a special meal to be prepared; not only was that day to be one of rest, but also other days when the weather was harsh. Lasrén's words brought comfort to the brethren, and the saint, hearing them in the spirit, for he was in Iona, ceased weeping and rejoiced wonderfully as he repeated to the brethren in that place all that had happened. He blessed Lasrén as the comforter of the monks.

### [I 30] *How the scholar Fiachnae*[139] *came as a penitent to St Columba, who foretold his arrival*

Once the saint was sitting at the top of the hill that overlooks our monastery from a little distance,[140] when he turned to his servant Diarmait and said:

'I wonder why it is taking so long for a ship coming from Ireland to get here. It brings a very learned man who has fallen into wrongdoing, but will soon come here to perform a fearful penance.'

It was not long after this that Diarmait, looking to the south, caught sight of the sail of a boat approaching the harbour. He pointed it out to St Columba, who quickly stood up, saying:

'We must go to meet the pilgrim, whose true repentance Christ accepts.'

St Columba had just reached the harbour when Fiachnae stepped off the boat and ran to meet him. Flinging himself at the saint's feet, weeping and grieving, he groaned bitterly and confessed in front of everyone the sins he had committed. St Columba was as full of tears as Fiachnae and said to him:

'Stand up, my son, and be comforted. Your sins have been forgiven, because, as it is written, "A broken and a contrite heart God will not despise."'[141]

Fiachnae stood up joyfully and was embraced by the saint. Some days later he was sent to Baithéne, who was at the time residing as prior of the church in Mag Luinge, and went in peace.[142]

## [I 31] *The saint's prophecy about his monk Cailtan*

Once St Columba sent two of his monks to take a message to another monk, Cailtan:

'Go quickly,' he said, 'hasten to Cailtan and tell him to come to me without delay.'

At that time, Cailtan was prior of the church of Diún, by the River Awe.[143] This church was actually named after his brother. The two monks, obedient to the saint's word, set out and came to the church of Diún, where they indicated to Cailtan the purpose of their visit. He lost no time but within the hour joined the messengers and they returned together to Iona at a good speed. When the saint saw Cailtan, he greeted him with these words:

'O Cailtan, you have done well to do what I asked so

quickly. Take a rest now for a while. I sent for you to come here because I love you as a friend and want you to be able to end your life here with me in true obedience. For before the end of this week you will go in peace to the Lord.'

Hearing the saint's words, Cailtan gave thanks to God and kissed St Columba, weeping as he did so. The saint blessed him, and he went to the guest-house. That night he was taken ill and before the week was over, as the saint foretold, he departed to Christ.

[I 32] *The saint's prophetic vision of two pilgrim brothers*

One Sunday there came a shout across the Sound. Hearing it, St Columba said to the brethren who were with him:

'Go quickly and bring at once to us the pilgrims who have arrived from a far-away district.'

They obeyed at once, took a boat over the Sound and brought the guests across. The saint greeted them with a kiss and asked for what reason they had come.

'We have come,' they answered, 'to live as pilgrims for a year in your monastery.'

'Here in my monastery,' said St Columba to them, 'you may stay as pilgrims for a year – as you say – only if you first take the monk's vow.'[144]

Those present were amazed to hear him speak so to guests who had only just then arrived. But the elder of the two pilgrim brothers replied:

'Although we did not have this purpose in mind until this hour, we shall do what you advise, for we think it must be God's will.'

Why say more? Immediately they went into the church with St Columba and, kneeling devoutly, they took the vow of a monk. Then the saint turned to the brethren and said:

'These two newcomers today offer themselves to God as a living sacrifice.[145] Within a short time they will have fulfilled the equivalent of years[146] as soldiers of Christ and within the space of one month they will depart in peace to Christ the Lord.'

Both brothers gave thanks to God when they heard this, and they were shown to the guest-house. One week later, the elder brother was taken ill and before the Saturday after, he departed to the Lord. Likewise after another seven days, the younger brother fell ill, and at the end of the next week he too passed happily to the Lord. So, in accordance with the true prophecy of the saint, both had ended this life before the end of a month.

### [I 33] *The saint's prophecy about someone called Artbranan*

When St Columba was staying for a few days on the island of Skye,[147] he struck with his staff a patch of ground by the seashore in a particular place, and said to his companions:

'Strange to tell, my dear children, today, here in this place and on this patch of ground, an old man – a pagan but one who has spent his whole life in natural goodness – will receive baptism, and will die and be buried.'[148]

Only an hour later – look! – a little boat came in to land on the shore, bringing in its prow a man worn out with age. He was the chief commander of the warband in the region of *Cé*.[149] Two young men carried him from the boat and set him down in front of the blessed man. As soon as he had received the word of God from St Columba, through an interpreter, he believed and was baptized by him. When the rite of baptism was finished, as the saint had predicted, the old man died on the same spot and they buried him there and raised a mound of stones over the place.[150] It is still visible there today by the seashore. The stream in which he had received baptism is even today called by the local people 'the water of Artbranan'.[151]

### [I 34] *How the saint ordered the boat to be moved at night*

Once, when St Columba made a journey at the other side of Druim Alban,[152] he lodged for the night in a little place they came upon among deserted fields. It was on the bank of a stream near the point where it flowed into the loch.[153]

That night, his companions had not been asleep for long when the saint woke them, saying:

'Now, quickly, now, go and move our boat from the house where you left it at the other side of the stream. Bring it to a little hut nearer here.'

They at once obeyed and did what he ordered. Some time later, when they were asleep again, the saint silently put his hand on Diarmait, saying:

'Stand outside the house now and look at what is happening at the houses where you first put your boat.'

Following the saint's command, he went outside the house and looked where they had been. He saw all the houses burning and destroyed by fire. Going back to St Columba, he told him what was happening at the other side. Then the saint related to the brethren how a rival had been in pursuit and had set fire to those houses that night.

[I 35] *About Gallán mac Fachtnai, who was in the district Colgu mac Cellaig came from*[154]

Again, once, the saint was sitting in his own hut and Colgu mac Cellaig was studying by his side, when he clairvoyantly said to him:

'At this moment devils are dragging off to hell one grasping leader from among the chief men of your district.'

Hearing what the saint said, Colgu wrote down the date and the hour on his tablet.[155] Months later, he returned to his own district and, questioning the local people, he discovered that Gallán mac Fachtnai had died at the exact time when St Columba had mentioned demons carrying someone away.

[I 36] *The blessed man's prophecy about Findchán, founder of the monastery called in Irish* Artchain *on the island of Tiree*[156]

Once, this priest called Findchán, a soldier of Christ, brought with him from Ireland to Britain a man of the race of Ulster and of royal stock yet wearing a cleric's habit. His name was Áed Dub, and it was intended that he should remain for a number of years as a pilgrim in Findchán's monastery. This Áed Dub had been a very bloody man and had killed many people, among them Diarmait mac Cerbaill, ordained by God's will as king of all Ireland.[157] This same Áed, having spent some time in pilgrimage, was ordained priest in Findchán's monastery, but the ordination was invalid even though a bishop had been brought. This was because the bishop had not dared to place his hand on Áed's head until Findchán (who had a carnal love for Áed) had first laid his right hand on his head in confirmation.[158]

When this ordination was later made known to the saint, he took it ill, pronouncing thereupon this fearful judgement on Findchán and Áed, now ordained, saying:

'That right hand which Findchán, against the law of God and of the Church, laid on the head of a son of perdition will soon grow rotten. It will give him great pain, and be dead and buried before him though he will live many years after his hand is buried.[159] Áed, however, who was ordained unfittingly, will return as a dog to his vomit; he will again be a bloody murderer and in the end, killed by a spear, he will fall from wood into water and die drowning. He deserved such an end to life long ago for having killed the king of all Ireland.'

The blessed man's prophecy concerning both of them was fulfilled. First, the right fist of the priest Findchán became rotten and preceded him into the earth, being buried on the island called *Ommon*.[160] The man himself, in accordance with St Columba's words, lived on for many years. Áed Dub, priest in name only, returned to his old wickedness and, being pierced by a treacherous spear, he fell from the prow of a ship into the waters of a lake and perished.

## [I 37] *How the holy man's spirit brought comfort to working monks on the road*

Among these noteworthy revelations of the spirit of prophecy, it seems not out of place to mention in our account the story of how St Columba brought spiritual refreshment to certain of his monks who felt that he came in spirit to meet them on the road.

For once the brethren were returning to the monastery after a day's work on the harvest. They had reached the place called *Cúl Eilne*, which is reckoned to be the halfway point between the machair on the west side of Iona and our monastery.[161] There, each of them seemed to feel a wonderful and strange sensation, but none of them dared to mention the subject to the others. Day after day the same thing happened in the same place at the same time.

St Baithéne was in charge of their work[162] at this period, and one day he spoke to them, saying:

'It is time, brethren, for each of you to declare if you have been conscious of anything unusual, even miraculous, here at the halfway point between the harvest fields and the monastery.'

One of them, an elder, said:

'As you bid us, I shall describe what has been revealed to me in this place. In the last few days and even now, I am conscious of a wonderful fragrance like all flowers gathered into one; and of heat like fire, not the fire of torment but somehow sweet. And I feel too a strange, incomparable joy poured into my heart. In an instant it refreshes me wonderfully and makes me so joyful that I forget all sadness, all toil. Even the load on my back, though it is not light, none the less from this point all the way to the monastery – I know not how – feels weightless so that I cannot tell I am carrying it.'

Why say more? All the harvest workers, each on his own account, admitted to feeling exactly what this one had openly described. Then with one movement all knelt on the ground and begged St Baithéne to try to explain to them what they did not understand: what was the cause, what was the source of this wonderful relief, which he felt as much as they did? So he gave them this answer:

'You know,' he said, 'that our elder, Columba, thinks anxiously about us, and is upset when we return home to him so late, for he knows we are hard at work. And so it is that, since he may not come to meet us in the body, his spirit meets us as we walk and refreshes us in this way so that we are joyful.'

Hearing these words, on their knees, they raised their outstretched arms to heaven and cried out for great joy, worshipping Christ in the holy and blessed man.[163]

No more should we pass over in silence what we have heard from some of those to whom it was well known about the sound of the saint's psalm-singing. When the venerable man was in church with the brethren, chanting, his voice could be heard sometimes as much as half a mile away, sometimes even a mile, for it was uplifted unlike any other.[164] And yet, strange to tell, it sounded no louder than an ordinary human voice to the ears of those standing with him in the church. But at the same time people more than a mile away could hear his voice so clearly they were able to make out every word of the verses he sang. His voice sounded the same to his hearers, whether near or far. This miracle is proven to have happened not on every occasion but only rarely, though it could not have happened at all but for the grace of the Holy Spirit.

Again, I cannot remain silent about the occasion when his voice was uplifted in this extraordinary way, so we are told, near the fort of King Bridei.[165] The saint was saying vespers as usual with a few brethren, outside the king's fort, and some wizards came quite close to them, trying as best they could to make them stop. For they were afraid that the heathen people would hear the sound of God's praise from the brethren's mouths. Knowing this, St Columba began to chant the forty-fourth psalm,[166] and at that moment his voice was miraculously lifted up in the air like some terrible thunder, so that the king and his people were filled with unbearable fear.

## [I 38] *About a rich man called Lugaid the Lame*

Once when St Columba was staying in Ireland for a time, he saw a cleric sitting in a chariot[167] and cheerfully driving over the plain of Brega.[168] At first he asked who this man was, and got this reply from the man's friends:

'This man is Lugaid the Lame, a rich man of high standing among the people.'[169]

'That,' answered the saint, 'is not how I see him. I see a poor, wretched fellow who on the day of his death has only three stray beasts[170] of his neighbours penned in a stone fold.[171] He will pick one from these stray cattle and have it slaughtered. He will ask for some of its meat to be cooked and served to him lying in bed with his whore.[172] But the first mouthful he takes will choke him to death.'

All this – so those who know say – was fulfilled in accordance with the saint's prophetic word.

### [I 39] *The saint's prophecy about Neman mac Gruthriche*

This man, when the saint reproached him for his bad deeds, took no notice but laughed under his breath. At which the saint said to him:

'In the name of the Lord, Neman, I shall tell you some words of truth. Your enemies will find you lying in bed with a whore, and there you will be cut down.[173] Devils will seize your soul and take you to the place of torments.'

Years later Neman was found in bed with a whore, in the district of *Cainle*,[174] and perished there, as the saint had said, and his enemies cut off his head.[175]

### [I 40] *The saint's prophecy about a priest*

Once when the saint was staying for a time in the part of Ireland we mentioned earlier, it happened to be a Sunday when he came to the little monastery of Trevet not far away.[176] The monks who lived there had chosen to perform the sacrament of the mass a priest who was considered to be deeply religious.[177] But that day, when St Columba heard this priest celebrating the sacred mystery of the Eucharist, he suddenly pronounced these terrible words:

'Clean and unclean are now seen mixed up together – the clean ministry of the sacred offering here administered by the unclean man who at the same time hides in his heart the guilt of a great sin.'

Those who were there and heard the saint were astonished and troubled. But the man of whom this was said was driven to confess his sinfulness in front of everyone. Those fellow-soldiers of Christ who stood on either side of the saint in the church marvelled to hear him disclose the secrets of another's heart, and glorified in him this God-given power of knowledge.

### [I 41] *The saint's prophecy about Erc moccu Druidi, a thief who lived in the isle of Coll*[178]

Once, when the saint was in Iona, he called for two of the brethren, Luigbe and Silnán,[179] and gave them instructions:

'Take a boat now across the Sound to Mull and seek out a thief called Erc among the grounds near the sea. He arrived from Coll last night, alone and in secret, and has made himself a hiding place under his upturned boat, which he has camouflaged with grass.[180] Here he tries to conceal himself all day so that by night he can sail across to the little island that is the breeding-place of the seals we reckon as our own.[181] His plan is to kill them, to fill his boat with what does not belong to him and take it away to his home. He is a greedy thief.'

Luigbe and Silnan listened and obeyed. They sailed out and found the thief hidden where St Columba had told them, and brought him to the saint as they were instructed. On his arrival the saint addressed him:

'To what end do you persistently offend against the Lord's commandment and steal what belongs to others? If you are in need, and come to us, you will receive the necessities you request.'

Fulfilling his words, so the man should not go home empty-handed, he had some sheep slaughtered and given to the wretched thief instead of the seals.

Some time later the saint foresaw in the spirit that the thief was on the point of death. At once he sent word to Baithéne, who was at the time prior of the house in Mag Luinge,[182] that he should dispatch a fat beast and six measures of grain as last gifts to the thief. Baithéne did so and the gifts arrived on the very day that the pitiful thief was overtaken by sudden death. The saint's gifts were used at the funeral.[183]

## [I 42] *The saint's prophecy about Crónán the poet*

Once the saint was in Ireland, sitting with some brethren beside Lough Key, near where the River Boyle flows into it.[184] An Irish poet approached them and after a little conversation he withdrew. When he had gone, the brethren asked St Columba:

'Why did you not ask, before the poet Crónán left us, that he should sing us a tuneful piece of his own composition, as custom allows?'[185]

The saint answered:

'Why ask such a pointless question? How could I have asked for a merry song from that unhappy fellow, who even now has reached the end of the line so soon? His enemies have murdered him.'

Columba had no sooner spoken than they heard a man shout from the other side of the river:

'That poet who left you a little while ago safe and well has in the past hour been attacked on the road and killed by enemies.'

All who were there at the time looked at one another in amazement and wondered greatly.

### [I 43] *The saint's prophecy about two rulers*[186] *who killed one another*

Likewise, once, when the holy man was in Iona, he suddenly broke off from his reading and groaned with deep sorrow and in great wonder. The man who was with him, Luigbe moccu Blai,[187] noticed this and began to ask the reason for this sudden display of grief.

'Two men of royal lineage,' St Columba answered sorrowfully, 'have died today in Ireland of wounds each inflicted on the other. This has happened near the monastery of Cell Rois in the territory of Mugdorna.[188] A week from today someone will shout to be brought across the Sound, coming from Ireland, and he will describe this incident I have mentioned.'

A week later there was a shout across the Sound. At once St Columba called for Luigbe and said to him softly:

'The man who calls across the Sound now is the old traveller whom I mentioned to you earlier. Go and bring him to us.'

Before long the man arrived and among other news had this to say:

'Two men of noble family from Mugdorna have died from wounds they gave one another. They were Colmán Cú mac Ailéni and Rónán mac Áedo maic Colgen of the Airthir. It happened on the boundary of the district, near where the monastery of Cell Rois is situated.'

When the man had told his story, Luigbe, himself a soldier of Christ, took Columba aside and began to question him, saying:

'Tell me, I beg you, about your prophetic revelations such as this. How are they revealed to you? By sight, or hearing, or in some way men know not?'

To which the saint replied:

'You are asking me now about a very delicate subject. I may tell you nothing, not the least word, unless you first kneel and promise me firmly in the name of God on high that you will tell no one of this most secret mystery so long as I am living.'

Luigbe at once knelt down and fell prostrate with his face to the ground and promised to obey in full everything the saint had ordered. Having made this promise, he stood up again and the saint went on:

'There are some people – few indeed – to whom the grace of God has given the power to see brightly and most clearly, with a mental grasp miraculously enlarged, at one and the same time as if lit by a single sunbeam, even the entire orbit of the whole earth and the sea and sky around it.'[189]

Although the saint appeared to attribute this miracle to others, there can be no doubt that he was speaking of his own experience, but obliquely as one reluctant to boast. Anyone who has read St Paul, himself a chosen vessel,[190] will remember what he has written, telling of such visions revealed to himself: not 'I know that I . . .' but 'I know a man, caught up to the third heaven.'[191] Although he appears here to speak of another, no one doubts that he is talking about himself in a humble and modest way. In this same way our Columba had followed St Paul's example in describing his visions of the spirit, a description which Luigbe, though held in great affection by the saint, was only able to wring from him with much pleading as he himself, after Columba's death, testified in the presence of other saints. It is from them that we learnt the account we have related, without any shadow of doubt.

[I 44] *About Bishop Crónán*

Once there came to the saint a stranger from the province of Munster who, so far as he was able, concealed his identity out of humility, for he did not want people to know that he was a bishop. But such a thing could not be hidden from St Columba, for on the Lord's day, when he was bidden by the saint to perform the sacrament of the body of Christ, he called on the saint that as two priests they should together break the Lord's bread. As Columba approached the altar, he suddenly saw into the man's face and spoke to him thus:

'Christ's blessing on you, my brother. Break this bread alone according to the rite of a bishop.[192] For now we know that is what you are. But to what end did you try to conceal your identity until now, so that you have not had from us the reverence due to you?'

The humble pilgrim was much surprised by the saint's words, and reverenced Christ in him, while all present were struck with wonder and glorified God.

[I 45] *The saint's prophecy about the priest Ernán*[193]

Likewise once the reverend man sent his elderly uncle, Ernán, a priest, to be prior of the monastery he had founded years before on the island of *Hinba*.[194] When he was ready to set out, St Columba kissed him and blessed him, speaking these prophetic words:

'I do not hope to see again in this earthly life this friend of mine now setting out on his journey.'

Not many days had passed before Ernán was taken ill, and by his own wish was taken back to Iona to St Columba. When told of his arrival, the saint was glad and set out to the harbour to meet him. Ernán, though he was a sick man, made every effort to try to go to the saint on his feet. But when there was less than fifty yards between them, death suddenly caught up with Ernán. He fell to the ground and breathed his last before the saint could set eyes on his face alive. Otherwise the saint's word would have proved false.

In the place where Ernán died, in front of the door of the corn-kiln,[195] a cross was set up, and another on the spot where Columba was standing at the moment of Ernán's death. These are still standing today.[196]

## [I 46] *The saint's prophecy about a layman's family*

Once the saint was staying as guest at *Coire Salcháin*.[197] Among the people who came to see him was a certain layman who arrived in the evening. When the saint saw him, he said:

'Where do you live?'

'In *Cruach Rannoch* near the shore of the loch.'[198]

'That district you name,' said the saint, 'is where savage marauders are now plundering.'

The poor layman, hearing this, began to grieve for his wife and children, but the saint comforted him in his sorrow, saying:

'Go, dear fellow, go. Your whole family has fled up the mountainside and escaped, though the cruel raiders have driven away with them your little herd, and have even taken as booty the furniture of your house.'

When the layman returned to his own district, he found that everything he had heard the saint say was fulfilled.

### [I 47] *The saint's prophecy about a layman called Guaire mac Áedáin*[199]

Likewise once a layman, at that period the strongest man in the whole of Dalriada,[200] asked St Columba how he would meet his death. The saint said to him:

'You will not die in battle nor at sea. But a companion of your journey, from whom you suspect nothing, will be the cause of your death.'

'Perhaps,' said Guaire, 'one of my entourage of friends plans to murder me; or my wife for love of a younger man may wish to kill me by witchcraft.'

'That is not the way it will come about,' said Columba.

'Why,' said Guaire, 'are you not willing to tell me now who will be my killer?'

'Because,' said the saint, 'if I were to speak out more plainly now and identify which one of your companions will cause your death, it would be a great trouble to you time and again to call that fact to mind. I will not have it so until the day comes when you shall see for yourself the truth of the matter.'

Why do we linger over words? Some years later this Guaire was sitting under an upturned boat, stripping the bark from a long straight stick[201] with his own knife. He heard a row break out among some of the men nearby, and quickly got up to stop the fight. But with the sudden movement he carelessly dropped his knife which cut him badly at the knee. This was the companion whose action caused his death. He realized at once what the saint's prophecy meant and was much perturbed. The wound did not heal, and some months later he died.

[I 48] *About another subject, though a little one, I think I should not pass over in silence the saint's happy foreknowledge and prophecy*

Once, when the saint was living in Iona, he called one of the brethren to him and said:

'Two days from the one now dawning, you should go to the west side of the island and sit up above the shore keeping watch. After the ninth hour[202] a guest will arrive from the north of Ireland, a heron, buffeted by the wind on its long flight, tired and weary. Its strength will be almost gone and it will fall on the shore in front of you. Take care how you lift it up, having pity for it, and carry it to the nearby house. Look after it and feed it there as a guest for three days and nights. Afterwards, at the end of three days, when the heron is revived, it will no longer want to stay as a pilgrim with us, but when its strength is recovered it will return to the sweet district of Ireland from which it came. This is the reason I am so solicitous you should do this, for the heron comes from my own homeland.'[203]

The brother obeyed. At the ninth hour of the third day he waited as he was told for the expected guest to come. When the bird arrived and collapsed, he lifted it from the shore and carried the weak, hungry creature to the house and fed it. He returned to the monastery in the evening, and the saint, not questioning but affirming, said to him:

'God bless you, my son. You have looked after the pilgrim guest well. It will not remain here but after three days will return home.'

What the saint foretold was borne out in the event. After three days as a guest, the bird first rose from the ground in the sight of the host who had looked after it; it flew upwards and for a while spied out its course through the air, then setting off over the ocean in a straight line of flight, it returned to Ireland in fine weather.

[I 49] *The blessed man's foreknowledge about the battle fought, many years later, at the fort of* Dún Cethirn, *and about a little spring near the land of that fort*

Once, after the meeting of the kings at Druim Cett, namely Áed mac Ainmirech and Áedán mac Gabráin,[204] the blessed man was on his way back to the coast when he and Abbot Comgall[205] sat down to rest one clear summer day not far away from this fort. Water for them to wash their hands was brought to the saints from a nearby spring in a bronze basin. St Columba took it and said to Abbot Comgall, who was sat beside him:

'The day will come, Comgall, when the spring from which this water was fetched for us will be unfit for men to use.'

'For what reason will the water of the spring be tainted?' said Comgall.

'Because it will be filled with human blood. For my near kindred and your kinsmen according to the flesh (that is the Uí Néill and the Cruithin) will make war on one another, fighting a battle at this fort of *Dún Cethirn* near here.[206] One of my kindred will actually be killed in this spring, and his blood with that of others will fill the site of the spring.'

This true prophecy was in time fulfilled, years afterwards. In that battle, as many people know, Domnall mac Áedo was raised up as victor, and a man from Columba's kin was killed in the spring as the saint foretold. A soldier of Christ called Fínán was present at that battle. He lived for many years an irreproachable life as an anchorite beside the monastery of Durrow, and it was he who reported to me some facts concerning this battle. He testified that he had seen in that spring a headless corpse, and that on the day of the battle he had returned to St Comgall's monastery at Camus, from where he had previously set out.[207] There he found two old men who had been monks since the time of St Comgall. He told them of the battle he had witnessed and of the spring tainted with human blood.

'A true prophet was St Columba,' they said at once; 'years ago, he foretold all this about the battle and the spring, which you now tell us is fulfilled today. We heard him as he sat with St Comgall near *Dún Cethirn*.'

[I 50] *Concerning the distinction between different offerings as revealed to the saint by the grace of God*

At the same time, Conall, bishop of Coleraine, collected almost innumerable offerings from the people of Mag nEilni and prepared a lodging for St Columba on his way home from the meeting of the kings with a great crowd of people around him. When the saint arrived, the many offerings of the people were set out in the open area of the monastery for him to bless them.[208] Looking at them as he blessed them, he pointed in particular at the gift of a rich man:

'The man,' he said, 'who gave this enjoys the mercy of God on account of his generosity and his mercies to the poor.'

Picking out another item among the many offerings, he said:

'Of this offering, the gift of a man both wise and greedy, I cannot so much as taste, unless he first truly does penance for his sin of avarice.'

This word was at once circulated among the crowd, and Columb mac Áedo, hearing it, recognized his guilt and came forward, to kneel before the saint and do penance. He promised too that henceforth he would renounce avarice, mend his way of life and practise generosity. The saint told him to stand, and from that hour his sin was healed and he was no longer grasping; for as the saint had recognized in his offering, he was a wise man.

The generous rich man whose offering we first mentioned, Brendan by name, heard what St Columba had said of him, and kneeling at the saint's feet he begged the saint to pray to the Lord on his behalf. Columba first reprimanded him for certain sins, for which the man did penance, promising that he would mend his ways. So both of them were corrected and healed of their particular faults.

On a different occasion, but with similar knowledge, the saint recognized the offerings of a grasping man called Diarmait, among the many offerings collected for his arrival at the church of Cell Mór Díthruib.[209]

These examples of St Columba's prophetic grace that I have set down in the first book of my work, though only a few out of many, must suffice. I say 'few' because it is beyond question that the venerable man experienced very many more inward revelations, which people could in no way know about, than those few that trickle out, the mere drips through the seams of a vessel full of newly fermenting wine. For saints and apostles, seeking to avoid the world's empty praise, hurry to hide as far as they can the inner mysteries revealed to them inwardly by God. But willy nilly, God publishes some of them and brings them out into the open one way or another. For he desires to glorify his saints who glorify him, the Lord himself, to whom be glory for ever and ever.

Here ends the first book.

# Now begins the second book, dealing with miracles of power which are often also prophetically foreknown.

[II 1] *Of wine made from water*

Once, when St Columba was still a young man studying the Holy Scriptures with St Uinniau,[210] the bishop, in Ireland, on a day when mass was to be said, by some mischance no wine could be found for the sacrificial mystery. Hearing the ministers of the altar complaining to one another about this problem, Columba picked up a pitcher and went to the well to draw water, in accordance with a deacon's duties, for the sacred service of the Eucharist. By this time he was certainly serving in the order of deacon. He called on the name of the Lord Jesus Christ, who at Cana in Galilee changed water into wine, and in faith he blessed the water that he drew from the well. With Christ's help, here once again the lowly nature of water was transformed at the saint's gesture into the more desired form of wine.

Columba returned from the well to the church and put the full pitcher down beside the altar.

'Here you have wine,' he said to the ministers, 'which the Lord Jesus has sent for the celebration of his mystery.'

When this was known, the holy bishop and his ministers gave great thanks to God, but the youthful saint ascribed it not to himself, but to the holy bishop Uinniau. And so Christ the Lord made this the first proof of power in his disciple, performing the same miracle that he himself had worked as the first of his signs at Cana of Galilee.[211]

Let it shine like a lantern at the entrance of this book, this miracle of God manifested through our own Columba, so that we may pass forward to other miracles of power shown through him.

[II 2] *How the bitter fruit of a tree was turned to sweetness by the saint's blessing*

There was a tree not far from the monastery of Durrow on the south side, which used to bear much fruit. But the inhabitants of the place complained of it, because the fruit was too bitter to eat. So one day St Columba went up to it in autumn. He saw that the tree had a heavy crop of fruit but it was useless, for everyone found it unpleasant to taste rather than pleasing. The saint raised his holy hand and blessed the tree, saying:

'In the name of almighty God, all your bitterness shall leave you, O bitter tree, and your fruit until now most bitter shall become most sweet.'

Marvellous to tell, not a moment after he said it, all the fruit of that tree lost its bitterness and was changed according to the saint's word into wonderful sweetness.

[II 3] *How, when St Columba was living in Iona, a crop was sown after midsummer and was harvested at the beginning of August, at the saint's prayer*[212]

Once St Columba sent his monks to bring bundles of withies from a plot of ground belonging to a layman so that they could be used in building a guest-house.[213] They went and did this, filling a boat with withies. On their return they came to the saint and told him that the layman was much distressed at his loss, so Columba at once gave instructions:

'We do not want to give offence to this man. Take him six measures of our own barley, and let him sow it at this time in ploughed land.'

As the saint commanded, this was sent to the layman, whose name was Findchán. It was handed to him with the saint's instruction, and the man received it gladly but said:

'What use is it to sow a crop after the middle of summer against the nature of the ground?'

His wife on the other hand said:

'Do what the holy man commands, for the Lord will give him whatever he asks.'

So too the men who were sent added these words:

'St Columba who sent us to you with this gift imposed this instruction concerning your crop, saying, "Let the man trust in God's omnipotence. Though his crop be sown when half the month of June has gone, it shall still be harvested at the beginning of August." '

The layman obeyed, both ploughing and sowing. And the harvest which he had sown so late and against hope he reaped to the wonder of all his neighbours, fully ripe as the saint had said, at the beginning of August. The place where this happened is called *Delcros*.[214]

## [II 4] *Of a disease-laden cloud and the healing of very many people*

Once again while St Columba was living in Iona, as he sat on the low hill of Dùn Ì,[215] he saw a heavy storm-cloud to the north rising from the sea on a clear day. Watching as the cloud rose, Columba turned to one of his monks sitting beside him, a man called Silnán mac Nemaidon, whose people were the moccu Sogin,[216] and said:

'This cloud will bring great harm to people and livestock. Today it will pass over here and tonight it will shed a deadly rain over that part of Ireland between the River Delvin and Dublin, a rain that will raise awful sores full of pus on the bodies of people and on the udders of cattle. All those afflicted with this poisonous infection will suffer a terrible sickness even to death.[217] But by the mercy of God it is our duty to take pity on them and help them. You, therefore, Silnán, come down with me now from this hill and prepare yourself to set sail tomorrow. For if life continue[218] and God will, you shall take from here bread that I have blessed in the name of God, you shall dip this bread in water and then sprinkle that water over both people and livestock, and they will soon recover health.'[219]

Why do we pause? All necessary preparations were quickly made, and the next day Silnán received from St Columba's hand the bread he had blessed and set sail in peace. In the hour of his departure St Columba gave him this additional word of encouragement, saying:

'Have confidence, my son. You will have a fair following wind day and night until you reach the area of Árd Ciannachta[220] so that without delay you may come to help the afflicted with this healing bread.'[221]

Why say more? Silnán did as St Columba had said. With the Lord's help his voyage was fair and fast, he landed where the saint had said, and found that the population of the district mentioned by St Columba had been wasted by the deadly rain from the cloud that had recently passed over. The first thing to happen was that Silnán found six men in one house by the sea, all close to death. But when he sprinkled them with the water of benediction, within the day they were happily restored to health. Accounts of this sudden cure rapidly circulated throughout the area affected by the disease, and attracted the sick to St Columba's representative, who, in accordance with the saint's command, sprinkled both people and livestock with water in which the blessed bread had been dipped. At once men and beasts regained their health, and praised Christ in St Columba with exceeding gratitude.

There are, I think, two significant elements in this story, namely the grace of prophecy in respect of the cloud, and the miracle of power in healing the sick. That the story is in every respect completely true we have the testimony of Silnán himself, a soldier of Christ, given in the presence of Abbot Ségéne and other elders.[222]

### [II 5] *Concerning the holy virgin Mogain, daughter of Daiméne, who lived in Clochar Macc nDaiméni*[223]

Once, while St Columba was living in Iona, he called to him in the first hour of the day one of the brethren, Lugaid nicknamed in Irish 'the strong',[224] and said to him:

'Make ready at once for a speedy voyage to Ireland, for it is essential that I send you as my representative to Clochar Macc nDaiméni. For in this night just past Daiméne's daughter, the holy virgin Mogain, has had an accident. As she returned home from the church after the night office, she stumbled, and her hip is broken in two.[225] Now she cries aloud and repeats my name constantly, hoping that I should bring her comfort from the Lord.'

Why say more? Lugaid did as he was bidden. When he was ready to set out, Columba handed him a little pinewood box with a blessing inside it,[226] and said:

'When you arrive to visit Mogain, the blessing contained in this box should be dipped in a jar of water and then the water of blessing should be poured over her hip. Then call on the name of God and at once her hipbone will be joined and knit together and her full health restored.'

Then the saint went on:

'Look, in your presence I write[227] on the lid of this box the number XXIII, which is the number of years which the holy virgin will continue in this present life after her cure.'

All of this was fulfilled as the saint foretold. For as soon as Lugaid came to the holy virgin, he sprinkled the blessed water on her hip, as the saint had said, and straightaway the bone was mended and Mogain was fully healed. She rejoiced at the coming of St Columba's representative and thanked him profusely. Thereafter, according to the saint's prophecy, she lived twenty-three years after her cure and continued in good works.

### [II 6] *On the healing of various ailments at Druim Cett*

The man of praiseworthy life by the invocation of Christ's name cured the ailments of various invalids during the brief period when he was at Druim Cett to attend the meeting of the kings. So the story is handed down to us by learned men. Many sick people put their trust in him and received full healing, some from his outstretched hand, some from being sprinkled with water he had blessed, others by the mere touching of the edge of his cloak, or from something such as salt or bread blessed by the saint and dipped in water.

### [II 7] *About a block of salt blessed by the saint which fire could not destroy*[228]

Likewise, on another occasion, Colgu mac Cellaig asked for and was given a block of salt which St Columba had blessed to help the man's sister, who had fostered him, for she was suffering from a severe affliction of the eye. That sister and foster-mother received this blessing from her brother's hand

and hung it on the wall above her bed. A few days later misfortune fell, and fire destroyed the entire village, including this woman's house. Marvellous to tell, a little section of the wall of this house remained standing unharmed though the rest of the house was completely burnt, and that which the holy man had blessed was still hanging there, for the fire did not dare to touch the two pegs on which this salt-block was hanging.

## [II 8] *Concerning one leaf of a book, written by St Columba, which water could not damage*

There is another miracle that I should not pass over in silence, one that concerns the opposite of fire, water. It happened many years after St Columba had died. A young man fell off his horse in the Irish River Boyne and was drowned, lying for twenty days under water. At the time of the fall he was carrying a leather satchel[229] of books under his arm, which he was still clutching when the body was found so many days later. When his body was brought to the bank, the satchel was opened and the pages of all the books were found to be ruined and rotten except one page, which St Columba had written out with his own hand.[230] This was found to be dry and in no way spoilt as though it had been all along in a book case.

## [II 9] *Another miracle of the same type*

Once a book of the week's hymns[231] written out by St Columba with his own hand fell into the water when the boy who was carrying it in a leather satchel on his shoulders slipped off a bridge over a river in the province of Leinster.

The book remained in the water from Christmas to Easter, until it was found on the river bank by some women out walking. They took it to a priest called Éogenán, a man of Pictish origin, to whom it had belonged.[232] The book was still in its satchel, which was not merely sodden but had rotted. When Éogenán opened the satchel, however, he found the book unharmed, as clean and dry as if it had never fallen into the water but had remained in its book case.

We have heard many other accounts about books written out by St Columba, reported in various places by people who knew the facts and did not doubt them. Such books were never spoilt by being submerged in water. But this particular story, about Éogenán's book, came to me from some men of exemplary honesty and good faith, who left no room for doubt that they had seen this book extraordinarily white and clean even though it had been so many days in the water.

These two different miracles, though concerned with things of little importance, were performed against the two opposed elements of fire and water. They bear witness to the honour of the blessed man and show how God held him to be a man of great and special merit.

### [II 10] *How the prayers of the saint drew water from hard rock*

While we are mentioning the element of water, we ought to speak also of the other miracles concerning it which the Lord worked at various times and places through St Columba.

Once during the saint's life of pilgrimage he was on a journey when a child was brought to him for baptism by his parents. But there was no water to be found in that spot. So the saint turned aside to the nearest rock, where he knelt and prayed a little while. When he stood up, he blessed the face of the rock, and at once water bubbled out from it in great quantity. Thereupon he baptized the child, making this prophecy concerning him:

'This little boy will live a long life, into extreme old age. In his youth he will be more or less a slave of the desires of the flesh, but afterwards he will devote himself to service as a soldier of Christ to the end of his days, and in old age will depart to the Lord.'

All this happened to the man as the saint foretold. His name was Ligu Cenncalad. The place where his parents were was in Ardnamurchan, and a little spring is still to be seen there which is powerful in the name of St Columba.[233]

### [II 11] *About another well with evil properties which St Columba blessed in Pictland*

Once, when St Columba spent some time in the land of the Picts, he heard reports of a well that was famous among the heathen population. Indeed the foolish people worshipped it as a god because the devil clouded their sense.[234] What used to happen was that anyone who drank from the well or intentionally washed his hands or feet in it was struck down by the devil's art (for God permitted this). Such people became leprous or half blind or crippled or were afflicted with some other infirmity when they left the well. These occurrences deluded the heathens into treating the well as a god. When St Columba learnt of this, he made his way fearlessly to the well. The wizards, whom he had often driven away in confusion and defeat,[235] saw what he was doing and were glad, for they expected that he too should suffer the effects of touching the harmful water. The saint first raised his hands and called on the name of Christ before washing his hands and feet. Then he and his companions drank from the water that he had blessed. Since that day the demons have kept away from the well. Instead, far from harming anyone, after the saint had blessed it and washed in it, many ailments among the local people were cured by that well.

[II 12] *How St Columba was in peril on the sea and how he stilled the storm by his prayer*

Once, when St Columba was at sea, he found himself threatened by danger. A great storm, with gusts of wind blowing from all sides, arose and his boat was tossed and buffeted by great waves. St Columba tried to help the sailors bail out the water that came into the boat, but they said to him:

'Your doing that does little to help us in this danger. You would do better to pray for us as we all perish.'

Hearing this, he stopped emptying the bitter water into the sea to no effect and began instead to pour out sweet prayers to the Lord.[236] Marvellous to tell, as soon as the saint stood up in the prow and raised his hands to heaven in prayer to almighty God, the stormy winds and the raging sea were still in less time than it takes to say it and at once all was fair and calm. The men on board the boat were amazed, and gave thanks in wonderment, glorifying God in his praiseworthy saint.

[II 13] *Of another similar danger at sea*

On another occasion St Columba's companions called on him during a wild and dangerous storm, that he should pray to the Lord for them. But the saint answered:

'Today it is not I who will pray for you in this danger, but the holy Abbot Cainnech.'

I shall tell you a wonderful thing now. That very hour, St Cainnech was at home in his own monastery of Aghaboe when the Spirit brought St Columba's words to the inward ear of his heart.[237] Nones[238] was already over and the saint was beginning to break the bread of blessing in the refectory.[239] But he instantly left the table and ran to the church, one shoe on his foot and the other left behind in his hurry.[240]

'We cannot have dinner at this time,' he said, 'for St Columba's boat is even now in peril on the sea. At this moment he speaks the name of this Cainnech, saying that he should pray to Christ for him and his fellows in time of trouble.'

So saying he entered the church where he knelt and prayed for a little time. The Lord heard his prayer and at once the storm ceased and the sea became calm.

At this point St Columba, who had seen in the Spirit the haste with which St Cainnech went to the church, though the two saints were miles apart, amazed everyone when from his pure heart he said:

'Now I know, O Cainnech, that God has heard your prayer. Now indeed you have helped us by your swift running to the church wearing only one shoe.'

In a miracle of this kind we believe that the prayers of the two saints worked together.

### [II 14] *Concerning St Cainnech's staff left behind at the harbour*[241]

Once, the same St Cainnech forgot to take his staff with him when he set sail from the harbour of Iona on his way to Ireland. When he had gone, the staff was found on the shore and was given to St Columba. Returning to the monastery, he took it with him into the church and stayed there a long while alone in prayer.

Cainnech had reached the southern part of Islay[242] before he realized that he had forgotten his staff and he was much dismayed. But after a little time he left the ship and knelt down on the ground to pray. There on the green grass of Islay he found lying in front of him the staff that he had left behind in the harbour of Iona. It could only have come there with the help of God, and he marvelled greatly and gave thanks.

### [II 15] *How Baithéne and Colmán mac Beognai,[243] both holy priests, asked St Columba to call on God to give them each a fair wind though they were sailing in different directions on the same day*

Once, these two holy men approached St Columba at the same time and with the same purpose, calling on him to ask for and obtain from the Lord that each be given a fair wind the next day, though they were to set sail in different directions. This is how St Columba answered them:

'Tomorrow, first thing in the morning, Baithéne will have a following wind for his journey from Iona to the harbour at Mag Luinge.'[244]

The Lord granted this according to the saint's word. For that day Baithéne crossed the whole expanse of sea to Tiree under full sail.

At the third hour of the same day St Columba sent for Colmán the priest and said to him:

'Baithéne has now arrived safely at the harbour he was wanting. Make your preparations to sail today. For soon the Lord will bring the wind round to the north.'

Within the hour the south wind had obeyed St Columba's word and had become a breeze blowing from the north.

So it happened that on one and the same day two men, parting from one another in peace, travelled under full sail with a following wind – Baithéne in the morning to Tiree, Colmán after noon beginning his voyage to Ireland. By the Lord's gift. This miracle was accomplished through the power of prayer by the famous saint, for it is written, 'All things are possible to him that believeth'.[245]

Later on the same day, after Colmán's departure, St Columba delivered this prophecy concerning him:

'The holy man Colmán whom we have blessed as he set sail will never see my face again in this world.'

This was fulfilled, for in less than a year from then St Columba departed to the Lord.

## [II 16] *How St Columba drove out a devil hiding at the bottom of a milk-pail*

Once a young man called Colmán Ua Briúin[246] was returning from milking the cows and carried on his back the wooden pail with the fresh milk in it. When he reached the door of the saint's hut, where St Columba was copying a manuscript, he stopped and asked the saint to bless the pail according to his custom. St Columba did not come near but raised his hand and made the saving sign of the cross in the air in the direction of the pail. He called on the name of God and blessed the vessel, which at once shook violently. The peg that held the lid to the pail was shot back through both holes and thrown some distance, the lid crashed to the ground, and most of the milk spilled on to the earth. The youth set the pail down on its base on the ground with what little milk was left, and knelt in supplication. St Columba said to him:

'Stand up, Colmán. Today you were careless in your work. There was a devil hiding in the bottom of the pail and, before you poured the milk in, you should have driven it off by making the sign of the Lord's cross. The devil could not withstand the power of that sign. Now his trembling has shaken the pail and as he escaped he has spilt the milk. Bring the pail nearer to me so that I may bless it.'

Colmán brought the pail to him and the saint blessed it. What was before nearly empty was in an instant found to be full; where only a little milk had remained in the bottom, under the blessing of the saint's hand it rose up to the brim.

[II 17] *About a pail that a sorcerer called Silnán filled with milk from a bull*

What follows is said to have happened in the house of a rich layman called Foirtgern, who lived on the hill of *Cainle*.[247] When St Columba was a guest there, he foresaw the arrival of two country people in dispute and with true judgement he acted as judge between them.[248]

One of them, who was a sorcerer, by the art of the devil drew milk from a bull nearby, at the saint's command. It was not in order to confirm these sorceries that the saint had ordered this to be done but in order to defeat them in the sight of the people. St Columba told the man to give him at once the pail, which seemed to be full of milk, and he blessed it with these words:

'Now it will be proven that this is not true milk as you all think, but is blood, deprived of its colour by the devil's cheating in order to deceive mankind.'

Straightway the milk-white colour was changed into its proper nature, namely into blood. The bull, also, in the space of one hour wasted away to a hideous leanness and came near to death. But when it was sprinkled with water blessed by St Columba it recovered with remarkable speed.

[II 18] *About Luigne moccu Min*[249]

One day a young man of naturally good disposition called Luigne (who later, in his riper years, was prior of the monastery in the island of *Elen*)[250] approached St Columba and complained of a discharge of blood that had often during many months past flowed uncontrollably from his nostrils. The saint called him closer, squeezed his nostrils between the thumb and forefinger of his right hand, and blessed him. There was never again a drop of blood from his nose, from the hour of that blessing to the last day of his life.

[II 19] *How God specially provided fish for St Columba*

Once when the praiseworthy man was in the company of hardy fishermen on the fishful River Shiel,[251] they had caught five fish in the net, and St Columba said:

'Again cast the net in the river, and you will quickly find a great fish which the Lord has provided for me.'

Obeying his instruction, they drew in with their net a salmon of wonderful size provided for him by God.[252]

Another time, St Columba spent some days on Lough Key.[253] His companions wanted to go fishing, but he delayed them, saying:

'Today and tomorrow there will not be a single fish caught in the river, but I shall send you fishing on the third day and you will find two great salmon caught in the net.'

So after two days of waiting they cast their net in the River Boyle, and when they drew it to the bank they found two salmon of very unusual size, for which St Columba and his companions gave hearty thanks to God.[254]

In these two stories about fishing the power of a miracle is manifest and is accompanied by prophetic foreknowledge.

## [II 20] *About Nesán the Crooked who lived in the district of Lochaber*

This Nesán, though he was a very poor man, rejoiced on one occasion to receive St Columba as his guest. When the saint had enjoyed one night's hospitality from Nesán, as far as his means would stretch, he asked how many cows he owned.

'Five,' said Nesán.

'Bring them to me,' said St Columba, 'so that I may bless them.'

They were brought, and St Columba blessed them, raising his holy hand, and said:

'From this day your little herd of five cows will grow until you have one hundred and five cows.'[255]

Since Nesán was a layman with a wife and children, St Columba made this addition to his benediction, saying:

'Your seed will be blessed in your sons and grandsons.'

All these things were fulfilled according to his word nor was anything diminished in any way.

[There was also a rich man called Vigen who was very tight-fisted, and who looked down on St Columba and would not receive him as a guest. About this man the saint made quite the opposite prophecy, saying:

'The riches of this miser, who has rejected Christ in the pilgrim visitors, will from henceforth be diminished little by little until there is nothing. He himself will be a beggar, and his son will run from house to house with a half-empty bag. A rival will strike him with an axe and he will die in the trench of a threshing-floor.'

All these things were fulfilled according to the saint's prophecies as they concerned the two men.][256]

[II 21] *A similar story about a layman called Colmán, whose cattle were few in number, but St Columba blessed them and thereafter they increased by one hundred*

At another time the saint was received as a guest one night by this Colmán, who at that period was a poor man.[257] Early in the morning St Columba questioned Colmán, just as he questioned Nesán in the previous story, about the kind and quantity of his wealth.

'I have only five little cows,' answered Colmán, 'but if you bless them, they will increase.'

The saint bade him bring them, which he did at once, and in the same manner as we described in the case of Nesán's five cows, so the saint blessed Colmán's little cows and said:

'God has granted that you will have one hundred and five cows, and there will be a blessing of fruitfulness on your sons and grandsons.'

Everything that St Columba foretold was fulfilled in Colmán's fields and herds and in his offspring. But this is the strangest part. For both men St Columba had fixed the number of his cattle at one hundred and five, and when this number was reached there was no further increase. Any beast which was in excess of the preordained limit was carried off by some mischance and never seen again, unless it could be made use of for the needs of his own household or in the work of charity.

In this story as in others a miracle of power is clearly connected with a prophecy. The power of blessing and of prayer are seen in the great increase of the cattle, and prophetic foreknowledge in the number set in advance.

## [II 22] *How men of evil who had scorned St Columba were destroyed*

St Columba held in great affection this Colmán whom the power of his benediction had brought from poverty to wealth, and Colmán in return showed his devotion in many services.

There was at that time a man of evil who persecuted good men. His name was Ioan mac Conaill maic Domnaill, who belonged to the royal lineage of Cenél nGabráin,[258] and he used to bring trouble upon trouble on St Columba's friend Colmán, attacking his house and taking all he could find there, not once but twice. Yet a third time, when this evil man had again plundered Colmán's house, he and his associates were returning loaded with booty to their boat. Suddenly and not undeservedly they were confronted by St Columba, whom they had discounted, believing him to be far away. Yet St Columba drew nearer, reproving the man for his evil deeds and urging him to give up his plunder. But the man remained hard and unyielding. He looked with contempt at the saint, and when he and his booty had all gone up the gangplank and into the boat, he scoffed at the saint and mocked him. St Columba followed him into the sea till the glassy water came up to his knees, then he raised both hands to heaven and earnestly prayed to Christ who glorifies his chosen ones who glorify him.[259]

He remained where he stood praying to the Lord for a little while after Ioan had sailed away from that bay, which is called 'Sharp bay' and is in Ardnamurchan.[260] Having finished his prayer, St Columba returned to dry ground and sat down with his companions in an elevated place. In that hour he spoke to them very terrible words, saying:

'This wretched fellow who has despised Christ in his servants will never return to this bay from which he has just now sailed away in front of your eyes, nor will he find the landfall he seeks. For he and those who share in his evil deeds will be cut off by sudden death. Today as you will soon see, a cloud will rise from the north and bring a violent squall which will overwhelm Ioan and his men so that no one will survive to tell what happened.'

It was only a short time after this that, though the weather was fine and clear, there came a cloud from the sea. Just as the saint had said, it brought a great squall of wind, which, finding the robber and his loot in the open sea between Mull and Coll, at once stirred up the waves and sank their boat. Again the saint was proved right, for no one from the boat survived. But the marvel of it is this, that while this one squall drowned the robbers and snatched them down to the depths of hell – a wretched end, but well deserved – all the sea round about remained perfectly calm.

### [II 23] *About someone called Feradach carried off by sudden death*

Likewise on another occasion there was a man named Taran, who belonged to a noble family in Pictland but who was living in exile.[261] St Columba in a friendly manner put him in the care of a rich man called Feradach, who lived in Islay, where Taran could live in his household as one of his friends for several months. Though Feradach received the man on trust from St Columba, only a few days passed before he acted treacherously and cruelly gave the order to murder Taran. News of this monstrous crime was brought by travellers to St Columba, who in response said:

'It is not only in my sight but in God's that Feradach has betrayed our trust. His name will be removed from the book of life. I say this to you now in the middle of summer, but in autumn when the pigs are fattened on acorns in the woods,[262] before he has his first taste of their meat, he will be overtaken by sudden death and carried off to hell.'

The holy man's prophetic saying was reported to the

wretched fellow, who made light of the saint and scoffed at his words. Autumn came and the pigs were fattening on mast when Feradach had a fattened sow slaughtered before any of his other pigs were killed. He ordered his servants to clean the sow quickly and to have some of its meat roasted immediately on a spit, for he was impatient to have his first taste of the meat and prove St Columba's prophecy false. As soon as a morsel of the meat was cooked, he called for it to taste it. He took the meat in his hand, but before he was able to bring it to his mouth he fell on his back and expired. Those who saw this and those who heard of it trembled greatly in wonder, glorifying Christ and honouring him in his holy prophet.

### [II 24] *Concerning another impious man, an attacker of churches, whose name means 'Right Hand'*[263]

Once, when St Columba was living in the island of *Hinba*, he set about excommunicating those men who persecuted churches, in particular the sons of Conall mac Domnaill. We have already told the story of one of them, Ioan.[264] Now, at the devil's prompting a man from the band of these men of evil attacked St Columba with a spear, meaning to kill him. To prevent this, one of the brethren, called Findlugán, stepped between them, ready to die instead of the saint. As it happened, he was wearing St Columba's cowl and miraculously this garment acted like a strong, impenetrable breastplate that could not be pierced, however sharp the spear or great the thrust of a strong man, but remained undamaged. The man wearing this protection was untouched and unharmed. But the wretched man, whose name means 'Right Hand,' thought he had pierced the saint with his spear and made off.

A year later, on the anniversary of that episode, St Columba was in Iona when he said:

'Today is exactly one year since the day when Lám Dess

did his best to kill Findlugán in my place, but this very hour, so I believe, he will himself be killed.'

This was happening at the very moment the saint made this revelation. Lám Dess was in a fight in the Long Island[265] when a spear, thrown – so it is said – in the name of St Columba by Crónán mac Báetáin, transfixed him. Out of all the men fighting on either side Lám Dess was the only one to die, and after he was killed they stopped their fighting.

### [II 25] *Again concerning another persecutor of innocents*[266]

When St Columba was a young man, still in deacon's orders, he lived in Leinster studying divine wisdom.[267] During this period it happened one day that a cruel man, a pitiless persecutor of innocent folk, was pursuing a young girl who was running away from him over the open plain. As soon as she saw Gemmán, St Columba's old teacher, reading his book out on the plain, she made straight for his protection as fast as she could run. Alarmed by these sudden events, Gemmán called to Columba, who was also reading a little distance away, so that with their joint strength they might do their best to save the girl from her pursuer. When he came close, he showed no reverence to the clerics but at once drove his spear into the girl, even as she clutched at their habits, and left her dead at their feet. Then he turned his back on them and began to walk away.

The old man was much distressed by this, and turned to Columba.

'How long, Columba, my holy son, will God the true judge let this crime and our dishonour go unpunished?'[268]

Whereupon the saint pronounced this sentence on the man who had committed the crime:

'In the same hour in which the soul of the girl he killed ascends to heaven, so be it that the soul of her killer shall descend to hell.'

He had no sooner spoken than, like Ananias in front of Peter,[269] so in the sight of St Columba that slaughterer of innocents fell dead on the spot. Reports of this sudden and terrible punishment were soon heard throughout the many districts of Ireland, and the holy deacon became famous.

This is enough of such stories about terrible vengeance on his opponents. Now we shall say a few things about animals.

[II 26]

Once, when St Columba was staying for a few days in Skye, he took himself off on his own, no little distance from the brethren with him, in order to pray. Entering a dense forest, he encountered a boar of amazing size which was being pursued by hunting-dogs.[270] Seeing this, the saint stood still and watched it from a distance. Then he raised his holy hand and called on the name of God with earnest prayer, and said to the boar:

'Go no further, but die where you are now.'

The saint's voice rang out in the forest, and the beast was unable to move any further but at once collapsed dead in front of him, killed by the power of his terrible word.

[II 27] *How a water beast was driven off by the power of the blessed man's prayer*

Once, on another occasion, when the blessed man stayed for some days in the land of the Picts,[271] he had to cross the River Ness. When he reached its bank, he saw some of the local people burying a poor fellow. They said they had seen a water beast snatch him and maul him savagely as he was swimming not long before.[272] Although some men had put out in a little boat to rescue him, they were too late, but, reaching out with hooks, they had hauled in his wretched corpse. The blessed man, having been told all this, astonished them by sending one of his companions to swim across the river and sail back to him in a dinghy that was on the further bank. At the command of the holy and praiseworthy man, Luigne moccu Min[273] obeyed without hesitation. He took off his clothes except for a tunic and dived into the water.[274] But the beast was lying low on the riverbed, its appetite not so much sated as whetted for prey. It could sense that the water above was stirred by the swimmer, and suddenly swam up to the surface, rushing open-mouthed with a great roar towards the man as he was swimming midstream. All the bystanders, both the heathen and the brethren, froze in terror, but the blessed man looking on raised his holy hand and made the sign of the cross in the air, and invoking the name of God, he commanded the fierce beast, saying:

'Go no further. Do not touch the man. Go back at once.'

At the sound of the saint's voice, the beast fled in terror so fast one might have thought it was pulled back with ropes. But it had got so close to Luigne swimming that there was no more than the length of a pole between man and beast. The brethren were amazed to see that the beast had gone and that their fellow-soldier Luigne returned to them untouched and safe in the dinghy, and they glorified God in the blessed man. Even the heathen natives who were present at the time were so moved by the greatness of the miracle they had witnessed that they too magnified the God of the Christians.[275]

[II 28] *How St Columba blessed the ground in this island so that thereafter the poison of snakes should not harm anyone here*[276]

One day of early summer, shortly before he passed to the Lord, St Columba went by cart to visit those brethren at work building a stone wall around the machair on the west coast of Iona.[277] He stood on a little knoll above them, and addressed them with words of comfort, which he ended with this prophecy:

'My children, today is the last time you will see my face here at the machair.'[278]

He could see that they were much distressed by these words, and he made every effort to console them. Then he raised both his holy hands and blessed all this island of ours, saying:

'From this hour, from this instant, all poisons of snakes shall have no power to harm either men or cattle in the lands of this island for as long as the people who dwell here keep Christ's commandments.'

[II 29] *Of a knife which St Columba blessed with the sign of the Lord's cross*

Once, one of the brethren, Molua Ua Briúin by name,[279] came to the saint while he was engaged in copying a manuscript and asked him:

'Please bless this implement which I have in my hand.'

St Columba did not look up, but continued to keep his eyes on the book from which he was copying. However, he reached his hand out a little way and, still holding his pen, made the sign of the cross. Molua took away the implement he had blessed, and later St Columba asked Diarmait, his loyal servant:

'What was the implement I blessed for our brother?'

'A knife,' said Diarmait, 'for the slaughtering of bulls or cattle.'

'I trust in my Lord,' added St Columba, 'that the implement I have blessed will not harm man or beast.'[280]

No more than an hour had gone by before the saint's word was proved entirely true. For Molua went outside the boundary bank of the monastery,[281] intending to kill a bullock. But though he tried three times, pressing very hard with the knife, yet he found he was unable to get through the skin. Having discovered this fact, the monks who knew the blacksmith's craft melted down the iron of that knife and then coated the liquid metal on to all the other iron tools in the monastery.[282] From then on, these tools were unable to harm any flesh, for the power of the saint's blessing remained in the metal.

## [II 30] *How Diarmait's sickness was healed*

Once, St Columba's loyal servant Diarmait fell ill and seemed likely to die. He was on the point of death when the saint came to visit him and as he stood at the bedside of the sick man he called on the name of Christ and prayed for Diarmait:

'My Lord, I beseech thee, hear my prayer, and while I live take not the soul of my loyal servant Diarmait from the habitation of this body.'

He was then silent for a time, before bringing this affirmation from his holy lips saying:

'This my child will not only survive on this occasion but he will outlive me by many years.'

The saint's prayer had been heard and found acceptable, for straightaway Diarmait regained his full health. He also lived many years after St Columba departed to the Lord.

### [II 31] *How Fintan mac Áedo was healed though on the point of death*

Also at another time, when St Columba was journeying at the other side of Druim Alban,[283] one of his companions was suddenly troubled with sickness and came close to death. He was a young man called Fintan, and his fellow soldiers in Christ were saddened and begged St Columba to pray for him. The saint took pity on them and at once spread out his holy arms towards heaven in earnest prayer, and blessed the sick man, saying:

'This young lad for whom you intercede will live a long life. Even when all of us here today are dead, he will still be living and will die in good old age.'

St Columba's prediction was fulfilled in every respect. For this youth, who in later life founded the monastery of *Cailli áufhinde*, ended this present life in good old age.[284]

### [II 32] *How St Columba in the Lord's name raised a boy from the dead*

During the time when St Columba spent a number of days in the province of the Picts,[285] he was preaching the word of life through an interpreter.[286] A Pictish layman heard him and with his entire household believed and was baptized, husband, wife, children and servants. A few days later one of his sons was seized with a severe pain, which brought him to the boundary of life and death. When the heathen wizards saw that the boy was dying, they began to make a mock of the parents and to reproach them harshly, making much of their own gods as the stronger and belittling the God of the Christians as the feebler.[287]

All this was made known to St Columba and it stirred him vigorously to take God's part. He set off with his companions to visit the layman's house, and there he found that the child had recently died and his parents were performing the rituals of mourning. Seeing their great distress, St Columba comforted them and assured them that they should not in any way doubt that God is almighty. Then he proceeded to question them, saying:

'In which of these buildings does the body of the dead boy lie?'[288]

The bereaved father led St Columba to that sad lodging, which the saint entered alone, leaving the crowd of people outside. Having gone inside, St Columba immediately knelt and, with tears streaming down his face, prayed to Christ the Lord. After these prayers on bended knee, he stood up and turned his gaze to the dead boy, saying:

'In the name of the Lord Jesus Christ, wake up again and stand upon thy feet.'[289]

At the saint's glorious word the soul returned to the body, and the boy that was dead opened his eyes and lived again. St Columba took hold of the boy's hand, raised him to his feet and, steadying him, led him out of the house. He gave the boy, now restored to life, back to his parents, and a great shout went up from the crowd. Mourning gave way to celebration and the God of the Christians was glorified.

One must recognize that in this miracle of power our St Columba is seen to share with the prophets Elijah and Elisha and with the apostles Peter and Paul and John the rare distinction of raising the dead to life. He has a seat of everlasting glory in the heavenly homeland as himself a prophet and apostle among the companies of the prophets and the apostles, with Christ who with the Father and the Holy Ghost reigns for ever and ever.[290]

### [II 33] *How Broichan, a wizard, was stricken with sickness when he refused to release a female slave, but was healed when he released her*[291]

At the same time St Columba asked a wizard called Broichan to release an Irish slave-girl,[292] having pity on her as a fellow human being. But Broichan's heart was hard and unbending, so the saint addressed him thus, saying:

'Know this, Broichan. Know that if you will not free this captive exile[293] before I leave Pictland, you will have very little time to live.'

He said this in King Bridei's house in the presence of the king.[294] Then leaving the house, he came to the River Ness, where he picked up a white pebble from the river and said to his companions:

'Mark this white stone,' he said, 'through which the Lord will bring about the healing of many sick people among this heathen race.'

After a moment's pause, he went on:

'Now Broichan has suffered a heavy blow. For an angel sent from heaven has struck him, breaking into fragments the glass cup in his hand just as he was drinking from it. He is now struggling to get his breath and is near to death. But we should wait here a little while. The king will send two messengers hurrying out to us to call on our help for Broichan, and urgently, for he is dying. This seizure has put fear into him. Now he is willing to release the slave-girl.'

The saint was still speaking when there came two men on horseback, sent by the king, who told what had happened to Broichan in the king's fortress. Everything matched St Columba's prediction: the breaking of the cup, the wizard's seizure, his readiness to release the slave-girl. And they added:

'The king and his household have sent us to you to call on your help for Broichan, who will soon die.'

The saint listened to their speech, and then sent two of his own companions to the king, handing them the stone that he had blessed and saying:

'If Broichan will first promise to release the Irish girl, then and only then dip this stone in some water and let him drink it. He will be well again immediately. But if he is intransigent and refuses to release her, he will die on the spot.'

The two men went to the king's hall and there, following St Columba's directions, they repeated to the king all he had said. The king and Broichan, his foster-father, were very much afraid when they learnt all this. Within the hour the slave-girl was set free and handed over to St Columba's messengers. The stone was dipped in some water, where, in defiance of nature, it floated miraculously on the surface of the water like an apple or a nut, for that which the saint had blessed could not be made to sink. When Broichan drank from it, though he had been near to death, he recovered completely his bodily health.

The stone itself was kept in the royal treasury. Whenever it was put in water, it floated, and by the Lord's mercy it brought about the healing of many ailments among the people. But if the sick person seeking help from the stone was one whose appointed term of life was finished, then – strange to say – no way could the stone be found. So it happened on the day King Bridei died. The stone was sought but it could not be found in the place where till then it had been kept.

### [II 34] *Of St Columba's resistance to Broichan the wizard, and of a contrary wind*

It was after these events that one day Broichan addressed St Columba, saying:

'Tell me, Columba,[295] when do you intend to sail?'

'God willing and life lasting,'[296] replied St Columba, 'we plan to start our voyage in three days' time.'

'You will not be able to,' said Broichan combatively, 'for I have the power to produce an adverse wind and to bring down a thick mist.'

'The almighty power of God rules all things,' said the saint, 'and all our comings and goings are directed by his governance.'

Why say more? On the same day as he had planned in his heart St Columba, with a great crowd of people following, came to the long loch at the head of the River Ness.[297] At this point the wizards began to congratulate themselves, seeing a great mist covered the loch and a stormy wind was blowing against them. One must not be surprised that such things happen occasionally by the art of devils – when God permits it – so that the wind and waves can be stirred up to a storm. For in this way St Germanus was once attacked by legions of evil spirits as he sailed from the bay of Gaul to Britain in the cause of man's salvation.[298] They rushed at him on the open sea, putting perils in his path, stirring storms and blotting out the daylight sky with a mist of darkness. But in an instant, at St Germanus's prayer, the mist was wiped away, the storms were stilled and all perils ceased.

Our own Columba, seeing that the elements were roused to fury against him, called upon Christ the Lord. Though the sailors were hesitant, he was steadfast. He boarded the boat and ordered them to hoist the sail into the wind. This was done, and all the crowd of people looking on saw his boat move off directly into the wind at marvellous speed. In only a little time the contrary wind backed round and, to everyone's wonder, turned in their favour. And so all day they enjoyed a gentle following breeze for their journey, and the boat arrived at its intended destination.

Consider, reader, how great was that venerable man, and what kind of man he was, in whom almighty God declared his glorious name in the sight of a heathen people through these miracles of power.

### [II 35] *How the gates of the royal fortress suddenly opened on their own*[299]

Once, the first time St Columba climbed the steep path[300] to King Bridei's fortress, the king, puffed up with royal pride, acted aloofly and would not have the gates of his fortress opened at the first arrival of the blessed man. The man of God, realizing this, approached the very doors with his companions. First he signed them with the sign of the Lord's cross and only then did he put his hand to the door to knock. At once the bars were thrust back and the doors opened of themselves with all speed. Whereupon St Columba and his companions entered.

The king and his council[301] were much alarmed at this, and came out of the house to meet the blessed man with due respect and to welcome him gently with words of peace. From that day forward for as long as he lived, the ruler treated the holy and venerable man with great honour as was fitting.

### [II 36] *About a similar opening of the church-door at Terryglass*

Likewise, on a different occasion when St Columba was staying for a time in Ireland, he had gone to visit the monks who lived at Terryglass and who had invited him.[302] But it happened by some misfortune that when he arrived the keys to the door of the church could not be found.[303] The saint heard the monks complaining to one another that the door was locked and the keys had not been found, and so he himself went up to the door.

'The Lord has the power,' he said, 'to open his house to his servants even without keys.'

At his word the bolts were forcefully drawn back and the door opened of itself to everyone's astonishment. St Columba was the first to enter the church. He was received as a guest and treated with honour and reverence by all the monks.

[II 37] *Of a certain layman, a beggar, for whom St Columba made a stake and blessed it for hunting wild animals*

Once, a layman who lived in the district of Lochaber, and who was very poor, came to St Columba. He had no means of providing food for his wife and children, and so St Columba took pity on him. He gave such alms as he was able to the poor man, who was begging, and said:

'My poor fellow, get a stick of wood from the forest here and bring it to me quickly.'

The dejected man obeyed the saint's command and fetched the piece of wood, which the saint took from him and sharpened to a point. He did this with his own hands, then blessed it and gave it to the needy man, saying:

'Keep this sharp stick carefully. It will not harm any man, I believe, nor any cattle, but with it you may kill wild animals and fish.[304] As long as you have this stake, your house will never be short of game for the table.'

The poor beggar was delighted to hear this and returned home. He set the sharp stick up in an out-of-the-way place where there were wild creatures, and after only one night he went to check his stake-trap in the early morning. There he found a stag of amazing size had fallen on the stake.

Why say more? It is said that no day could pass but he found a stag or a hind or some other creature had fallen on the stake where it was fixed. Also, when the house was filled with game, he sold to neighbours the surplus that the hospitality of his house could not use. But the devil's hatred reached this pitiable man, as it did Adam, through his wife. She, like a fool without any sense, spoke to her husband saying this kind of thing:

'Take up that stake from the ground, for if any person or cattle should be killed by it, then you and I and our children will be killed or led into slavery.'[305]

'Nothing like that will happen,' said her husband, 'for St Columba said to me when he blessed the stake that it would never harm people or cattle.'

But after exchanges of this kind, the beggar gave in to his wife and went to take up the stake, which he brought back to the house as though he loved it and kept it inside by the wall. However, not long afterwards, a house-dog fell on it and died. At this the wife resumed her complaint:

'One of your children,' she said, 'will fall on that stake and be killed.'

So the man took the stake from the wall and carried it back to the woods, and he set it in a place where the brambles grew so thick, he thought no living creature could be hurt by it. But the next day he went back and found that a goat had fallen on it and been killed. He again moved the stake and set it where it was hidden underwater, though near the bank, in the River Lochy.[306] Again, returning to it one day, he found a salmon of amazing size stuck on the stake. Indeed, it was so big he could hardly lift it from the river and take it home. He took the stake away with him too and this time set it on top of his roof outside. Here a raven flying past dropped on to it and died. After this, the poor man, ruined by the advice of his foolish wife, took the stake down, chopped it into pieces with his axe, and threw the fragments in the fire. From then on he returned to begging, a fate he deserved, for he had thrown away the means of no small relief from his poverty; for this relief from penury had depended on that stake which had stood him in good stead as snare or net or any other means of hunting or fishing, because it had been blessed and given by St Columba. But now that it was thrown away, the wretched layman and his whole family, to whom it had brought prosperity for a time, regretted its loss too late during all that remained of his life.

[II 38] *How a milk-skin was carried away on the ebb and brought back to the same place on the next tide*

Once, St Columba sent a man called Lugaid Láitir to sail to Ireland as his representative.[307] In making his preparations Lugaid looked for a milk-skin among the equipment of the saint's boat. Having found one, he put it in the sea, weighted down with large stones, in order to saturate it.[308] When he went to St Columba, he told him what he had done with the skin, but the saint smiled and said:

'This time, I think, that skin which you say you have put to soak will not accompany you to Ireland.'

'Why,' he said, 'should I not be able to have it with me in the boat?'

'Tomorrow,' said St Columba, 'you will see what happens.'

So, early next day, Lugaid went down to the sea to recover the skin. But overnight the ebbing tide had washed it away. Not finding it, he returned sadly to St Columba and, kneeling on the ground, admitted his negligence. The saint reassured him, saying:

'Do not grieve, brother, over such perishable things. The skin that the ebb-tide washed away will come back to where it was on the flood.[309] But you will have sailed by then.'

The same day, though after Lugaid's departure from Iona, St Columba spoke to those standing near him after Nones, and said:

'Now one of you go down to the sea. Yesterday Lugaid was complaining about a skin that had been carried away on the ebb-tide, but now the flood has returned it to the spot where it was.'

A young man who heard him say this quickly ran to the shore. He found the skin as the saint had foretold, and ran back carrying it, happy to return it to St Columba. All who were present marvelled.

In these two stories, as we have often remarked before, though their subjects be as trivial as a stake or a skin, yet prophecy and a miracle of power are seen together. Now let us go on to other matters.

## [II 39] *St Columba's prophecy about Librán of the reed-bed*

Once, during the period when St Columba lived in Iona, a layman who had only lately assumed the clerical habit crossed by sea from Ireland to the blessed man's island monastery. One day the saint encountered him sitting alone in the guest-house where he was lodged, and spoke to him. He asked first about where the man came from, who his people were and what was the reason for his journey. The man replied that he belonged to the province of the Connachta, and that he had made the effort of the long journey in order to wipe out his sins on a pilgrimage.[310] St Columba then set out for him how strict and burdensome were the demands of monastic life, for he wanted to test the strength of his penitence. The man's answer to the saint came without hesitation:

'I am ready for anything you choose to demand of me, however harsh, however degrading.'

Why say more? There and then he confessed all his sins[311] and kneeling on the ground gave his word that he would do whatever the rules of penance required.

'Rise,' said St Columba, 'and have a seat.'

When the man was seated, the saint continued:

'You must spend seven years in penance in Tiree. But by God's gift you and I shall both live to see those seven years through.'

The saint's words gave the man strength, and he thanked God. Then he said:

'What should I do about an oath I once swore but which I did not keep? For while I still lived in my own district, I killed a fellow. After this I was held in chains as a guilty man. But a relative of mine, in fact one of my immediate kindred, who was extremely rich, came to my rescue in the nick of time. He paid what was needed to get me off though I was bound in chains, and he saved me, though guilty, from death. After he had bought my release, I promised to him with a binding oath that I should serve him all the days of my life. I had only been in this servitude for a matter of days when, disdaining to serve any man and preferring to live in obedience to God, I broke my oath and went away, a fugitive from my worldly master.[312] The Lord favoured my journey and now I have come to you.'

St Columba could see that these matters were causing the man real anxiety, and returned to his previous prophecy, saying:

'As I said to you, when a term of seven years is completed, you shall come to me here during Lent so that at the Easter festival you may approach the altar and receive the sacrament.'

Why dwell on words? The repentant pilgrim obeyed St Columba's instructions in everything. At that date he was sent to the monastery in Mag Luinge, and there he spent seven whole years in penance.[313] Then during Lent he returned in accordance with the saint's previous prophetic command, and during the celebration of the Easter festival, he approached the altar as he was bidden. After Easter, the man came to St Columba and again questioned him about his oath. This was the saint's prophetic answer to him:

'Your worldly master, of whom you once spoke to me, is still living. So are your father and mother and your brothers. Now therefore you must prepare yourself for a voyage.'

As he was saying this, he produced a sword decorated with carved ivory,[314] and continued:

'Take this to carry with you as a gift that you can offer to your master in return for your freedom. He has a wife with many virtues, whose sound advice he will follow. Without delay he will grant you your freedom, untying according to custom the slave's belt from your loins, and he will do it without taking payment.[315] Though you will be released from this cause of anxiety, there will be another near at hand from which you will not escape. For your brothers will force you to make good the service due from son to father which you have for so long neglected.[316] But you must obey their will without hesitation and take your old father into your dutiful care. Though this may seem to you a heavy burden, you should not be disheartened for you will soon have discharged the debt. One week from the day when you begin to look after your father, you will lay him in his grave. When your father is buried, your brothers will again press you to be a dutiful son to your mother also, and serve her. Your younger brother, however, will deliver you from this obligation, for he will be ready to do all that you ought in the way of filial duty and to serve her in your place.'

The brother, whose name was Librán, took the sword and set out, after the saint had bestowed his blessing on him. When he reached his native district he found that everything the saint predicted was proved true. He showed the sword to his master, offering it as the price of his freedom; the master would have taken it, but his wife at once refused, saying:

'How can we accept this precious gift which St Columba has sent? We are not worthy of this. Let this dutiful servant be delivered to the saint without payment. For the holy man's blessing will bring us more benefit than this gift which is offered.'

The husband listened to his wife's sound advice and readily freed his slave without payment.

After that, according to St Columba's prophecy, Librán was made by his brothers to serve their father, whom seven days later he laid in his grave. Next he was made to serve his mother also, but with the help of his younger brother, who took his place, he was released from this duty as St Columba had indicated. This is what the younger one told the brothers:

'It is not right that we should hold back our brother in this district who has for the last seven years been with St Columba in Britain, working for the salvation of his soul.'

Librán was now released from all his burdens, and taking his leave from his mother and brothers, he returned as a free man to Derry. There he found a ship under sail and just drawing away from the mooring. He shouted from the shore, begging the sailors to take him with them since he wished to sail across to Britain. But they refused him, for they did not belong to the community of St Columba.[317] At this point, Librán spoke to the saint – for although he was a long way away, he was present in the spirit, as the event soon showed – saying:

'Does it please you, St Columba,' he said, 'that these sailors have full sails and a following wind for their voyage, though they refuse to take me, your friend, with them?'

He had hardly finished speaking before the wind, which had until then been favourable, swung round against the boat. Meanwhile, the sailors saw that Librán was running along the riverbank beside them. Discussing the situation with one another, they called after him from their boat, saying:

'Perhaps it is because we refused to take you with us that the wind has turned round against us so quickly. But if we now ask you to join us in the boat, you will have power to change the wind again, so that what is now a head wind will become a following wind.'

Hearing this, the traveller said to them:

'St Columba, to whom I am going and whom I have obeyed for the last seven years, will be able to get you a favourable wind from his Lord by the power of prayer if you take me with you.'

On the strength of this they brought their boat to the bank and asked him to get in with them. As soon as he had climbed on board, he said:

'In the name of the Almighty, whom St Columba serves without blame, hoist the sail and fix the sheets.'

At once the wind which had been blowing against them veered round, and they had a fair voyage to Britain with their sails full.

On reaching Britain, Librán left the boat and, after blessing the sailors, made his way to Iona, where St Columba was living. The saint welcomed him joyfully and related, though no one had brought him news, everything that had happened to Librán on his journey: of his master and the wife's sound advice, how he was freed by her persuasion, of his brothers, of his father's death and burial within a week, of his mother and the timely help of his younger brother, and of the events during his return journey, the change of wind, the words of the sailors who would not take him, his promise of a favourable wind and how the wind improved when he was taken on board. In fact, all that the saint had said would happen, he now described as it had happened. After this, the traveller returned to St Columba the price of his deliverance which he had received from the saint. At that time the saint gave him a name, saying:

'You will be called Librán because you are free.'

During the next few days Librán took the monastic vow. St Columba sent him back to the monastery where he had served the Lord for seven years before as a penitent, taking his leave with these prophetic words:

'You will enjoy long life, and will end this present life in good old age. Nevertheless your resurrection will not be in Britain but in Ireland.'[318]

These words made Librán weep bitterly kneeling in front of the saint. The saint was sad to see him so, and began to comfort him, saying:

'Stand up, and do not distress yourself. You will die in one of my monasteries and you will have your share in the Kingdom among my elect monks, with whom you will awake from the sleep of death into the resurrection of eternal life.'

This was no little comfort, and Librán was much cheered to hear it. Then enriched with St Columba's blessing, he went away in peace.

What the saint had truly foretold about him was in due course fulfilled. He served St Columba as a monk in the monastery at Mag Luinge for many years, even after St Columba had passed from this world. When he was a very old man, he was sent to Ireland on some business of the community. He left the boat on the coast of Brega and crossed the plain to the monastery of Durrow. There he was hospitably received and given lodging in the guest-house, where he fell ill and after a week of illness he went to the Lord in peace. There he was buried among the elect monks of St Columba, where he will rise again to eternal life in accordance with the saint's prophecy.

These true prophecies that I have written about Librán must be enough. He was known as Librán of the reed-bed because for many years he worked gathering reeds in the reed-bed.[319]

[II 40] *Concerning a certain young woman who as a daughter of Eve suffered great pains during a difficult childbirth*

One day, on Iona, St Columba suddenly got up from his reading and said with a smile:

'Now I must hurry to the church to beseech God on behalf of a poor girl who is tortured by the pains of a most difficult childbirth and who now in Ireland calls on my name. For she hopes that through me the Lord will release her from her anguish, because she is related to me, for her father belonged to my mother's kindred.'

St Columba was moved by pity for the girl and ran to the church where he knelt and prayed to Christ the Son of Man. Then after praying he came out and said to those of the brethren who met him:

'Now has our Lord Jesus, who was born of woman, shown favour on the poor girl and brought timely help to deliver her from her difficulties. She has safely given birth and is in no danger of death.'

At exactly that time, as St Columba predicted, the poor woman who had called on his name was relieved and regained her health. The story was confirmed by people coming from the district of Ireland where the woman herself lived.

[II 41] *Concerning a man called Luigne 'the little hammer', a steersman, who lived in* Rathlin,[320] *whose wife hated him for his ugliness*

Once when St Columba stayed as a guest in Rathlin Island, a layman came to him and complained that his wife had an aversion to him, so he said, and would not allow him to lie with her. The saint called the wife to him and, so far as he was able, began to reproach her, saying:

'Why, woman, do you attempt to deny your own flesh? For the Lord says, "Two shall be in one flesh". Therefore your husband's flesh is your flesh.'[321]

To which she answered:

'I am prepared to do anything you order me to, however much of a burden, except one thing. Do not make me share a bed with Luigne. I do not shirk from all the work of the house, or if you tell me to cross the seas and remain in some woman's monastery I would do it.'

'It cannot be right to do what you say. For as long as your husband is alive, you are subject to the law of your husband. It is unlawful to put apart those whom God has joined together.'[322]

Having said this, he went on with this suggestion:

'Today, the three of us – husband and wife and I – shall fast and pray to the Lord.'

'I know,' she said, 'that things which seem difficult or even impossible will be possible for you, for God will grant you what you ask.'

Why say more? Both husband and wife consented to fast that day with St Columba. That night, while the couple slept, St Columba prayed for them. The next day, in this husband's presence, he charged the wife:

'Woman, will you today do what yesterday you said you were ready to do and enter a monastery of women?'

'Now,' she said, 'I know that the Lord has heard your prayers for me. For the husband whom I hated yesterday I love today. For during last night, I know not how, my heart was changed within me from loathing to love.'

Why linger? From then until the day of her death, the heart of the wife was fixed entirely on her husband's love, so that she never afterwards refused the dues of the marriage bed as she used to.

### [II 42] *St Columba's prophecy concerning the voyage of Cormac Ua Liatháin*

Once, Cormac, a soldier of Christ about whom we said a few words in Book One of this work, tried again, a second time, to find a place of retreat in the ocean.[323] It was after he had set sail over the boundless ocean with his sails full that St Columba stayed for a time at the other side of Druim Alban. While there, he commended Cormac to King Bridei, in the presence of the under-king of the Orkneys, saying:

'Some of our people have sailed off hoping to find a place of retreat somewhere on the trackless sea. Commend them to the care of this sub-king, whose hostages you hold, so that, if by chance their long wanderings should bring them to Orkney, they should meet with no hostility within his boundaries.'[324]

The saint said this because he already knew in the spirit that Cormac would arrive in Orkney after several months. This afterwards came about, and, thanks to the saint's commendation, he was delivered from imminent death there.

Several months later, when St Columba was back at home in Iona, the brethren were talking to one another in his presence, and at one point the name of Cormac came up in the conversation. Someone said:

'No one knows whether Cormac's voyage turned out to be successful or not.'

St Columba heard this and said:

'Today, you will soon see this Cormac whom you talk of, for he will arrive here.'

It was only perhaps an hour later that, strange to tell, look, there was Cormac. Quite unexpectedly he arrived in the church to give thanks, to the astonishment of everyone there.[325]

Since we have briefly talked of this prophecy concerning

Cormac's second voyage, we shall now set down a few words about St Columba's clairvoyant knowledge of his third voyage.

When this Cormac was travelling on the ocean for the third time, he found himself in such danger that he came close to death. His ship had been driven with full sails by a steady wind from the south for fourteen summer days and nights, so that a straight course brought them to an area under the most northerly skies. They reckoned that they had passed beyond the range of human exploration, and had reached a place from which they might not be able to return. There it happened, after the tenth hour of the fourteenth day, that a source of terror appeared, rising up on all sides, most fearsome, almost unendurable. To that day, assuredly, no one had ever seen such a thing: the whole sea was covered with deadly loathsome little creatures. They struck with horrible force against the keel, against the sides of the boat, against the stern and the prow, and the pressure of them was so great that it was thought they would pierce the skin covering of the boat. These creatures (as those who were present afterwards described) were about the size of frogs, but exceedingly troublesome because they had spines, though they did not fly but merely swam.[326] They were also a great nuisance to the blades of the oars. Nor were these the only prodigies that Cormac and his fellow sailors saw, though there is not time here to describe them.[327] They were greatly disturbed and frightened, and with tears they prayed to God, who is a loyal and ready helper in time of trouble.

At that time our own St Columba was there in spirit, in the boat with Cormac, though his body was far away. In the moment of their worst trouble he sounded the bell to call the brethren to come to the church. Then entering the church, he gave this prophecy to those standing there, according to his usual practice, saying:

'Brethren, pray with all your might for Cormac, who is

sailing out of control and has now passed beyond the limit of where man has gone before. There he suffers horrific terrors, monstrous things never seen before and almost indescribable. We should therefore share in our minds the sufferings of our brethren, members of the same body as ourselves, who are placed in unendurable danger. Now, behold, I see Cormac and his fellow sailors earnestly imploring Christ's help, their faces streaming with tears. We too must help with our prayers and call on him to have pity on our brethren, to turn the wind that has driven them northwards now for fourteen days, and to give them a wind from the north, which would bring Cormac's boat back out of danger.'

So saying, he knelt before the altar, praying to almighty God, who governs the winds and all things. After praying, he rose quickly, wiping away his tears, and joyfully gave thanks to God, saying:

'Now, brethren, we may share in the joy of those of our dear ones for whom we pray. The Lord has now turned the wind from the south to a north wind, which will carry our fellow members out of danger and bring them back once more to us here.'

At once, the south wind ceased, the wind blew day after day from the north, and Cormac's boat was brought back to land. Cormac himself came to St Columba, and by God's gift they looked again on each other's face, while everyone wondered and rejoiced greatly.

The reader should therefore ponder how great and of what nature was this blessed man who possessed such prophetic knowledge and who was able, by invoking Christ's name, to command the winds and the ocean.

### [II 43] *How St Columba rode in a chariot without the necessary protection of linchpins*

Once, when St Columba spent a number of days in Ireland, travelling in the interests of the church, it was necessary for him to mount into a chariot, which he first blessed. It was already hitched up, but by some extraordinary oversight the necessary linchpins had not been fitted into the slots for them at the ends of the axles. That day the chariot was driven by Colmán mac Echdach, a saintly man who had founded the monastery of Slanore.[328] Though shaken about by a whole day's driving over a long distance, the wheels did not separate from the axle-shoulders, nor did they slacken even though they were secured by no linchpins.[329] But it was the Grace of God which alone preserved the saint so that the chariot in which he sat kept to a straight course, safely and without hindrance.

To this point we have written about those miracles of power which almighty God worked through this praiseworthy man while he lived in this present life. We have given sufficient examples of these. Now we must record a few of those which were granted by the Lord after St Columba had passed from the flesh.[330]

### [II 44] *How in honour of St Columba the Lord brought rain to ground parched by months of drought*[331]

[The miracle which by God's favour we are now about to recount took place in our own time and we witnessed it with our own eyes.][332] It happened about seventeen years ago. Right through the spring a severe drought lasted unrelieved so that our fields were baked dry. It was so bad that we thought our people were threatened by the curse which the Lord imposed on those who transgressed, where it says in Leviticus: "I will make your heaven as iron, and your earth as brass. And your strength shall be spent in vain: for your land shall not yield her increase, neither shall the trees of the land yield their fruit", and so forth.[333] As we read this and thought with fear of the blow that threatened, we debated what should be done, and decided on this. Some of our elders should walk around the fields that had lately been ploughed and sown, carrying with them St Columba's white tunic and books which the saint had himself copied. They should hold aloft the tunic, which was the one he wore at the hour of his departure from the flesh, and shake it three times. They should open his books and read aloud from them at the Hill of Angels, where from time to time the citizens of heaven used to be seen coming down to converse with the saint.[334]

When all these things had been done as we had decided, on the same day – wonderful to tell – the sky, which had been cloudless through the whole of March and April, was at once covered, extraordinarily quickly, with clouds rising from the sea, and heavy rain fell day and night.[335] The thirsty ground was quenched in time, the seed germinated and in due course there was a particularly good harvest. In this way the commemoration of St Columba's name, using his tunic and his books, on that occasion, brought help to many districts and peoples in time to save their crops.

### [II 45] *How the intercession of St Columba changed contrary winds into favourable winds*

The present-day miracles that I have seen myself confirm my faith in such events in the past, which I have not seen.[336] For example, the changing of a contrary wind to a favourable one I have myself witnessed on three occasions.

On the first of these, pine trees and oaks[337] had been felled and dragged overland. Some were to be used in the making of a longship,[338] and besides ships' timbers there were also beams for a great house to be brought here to Iona.[339] It was decided that we should lay the saint's vestments and books on the altar, and that by fasting and singing psalms and invoking his name, we should ask St Columba to obtain for us from the Lord that we should have favourable winds. So it turned out, that God had granted it to him; for on the day when our sailors had got everything ready and meant to take the boats and curraghs and tow the timbers to the island by sea, the wind, which had blown in the wrong direction for several days, changed and became favourable. Though the route was long and indirect, by God's favour the wind remained favourable all day and the whole convoy sailed with their sails full so that they reached Iona without delay.

The second time was several years later. Again, oak trees were being towed by a group of twelve curraghs from the mouth of the River Shiel to be used here in repairs to the monastery.[340] On a dead calm day, when the sailors were having to use the oars, a wind suddenly sprang up from the west, blowing head on against them. We put in to the nearest island, called Eilean Shona, intending to stay in sheltered water. All the while I complained of this inconvenient change of wind, and began after a fashion to chide our St Columba, saying:

'Is this troublesome delay in our efforts what you wanted, St Columba? To this point I had hoped that by God's favour you would bring help and comfort in our labours, since I thought you stood in high honour with God.'

Hardly a minute had passed when the west wind dropped and, strange to say, a wind immediately blew from the north-east. Then I told the sailors to hoist the yards cross-wise, spread the sails and draw the sheets taut. In this way we were carried by a fair, gentle breeze, all the way to our island in one day quite effortlessly, and all who were with me in the boats, helping to tow the timbers, were greatly pleased.

My little complaint against St Columba, trivial though it was, brought us considerable advantage. It is obvious how great and how special is the saint's merit with the Lord, who made the wind change as soon as he heard.

The third time this happened was during the summer, when I had been to the meeting of the Irish synod,[341] and on the return journey found myself delayed for some days by contrary winds among the people of Cenél Loairn.[342] We had reached the island of *Saine*,[343] and the eve of St Columba's solemn feast saw us still held up there. I was much disappointed by this, for I very much wanted to be in Iona for this joyful day. So, as on the previous occasion, I complained, saying:

'Is it your wish, O saint, that I should stay here among the lay people till tomorrow, and not spend the day of your feast in your own church? It is such an easy thing for you on a day like this to change an adverse wind into a favourable one, so that I might partake of the solemn masses of your feast day in your own church.'

When night had passed and we rose at first light, we realized that the wind had dropped completely and we set out in the boats in still weather. Soon a south wind rose behind us, and the sailors shouted for joy and raised the sails. In this way God gave us a fast and fair voyage without the labour of rowing for St Columba's sake, so that we achieved our desire and reached the harbour of Iona after the hour of Terce. So we were able to wash our hands and feet before entering the church with the brethren to celebrate together the solemn mass at the hour of Sext, for the feast of St Columba and St Baithéne.[344] It was the same day that we had sailed all the way from *Saine* since early morning.

The law requires two or three witnesses,[345] but there are a hundred and more who will testify to the truth of this account.

[II 46] *About the plague*

This story too, I think, should be counted among the major miracles of power. It concerns the great plague which twice in our time has ravaged a large part of the world.[346] Though I do not speak of the broader regions of Europe – Italy or the city of Rome, Cisalpine Gaul or the province of Spain beyond the Pyrenees – yet the islands of the ocean, Ireland and Britain, have been twice ravaged by a terrible plague. Everywhere was affected except two peoples, the population of Pictland and the Irish who lived in Britain, races separated by the mountains of Druim Alban.[347] Although neither of these peoples is without great sin, by which the eternal Judge is moved to anger, none the less to this date he has been patient and has spared them both. Surely this grace from God can only be attributed to St Columba? For he founded among both peoples the monasteries where today he is still honoured on both sides.[348]

It is not without sorrow now that I say this, that there are in both nations many foolish people who ungratefully fail to recognize that they have been protected from the plague by the prayers of saints, and who abuse God's patience. But we often thank God that through the intercession of our holy patron he has preserved us from the onslaughts of plague, not only at home among our islands, but also in England. For I visited my friend King Aldfrith[349] while the plague was at its worst and many whole villages on all sides were stricken. But both on my first visit after Ecgfrith's battle[350] and on my second two years later, though I walked in the midst of this danger of plague, the Lord delivered me, so that not even one of my companions died nor was any of them troubled with the disease.[351]

Here we must end the second book concerning St Columba's miracles of power. Readers should take notice that I have omitted many well attested examples so that they should not become weary.

# Here begins Book Three, concerning visions of angels

In the first of these three books, as is noted above, there is a short and succinct account of St Columba's prophetic revelations, set down in writing with the help of God. In the second book the miracles of power are described that were manifested through him and which were often accompanied by the grace of prophecy. Now this third book is concerned with angelic apparitions that were revealed to others about the saint, and to him about others, and also those that were visible to both though in different measure. For he experienced them directly and fully but others saw them only indirectly and in part, that is to say from the outside or by looking on surreptitiously. I shall include visions of angels and manifestations of heavenly light. The differences between these phenomena will be made clear below, in the places where they are recounted.

Let us now begin to describe these angelic apparitions from the very beginning of St Columba's life.

[III 1]

An angel of the Lord appeared in a dream to St Columba's mother one night after his conception but before his birth. He seemed to stand beside her and to give her a robe of marvellous beauty, decorated with what looked like the colours of every flower. After a little time, he asked for it back and took it from her hands. Then he raised the robe and spread it out, letting go of it on the empty air. She was disappointed that it was taken away from her and spoke to the man of holy appearance:

'Why do you take away from me so quickly this delightful mantle?' she said.

'Because,' he answered, 'this is a cloak of such glorious honour that you will no longer be able to keep it with you.'

Then the woman saw the robe moving further and further from her as if in flight, growing greater and greater so that it seemed to be broader than the plains and to exceed in measure the mountains and the forests. Then she heard a voice which said:

'Woman, do not be distressed, for you shall bear to the man to whom you are joined in marriage a son of such flower that he shall be reckoned as one of the prophets. He is destined by God to lead innumerable souls to the heavenly kingdom.'

As she heard these words, his mother woke up.

### [III 2] *On a ray of light seen over the face of the sleeping boy*

One night St Columba's foster-father, a priest of admirable life, whose name was Cruithnechán, was returning to his house from the church after the office, when he saw the whole house bathed in a bright light, and poised over the face of the sleeping child was a fiery ball of light.[352] He began to tremble, and bowed his face to the ground for he recognized that the grace of the Holy Ghost was poured from heaven upon his foster-son, and he stood in awe.

### [III 3] *How St Brendan saw an apparition of holy angels walking with St Columba over the plain*

Many years after this, St Columba was excommunicated for some trivial and quite excusable offences by a synod that, as eventually became known, had acted wrongly. The saint himself came to the assembly that had been convoked against him.[353]

When St Brendan, the founder of the monastery of Birr,[354] saw St Columba approaching though still a little distance away, he rose quickly to meet him, bowed his face and kissed him with reverence. Some of the elders of that synod, moving the others to one side, berated him, saying:

'Why do you not shrink from rising before an excommunicate and kissing him?'

'If you,' replied Brendan, 'had seen what the Lord deigned to disclose to me today, concerning this chosen one whom you refuse to honour, you would never have excommunicated him. For in no sense does God excommunicate him in accordance with your wrong judgement, but rather glorifies him more and more.'

'How, we should like to know,' said the elders, bridling, 'does God glorify him, as you say, whom we have excommunicated for a good reason?'

'I saw a very bright column of fiery light going in front of the man of God whom you despise, and holy angels as his companions travelling over the plain. Therefore I do not dare to spurn this man whom God, as I have had visible proof, has predestined to lead the nations to life.'

After this statement, the elders dropped their charge, for they dared not continue with their excommunication. Instead, they honoured him with great reverence.

This statement was made at Teltown.[355]

[During this period, St Columba crossed to Britain with twelve disciples as his fellow soldiers.][356]

[III 4] *How St Uinniau saw that the saint's travelling companion was an angel of the Lord*

Once, in his youth, St Columba went to his master, the holy bishop Uinniau, who was an old man.[357] When St Uinniau saw him approach, he noticed also that the companion walking by his side was an angel of the Lord. St Uinniau, so the story is handed down to us by learned men, drew this to the notice of those monks who were near by, saying:

'Look. Do you see now, St Columba is coming here, who has deserved to have as the companion of his journey an angel out of heaven.'

[III 5] *Of the angel of the Lord who was sent to St Columba to bid him ordain Áedán as king, and who appeared to him in a vision while he was living in the island of* Hinba[358]

Once, when the praiseworthy man was living in the island of *Hinba*, he saw one night in a mental trance an angel of the Lord sent to him. He had in his hand a glass book of the ordination of kings, which St Columba received from him, and which at the angel's bidding he began to read.[359] In the book the command was given him that he should ordain Áedán as king, which St Columba refused to do because he held Áedán's brother Éoganán in higher regard. Whereupon the angel reached out and struck the saint with a whip, the scar from which remained with him for the rest of his life. Then the angel addressed him sternly:

'Know then as a certain truth, I am sent to you by God with the glass book in order that you should ordain Áedán to the kingship according to the words you have read in it. But if you refuse to obey this command, I shall strike you again.'

In this way the angel of the Lord appeared to St Columba on three successive nights, each time having the same glass book, and each time making the same demand that he should ordain Áedán as king. The holy man obeyed the word of the Lord and sailed from *Hinba* to Iona, where Áedán had arrived at this time, and he ordained him king in accordance with the Lord's command. As he was performing the ordination, St Columba also prophesied the future of Áedán's sons and grandsons and great-grandsons, then he laid his hand on Áedán's head in ordination and blessed him.

[Cumméne the White in the book which he wrote on the miraculous powers of St Columba gives this account of St Columba's prophecy about Áedán and his descendants and his kingdom:[360]

'Make no mistake, Áedán, but believe that, until you commit some act of treachery against me or my successors, none of your enemies will have the power to oppose you. For this reason you must give this warning to your sons, as they must pass it on to their sons and grandsons and descendants, so that they do not follow evil counsels and so lose the sceptre[361] of this kingdom from their hands. For whenever it may happen that they do wrong to me or to my kindred in Ireland, the scourge that I have suffered for your sake from the angel will be turned by the hand of God to deliver a heavy punishment on them. Men's hearts will be taken from them, and their enemies will draw strength mightily against them.'

This prophecy was fulfilled in our own time, at the battle of Mag Roth, when Áedán's grandson Domnall Brecc laid waste the territory of the saint's kinsman Domnall Ua Ainmirech.[362] From that day to this the family of Áedán is held in subjection by strangers, a fact which brings sighs of sorrow to the breast.]

[III 6] *How angels were seen carrying the soul of a saintly Briton to heaven*

Once when St Columba was living in Iona, one of his monks, a Briton, dedicated to good works,[363] was taken ill with a bodily affliction and came close to death. The holy man came to visit him in his last hour, standing for a time beside his bed and blessing him. But he soon left the monk, for he wished not to see the man die.[364] The end came as soon as the saint had left the house.

Then St Columba, as he walked across the open area of his monastery, stopped and looked up to heaven, standing awe-struck for some time. One of the brethren, Áedán mac Libir, a devout man of natural goodness, was the only person with him at that moment. He knelt down and began to ask the saint to share with him the reason for his wonder.

'I have just now seen holy angels fighting in the air against the powers of the Adversary. I give thanks to Christ, who watches over the contest, for the angels are victorious and they have carried to the joys of the heavenly kingdom the soul of this pilgrim who is the first of us to die here in this island.[365] But I beg you, do not reveal this mystery to anyone while I am living.'

[III 7] *Concerning a vision revealed to St Columba in which angels led the soul of a man called Diarmait to heaven*

There was once an Irish pilgrim who came to visit St Columba and stayed several months with him in Iona. One day the saint said to him:

'Now a man from your own territory, a cleric, is being carried to heaven by angels, though I do not yet know his name.'

When the brother heard this, he began to search his memory about his territory, that of the Easterners or in Irish the Airthir,[366] looking for the name of this blessed man.

'I know a soldier of Christ,' he said, 'who built a little monastery for himself in the district where he and I used to live.[367] His name was Diarmait.'

'That is the man,' said St Columba, 'who is now brought to paradise by the angels of God.'

I mention here something that should not be overlooked. God revealed to this holy man many sacred mysteries that are hidden from others, but St Columba would not allow them to come to public notice. This was for two reasons, as he disclosed one time to a few of the brethren. First, he wanted to avoid boasting, and, second, so that widespread reports of these revelations should not attract unmanageable crowds of people, wanting to put their questions to him.

### [III 8] *Of a fierce fight with demons in which St Columba received timely help from the angels*

One day, when St Columba was living on Iona, he set off into the wilder parts of the island to find a place secluded from other people where he could pray alone.[368] There, soon after he had begun his prayers – as he later disclosed to a few of the brethren – he saw a line of foul, black devils armed with iron spikes and drawn up ready for battle. The holy man realized in the spirit that they wanted to attack his monastery and slaughter many of the brethren with their stakes. Though he was alone against such an army of countless opponents, he was protected by the armour of St Paul[369] and flung himself into a great conflict. The battle continued most of the day, and the hosts were unable to vanquish him while he could not drive them away from Iona on his own. Then the angels of God came to his aid, as he afterwards told a few of the brethren, and the devils were terrified of them and left the place.

That same day, after the demons had been driven off the island, St Columba returned to the monastery, and gave this account of those hosts of the Enemy, saying:

'Those deadly opponents which have today by God's favour and with the help of angels, been banished from this island have gone to Tiree. They will invade the monastery there, and attack the monks cruelly and bring deadly plagues. Many of those afflicted will die.'

That is what happened at the time, as St Columba had foreknown. But two days later, the Spirit revealed to him the outcome, and he said:

'With God's help, Baithéne has managed everything well, so that the community in that church over which he presides in Mag Luinge has been saved by prayer and fasting from the attack of the demons. One man has died, and on this occasion he will be the only one.'

This prophecy was fulfilled. For though many died of the same disease in the other monasteries of Tiree, no one but the man mentioned by St Columba had died in Baithéne's community.[370]

### [III 9] *How angels appeared to St Columba carrying to heaven the soul of a blacksmith called Columb Cóilrigin*[371]

There was a blacksmith who lived in Mide[372] in Ireland, whose name was Columb Cóilrigin. He was conscientious in works of charity and performed many other acts of righteousness. When, in good old age, this man came to the end of his life, in the same hour that his soul parted from his body, St Columba, who was living in Iona, said to the handful of elders who were standing near him:

'Columb Cóilrigin the blacksmith has not laboured in vain, for he has obtained by the labour of his own hands the heavenly rewards he would have bought, and is now in bliss. Look, now, how his soul is carried to the delights of the heavenly kingdom by holy angels. For whatever he was able to gain by the practice of his craft, he spent in alms for the needy.'

[III 10] *Of a similar vision, in which St Columba beheld angels bearing to heaven the soul of a virtuous woman*

Likewise, on another occasion, when St Columba was dwelling in Iona, one day he suddenly looked up towards heaven and said:

'Happy woman, happy and virtuous, whose soul the angels of God now take to paradise!'

One of the brothers was a devout man called Genereus the Englishman, who was the baker.[373] He was at work in the bakery where he heard St Columba say this. A year later, on the same day, the saint again spoke to Genereus the Englishman, saying:

'I see a marvellous thing. The woman of whom I spoke in your presence a year ago today – look! – she is now meeting in the air the soul of a devout layman, her husband, and is fighting for him together with holy angels against the powers of the Enemy. With their help and because the man himself was always righteous, his soul is rescued from the devils' assaults and is brought to the place of eternal refreshment.'

[III 11] *How St Columba saw the holy angels who came to meet the soul of St Brendan, the founder of Birr, at the time of his passing away*[374]

Likewise, one day, the holy man was living in Iona when, in the early morning, he called for his servant Diarmait, whom we have often referred to, and gave him these instructions, saying:

'Have everything made ready for the sacred mystery of the Eucharist as quickly as possible. For today is the feast day of St Brendan.'

'Why,' said his servant, 'do you give orders for the celebration of this solemn feast today? No one has come from Ireland bringing news that this saint has died.'

'Go,' said St Columba, 'you must do what I have ordered. For last night I saw heaven opened and choirs of angels descending to meet the soul of St Brendan. In that hour the whole world was lit up by the peerless light of their brightness.'

[III 12] *Of a vision in which holy angels carried to heaven the soul of the holy bishop Colmán moccu Loígse*[375]

Likewise, one day, when the brethren were putting on their shoes[376] in the morning ready to go out to their various tasks about the monastery,[377] St Columba stopped them and gave orders that there should be no work that day. Instead they should prepare for the rite of the sacred offering, and there should be a special meal as on the Lord's day.[378]

'And I who am so unworthy,' he said, 'must today celebrate the sacred mystery of the Eucharist, out of reverence for the soul that last night was carried away among the choirs of angels and ascended beyond the starry heavens to paradise.'

The brethren were obedient to his words. That day was made a holiday, the preparations were made for a celebration of the sacred liturgy, and they all went to the church clothed in white as for a major feast. As they were singing the office, they reached the point where the prayer is usually chanted, which mentions the name of St Martin.[379] Here St Columba suddenly said to the singers:

'Today you must chant "for St Colmán the bishop".'

At this, all who were present realized that Bishop Colmán in Leinster, St Columba's friend, had gone to the Lord. Some time later, travellers arrived from Leinster bringing the news that the bishop had died on the night when this was revealed to St Columba.

[III 13] *How angels appeared coming down to meet the souls of some of St Comgall's monks*

Once, when St Columba was living in Iona, he was suddenly aroused and had the brethren gathered together by ringing the bell.

'Now,' he said to them, 'we must bring the help of our prayers to some of St Comgall's monks who are drowned in Belfast Lough[380] at this time. See, even now, they are battling in the air against the powers of the Adversary who are seeking to snatch away the soul of a visitor who was drowned along with them.'

He prayed earnestly, not without tears, then rose quickly in front of the altar while the rest of the brethren were still lying on the ground in prayer. His face was lit up with joy, and he said:

'Give thanks to Christ. For holy angels have met the souls of these saints and have been victorious in the battle. Even the visitor who was seized by the battling demons has been delivered.'

### [III 14] *How angels appeared to meet the soul of Emchath*

When St Columba was travelling to the other side of Druim Alban, suddenly, at the side of Loch Ness, he was inspired by the Holy Spirit.

'Let us make haste,' he said to those of the brethren who were with him, 'to meet the holy angels who have come from the heights of heaven to bear away the soul of a heathen man, who has spent his whole life in natural goodness and is now very old. But they must wait till we reach the place, so that we may bring timely baptism to him before he dies.'

Though St Columba was an old man, he hurried on as fast as he could ahead of his companions, till he reached the fields of Glen Urquhart.[381] There he found an old man called Emchath, who heard and believed the word of God preached to him by the saint, and was baptized. Thereupon, he departed happily and safely to the Lord in the company of the angels that had come to meet him. His son Virolec also believed and was baptized with his whole household.

### [III 15] *How an angel of the Lord brought swift and timely help to a monk who fell from the top of the round house in the monastery of Durrow*

Once, while St Columba was sitting in his hut copying a book, his expression suddenly changed, and from his pure heart he cried out:

'Help! Help!'

The two brethren standing by the door, Colgu mac Cellaig and Luigne moccu Blai,[382] asked him why he had suddenly cried out. St Columba answered them, saying:

'There was an angel of the Lord just now standing between

you, whom I have sent as fast as possible to help one of our brethren falling from the very top of the great house which is now under construction at Durrow.'[383]

Then the saint continued:

'One cannot describe but only wonder at the speed with which an angel flies, for it is as fast as lightning, I think. That heavenly citizen, who flew away from here just now as the man began to fall, came to the rescue in the twinkling of an eye and was there to hold the man before he hit the ground. Nor did the man who fell suffer any broken bones or other injury. How amazing, I say, is this most speedy and timely help which could be brought so very quickly though so many miles of sea and land lay between.'

[III 16] *How a great number of holy angels were seen, coming down from heaven to confer with St Columba*

Likewise, on another occasion, when St Columba was living in Iona, he addressed the assembled brethren, making his point with great emphasis, saying:

'Today I shall go to the machair on the west coast of our island, and I wish to go alone. No one is to follow me therefore.'

They obeyed and he set out alone as he desired. But one of the brethren, who was an artful scout, took a different route and hid himself on the top of a little hill that overlooks the machair, for he was eager to find out why the saint had gone out alone. From his vantage point, he could see St Columba standing on a knoll among the fields and praying with his arms spread out towards heaven and his eyes gazing upwards. Strange to tell – look! – there was suddenly a marvellous apparition, which the man could see with his own bodily eyes from his position on that nearby hill. This cannot have happened, I think, without the permission of God, who desired that the reputation and glory of St Columba, notwithstanding his own reluctance, should be made more widely known among the peoples because there had been a witness to this vision. For holy angels, the citizens of the heavenly kingdom, were flying down with amazing speed, dressed in white robes, and began to gather around the holy man as he prayed. After they had conversed a little with St Columba, the heavenly crowd – as though they could feel that they were being spied on – quickly returned to the heights of heaven.

St Columba himself, after this conference with angels, went back to the monastery, where he again called the brethren together. He reproached them severely and asked which of them was guilty of disobedience. They protested that they did not know what he referred to, but the man, who was aware of his own inexcusable disobedience, could not bear to hide his sin any longer. He knelt in front of St Columba in the sight of all the brethren and begged his forgiveness. The saint took the brother aside, laying stern threats on him, as he knelt, and charged him never to give away to anyone the least part of this secret concerning his angelic vision so long as the saint should live.

After St Columba had left the body, the man disclosed to the brethren how he had seen the apparition of the heavenly host, and publicly affirmed what he said.[384] Hence today the knoll where St Columba conferred with angels affirms by its very name what took place there, for it is called Cnoc nan Aingel, that is, the angels' knoll.[385]

One should take notice of this story, and carefully think about the extent and nature of the sweet visits by angels that no one could know about but which, without doubt, were very frequent, for they generally came to him as he remained awake on winter nights or as he prayed in isolated places while others rested. Though a few of them were observed by someone, one way or another, day or night, these were most certainly very few in comparison with the numbers of those visitations about which no one could know.

The same applies to certain manifestations of light, of which only a few were observed. We shall now describe these.

[III 17] *How a column of light seemed to shine from St Columba's head*

Once, four saints who had founded monasteries in Ireland came to visit St Columba. When they arrived at *Hinba*, they found him there. The names of these famous men were Comgall moccu Araidi, Cainnech moccu Dalann, Brendan moccu Altae and Cormac Ua Liatháin.[386] When the sacred mysteries of the Eucharist were to take place, with one accord they chose St Columba to act as celebrant. He obeyed their command, and with them he entered the church as usual on the Lord's day after the Gospel had been read.[387] There, while the sacrament of the mass was celebrated, St Brendan moccu Altae saw a radiant ball of fire shining very brightly from St Columba's head as he stood in front of the altar and consecrated the sacred oblation. It shone upwards like a column of light and lasted until the mysteries were completed. Afterwards St Brendan disclosed what he had seen to St Comgall and St Cainnech.

[III 18] *How the Holy Spirit descended to visit St Columba in the same island, and remained over him for three days and nights*

On another occasion when St Columba was living in *Hinba*, the grace of the Holy Spirit was poured upon him in incomparable abundance and miraculously remained over him for three days. During that time he remained day and night locked in his house, which was filled with heavenly light. No one was allowed to go near him, and he neither ate nor drank. But from the house rays of brilliant light could be seen at night, escaping through the chinks of the doors and through the keyholes. He was also heard singing spiritual chants of a kind never heard before. And, as he afterwards admitted to a few people, he was able to see openly revealed many secrets that had been hidden since the world began, while all that was most dark and difficult in the sacred Scriptures lay open, plain, and clearer than light in the sight of his most pure heart.

St Columba regretted that his foster-son Baithéne was not there. If he had been present for those three days, he could have recorded from the saint's lips a great number of mysteries, both of ages past and future, unknown to other men, together with some interpretations of the sacred books. However, Baithéne was held up by adverse winds in Eigg,[388] and could not be present until those three days and three nights of unique and glorious visitation had come to an end.

[III 19] *How the brightness of angelic light was seen shining down on St Columba in church, one winter night while the brethren were sleeping in their chambers, by Fergnae, a young man of natural goodness, who by the will of God later was the head of this church that I too, though unworthy, serve*[389]

One winter night, this Fergnae was so moved by the love of God burning within him that he entered the church alone to pray while the others slept, and there in a side-chapel[390] attached to the wall of the church he devoted himself to his prayers. Some time had passed, perhaps an hour, when St

Columba too entered the Lord's house. With his arrival the whole church was filled with a golden light shining from the heights of heaven. Even in his shut-off side-chapel, where Fergnae tried as best he could to lie concealed, the brilliance of that heavenly light came through the inner door of the chamber, which was not completely closed, and filled the room, causing Fergnae no little sense of fear. In the same way that no one is able to look directly at the sun at midday in summer without being dazzled, so Fergnae could not bear that heavenly brightness, for it was brighter than any light and completely dazzled his sight. Its radiance filled him with fear, so that his strength failed him utterly.

St Columba prayed for a little time only before leaving the church again. But on the following day he called Fergnae to him, though he was still much afraid, and addressed him with these words of comfort:

'O my dear son,' the saint said, 'what you did last night was well pleasing in the sight of God, lowering your eyes to the ground for fear of his brightness. If you had not done so, your eyes might have been blinded by the sight of that unimaginable light. But you must take care never to reveal to anyone that you witnessed this manifestation of light so long as I may live.'

So it was that only after the blessed man had passed away Fergnae told the story of this praiseworthy and marvellous event to many people. I, Adomnán, who have written this account, heard it in testimony from the worthy priest Commán, who was the son of Fergnae's sister.[391] He had heard it at firsthand from his uncle Fergnae, who had himself seen the event inasmuch as his strength permitted.

## [III 20] *A very similar vision of light from above*

Likewise, on another night, a similar thing happened to one of the brethren whom we mentioned in Book One, namely Colgu mac Áedo Draigniche, who came from the district of Uí Fiachrach.[392] He happened to come to the door of the church when everyone else was asleep, and he stood there in prayer for a little time. Then suddenly he saw the entire church filled with heavenly light, instantaneously, as if it were lightning, and then it was gone. He was unaware that St Columba was at that time inside the church praying. The sudden flash of light had made him afraid, and he returned to his lodging.

Next day, St Columba called for Colgu and reprimanded him somewhat harshly, saying:

'In future, my son, take care that you do not attempt to see surreptitiously the light from heaven which is not given to you, for it will vanish from you. And do not tell anyone what you have seen in my lifetime.'

## [III 21] *Concerning another similar apparition of divine light*

Likewise, once, St Columba earnestly warned a foster-son of his, who was studying wisdom,[393] called Berchán Mes loen, saying:

'Beware, my son. Do not come to my lodging tonight as you usually do.'

Though Berchán had been told this, he did what he was forbidden to do, and when everyone was asleep he came in the silence of the night to St Columba's house. He contrived to spy on the saint by looking through the keyhole, for he reckoned – as the facts proved to be true – that a heavenly vision was revealed to the saint inside the house. In that hour the lodging of St Columba was completely filled with the radiance of heavenly light. The disobedient youth could not endure the sight and immediately ran away.

St Columba took him aside next day and reproved him very severely, saying:

'Last night, my son, you sinned in the sight of God. For you foolishly thought that your crafty attempt to spy – though you deny it – could be hidden from the Holy Spirit. Surely I saw you coming to the door of my house and going away from it? If I had not in that instant prayed for your sake, you would have dropped dead by the door or else your eyes would have been torn from their sockets. But the Lord spared you this time because of my intercession. And know this too: you will live lecherously all your days in Ireland, in your own district, and you will be reviled to your face. But I have won from the Lord by my prayers that because you are our foster-son, you shall do penance before your death and receive mercy from God.'

All of this came to pass as the saint predicted it would.

### [III 22] *How St Columba had a vision of angels setting out to meet his holy soul as though it were soon to leave his body*

The blessed man was living in Iona when one day his holy face was suddenly lit up with marvellous, blissful joy, and he raised his eyes to heaven as he was filled with incomparable gladness. But hardly a moment later that sweet rejoicing had turned to sad distress.

At that time, there were two men standing by the door of his hut, which had been built in an elevated position.[394] Their names were Luigne moccu Blai and Pilu the Englishman. They grieved with him, and asked the reason for his sudden joy and the sadness that followed it. But in answer, he said only this:

'Go in peace. Do not ask to be shown the cause of either my gladness or my sorrow.'

Hearing this, they were filled with tears and fell to their knees, prostrating themselves on the ground in supplication, and begging to be told what had been disclosed to the saint in that hour. Seeing how distressed they were, St Columba said:

'Since I love you, I do not want to grieve you. You must promise me first that you will not betray to anyone, as long as I am living, the mystery that you seek to know.'

They readily promised what he imposed on them, and he went on:

'Today is the thirtieth anniversary since I began to live in pilgrimage in Britain. A long time ago I earnestly asked the Lord that at the end of this thirtieth year he would release me from this dwelling and call me straightaway to the heavenly kingdom. This is why I was so glad, which you sadly seek to know, for I saw the angels sent from the throne on high to lead my soul from this body. But see, now they are suddenly delayed, and wait standing on a rock across our island Sound. It is as though they wish to draw near me to call me from the body but they are not allowed to come any closer and they will soon hasten back to the heights of heaven. Though the Lord had granted what I desired with all my strength, that I should this day leave this world and go to him, none the less he has answered the prayers of many churches concerning me, and quicker than speech has caused this change. For these churches have prayed the Lord that, even though I do not want it, four years longer must I remain in this flesh. This sorrowful delay is the reason for my great distress today, and rightly so. But by God's favour, at the end of these four years more in this life, my end will come suddenly and without physical pain, when his holy angels will meet me at the time and I shall be glad to depart to the Lord.'

These words were spoken with much lamentation and sadness and with floods of tears, so we are told. And in accordance with them, he remained in the flesh for four further years.

[III 23] *How our patron St Columba passed to the Lord*

When the end was approaching of this four-year period, a time when the foreteller of truth had long ago foreknown that his present life would end – it was May, as we have already stated[395] in Book Two – one day the saint was going in a cart (for he was an old man, worn out with age) to visit the brethren at their work. They were labouring on the west side of Iona. That day the saint began to speak to them, saying:

'At Easter in the month of April just past, I longed deeply[396] to depart to Christ the Lord. He would have allowed me this if I had chosen it. But so as not to make the festival of gladness into one of sorrow for you, I preferred to put off a little longer the day of my departure from the world.'

Hearing him tell this mournful news, the monks of his community became very sorrowful, and he began to cheer them as far as he could with consoling words. Then, sitting in his cart, he turned his face eastwards and blessed the island and the islanders dwelling there. (Since when, even to the present day, the venom of vipers' three-forked tongues has been unable to harm man or beast, as we wrote[397] in a previous book.) After pronouncing this blessing, the saint was carried back to the monastery.

A few days later, while mass was being celebrated as usual on Sunday, the venerable man's face, with his eyes gazing upwards, looked suffused with a ruddy bloom – as it is written, 'A merry heart maketh a cheerful countenance';[398] for in that hour he alone could see an angel of the Lord flying above actually inside the house of prayer. Since the loving and gentle appearance of holy angels pours joy and exultation into the hearts of the elect,[399] so this was the reason why the blessed man was filled with a sudden gladness.

When those who were with the saint asked him why he was so inspired with gladness, he looked upwards and answered:

'How wonderful and without compare is the fineness of an angel's nature. Look how an angel of the Lord, sent to recover a loan[400] dear to God, has been here inside the church watching and blessing us, and has gone out through the roof[401] of the church leaving no trace of his passing.'

These were the saint's words, but no one among the congregation understood what loan the angel had been sent to recover. For our patron used the word 'loan' to describe the sacred soul entrusted to him by God which would within the week (as we shall tell) depart to the Lord on the Lord's night following.[402]

So, on the Sabbath at the end of that week, the venerable man and his faithful servant Diarmait went to bless the nearest barn. As he entered, the saint blessed it and the two heaps of grain stored there. With a gesture of thankfulness, he said:

'I am very glad for the monks of my community, knowing that if I have to go away somewhere you will have bread enough for a year.'

Hearing this, the servant Diarmait was saddened and said:

'Father, this year you make us sad too often as you speak frequently about your passing.'

The saint answered him:

'I can tell you more plainly a little secret about my going away if you will promise faithfully not to tell anyone till I am dead.'

When the servant had given his promise on bended knees, as the saint desired, the venerable man went on to tell him:

'Scripture calls this day the Sabbath, which means "rest". Today is truly my sabbath, for it is my last day in this wearisome life, when I shall keep the Sabbath[403] after my troublesome labours. At midnight this Sunday, as Scripture saith, "I shall go the way of my fathers."[404] For now my Lord Jesus Christ deigns to invite me,[405] and I shall go to him when he calls me in the middle of this night. The Lord himself has revealed this to me.'

The attendant hearing these sad words began to weep bitterly, and St Columba tried as far as he was able to console him.

After this the saint left the barn and made his way back to the monastery. Where he rested halfway, a cross was later set up, fixed in a millstone;[406] it can still be seen today at the roadside. As the saint was sitting there for a few minutes' rest (for he was weary with age, as I have said), behold, a white horse came to him, the loyal work-horse which used to carry the milk-pails from the booley[407] to the monastery. It approached the saint and – strange to tell – put its head against his bosom, inspired I believe by God for whom every living thing shows such understanding as the Creator bids; it knew that its master would soon be going away so that it would see him no more, and it began to mourn like a person, pouring out its tears in the saint's bosom and weeping aloud with foaming lips.[408] The servant seeing this started to drive off the weeping mourner, but the saint stopped him, saying:

'Let him be! Let him that loves us pour out the tears of bitterest mourning here at my breast. Look how you, though you have a man's rational soul, could not know of my going if I had not myself just told you. But according to his will the Creator has clearly revealed to this brute and reasonless animal that his master is going away.'

So saying, he blessed the horse his servant as it turned away.

Going on from there, he climbed a little hill overlooking the monastery and stood a little while on the top.[409] Standing there, he raised both his hands and blessed the monastery, saying:

'This place, however small and mean, will have bestowed on it no small but great honour by the kings and peoples of Ireland, and also by the rulers of even barbarous and foreign nations with their subject tribes. And the saints of other churches too will give it great reverence.'

When he had come down from the hill and returned to the monastery, he sat in his hut writing out a copy of the psalms. As he reached that verse of the thirty-fourth psalm where it is written, 'They that seek the Lord shall not want for anything that is good,'[410] he said:

'Here at the end of the page I must stop. Let Baithéne write what follows.'

The last verse he wrote was very appropriate for our holy predecessor, who will never lack the good things of eternal life. The verse that follows is, 'Come, my sons, hear me; I shall teach you the fear of the Lord.' This is appropriate for Baithéne his successor, a father and teacher of spiritual sons, who, as his predecessor enjoined, followed him not only as a teacher but also as a scribe.

When the saint had finished his verse at the bottom of the page, he went to the church for vespers on the night before Sunday. As soon as it was over, he returned to his lodgings and rested on his bed, where at night instead of straw he had bare rock and a stone for a pillow, which today stands as a memorial beside his grave.[411] There he gave his last commands to the brethren, with only his servant to hear:[412]

'I commend to you, my little children, these my last words: Love one another unfeignedly. Peace. If you keep this course according to the example of the holy fathers, God, who strengthens the good, will help you, and I dwelling with him shall intercede for you. He will supply not only enough for the needs of this present life, but also the eternal good things that are prepared as a reward for those who keep the Lord's commandments.'

Our story has now reached our venerable patron's last words briefly recounted at the point when he was crossing over from this weary pilgrimage to the heavenly home.

Now the saint was silent as his happy final hour drew near. Then, as the bell rang out for the midnight office, he rose in haste and went to the church, running in ahead of the others and knelt alone in prayer before the altar. In the same instant his servant Diarmait following behind saw from a distance the whole church filled inside with angelic light around the saint. As he reached the door, the light quickly vanished, though some of the other brethren had seen it from further off.

So Diarmait entered the church crying in a tearful voice:

'Father, where are you?'

The lamps of the brethren had not yet been brought, but feeling his way in the dark he found the saint lying before the altar. Raising him up a little and sitting down at his side, he cradled the holy head on his bosom. Meanwhile the monks and their lamps had gathered and they began to lament at the sight of their father dying. Some of those who were present have related how, before his soul left him, the saint opened his eyes and looked about him with a wonderful joy and gladness in his face, for he could see the angels coming to meet him.[413] Diarmait held up the saint's right hand to bless the choir of monks. The venerable father himself, insofar as he had the strength, moved his hand at the same time so that by that movement he should be seen to bless the brethren, though in the moment of his soul's passing he could not speak. Then at once he gave up the ghost.

But even after the soul had left the body that had been its tabernacle, his face remained ruddy with the joy of seeing an angel so that it seemed to belong to a living sleeper, not to a dead man. Meanwhile the whole church was filled with the sound of sorrowful lamentation.

I should not fail to mention here that in the hour of his soul's passing this revelation occurred to a saint in Ireland.

In the monastery of *Cluain Finchoil*[414] there was a holy man, a soldier of Christ advanced in years, called Lugaid mac Tailchain, a just man and a sage. At first light this man, groaning deeply, related to a fellow soldier of Christ called Fergnae this vision:

'During the night just past, St Columba, the pillar of many churches, passed to the Lord. And in the hour of his blessed going, I saw his island of Iona. Though I have never been there in the flesh, yet in the Spirit I could see it, bathed in the bright light of angels. And all the air and sky above even to the heavenly ether was filled with the radiance of the countless angels sent down from heaven to carry home his soul. I heard the most sweet songs of the angelic hosts singing on high in the very moment when his soul departed and was carried up among the choirs of angels.'

Fergnae soon afterwards left Ireland and sailed to *Hinba*, where he spent the rest of his days. Here he used often to tell the monks of St Columba this story, which he had learnt, as we have said, directly from the lips of the aged saint to whom the vision was itself disclosed. Fergnae remained for many years in obedience among the brethren and lived faultlessly. For a further twelve years he withdrew to live in isolation at the place of the anchorites in *Muirbolc Már*,[415] and died a victorious soldier of Christ.

This vision we have found recorded in writing, and we have also learnt it from some of those old men to whom Fergnae himself had told the story, and who repeated it without hesitation.

There was another vision seen in the same hour. One of those who had himself seen it, a soldier of Christ called Ernéne moccu Fir Roíde, when he was an old man, told the story to me, Adomnán, when I was a young man. This Ernéne was himself a holy monk and is buried in the burial ground of the monks of St Columba at Druim Tuamma, where he awaits with the saints the resurrection of the dead.[416] This is the account which he told me, firmly attesting its reliability.

'On the night of St Columba's blessed and blissful passing from the world to the heavens, I and the men with me were hard at work, fishing in the fishful River Finn when all at once we saw the whole sky lit up.[417] The miracle quite took us by surprise. When we looked eastwards, there seemed to be some sort of huge fiery pillar rising upwards in the middle of the night, which lit up the whole world like the summer sun at midday. When the column passed beyond the sky, darkness returned just as follows sunset. Those of us who were there together at that time looked on the brilliance of that praiseworthy column of light with huge astonishment. But later we learnt that many other fishermen, fishing in various places along the same river, saw a similar apparition, and they were seized with great fear.'

The miracles of these three visions all seen in the hour of St Columba's passing proclaim how much honour God has conferred on him. But we must return to our narrative.

After the departure of the saint's soul, the morning hymns were sung, and his sacred body was carried from the church to his lodging, from where a little before he had walked out alive, to the sweet sound of the brethren's chanting. For three days and nights the funeral rituals befitting one of his honour and status were duly carried out. These were concluded with the sweet praises of God, and the venerable body of our holy and blessed patron was wrapped in pure linen and was buried in the chosen grave with all due reverence, from where he will arise in bright, everlasting light.[418]

Before putting an end to this book, we shall recount what

we have been told by learned men about those three days of funeral ceremonies performed in accordance with the good custom of the church.

Once, one of the brethren had foolishly said in the presence of St Columba:

'When you are dead, it is reckoned that all the population of these provinces will row here and fill the whole island of Iona to attend your funeral ceremonies.'

Hearing this said, St Columba commented:

'O my dear son, when the time comes it will prove not to be as you say. The men and women of the lay population will not be able to come to my funeral at all. Only the monks of my own community will carry out my burial and perform the funeral duties.'

The almighty power of God made sure that this word of prophecy was fulfilled straightaway after St Columba's death, for there was a great storm of wind and rain which lasted through the three days and three nights of the funeral. This prevented anyone from coming across the waters in a small boat from any direction. When the burial was completed, at once the wind dropped, the storm was stilled and the whole sea was calm.

The reader should contemplate how great and how special is the honour in which our glorious patron stands with God:[419] while he yet lived in mortal flesh, God deigned to hear his prayers so that storms were stilled and seas were made calm; or, at his need as we have told, winds were raised up and seas stirred when he wished it, which afterwards, as we have described, when the services of his burial were over, were transformed into a great calm.

This then was the end of our praiseworthy patron's life and the beginning of his rewards.[420] In the language of the Scriptures he is added to the fathers as a partaker in eternal triumphs, he is joined with the apostles and prophets, he is enrolled in the number of the thousands of white-robed saints who wash their garments in the blood of the Lamb, he is one of the company that follows the Lamb, a virgin without stain, pure and whole without fault, through the grace of our Lord Jesus Christ himself, to whom with the Father be all honour and power and praise and glory and everlasting kingdom in the unity of the Holy Spirit, for ever and ever.

Every conscientious reader who has finished reading this three-part book should mark well how great and special is the merit of our reverend abbot; how great and special is his honour in God's sight; how great and special were his experiences of angelic visits and heavenly light; how great was the grace of prophecy in him; how great and how frequent was the brilliant light of heaven which shone on him as he dwelt in mortal flesh and which, after his most gentle soul had left the tabernacle of the body, does not cease even today. For the place where his bones rest is still visited by the light of heaven and by numbers of angels, as is known from those of the elect who have themselves seen this.[421]

This too is no small favour conferred by God on the man of blessed memory, that one who dwelt in this little island on the edge of the ocean should have earned a reputation that is famous not only in our own Ireland and in Britain, the largest of ocean's islands, but has also reached the three corners of Spain and Gaul and Italy beyond the Alps, and even Rome itself, the chief of all cities.[422] This great and special renown is known to have been bestowed on St Columba along with other divine gifts by God himself, who loves them that love him and who raises to the heights with honour and glory them that magnify him with sweet praises, who is blessed for ever.
Amen.

I beseech any who wish to copy these books, nay rather I call on them in the name of Christ, the judge of the ages, that when the copying has been done with care, they should then diligently compare what they have written with the exemplar and correct it, and they should add this injunction here at the end of what they have written.[423]

*Whoever may read these books about St Columba's miraculous powers, pray to God for me Dorbbéne that after death I may have life eternal.*[424]

# Notes

*Abbreviations*

*CGSH Corpus Genealogiarum Sanctorum Hiberniae*
*Hib. Hibernensis, Collectio canonum*
MTall Martyrology of Tallaght
RCAHMS Royal Commission on the Ancient and Historical Monuments of Scotland

MANUSCRIPTS AND EDITIONS Texts from the seventh century very rarely survive in contemporary copies and have usually to be reconstructed by comparing several copies made at later dates, many of them probably copies of copies, several stages removed from the original. The Life of St Columba by Adomnán is one of the rare cases.

In 1621 an Irish Jesuit called Stephen White was Professor of Theology at the University of Dillingen in Germany. He had a keen interest in Irish history, and especially in the early history of the Irish church; whenever he had the opportunity, he searched the libraries within his reach for ancient manuscripts relating to Ireland. In the monastery of Reichenau, on an island in Lake Constance, he made his most important discovery – a small book containing Adomnán's Life of St Columba copied by a monk of Iona who gives his name as Dorbbéne. By a happy chance we know from the annals that Dorbbéne was one of the most senior members of the community when he died in 713. His manuscript could easily have been written ten years earlier, when, as an ordinary monk, he was engaged in the task of copying books. It may therefore have been seen in Iona by the author himself. Reichenau was a popular destination with Irish monks who set out to live and study in the monasteries of France, Germany and Switzerland. One of these travellers must have brought this book with him from Iona, perhaps in the eighth or ninth century, and it remained in the library at Reichenau for centuries. Stephen White was allowed to borrow the manuscript and at Dillingen he made a copy from the original. His copy was dated 31 May 1621; it is now lost.

Through Stephen White the complete text of Adomnán's Life became known to scholars: he supplied a copy to the Irish Franciscans at St Anthony's College, Louvain, who were then engaged in collecting and studying historical texts from Ireland. There John Colgan published the Life in 1647, the first edition of the complete text, in a book called *Trias Thaumaturga*, which dealt also with St Patrick and St Brigit. An abstract was made from White's copy by James Ussher about 1639. Ussher was archbishop of Armagh and the leading protestant authority on Irish church history, but he met White too late to be able to make full use of his text of Adomnán's Life. Some references were included in the addenda to Ussher's *Britannicarum ecclesiarum antiquitates* (1639), and Ussher's abstract has by chance survived, and is now in a private library in Wales. Another copy made from White's transcript formed the basis of the next published edition, in the volume of the Bollandists' *Acta Sanctorum* that covers the 9 June, the feast day of St Columba. Published in 1698 this edition is neither as accurate nor as carefully annotated as Colgan's.

Meanwhile the manuscript written by Dorbbéne was presumably returned to Reichenau by Fr White. At some point, however, it became separated from the main collection of ancient manuscripts at Reichenau (now kept in the public library at Karlsruhe), but it turned up again in the eighteenth century in the nearby town of Schaffhausen, where it has been kept in the public library for some two hundred years. The manuscript is still there and has been used by the modern editors of the text. The Revd William Reeves published a monumental edition, to which I refer constantly in my notes, at Dublin in 1857. The later editions by Skene and Fowler, and the translations by Bishop Daniel MacCarthy (1860), A. P. Forbes (1874), J. T. Fowler (1895), and Wentworth Huyshe (1906) all used Reeves's text. A new and more exact text, founded on a very careful scrutiny of the manuscript in Schaffhausen, was brought out in 1961 by Dr Alan Orr Anderson and his wife Dr Marjorie Ogilvie Anderson. The scrupulous exactitude of this text was a remarkable achievement, and I have used it as the basis of my translation.

The Schaffhausen manuscript is conventionally designated as MS A, and its importance lies in the fact that it allows us to see the exact form in which the Life was originally read: the size of page, the handwriting, the spelling, even the punctuation. Yet it is not the only witness to the text. There are three copies now in the British Library, London, which agree closely on a text differing in a number of particulars from that of MS A. At several points these B MSS contain additional sentences, quite evidently by Adomnán himself; this gives them considerable importance, since it becomes apparent that Adomnán allowed copies to be made from his own working copy both before and after some final revisions. Where MS A and the B MSS differ in a minor way, the fact that MS A was written in Iona about 700 does not mean that it is necessarily a better witness than the B MSS, which must ultimately go back to the exemplar corrected and revised by Adomnán.

Of these B MSS the most significant is B1, now London, British Library, MS Additional 35110. The book was copied at Durham towards the end of the twelfth century and then carefully corrected against the exemplar from which the copy was made. The library at Durham had been growing during the twelfth century, but as early as the 1150s it already included a copy of the Life, the copy that was used by Reginald, a monk of Durham who wrote Lives of several saints, including one of King Oswald of Northumbria. The copy from which Reginald quoted Adomnán is now lost, but it presumably served as the model from which B1 was transcribed about forty years later. Later still, perhaps in the late thirteenth or fourteenth century, B1 left Durham, for it bears the medieval library-mark of the Augustinian or Austin Friary at Newcastle. Another manuscript, B3, is related to B1: its text could have been copied from B1, for the two agree closely. B3 was written in the late fifteenth century at a house of Augustinian canons; shortly before 1609 it belonged to a nobleman in Co. Durham, Lord Lumley, whose books were soon afterwards transferred to the Royal collection, where it still is, London, British Library, MS Royal 8 D. IX. From this volume the B text was used by John Pinkerton in 1789, but without adequate attention; his edition, even at the time of its appearance, was of less use than Colgan's. The remaining witness to the B text, known as B2, is London, British Library, MS Cotton Tiberius D. III. The handwriting of this book is of a date similar to B1; its text agrees with B rather than A, but it is not as closely related to either B1 or B3 as they are to each other. In any case B2 was badly damaged by the fire that decimated the Cotton Library in 1731.

There is sufficient agreement between B1, B2, and B3 for us to suppose that they have a common ancestor, B. Because B contains passages written by Adomnán but missing from A, it is necessary to infer that A and B reflect two stages in the author's intentions. Where either one does not yield acceptable sense, it should be possible to correct it from the other. For this reason, I have commented in the notes at points where I have preferred the reading of B over that of A.

There are many other manuscripts that present a later, shorter form of the text. I have followed the Andersons in not taking them into consideration for textual purposes.

PERSONAL NAMES In his preface Adomnán apologizes to his Latin readers for the number of Irish names in his work. Readers of English may find them difficult to pronounce, but I have tried to reduce this difficulty by adopting the standard spelling of Old Irish as used by modern historians. For one or two names, used by Adomnán but obsolete thereafter, I have kept close to his early spelling, dropping the case-endings of Latin. Only one grammatical inflection is retained, namely the genitive or possessive case: where someone is called 'X son of Y' the Irish word *mac* 'son' is followed by the genitive form of the name Y. In most cases this will mean the insertion of the letter *i*, e.g., Domnall mac Domnaill, Fintan mac Fintain; sometimes the change is greater, e.g., Áed mac Áedo, Ainmire mac Ainmirech, Eochaid mac Echdach. I have retained these Irish forms for the sake of authenticity and to avoid the ambiguity in English of writing 'X, the son of Y, who . . .'.

With the few non-Irish personal names I have sought to adopt the most appropriate form, not necessarily that used by Adomnán. Thus, where possible, English persons have English names (Oswald, Ecgfrith, Aldfrith); the names of British-speaking rulers are given in modern Welsh spelling (Cadwallon, Rhydderch). The Pictish language (or languages) died out nearly a thousand years ago, and no texts remain. The names of kings, however, are preserved in a Pictish king-list, which provides better spellings than those used by Irish annalists. These names take the patronymic form 'Bridei f. Bili', which I have retained; here 'f.' represents the Latin *filius* 'son', followed by what is presumably the genitive case of the father's name. For minor individuals, in the absence of other information, I have retained Adomnán's spelling, knowing that it may not accurately reflect Pictish usage.

When Adomnán names an Irish man in the Life, it is his practice to give also the man's father's name (introduced by *mac*) and some indication either of the dynasty to which he belonged or of his tribal group. These facts served to differentiate individuals of the same name and they told the audience where the person came from and (in many cases) where he stood in the social hierarchy.

PEOPLES AND DYNASTIES For the great majority of people mentioned, the name of their tribal group or people is a phrase beginning with the word *moccu*; thus in I 5 St Colmán is called 'Colmán mac Beognai' (indicating his father) and 'Colmán moccu Sailni' (indicating his people). Population groups with names in *moccu* seem to have been quite small, associated with a particular area and possibly, but not necessarily, related. No author later than Adomnán uses so large a number of *moccu* names, so that it appears that this way of identifying people became obsolete during the eighth century. Later writers mistakenly thought *moccu* was made up of two distinct words *mac* 'son' and *ua* 'grandson'.

Groups known by *moccu* names seem to have been of little political importance in Adomnán's time. Ruling families preferred to use a dynastic name, introduced by words such as *cenél* 'kindred' or *síl* 'seed, issue'. In the course of generations, as the family tree branched out, new dynastic names came into use, identifying the younger branches by a nearer ancestor. Some names of this kind, however, remained the same for hundreds of years and designated large dynastic groups with many sub-dynasties. The Uí Néill, for example, all claimed to be descendants (*ua* 'grandson' has the plural *uí*) of Niall, gen. Néill, through many sons, in different parts of Ireland. These dynastic names were used to define not only members of the dynasty but also the area that they ruled. Some of them survive in modern place names: Co. Offaly, for example, preserves the dative case of the dynastic name Uí Failgi. Of course, only a minority of the population in the area were blood-related to the ruling dynasty that gave its name to the territory.

Some areas were called by names that designated larger, non-dynastic population groups. These include simple group-names such as the *Airthir* (I 44), which means 'Easterners'. Some terms are intermediate between dynastic names and wider designations; the *dál* in Dál Riata and similar names means 'division, share'; the Dál Riata were the people who took their name and identity from Riata rather than those who descended from him. The idea of common descent may have been present, but it was descent from a remote, generally fictitious ancestor, whose role was to give a sense of identity and unity. Such group-names are not dynastic in the sense of designating the ruling family; they refer to whole populations, which would subsume a considerable number of *moccu* groups and one or more prominent dynastic *cenéla*.

PLACE-NAMES For identifiable and well-known places I have generally subsitituted a modern name for the form used by Adomnán. Sometimes, however, I have retained in standardized spelling a vernacular name. This has been done in cases such as Druim Cett, which are more familiar in historical use than any identification on the map. In the case of Clochar Macc nDáiméni (modern Clogher) it seemed desirable to retain the reference to the family of Dáiméne which is relevant to the story. Place names for which no identification is agreed and where there is no standard spelling are printed in italics in a form as close as possible to that of Adomnán.

DATES Whenever I refer to years derived from the various annal collections, I have given the date as it can best be converted to Anno Domini; the source, however, is specified as AU or AT. The Annals of Ulster, in their extant sixteenth-century form, incorporate Anno Domini dates, though for the period with which we are concerned there was an accidental misnumbering by one year; this error is rectified in references to AU. The Annals of Tigernach do not specify years Anno Domini but have to be converted; there are from time to time anomalies between dates in AU and AT, which show up in the conversion. For Iona entries, both collections go back to a set of annals kept at Iona through the seventh century and after. These original annals would have been kept in a form that did not use dates Anno Domini. They may simply have counted the years of each abbot's tenure, or the years of a king's rule, but a good case can be made out for thinking that the original entries were made in a table showing the successive years of the cycle by which the date of Easter was worked out. The conversion of these entries to dates Anno Domini was carried out much later, after more than one merger of different annal collections. Exact dates from the annals are thus not always reliable. The date of an eclipse, however, in the year 664 shows that annal dates can work out exactly (see n. 346). Even where a majority of entries in the annals offer dates that are near enough dependable, there are some entries that were made retrospectively, many years after the event and sometimes without any accurate information on the date (see nn. 54, 204). Unfortunately, it is not always possible to tell the difference between these retrospective entries and trustworthy contemporary ones.

1 These sentences borrow from two separate passages in the Life of St Martin by Sulpicius Severus, the text that was Adomnán's primary literary model. The first sentence cites Sulpicius's Life of St Martin, 1. 9: 'I beg those who read this to put their faith in these statements'; the second cites Sulpicius's preface § 3: 'They should give more thought to the subject than to the words, . . . for the Kingdom of God stands not on eloquence but on faith.' The latter statement depends in turn on St

Paul, 1 Cor. 4:20. Adomnán's paraphrase was itself quoted in the preface to a Life of St Kentigern of Glasgow, written between 1147 and 1164.

**2** Adomnán's apology to his Latin readers for his use of Irish names is no doubt just as valid for modern English readers. One may compare another passage, originally written in Latin in the late seventh or eighth century, and preserved in the Book of Armagh, fol. 18vb:

Here end these few pieces, written imperfectly in Irish. It is not that I was unable to put them into Latin, but that these stories can scarcely be understood even in Irish. If they had been translated into Latin, no one would have been better off. The reader would hardly even know what language he was reading on account of the number of Irish names for which there are no equivalents in Latin.

On occasion, Adomnán did put Irish names into Latin, such as *mediterranea pars* 'the midland part' for Irish *Mide* 'Meath'. More often he added a Latin suffix to an Irish name, and in doing so sometimes chose a Latin declension that paralleled the Irish. For anyone interested in Irish names, or in the early history of the Irish language, the forms used by Adomnán and retained by Dorbbéne are of very great interest. They represent the earliest written record of any quantity of names, and are revealing both on matters of spelling and phonetics. (See discussion by Anderson and Anderson, pp. 124–61, 2nd edn, pp. lxxii–lxxix; Binchy [review of Anderson and Anderson], pp. 193–5; Harvey, 'Retrieving the pronunciation of early insular Celtic scribes').

Bullough, 'Columba, Adomnan', p. 127, compared Adomnán's words *quae ut puto inter alias exterarum gentium diuersas uilescunt linguas*, with a phrase used by the sixth-century British polemicist Gildas, *De Excidio Britanniae*, c. 17: *ne . . . nomen Romanorum quod . . . exterarum gentium opprobrio obrosum uilesceret* 'that the name of Rome . . . should not be cheapened, gnawed by the insult of foreign races'. Adomnán shows no other acquaintance with Gildas's *De Excidio*, but that work was familiar to St Columbanus at Bangor in the late sixth century and to Bede in the eighth. It is possible that Adomnán too had studied it.

**3** This apology is of a very conventional type, and the wording here may be compared with the apology at the end of Book II. Both are modelled on words of Sulpicius's Life of St Martin, 1. 8, 19. 5.

4 Here Adomnán has a short phrase, *minima ... de maximis*, which he perhaps borrowed from the prologue to Evagrius's Life of St Antony – a text from which he quotes occasionally through the Life and which infuses much of his account of St Columba's last days (II 28, III 23); I say perhaps because it may be regarded as a cliché.

5 The conventionality of saying that the saint did much more than there is space to retell makes it difficult to assess the implication of this statement. In saying that there is much to tell, that he can give only a small part of it, yet even that is more than is widely known, Adomnán appears to indicate that St Columba's life-story had been slow to spread, slower than his reputation. Almost all other evidence is later than Adomnán, so that it is possible that the Life played a major role in the dissemination of stories about the saint; but the extent of the community in Scotland, Ireland and Northumbria makes it certain that his cult was widely known in the seventh century.

6 There are several Latin saints' Lives that begin with two prefaces, a literary tradition that began because Evagrius, who translated Athanasius's Life of St Antony from Greek into Latin, added his own translator's preface to that by the original author. Subsequently, Sulpicius Severus made a feature of the double preface in imitation of Evagrius: in his first preface he justified the style in which he presented his Life of St Martin, and in the second he explained the organization of the work in relation to St Martin's life. Adomnán quotes from both Evagrius and Sulpicius in his first preface, and from Sulpicius in his second; in the content of his prefaces Sulpicius was much the nearer of the two models. Another insular Latin saint's Life, the anonymous Life of St Cuthbert, was written at Lindisfarne between 699 and 705 – very much at the same time as Adomnán's Life. This too begins with two prefaces: the first, concerning the author's obedience to the command to write the Life, quotes from the first preface to the Life of St Antony; the second, which deals with the quantity of Cuthbert's miracles and the good authority on which they are reported, is largely lifted from Sulpicius. This feature of the Life is discussed by Picard, 'Structural patterns', p. 75.

7 ST COLUMBA'S NAME The name *Columba* is Latin and means 'dove', but it is used conventionally to express the Irish name *Columb*; similarly the common Irish name *Colmán*, a diminutive, is Latinized as *Columbanus*. The Irishman Columbanus (who died in 615, a few years later than

Columba), writing to Pope Boniface IV, makes the same play on words with his name: 'the last to the first, the foreigner to the native, a poor creature to a powerful lord, (strange to tell, a monstrosity, a rare bird) the Dove dares to write to Pope Boniface' (Letters 5. 1); 'I am called *Jona* in Hebrew, *Peristera* in Greek, *Columba* in Latin, yet so much is my birthright in the idiom of your language that I use the ancient Hebrew name of Jonah, whose shipwreck I have almost undergone' (Letters 5. 16). Columbanus himself preferred to use the form Columba; his biographer, who as a monk took the name Jonah, uses both indifferently. Adomnán uses the form Columbanus for Colmán on a number of occasions (I 5, 14; II 15, 16, 21, 22, 43; III 12).

Adomnán is at pains in this paragraph to show that the name meaning 'dove' was given to Columba 'from the days of his infancy' by divine providence. Irish writers of later date thought that this was a name he acquired at a later stage, and give his original name as *Crimthann*. This name is not uncommon in early medieval Ireland; it means 'fox'. There is a story, recorded in a later medieval commentary on the *Félire* of Oengus (a poem on the feast days of saints, composed about AD 830), of how the saint was given the Irish name Columb Cille 'dove of the church'. The story is incorporated in Manus O'Donnell's *Life*, § 53.

**8** The Gospel passages referred to are Matt. 3:16, Mark 1:9–11, Luke 3:21–2, John 1:32–4; in all these accounts it is explicitly stated that the Spirit came down in the form of a dove. Adomnán, the biblical scholar, refers also to the wider allegorical interpretation, popular in Ireland in his day, that doves mentioned elsewhere (as, e.g., Gen. 8) allude to the Holy Spirit.

**9** Compare Matt. 10:16. According to a note in Irish on a hymn in the Irish *Liber Hymnorum* (eleventh century), 'he was called dove for his simplicity' (*Liber Hymnorum*, I 30, II 122); the same explanation is given in a commentary on the *Félire* of Oengus (Stokes, *Félire*, p. 146).

**10** Compare Prov. 22:1. Adomnán, in a play on words, interprets the Vulgate *nomen* 'name' literally, though the passage is usually taken to signify a good reputation.

**11** The phrase *filius repromissionis* alludes to Gal. 4:28: 'Now we, brethren, are the children of promise [*promissionis filii*]', referring back to the story of Isaac, the son promised by God to Abraham. Columba likewise is promised by God through prophecy.

12 ST MOCHTA'S PROPHECY The prophecy is more or less a commonplace. Most saints' births were foreknown and foretold, so that in its general implication of future sanctity, there is nothing remarkable. The reference to Maucteus (Mochta), however, is both interesting and problematic; I have discussed it in detail in an article, 'Saint Mauchteus, *discipulus Patricii*'. St Mochta is mentioned in the Annals of Ulster in the year 535: 'The death of Mochta, disciple of Patrick, on 19 August. This is how he refers to himself in his letter: "Mauchteus, a sinner, priest, disciple of St Patrick, sends greetings in the Lord." ' (The letter quoted by the annals does not itself survive.) He is also cited as the authority for a Saxon raid on Ireland in AU 471. On the early testimony of these annals and Adomnán's saying that he was from Britain, we may suppose that he came, like Uinniau, to Ireland sometime before or after 500; the date given for his death, if reliable, would place him in a period when the British church was highly influential in the conversion of Ireland. The reference to a letter reminds one of those between Uinniau and Gildas, of which only fragments survive; Sharpe, 'Gildas as a Father of the Church'.

The date of Mochta's death was a problem to Bury and his followers, who argued that St Patrick died in 461. Could a disciple of his have lived on for more than seventy years? Even those who favour a date for St Patrick's death in the 490s may have anxieties over Mochta's longevity. But the chronological question apart, students of St Patrick and his mission have always been delighted with these statements, in sources of impeccable authority, which support the view that St Patrick played the major role in the conversion of Ireland and left disciples to continue his work. St Mochta, however, is not mentioned in the seventh-century Lives of St Patrick.

Entries for persons associated with St Patrick form a distinct group in the annals, probably entered retrospectively in a collection compiled at Armagh, which included a list of St Patrick's successors. Mochta's absence from Patrician Lives and his anomalous placing in relation to Patrician chronology separate him from this tradition. The close similarity between the description of Mochta in Adomnán's *Life* and at the start of his own lost letter may suggest that Adomnán knew either the letter itself or the quotation from it in the annals. This may further suggest that a copy of the letter was preserved at Iona, and that Mochta's obituary derives from the annals originally kept at Iona.

Later sources agree in associating St Mochta with the church of Louth in north-east Ireland. No church of St Columba, however, is known at any date adjacent to this. The most probable way out of this difficulty may be that St Mochta's association with Louth (a church not referred to in the Annals of Ulster until 662) began at a later date, and that he had previously been associated with another church known to Adomnán and near one of St Columba's monasteries.

13 On Adomnán's plan for the Life, see Introduction, pp. 55–65.

14 The sentiment but not the words here are founded on Sulpicius's Life of St Martin, I. 9.

15 ADOMNÁN'S INFORMANTS Several times Adomnán attributes his information to *experti* 'informed people', 'learned men': 'we have learnt of it . . . from informed people' (I 1), 'so the learned say' (I 38), 'so the story is handed down to us by learned men' (II 6), 'reported in various places by people who knew the facts' (II 9), 'so the story is handed down to us by learned men' (III 4), 'what we have been told by learned men' (III 23, p. 232). The word *expertus* may simply mean 'expert, skilled', but in British- and Hiberno-Latin it can carry a more precise meaning: *peritia* 'skill' is used to translate OIr. *senchus* 'lore, tradition', a term that embraces historical and especially genealogical tradition; *experti* could mean those with a particular knowledge of the community's tradition, though not, I think, in I 38 or II 6, and not necessarily therefore in other contexts. Sometimes the author is more specific about the qualifications of his informants: 'from some men of exemplary honesty and good faith who left no room for doubt that they had seen . . .' (II 9), 'some of those who were present have related how . . .' (III 23, p. 229), and 'as is known from those of the elect who have themselves seen this' (III 23, p. 233). One of these examples raises a problem: when he cites 'those who were present' at the hour of the saint's death, he can hardly mean that these were his direct informants, unless he was collecting information in his youth or, perhaps, unless he is repeating a source of earlier date.

More often, Adomnán is specific about how the information reached him, sometimes naming his source, other times naming the original witness. His wording in these cases can be particularly striking, affirming not only the reliability of his information but also the circumstances in which it was collected. The story of King Oswald's vision (I 1) came to Adomnán from his predecessor Abbot Failbe, who testified (*protestatus est*) that he heard King Oswald himself tell Abbot Ségéne. The saint's prophecy to St Fintan and its fulfilment (I 2) were described by Fintan to his monk Oisséne, who, in old age told Adomnán. His prophecy about Ernéne (I 3) was related by Ernéne himself to Abbot Ségéne, and again Failbe was present and reported it to Adomnán. Máel Odrain, who witnessed the fulfilment of the saint's prophecy about Báetán (I 20), told Adomnán, but in this case the prophecy itself 'was reported many years ago'. Luigbe 'testified in the presence of other saints' to Columba's description of his clairvoyance (I 43), and Adomnán heard it from them. The prophecy known to the monks of St Comgall and fulfilled years later (I 49) was revealed by Fínán, a witness to its fulfilment, who more than forty years later testified to Adomnán about what he had seen and heard. In most of these cases Adomnán has a need to show how the prophecy was recognized as being fulfilled as well as how word came to him. The miracles of power generally need less elaborate explanations, but the one for which a witness is cited is particularly striking: Silnán who experienced the saint's power (II 4) gave testimony 'in the presence of Abbot Ségéne and other elders'. The saint's heavenly radiance seen by the young Fergnae (III 19) was described to his nephew, the priest Commán, who gave testimony to Adomnán. Finally, two stories about Columba's passing are explained. In one case the original witness Lugaid told another monk, Fergnae, who came to Hinba, where he used to tell his story to members of the community; Adomnán heard it from some of these old men, but he had also 'found [it] recorded in writing' (III 23, p. 230). Another miracle at the time Columba died was witnessed in Ireland by Ernéne, who described it to the young Adomnán, still in his home district, 'firmly attesting its reliability' (*cum grandi testificatione*) (III 23, p. 231).

Now there are two problems in all this. One is the word *seniores*: Silnán gave his testimony in front of the elders of the community, the leading senior monks (mentioned also in II 44); but those elders who told Adomnán what they had heard years before from Fergnae are so described not for their seniority but because they are old enough to have known the witness. So, where Adomnán mentions 'the account handed down by our elders' and by 'informed and reliable old men' in the second preface, it is hard to know where his emphasis lies.

The other problem is the language of witness and testimony. In the case of Silnán, Adomnán says very formally 'We have the testimony of Silnán himself given in the presence of Abbot Ségéne and other elders.' Taken with two other references to statements made to Abbot Ségéne, this led Dr Herbert to argue that there may have been an effort in Ségéne's time to collect sworn witness to Columba's miracles while the witnesses were still alive (*Iona, Kells, and Derry*, pp. 16–26). She goes on to suggest that these statements may have formed the basis of

Cumméne's book. A difficulty with this tempting hypothesis is that Adomnán uses the same language of sworn witness with reference to statements made to him (see n. 391), and, in particular, with reference to what he heard as a youth from Ernéne. In this last example formal testimony cannot be involved, so it must make us wonder whether Adomnán ever uses this language in a strong formal sense.

Silnán's testimony, however, is also significant because Adomnán does not say how the story was transmitted thereafter. It is as though citing his testimony before Ségéne and the elders was sufficient for everyone to know that he meant a particular authoritative record. But for the other statements made to Ségéne Adomnán relies on word of mouth through Abbot Failbe. The relationship between written record and oral testimony about Lugaid's vision is similarly unclear. In the end, I do not feel confident that we can infer any clear generalizations about how the community preserved the memory of its founder beyond the obvious inference that it did, and in a variety of ways. The amount of circumstantial detail, including the names and family connections of people mentioned in stories relating to the community, is remarkable. It is debatable whether it is evidence of the extent to which Adomnán had written evidence to work from.

**16** ST COLUMBA'S LINEAGE St Columba's family belonged to the lineage of Cenél Conaill, who claimed descent from Conall Gulban, son of Niall of Nine Hostages. As a lineage, the Cenél Conaill were one of the most powerful groups among all the descendants of Niall, who were known collectively as the Uí Néill. During the sixth and seventh centuries the Cenél Conaill often dominated the other lineages of the Uí Néill in the north-west of Ireland, and were sometimes able to exert authority over the southern branches of the Uí Néill in Brega. The rulers of Cenél Conaill, St Columba's close cousins, were therefore among the most powerful kings in Ireland. St Columba's position in the lineage can be seen from the genealogical table (pp. xvi–xvii).

Irish genealogical sources are in agreement in saying that St Columba was the son of Fedelmid, son of Fergus, son of Conall Gulban, son of Niall of Nine Hostages. Little is known of the saint's mother's lineage; the eleventh- or early-twelfth-century genealogies in MS Rawl. B. 502 fol. 128b1–8 refer to her as daughter of Oengus or Dimma, son of Noe, son of Fechin, of a lineage known as Cland Ailello, who belonged to the Manaig of Lough Erne, a people whose territory lay in what is now Co. Fermanagh. The uncertainty as to Eithne's father's name may have arisen because he was known as Mac Noe 'son of a ship'. The Middle Irish homily favours Dimma mac Noe. Modern tradition (first attested in the nineteenth century) has given the name Eithne's Grave to a cross-marked site associated with the early monastic remains on Eileach an Naoimh; see RCAHMS, *Islay and Jura*, p. 176.

**17** On the battle of *Cúl Drebene* and explanations of St Columba's pilgrimage, see Introduction, pp. 12–14. For details of the chronology, see I 7 and n. 77.

Adomnán's phrase would appear to identify St Columba as a *deorad Dé* 'stranger of God'. It is, however, not clear that this is so: the choice of a life of pilgrimage was not necessarily sufficient to earn the status of 'stranger of God'. How one qualified for this title is not clear, but the stranger of God enjoyed very high status in Irish law, the equal of a bishop or a local king according to *Bretha Crólige*, § 4. Later legal commentators expected the stranger of God to have the power to perform miracles; *Bretha Crólige* itself, written after Columba's time but before Adomnán's, mentions in § 12 'the stranger of God whose miracles are made known'. The term appears therefore to be a legal one for a holy man with special divine gifts; it accords special status to someone who may otherwise fall outside the system of legal status. Such a man was required to act to enforce any contracts in law bound by the men of heaven or by the gospel of Christ, according to the tract *Coibnes Uisci Thairidne*, § 7.

**18** This passage is a quotation from the *Actus S. Siluestri*: 'Placed on earth, he showed by his way of life that he was fit for the life of heaven. He was an angel in demeanour, blameless in what he said, godly in what he did, pure in body, brilliant in intellect, and great in counsel.' The same passage is quoted and continued in the anonymous Life of St Cuthbert (see n. 6), II 1; Levison has pointed out that it is also used elsewhere of other saints, 'Konstantinische Schenkung und Silvester-Legende', pp. 213–14.

**19** On the duration of St Columba's life of pilgrimage, see III 22 and n. 395.

**20** The second half of this sentence is based on Sulpicius's Life of St Martin, 26. 3, but with the addition of writing as an approved activity. On St Columba's interest in the copying of books, see n. 125.

**21** Here again Adomnán borrows a short phrase, *hilarem semper faciem ostendens sanctam*, from Evagrius's Life of St Antony, c. 40: *semper hilarem faciem gerens.*

**22** These chapter headings differ from those at the head of each chapter, and, as will be clear from my added references, several chapters are grouped, others are omitted. More importantly, the heading for I 34 mentions a place-name not actually given in the title or the text of the chapter. Reeves, p. 10n., was the first to draw the inference that this table is by the author himself.

**23** The reading of A is clearly *binc*, which is inexplicable in Latin or Irish; the reading of B was read by Reeves as *biui*, which is no better. B. MacCarthy, in the review of J. T. Fowler's edition, p. 473, suggested that one should read *biuc*, the dative of Old Irish *bec* 'little', as a nickname 'Little Fiachnae'. This plausible suggestion was also made by Anderson and Anderson, p. 556, without reference to MacCarthy; in the second edition, p. 250, Mrs Anderson notes that the reading of B2 appears actually to be *biuc*. The nickname is given only here, not in the body of the chapter.

**24** In I 39 his name is given as Neman mac Gruthriche; the error 'Enan' is found in both the A and the B MSS.

**25** This alludes to the story at III 8. Adomnán's words here clearly show the leading position of Iona among St Columba's island churches; he uses the same word, *primarius*, in *De Locis Sanctis* III 5, referring to Constantinople as 'the principal city of the Roman Empire'. Compare also II 5, where Iona is described as St Columba's 'mother church'.

**26** See II 26–7.

**27** See II 12.

**28** See II 34.

**29** See I 4, II 15, 45.

**30** See II 33.

**31** See II 32.

32 See II 1.

33 For manifestations of heavenly light, see below, III 17–21; for angels, see III 3–5, 16, 22.

34 See III 6–7, 9–12, 14.

35 See I 35, 39, II 23, 25.

36 See I 7–8, 12.

37 This is a striking claim, apparently addressed to kings, as an invitation to them to seek the support of St Columba's prayers, and to those other saints to whom God did not give this special privilege, perhaps warning their churches not to come between the abbot of Iona and his royal friends. See Introduction, pp. 61–3; Enright, 'Royal succession', p. 100.

38 This story is told nowhere in the body of the Life, but only here. It is possible that it was added as an afterthought, as suggested by Anderson and Anderson, p. 6. It is perhaps more likely that it was placed here for special prominence. First, it is given a vigorous introduction, claiming for St Columba a special privilege in relation to kings. Second, Oswald was one of the most powerful kings between the saint's time and the author's, claiming hegemony over all the other English kings, and some authority over the Britons, the Picts and the Irish of Dalriada (see n. 42); a king whom Adomnán calls 'emperor', perhaps recognizing his power as greater than that of a king of Tara. Third, Adomnán was aware of an important series of connections: Columba's prayers helped Oswald gain his kingdom; this introduced Christianity to Bernicia, and for its development Oswald turned to Abbot Ségéne and asked for a bishop to be sent from Iona. Iona's influence in the Northumbrian church declined after the synod at Whitby in 664, but Adomnán may still have expected a Northumbrian audience. Fourth, even in Ireland there may have been a particular interest in King Oswald. He was killed in battle in 642 by the pagan king of Mercia, Penda; miracles were reported at the site of his death near Oswestry, his relics worked many miracles, and already Bede refers to him as St Oswald (III 12). In the 680s in Ireland an unnamed Irish biblical scholar told the Englishman Willibrord, 'I have heard the well-known story of your most saintly King Oswald, whose wonderful

faith and virtue have become renowned . . .'; this Irishman was cured by a relic of Oswald and further helped to spread Oswald's reputation in Ireland (Bede, III 13).

The story of Oswald's victory (which is also told by Bede and later Northumbrian writers) would have had the historical interest of providing background to Iona's role in the conversion of Northumbria. The battle marked the culmination of a period of complicated infighting. Oswald (b. 604) was the son of the Northumbrian king Æthelfrith (d. 617), but did not succeed his father directly. When Æthelfrith had become king, his rival's heir, Edwin, withdrew into exile, but with the support of King Rædwald of East Anglia he returned and killed Æthelfrith, becoming king himself. Now it was the turn of Æthelfrith's sons to go into exile; Oswald and his elder brother, Eanfrith, spent fifteen years 'among the Irish or the Picts' (Bede, III 1). Eanfrith spent some time in Pictland, where he married a Pictish princess and fathered the future king Talorcen f. Anfrith (653–7). Bede also indicates that both were baptized, evidently in Iona (see n. 41). Meanwhile, the Welsh king, Cadwallon, whose territory had earlier been invaded by Edwin and who was nominally a subject, rebelled against the Northumbrian king and, aided by the king of Mercia, defeated and killed Edwin in 633. Eanfrith, Oswald's elder brother, then claimed the kingdom of Bernicia, the northern part of Northumbria, while Edwin's cousin Osric took the southern part, Deira. Both Eanfrith and Osric reverted to paganism. Osric was defeated and killed by Cadwallon, who also murdered Eanfrith. So in 634 Oswald, now about thirty years old, gathered a small army, 'strong in the faith of Christ' (according to Bede), and marched against Cadwallon. Adomnán here tells how St Columba promised Oswald victory in a vision; Bede, though his story is quite different (Bede, III 2), also attributes Oswald's success to the special help of God against the Welsh king, whom both the English (of a later generation) and the Irish regarded as apostate. Oswald's victory in the battle, which took place at 'Heavenfield' near Hexham, secured his control over Northumbria.

39 Josh. 1:9.

40 The Latin word used by Adomnán was *expergitus*, but in one of the surviving manuscripts, B1, written at Durham in the twelfth century, the copyist altered this to *expergefactus*. This slight change enabled Anderson and Anderson, p. 4, to argue that this particular manuscript, now London, British Library, MS Add. 35110, may have been the very

book used by Reginald of Durham in writing his Life of St Oswald, the Northumbrian king in this story. The date of the handwriting, however, appears to be about thirty or forty years later. This volume is therefore likely to be a copy made at Durham and 'corrected' against the older copy used by Reginald. (See Anderson and Anderson, 2nd edn, p. lvi.)

41 Adomnán here differs from Bede as to whether Oswald's army was or was not Christian. The Irish author has it that Oswald and twelve companions had been baptized previously during his exile, and that the rest of his force was baptized only after the battle. Bede, on the other hand, emphasizes that the altar and cross erected by Oswald at a place called Heavenfield before the battle were the first ever set up in Bernicia, and that the site was therefore revered; in his own time a church had 'recently' been built there. Bede also indicates that all of Oswald's soldiers were Christians already and that all knelt in prayer before battle. It is not possible to know what proportion of Oswald's troops were Christian, nor indeed from where they were drawn. If the English of Bernicia were still pagan, at least some of those of Deira were Christian. There was probably also a substantial British population in Bernicia, who would presumably have been Christians, but they would be unlikely to support a recently converted English king against their fellow-national Cadwallon, whose line had been Christian for generations. It is worth bearing in mind that Bede would not wish to admit that this battle, so important in Oswald's career as the king who provided for the conversion of Bernicia, was a victory of pagan English over Christian Britons. It would go right against the theme of his work.

KING OSWALD'S BAPTISM Oswald and his elder brother, Eanfrith, were baptized in exile before Oswald gained the crown. We can infer from Bede that this was actually in Iona. Having gained the kingdom, Oswald 'sent to the Irish elders among whom he and his thegns had received the sacrament of baptism when he was an exile' (Bede, III 3). They sent him Bishop Áedán, or Aidan, who was himself a monk 'from the island of Iona, whose monastery was for a considerable time the chief among the monasteries of the northern Irish and the Picts'. The elders who sent Aidan were presumably those of Iona, where we gather Oswald and his close companions received baptism. From Bede we may also infer that Oswald's younger brother, Oswiu, was also baptized here. This is entirely compatible with what little Adomnán says on the subject. The exiled princes were presumably baptized by Abbot Fergnae

(608–24) or by Abbot Ségéne (624–52); such baptisms would surely have maintained a sense of mission at Iona between the founder's time and the period of the mission to England.

**42** Bede (III 6) also says: 'Oswald obtained from the one same God who made heaven and earth a more extensive kingdom than any of his ancestors; he had under his rule all the peoples and provinces of Britain, though they spoke four different languages – I mean the British, the Picts, the Irish, and the English.' Bede's reference to God's patronage is less strongly worded than Adomnán's 'ordained by God' (with which compare similar remarks below, I 36 and III 5). The nature of Oswald's hegemony has been much discussed by historians but it remains elusive.

**43** It would appear from this that after his victory in 634 King Oswald travelled to Iona and gave this account to the abbot in the presence of other monks. He may have done this at any time before his death in 642 – we know nothing of Oswald's movements, but, given the extent of his authority, he probably had to visit Pictish and Scottish territory from time to time. One would like, perhaps, to see this return visit to Abbot Ségéne in 634–5, when the king was arranging with the elders of Iona for a bishop to come to Bernicia. As Bede describes it, this involved the initial request and a second discussion after an unsuitable candidate gave up the task. Aidan was Ségéne's second nominee.

**44** This story too is told here but not in the body of the Life. The phrase with which it is introduced is a cliché in saints' Lives.

**45** The Latin text literally means 'certain men guilty of a lay (*laicus*) way of life and bloodstained', but I do not think Adomnán meant to imply that to be a layman was itself wicked. For layman, Adomnán generally writes *plebeus*, and I have here followed my own interpretation of the Hiberno-Latin use of *laicus* 'brigand, man of evil' to translate OIr. *díbergach*; Sharpe, 'Hiberno-Latin *laicus*, Irish *láech*, and the Devil's men'. We encounter a band of such *díbergaig* below, II 22, 24.

**46** The reference to songs in praise of St Columba has attracted attention from Irish scholars. Colgan (it seems) took it to refer to *Amrae Coluimb Chille*, an Irish eulogy of the saint, which was composed soon after his death in an arcane style, and which had the status of a classic in medieval Ireland. He has generally been followed, but we cannot be sure that Adomnán was not thinking of other eulogies now lost. This interpretation first appears in Colgan's translation of Manus O'Donnell, *Trias*, p. 444, but it is not O'Donnell's; it is part of a series of passages derived from the longer version of Adomnán and appended, apparently by Colgan, to O'Donnell's work. This misled Reeves, p. 17n., and those who followed him without firsthand knowledge of O'Donnell's *Life*.

**47** Adomnán makes the point again at II 45. He refers to the Mosaic Law, Deut. 19:15: 'One witness shall not rise up against a man for any iniquity . . .; at the mouth of two witnesses, or at the mouth of three witnesses shall the matter be established'. This principle is frequently cited in the New Testament (Matt. 18:16, John 8:17, 2 Cor. 13:1, 1 Tim. 5:19), and was included in the section on testimony in the Irish canon collection, *Hib.*,16. 7.

**48** The fact that the songs were in Irish shows that Adomnán here uses Britain to refer to the Irish-speaking parts of Scotland.

**49** This is a recurrent expression in the Life, though the wording varies a little: *quamuis absens corpore praesens tamen spiritu* in this passage, elsewhere *quamlibet longe absentem tamen spiritu praesentem* (II 39, p. 191) and *quamlibet longe absens corpore spiritu tamen praesens* (II 42). The source is clearly St Paul, 1 Cor. 5:3, *absens corpore praesens autem spiritu*, 'absent in body but present in spirit'. The same idea takes a different form in I 37, where the saint's spirit meets his monks to refresh them though in the bodily sense he is nowhere near.

**50** 1 Cor. 6:17.

**51** See below, I 43 and n. 189.

**52** Structural sentences, or *diuisiones*, such as this are used at intervals throughout the *Life* (I 1, 50; II 10, 19, 21, 34, 38, 43, 46; III 1, 16). They highlight where Adomnán has grouped stories by similarity of subject-matter. Both in this arrangement and in the use of *diuisiones*, Picard detects 'a definite touch of the grammarian'; 'Structural patterns', p. 78.

**53** ST MUNNU OF TAGHMON St Fintan mac Tulcháin, who is better known by the hypocoristic form of his name as St Munnu, died in AU 635. This story, set in 597, the year of St Columba's death, when Fintan was a young man, takes place in the far north of Ireland where Fintan was living with Columb Crag only one day's journey from Derry. Nothing further is known of Columb Crag. Adomnán, in referring to Fintan as abbot at this stage, has backdated his position in later life.

Different sources give different versions of St Fintan's lineage. Adomnán is the oldest witness, and he says that Fintan mac Tulcháin belonged to the moccu Moie, a population group mentioned only here and below (I 18). From these two passages one can infer that the moccu Moie lived near Derry, at a convenient landfall for a boat from Iona. The Life of St Fintan or Munnu, which probably dates from the eighth century, provides a different ancestry, saying that the saint's father's kin were the Cenél Conaill, the same lineage as St Columba, while his mother's were the Uí Maini, another branch of the Uí Néill but a minor one, settled at this date in Tethbae. The Genealogies of Saints (as collected in the early eleventh century, and perhaps therefore representing a later view) are different again, tracing St Fintan's paternal descent back to Fiacha Riatai, i.e., Fiachu Roíde, ancestor of the Corco Roíde, a lineage subordinate to the Uí Néill in the midlands.

St Fintan's principal church, Tech Munnu (now Taghmon, Co. Wexford), is situated in the south of Leinster, but his Life tells of a good deal of travelling before he established his monastery there. Another Tech Munnu, now Taghmon, Co. Westmeath, is situated in the territory of Corco Roíde. The Life (§ 7) includes a shorter telling of the story here about his coming to Iona, focusing on St Columba's prophetic words to Baithéne. A rather different story is told in the Life of St Cainnech, § 26.

54 THE FOUNDATION OF DERRY Adomnán mentions Derry three times: here and in the story of Librán (II 39) we see monks travelling between Iona and Derry, and in I 20 the holy man Báetán is said to have been buried close to the church at Derry. The fact that Adomnán does not explicitly mention the monastery of Derry is probably insignificant; he was not concerned with the particulars of church-foundations. He calls the place *Daire Calgaich*, a name that continues in use in the annals from the seventh to the tenth century; the place was later known as *Daire Coluimb Chille*, and in the twelfth century the abbot of Derry was the coarb of St Columba. The Annals of Ulster record in 546 that '*Daire Coluimb Chille* was founded', but the form of name shows that this is a late retrospective entry, and the date is therefore unreliable. In 620 the death of Fiachra mac Ciaráin is entered in the Annals of Ulster, and the same entry in Tigernach describes him as 'second founder of

*Daire Calgaich*'. Fiachra's father, Ciarán, was the brother of Áed mac Ainmirech, king of the Northern Uí Néill (see n. 204) and a kinsman of St Columba. This Áed was reputed to have first given Derry, previously a royal fort, to the saint, but the story is not found before the eleventh or twelfth century. In any case, the story as told in the *Liber hymnorum* preface to the hymn *Noli pater indulgere* and in the Middle Irish homily (§ 32) involves not only King Áed but also St Mobí, a saint of the generation before Columba. If the connection with Áed is accepted, the date of Derry's foundation cannot have been before the death of Áed's father Ainmire in 569; it would therefore have been subsequent to the founding of Iona. Áed himself did not become king until the 580s, pointing to a still later date. But, since his involvement is unproven, these dates are entirely speculative.

The Middle Irish homily, written at Derry in the twelfth century, treats Derry as St Columba's first monastery, but this is a *parti pris* view. It cannot be consistent with Áed's role but explains the late-entered annal claiming a foundation as early as 546. The site was perhaps donated by Áed mac Ainmirech; his donation may have been confirmed or enhanced by his nephew before 620. It appears from Adomnán's account that Derry served as the Irish point of departure for sailing between Northern Uí Néill lands and Iona. Since much less is said about Derry than about Durrow, we may perhaps infer that Derry's major development happened at a later date.

55 ST BAITHÉNE, SECOND ABBOT OF IONA Baithéne's father and St Columba's were brothers; the two holy men were therefore first cousins. Baithéne and his brother Cobthach were counted as two of St Columba's companions in the founding of Iona (see n. 356), and Baithéne is mentioned many times in the Life. He appears as St Columba's disciple (*alumnus*) here and in III 18; Adomnán uses the same word of St Columba at III 2 in relation to Cruithnechán, his foster-father (*nutritor*), and it may be legitimate to suppose that Adomnán regarded Baithéne as the saint's foster-son. Like St Columba, Baithéne was a monk in priest's orders (II 15). He seems to have been the saint's right-hand man, sharing authority with the saint on *Hinba* (I 21), directing the work of the monks in Iona (I 37), and even advising the saint on how to deal with a penitent (I 22). He is most often mentioned in connection with Tiree (I 19, II 15), where he was prior of the monastery at Mag Luinge (I 30, 41). He also, like St Columba, put his hand to copying manuscripts (I 23) and was knowledgeable in the Scriptures (I 22). Baithéne's absence in Eigg at one point left no one with the saint who was able to

record his inspired prophecies and teachings (III 18). His succession to St Columba seems to have been appropriate in terms of his kinship with the saint, his personal relationship, and his natural qualities and ability (III 23, p. 228). One may perhaps compare the statement attributed to an Irish synod: 'It is right that who would be abbot should be first a monk, that who would succeed be first a loyal son, and that who would teach be first a pupil' (*Hib.*, 37. 7).

Baithéne was born in 536 according to the Annals of Tigernach, where he is called *daltae Coluimb Chille*, the Irish equivalent of *alumnus*, with the same dual meaning, 'foster-son, pupil'. The date of his death was probably 600; although the Annals of Ulster give 598, this is three years after their incorrect obit for St Columba. If these entries reflect annal-keeping at Iona, one can hardly admit an error in the length of Baithéne's tenure of the abbacy, whereas an error in converting to Anno Domini is easily accepted. Three years from the true date would be 600. The Annals of Tigernach favour 601, saying that Baithéne was in his sixty-sixth year. In Adomnán's time he was commemorated on 9 June, the feast day of St Columba himself (II 45). Although coincidence cannot be ruled out, it seems remarkable that both St Columba's successor and St Brigit's should have died on the anniversary of their patron's death; it was perhaps rather a convention that the saint's disciple be commemorated along with the saint.

56 THE NAME OF IONA This is the first reference by name to *Ioua insula*; the mention is entirely casual, and at no stage does Adomnán enter into an account of the foundation, or a description of the island or the monastery.

The name 'Iona', which I have used throughout this translation, is relatively modern, being found in manuscripts of the fourteenth century and later. It was also used in late medieval inscriptions, but its origin seems to have been a misreading of *Ioua insula*, Adomnán's name for the island. Its adoption in common use, however, is much more recent, apparently dating from the late eighteenth century, perhaps under the influence of Dr Johnson's use of this name in his much quoted panegyric.

From the ninth century for nearly a thousand years the island was generally called *Ì Coluimb Chille* (in various spellings). The word *Ì* 'island' entered Scottish Gaelic from Old Norse *ey*, but the name of the island appears as *Hii* or *Ie* at a date much earlier than Norse influence was felt. Thus, although *Ì Coluimb Chille* was for centuries understood as 'the island of Columb Cille', its original meaning was different. The importance of St Columba's monastery insured that the name is frequently mentioned in the records of the seventh and eighth centuries, and all the spellings are collected by Reeves, pp. 258–62. They were analysed by Watson, *Celtic Place-names*, pp. 87–90, who divides the forms into two series: *Io* or *Eo*, deriving from **iuo-*, is related to OIr. *eó* 'stem, trunk', which in MIr. was chiefly used of yew trees; the second series, *Hii*, *Ia*, *Ì*, may be from the same stem.

The question of meaning has never been adequately answered.

A traditional explanation told in the island and recorded about 1700 by Martin Martin, p. 256, is that *Ì* derives from the feminine object pronoun, as Columba cried on approaching Iona, *Chim ì* 'I see her'. The same story is given in 1771 by 'An Irish tourist', though the phrase is there given as *Sud ì* 'Yonder she'. These versions may dimly recollect a stanza quoted in Manus O'Donnell's *Life of St Columba*, § 202, in which on landing at Iona Columba says *Dochím hÍ, bendacht ar gach súil docí* 'I see Iona, a blessing on each eye that sees it.' The name has, in fact, been mistaken for the pronoun. Such homespun etymology was soon overlaid with more poetical inspiration.

The only native explanation of the form Iona appears to be *Ì Eòin* 'St John's Island'; this is cited by John Walker in 1764, who comments on the strength of oral tradition in the island, and by 'An Irish tourist' in 1771.

When Romantic interest in Iona began, from Pennant onwards, there sprang up in the late eighteenth and early nineteenth centuries a number of bogus 'Gaelic' explanations of Iona, which will be found in old guide-books and occasionally in more recent popular literature. The Revd Dugal Campbell, for example, in 1792, calls the island I or Icolumkill, adding: 'In monkish writers, it is called Iona, which signifies Island of Waves. . . . The name Iona is now quite lost in the country, and it is always called I, except when the speaker would wish to lay an emphasis upon the word, when it is called Icolumkill' (p. 298). He adds in a note: 'Iona is, in Gaelic, spelt I-thonn' (pronounced 'ee honn'). This would indeed mean 'island of waves', but Campbell has admitted that the name was not used in Gaelic but by monkish writers (whose language was Latin, where it does not have this meaning). Another less widely cited explanation, equally bogus, is *Ì shona* 'blessed island' (Gael. *sona* 'fortunate, happy'; the combination is pronounced 'ee honna'), a derivation I have not noted before 1850, when it is mentioned by Graham and Keddie in the same year. It was probably coined by a contemporary guide.

Fordun and Pennant made the equation between Iona and the

Hebrew *jona* 'dove', already mentioned in connection with St Columba's name. Pennant sometimes names the island *Jona* in allusion to this. The author of *The Native Steam-boat Companion* (1845) thought this was a mere joke: 'Some wag, I suppose, by way of gaggery, put it into the noddle of Mr Pennant that Iona comes from the Hebrew, and signifies a dove!' (p. 124). Fanciful though this is, it may have helped to popularize the form Iona, which has now supplanted all others in the English language.

57 Oisséne mac Ernáin is not recorded elsewhere (unless he be the priest Oissíne mentioned in the list of priests, *CGSH*, § 705. 235). The moccu Néth Corb were presumably the lineage descended from Nia Corb, an ancestor-figure of the Osraige, who occupied an area on either side of the River Nore, the boundary of Leinster and Munster. One cannot guess how or where Oisséne and Adomnán met, but the statement that Oisséne was a monk of St Fintan/Munnu must presumably connect him with the Leinster monastery of Taghmon. There are two men named Oisséne mentioned in a list of the community of Taghmon contained in the Martyrology of Tallaght (*Book of Leinster*, VI, 1642).

58 Ernéne mac Craséni died in AU 635; his obit is part of the same entry as St Munnu's. For this reason Dr Smyth conjectured that Adomnán ordered these two chapters (I 2–3) in the light of the obit, 'Death of Fintan mac Tulcháin and of Ernéne mac Craséni'. This led him to infer further that the Iona chronicle, which was later incorporated into the Annals of Ulster, contained this entry and that it was available to Adomnán; Smyth, 'The earliest Irish annals', pp. 38–40.

Columba prophesied that Ernéne would be 'famous through all the churches of Ireland', and one may suppose that to Adomnán and his audience the prophecy appeared fulfilled. Although Ernéne's reputation lasted at least a century, it has made little impression on the historical record, so that we know nothing of his achievements. He is commemorated in MTall. at 18 August as Erníne mac Cresíne of Ráith Noí in Uí Garrchon. He is probably the person listed under the hypocoristic form Moernóc mac Cruisíne in the list of homonymous saints (*CGSH*, § 707. 766).

59 THE FOUNDATION OF DURROW The date of the founding of Durrow is far from certain. The reference to Ailither as abbot of Clonmacnoise (see n. 60) provides guidelines, since he became abbot in

AU 585 on the death of Mac Nisse and died in AU 599. Reeves, p. 24n., identifies Ailither with a saint of Muicinis, a church in Lough Derg, who was commemorated on 12 May, but in this he was in error; Ailither of Clonmacnoise was commemorated on 7 January, MTall. Nothing is known of Ailither's work; Ryan, 'Abbatial succession', p. 494. At AU 589 the death is recorded of Áed mac Brénainn, king of Tethbae, and a note added by Scribe H[2] in the margin says: 'It is he who granted Durrow to Columb Cille'; this corresponds to the entry in the Annals of Tigernach, which may date from the tenth century. Moreover, a Middle Irish poem, *Dia do beth, a Chormaic cáin*, preserved in a sixteenth-century collection of poetry related to St Columba, refers to Durrow as 'the monastery (*cathair*) of Áed mac Brénainn'. Although his own territory lay some way north of Durrow, Áed had been successful as king of Tethbae, and as early as 562 had defeated the king of Tara, the harassed Diarmait mac Cerbaill (see n. 157), at the battle of Cúl Uinsen. There is, however, no other evidence to corroborate his exercising dominion in Uí Failge, the territory where Durrow lay. A date between 585 and 589 for the foundation, therefore, depends on some uncertain evidence. It is perhaps possible to explain the Tethbae connection in another way: in the late tenth and eleventh centuries, the Uí Tadgáin dynasty of Tethbae was associated with Durrow; their influence may have led to the formulation of a supposed historical involvement in the founding of the monastery. See Herbert, *Iona, Kells, and Derry*, p. 32.

Bede (III 4) specifically says that Columba had founded Durrow before he left Ireland: 'Before he came to Britain, he had founded a noble monastery in Ireland known in the Irish language as *Dearmach*, the field of oaks, because of the oak forest in which it stands.' As often in these matters the Irish evidence is preferable.

For what it is worth, the Middle Irish homily on St Columba says that the site of Durrow was given by the king of Tethbae, but the fact that this text arranges Columba's Irish foundations on the basis of a circular route from Derry makes their order debatable, and the text useless from the point of view of dating.

**60** Clonmacnoise was founded in AU 548 by St Ciarán, who died in the following year. (Ryan, 'Abbatial succession', pp. 492–3, argued instead for a foundation in January 545, but in so doing he sets too much store by the reference to the day of the week in the Middle Irish homily on St Ciarán.) Clonmacnoise was rapidly established as a large and important monastery. Its position where two major routes crossed – the north–south route by the River Shannon and an important east–west route along a glacial ridge or esker – must have helped in this development.

61 The Latin text merely says 'those who were in the fields' and 'those who were inside' followed *their* abbot. Reeves, p. 24n., takes those in the fields as 'external dependants' rather than monks, and Forbes, p. 9, and MacCarthy, p. 16, both translate 'all flocked from their little grange farms'; but the context is their coming together to lead Columba to the church, and the later reference to 'the pressing crowd of brethren' suggests that all were members of the monastic community. Adomnán several times mentions monks working in the fields (I 37, II 28, 44).

62 The *uallum monasterii* was generally a bank marking the limits of the monastic enclosure. Its function was more as a boundary than a defensive rampart. The line of the vallum at Clonmacnoise has not been identified, even from aerial photographs. On the vallum at Iona, see n. 281.

63 Reeves, p. 24n., interprets the words *de lignis piramidem* as referring to a canopy, following an example from Du Cange. Fowler, p. 19n., points out that in *De Locis Sanctis* II 4 and 7 Adomnán uses the word for the enclosure around a tomb; in these instances, Meehan, *Adamnan's De Locis*, pp. 77, 79, translates *lapidea piramis* as 'stone coping'. The most common use of the word in Hiberno-Latin is to designate a tomb or grave – a reference to the function rather than the shape of ancient pyramids. Adomnán, however, appears to use the word to mean a rectangular enclosure, here made of wooden staves and designed to protect the saint from the crowd; 'a kind of barrier of branches', as Anderson and Anderson translate the phrase.

64 Compare Matt. 9:20, 14:36.

65 I have here interpreted rather than translated the Latin: *lingua quoque eius salubri et doctrina eloquentia a Deo donabitur* is the reading of A, later altered to *et doctrina et eloquentia*. Anderson and Anderson translate: 'his tongue also will receive from God eloquence, with healthful doctrine'. Bullough, 'Columba, Adomnan, Iona', p. 120n., and Bieler [review of Anderson and Anderson], p. 180, preferred the reading of B, *salubri et doctrinali eloquentia* 'with salutary and didactic eloquence', an interpretation that the Andersons, p. 218n., rejected as unsatisfactory (though in

the second edition, p. 26n., Mrs Anderson has changed her mind). I agree with Bullough, and regard the sense as clear. *Salubris* does not mean merely 'healthful' but also 'saving', 'leading to salvation' (compare II 4 and n. 221); *doctrinalis* means 'for teaching', *doctrina* that which is taught, especially Christian doctrine. The expression is no more than a little elliptical, 'eloquence in teaching and bringing salvation'.

**66** On Ségéne and Failbe, see Introduction, pp. 36–41, 43

**67** This is Adomnán's only mention of the Easter controversy (see Introduction, pp. 36–8, 42, 48–51, 53, 76), and it is especially interesting that he does not put forward his own convictions.

**68** ST CAINNECH OF AGHABOE. St Cainnech, founder of Achad Bó (see II 13, III 17), died about 600 – his 'repose' is entered twice in the annals, at AU 599 and AU 600. The Annals of Tigernach say that he was in his eighty-seventh year, but the Annals of Ulster calculated his birth to 527 or 521.

Adomnán is probably the earliest witness to the cult of St Cainnech, whom he presents as a monastic founder (III 17), naming his monastery as Achad Bó (II 13), now Aghaboe, Co. Laois, which lay in the territory of Osraige, between Leinster and Munster. In III 17 Adomnán identifies Cainnech's lineage as the moccu Dalann. There exists a Life of St Cainnech in *Codex Salmanticensis*, probably composed in the eighth century. From this we learn that the moccu Dalann, there called Corco Dalonn, came from the north of Ireland and were one of the families of the Ciannacht (whose name survives in the barony of Keenaght, Co. Derry; Reeves, p. 121n.). His own Life names his birthplace in Latin as *in Valle Pellis*, but this has not been identified. It is clear, however, that Cainnech's lineage was one of those subject to the Northern Uí Néill. Cainnech was fostered among his mother's people in Leinster, and his principal church lay in the south.

The Life of St Cainnech describes a period in his career when he lived in Britain. It includes an episode 'at the other side of Druim Alban' (§ 24), using a phrase borrowed from Adomnán (see n. 283). There are several stories involving St Columba (§§ 20, 26–8, 54). One of these, § 28, corresponds to the present story in the Life of St Columba, and is actually a verbal adaptation of Adomnán's words. Another, § 54, is based on Adomnán's Life, II 13, but the wording in that case is less close. These passages constitute the best evidence for the circulation of Adomnán's Life in Ireland soon after it was written, and also show that the Life of St Cainnech cannot be earlier than *c.* 700.

69 Hospitality to visitors is a constant theme in the Life, and Adomnán several times mentions the monastic guest-house. In Columba's time this was built of withies (II 3), probably on a frame of larger timbers. Strangers were lodged in the guest-house (I 32, II 39, p. 188), sometimes for several months at a stretch (III 7). It was presumably large enough to accommodate quite a few visitors at once; lay visitors of high status, however, accompanied by their retainers, were not necessarily housed here (II 23). Members of the *familia* who were normally resident outside Iona also lodged in the guest-house (I 31). Compare II 39, p. 193, where a monk from the Columban house in Tiree dies while staying in the guest-house at Durrow.

70 ST COLMÁN ELO OF LYNALLY Colmán is given his patronymic, 'mac Beognai', in the text of the chapter here and at II 15, but in the chapter heading he is identified by his lineage, 'moccu Sailni'. In the later story Colmán is described as a priest on the occasion of his last meeting with St Columba, in the year before the saint's death. Yet here Adomnán refers to him as a bishop, which Reeves, p. 125n., took to be an error.

He is best known as St Colmán Elo, founder of Lann Elo or Lynally, Co. Offaly, a church not many miles from St Columba's monastery at Durrow. At his obituary notice in the Annals of Tigernach, he is called Colmán Elo moccu Seilli; he died in AU 611, aged 55 according to AT. The Life of St Colmán Elo, which is best preserved in the *Codex Salmanticensis*, and which may date from the late seventh or eighth century, gives him the patronymic 'mac Beugne', but says that he belonged to the Uí Néill; the latter statement is not corroborated by other sources, but probably reflects the fact that Lynally is situated among the Southern Uí Néill. It has been suggested that his people may be identified with the Dál Saillni, located in Co. Antrim according to the genealogies in the Great Book of Lecan; this would make St Colmán belong to the Dál nAraide (Doherty, 'Cult of St Patrick', pp. 89–90). This may be confirmed by a passage added when his Life was revised by an unknown scholar from Leinster in the early thirteenth century; according to this addition in the D-text, Colmán was considered the second patron after St Mac Nisse of Connor, the principal church of Dál nAraide. The early Life seeks to bring Colmán into contact with St Columba several times: one story parallels this one (see n. 73), another suggests that it was at St Columba's request that Áed Sláine, overking of the Southern Uí Néill, gave Lann Elo to St Colmán (§ 14), and in a third Colmán turns aside an imponderable question with the words,

'Surely you do not want to make me a prophet like Columb Cille?' (§ 42).

Colmán is said to have been the author of an ancient devotional work *Apgitir Chrábaid* 'the Alphabet of Piety'. The manuscripts of the work that supply this attribution cannot be shown to have any sound basis for it; nevertheless, students of Irish philology have long accepted that the language of the text is compatible with a very early date, around the beginning of the seventh century. P. Ó Néill, 'The date and authorship of *Apgitir Chrábaid*', has further argued that the sources of ideas in the Alphabet, which include John Cassian, are also compatible with this date. Another work claimed for St Colmán is the Latin hymn to St Patrick, *Audite omnes amantes*; the early Life of St Colmán does not deal with the question of authorship, but it tells how he had a vision of St Patrick during the singing of this hymn (§ 33).

71 Adomnán uses the name *Rechru* here and the adjectival form *Rechrea insula* at II 41; there can be no doubt that the island is Rathlin Island off the coast of Antrim, used as a port of call on the voyage between Iona and Ireland.

The same name *Rechru*, however, is also used of Lambay Island off the coast of Co. Dublin. The church of *Rechru* was founded in 635 according to AU, to which AT adds that the founder was Ségéne, abbot of Iona. The Middle Irish homily on St Columba attributes the foundation to Columba himself, but identifies the island as lying off the coast of Brega, i.e., as Lambay Island; see Reeves, pp. 164–5n. St Comgall of Bangor also tried to found a church on *Rechru* according to his Life (which is now known only in versions dating from the thirteenth century).

Anderson and Anderson, pp. 48, 91, advanced an argument that after 661 Abbot Cumméne lived in Irish Dál Riata, on Rathlin Island (mistaking this for the site of the church founded by Ségéne), when writing his book on the miracles of St Columba (see n. 360). I find the argument impossible to accept. It hinged, first, on an interpretation of the words *huius regni* in the extract from Cumméne as a reference to Irish Dál Riata, which Mrs Anderson has now withdrawn (*Kings*, p. 153); and, second, on the supposition that *Rechru* was a Columban church in that district, which is not established.

72 THE WHIRLPOOL OF CORRYVRECKAN Adomnán locates the whirlpool of Corryvreckan near Rathlin Island; other Irish sources of later date are in agreement with him, placing it on the route between Ireland

and Scotland. Here tides and counter-tides create a swirling of water at the west end of the island, more recently known as *Slog na mara* 'Swallowing of the sea'. The legend of its ancient name is first told in a short Irish dictionary or encyclopaedia, *Sanas Cormaic* 'Cormac's Glossary', which is usually dated to about 900:

Coire Breccáin, i.e., a great whirlpool which is between Ireland and Scotland to the north, i.e., a meeting place of many seas: the sea which surrounds Ireland from the west, the sea which surrounds Scotland from the north-east, and the sea from the south between Ireland and Scotland. Then it takes them each in turn just like whirling spirals and puts each one in the place of another, just like the paddle of a mill-wheel as it goes past, and sucks them down into the depths, so that there is an open-mouthed cauldron which would suck down the whole of Ireland and would put it in all together. Again it vomits up that mouthful and its thunderous belching and its crashing and roaring can be heard among the clouds just like a cauldron boiling on the fire.

Breccán then was a fine merchant of the Uí Néill and was trading with fifty currachs between Ireland and Scotland. They happened upon that whirlpool and it swallowed them all up so that no one escaped from it to bring news of the destruction.

Breccán mac Máine maic Néill then, so other books tell, used to trade between Ireland and Scotland with fifty currachs when on one occasion they fell into the whirlpool and no one escaped from it to bring news of the destruction, and their death was not known until Lugaid Dalléices came to Bangor. His followers then came to the strand of Inber Becc and they found there a small bare skull and they took it with them to Lugaid. They asked him whose it was and he said to them: 'Put the end of the poet's wand upon it.' They did this and Lugaid said: 'By a death from the high seas has Breccán perished, either by water or the whirlpool. This is the head of Breccán's lap dog and this is a small thing from something great, for Breccán and all his followers have perished in yonder whirlpool.'

It should be remembered that mill-wheels at this date turned horizontally around a vertical axle.

Later accounts are given by Reeves, pp. 262–3, from the prose *Dindsenchus* (Place-name stories) in the Great Book of Lecan, fol. 253, and from Manus O'Donnell's *Life of St Columba*, § 352. By the fifteenth century, when the Scottish chronicler Fordun described the Hebrides, the name had been transferred to the now famous 'whirlpool', the Gulf of Corryvreckan, between the islands of Jura and Scarba. The geographical indicators here show that Adomnán cannot have meant this tidal overfall.

73 The earliest version of the Life of St Colmán, § 13, has a less detailed but more complete account:

Once when St Colmán was sailing away into exile, it chanced that he and his companions came into Corryvreckan. At that point St Colmán prayed and made the sign of the Cross, and in that hour St Columba in Iona said: 'Pray all of you that Colmán Elo be not drowned to the bottom of the sea.' For the sake of both saints, the brethren were saved and came to Iona, and on their arrival St Columba and his monks rejoiced.

The story goes on to say how St Columba sent Colmán back to Ireland, where his future lay.

74 Cormac Ua Liatháin (see n. 323) is mentioned three times by Adomnán, here, at II 42, and III 17. The territory of Uí Liatháin lies east of Cork, between Cork Harbour and the estuary of the Blackwater. On the pursuit of a retreat at sea, see n. 109.

75 The River Moy forms the boundary between Co. Mayo and Co. Sligo before entering the Atlantic in Killala Bay; it is mentioned by Tírechán, §§ 42, 45. Erris lies still further west, on the coast of Co. Mayo.

76 The Benedictine vow of lifelong stability in one monastery did not apply in the Irish church, but monks were supposed not to leave a religious house without the consent of the abbot. An exception would be allowed if the abbot were openly irreligious. In the middle of the sixth century this principle and its exception were set out by Gildas in his letter to Uinniau (on whom see n. 210):

Where an abbot has so far fallen away from the work of God that he deserves to be barred from the table of holy men and even to be loaded with the charge of fornication, not on suspicion but as a clearly detected evil, you should welcome his monks with no scruple as ones taking refuge from hell fire, without any consultation with their abbot. But as for those whose abbot we do not, for any ill reputation, bar from the table of holy men, we ought not to take them if he does not agree. Still less should we welcome those who come from holy abbots, under suspicion only because they possess animals and vehicles because it is the custom of their country or because of their weakness (Gildas, fragments of letter to Uinniau, § 4, tr. Winterbottom, p. 81).

Similarly, an early Irish text of uncertain date but perhaps sixth-century, *Synodus Episcoporum*, § 34, says: 'A monk who goes wandering without consulting his abbot is to be punished' (Bieler, *The Irish Penitentials*, p. 59). Another text, of the same or slightly later date, *Synodus Patricii*, § 21, says: 'Of monks to be retained or sent out. Let everyone enjoy his fruit in the church in which he has been instructed, unless the cause of greater success requires that he should bear fruit in another's church with the permission of his abbot' (Bieler, ibid., p. 193).

77 Adomnán twice dates St Columba's pilgrimage from the battle of Cúl Drebene, which we know to have taken place in AU 561. On the first occasion, in the second preface, his words are *anno secundo post . . . bellum* 'in the year following after the battle'; here he says *duobus transactis annis* 'when two years were past'. We know by subtracting thirty-four years of Columba's pilgrimage from 597, the year of his death, that his pilgrimage began in 563. When Adomnán says 'in the year following after the battle' (i.e., the second year in inclusive reckoning), he does not mean 562, for that would contradict what he says here. I take it that he is measuring time from the battle and not referring to calendar years. If St Columba began his pilgrimage in 563 before the second anniversary of the battle, Adomnán's expression is compatible with the chronological data.

78 The identification of the battle mentioned here, *bellum quod Scotice dicitur Ondemmone*, with the battle of Móin Daire Lothair (AU 563), goes back to Colgan, *Trias*, p. 374 n. 37, but was based on a conjecture in White's transcript of A, 'Mona-moire' (so printed by Colgan and the Bollandists). The association of *Ondemmone* with Móin Daire Lothair rests, first, on the fact that both happened in 563; second, both were victories for an alliance of the Northern Uí Néill over the Cruithin. The second element of the name as given by Adomnán, *móne*, is the genitive of *móin* 'bog'; the first element is probably *ond* 'stone'. The 'stone of the bog' was perhaps a landmark in the bog of Móin Daire Lothair. The information in the Annals of Ulster led Reeves, p. 32n., to locate the site in Eilne, near Coleraine.

79 Strictly read, this passage indicates that in 563, at the time of his first departure from Ireland, Columba visited King Conall mac Comgaill, the ruler of Scottish Dalriada. It has often been observed that an immediate visit to the king, before the foundation of a new monastery, may have been the occasion for Conall to grant the island of Iona to Columba, as

mentioned retrospectively by the annals in their notice of the king's death in 574: 'The death of Conall mac Comgaill, who granted Iona to Columba, after fifteen years as king'. See Introduction, p. 16.

**80** Ainmire mac Sétna, king of Cenél Conaill and Columba's first cousin, also fought in the battle of Cúl Drebene. Mac Ercae is a byname of Muirchertach mac Muiredaig, king of Cenél nÉogain, who died in AU 536. His sons Domnall and Forcus were on the winning side in a series of battles from the 540s (see Byrne, *Irish Kings*, pp. 102–3), and may – if later regnal lists may be trusted – have held the kingship of Tara jointly for a year after the death of Diarmait mac Cerbaill. Their last success is recorded in AU 566, the year of Domnall's death. The high kingship then passed to Ainmire mac Sétna.

The Annals of Tigernach indicate that a considerable grouping of the Cruithin was involved in the battle of Móin Daire Lothair, and that Áed Brecc and several other Cruithin kings died. Eochaid Laib, who survived the battle, is not mentioned in either annals or genealogies – his lineage must have been of little importance among the different groups of the Cruithin. His son Éogan mac Echdach Laib died in AU 611. The annals indicate that the battle was in origin an internal struggle among the Cruithin, from which Báetán mac Cinn emerged with advantage. He persuaded both branches of the Northern Uí Néill to intervene, rewarding them with territory. There is a short poem on the battle incorporated in the Annals of Ulster.

Byrne, on the basis of the last sentence of this chapter, comments: 'This seems to be the latest mention of the use of chariots in battle' ('Ireland of St Columba', p. 55, n. 50). I know little of early Irish battlefield methods, but Adomnán does not say Eochaid fought from a chariot, merely that he escaped in one. The two-wheeled chariot continued for many years as a means of quick transport for persons of rank (see n. 167).

**81** The date and circumstances of this battle are a matter for guesswork. First, the *Miathi* are called 'barbarians' by Adomnán, so we must infer that they were not an Irish-speaking group from Dalriada. He does not explicitly associate them with the Picts, a term that Adomnán uses only of the people of northern Pictland. Ussher ingeniously suggested, as long ago as 1639, that the name represents the tribe called *Maeatae*, mentioned by the Greek writer Dio Cassius in his account of events on the northern frontier of Roman Britain in AD 197–211. Their territory has been located on the basis of two place-names that are thought to preserve the name: Dumyat, north-east of Stirling in the Ochil Hills, and Myot Hill, south of the town.

Adomnán indicates that the battle was a costly victory, and on this basis Anderson and Anderson, p. 42, inferred that 'the high losses incurred . . . suggest that the assault was made against a well-defended fortress'. Both Dumyat and Myot Hill bear traces of fortifications on the summits (Wainwright, 'The Picts and the Problem', pp. 23–4), and Feachem has suggested that the fort at Dumyat was the principal centre of the *Miathi* ('Fortifications', p. 78). The Andersons therefore comment that this may have been the site of the battle. I doubt this argument: Adomnán says that the *Miathi* 'were turned in flight', which suggests they were not defending their main stronghold.

The association of the battle against the *Miathi* with the battle of Manu, 'in which Áedán mac Gabráin was victor' (AU 582 or 583), seems to me weaker than Anderson and Anderson, p. 43, allowed (and in the second edition, p. xx, Mrs Anderson has revised accordingly). *Manu* in Irish represents Welsh *Manaw*, the name of a British territory occupied by the *Votadini* (Welsh *Gododdin*), which extended from the environs of Stirling south and eastwards along the River Forth. Inasmuch as the arguments for localizing the *Miathi* may be trusted, their territory and *Manaw* may have bordered or overlapped. Yet it is hard to imagine Adomnán calling the *Votadini* barbarians, considering that they seem to have been Christian for more than a century. The very obscurity of the term *Miathi*, a whole tribal group beyond the grasp of history, suggests more an isolated highland group than a branch of the Pictish or British kingdoms.

**82** Early Irish and Scottish bells were handbells, varying from a few inches to over a foot in height. In St Columba's time such bells were made of iron, beaten flat then wrapped to form a flattened pyramid shape with a ring or grip at the top to hold the bell. There was no clapper and the bell was rung by striking it on the outside. Several such bells have been preserved both in Scotland and Ireland. The Irish examples have been discussed by Bourke, 'Early Irish hand-bells'.

In the *Life* the ringing of the bell is mentioned three times when the brethren were summoned to assemble in the church under exceptional circumstances (I 8, II 42, III 13). Only once do we hear of its use to call them to service (III 23, p. 229 ), but this was clearly its principal use.

**83** As mentioned in the table of chapter headings (p. 107), I 9–15 are all concerned with kings – the idea that links the chapters but which is not overtly indicated in the text.

84 ÁEDÁN MAC GABRÁIN, KING OF DALRIADA Áedán mac Gabráin is the first king of Scottish Dalriada to be more than a shadowy figure, though even here we know little more than a poor outline of his career as a political fighter. His father, Gabrán, had been leader of the Dalriada in the middle of the sixth century, and had been succeeded by his nephew, Conall mac Comgaill (d. 574). Áedán followed him as king, though the succession may have involved warfare, for the annals record a *bellum Telocho* in Kintyre, 'in which fell Dunchad son of Conall mac Comgaill and many others of the supporters of the sons of Gabrán'. The dating of this and other events in Áedán's reign is confused in the Annals of Ulster, there being sometimes two entries for the same event. Thus in 580 or 581 he led an expedition against the Picts in Orkney (see n. 324). In 582 or 583 he was the victor in a campaign described as *bellum Manonn* or *bellum Manand* 'the battle of Manu', which might have been against the people of Manaw Gododdin in the valley of the River Forth (see n. 81); Bannerman, *Studies*, pp. 83–4, has argued that this may have been one of several battles over the Isle of Man. Áedán's pyrrhic victory over the *Miathi* is mentioned by Adomnán (I 8–9); in it two of his sons, Artuir and Eochaid Find, were killed.

In 590 Áedán was involved in another unlocated battle, *bellum Leithreid*. In the year after Columba's death the annals record a battle in the Pictish province of Circhenn, in which Áedán was defeated. In the same year his sons Bran and Domangart fell in battle; Adomnán mentions only Domangart's death, in battle against the English. It is difficult to disentangle the entries for this year, but we know from Bede that Áedán was heavily defeated in 603, at a place called *Degsastan*, thought to have happened near Lochmaben in Dumfriesshire; it appears that he had led a considerable expeditionary force through the British kingdoms of the north to attack King Æthelfrith, and it may be supposed he acted in alliance with the Britons. Áedán is himself mentioned several times in Welsh texts dealing with the old British north, but it is not clear that his relations with the Britons were always peaceful (see n. 97). His last years are wholly obscure. His death is recorded in AU 606, but Bannerman has suggested that this obit, like those of Columba and Baithéne, was entered two or three years too early.

The three events of his reign to which Adomnán attaches great importance are all problematic. That Áedán was a participant in the meeting of kings at Druim Cett is hardly in doubt, though I have argued that this took place rather later in his reign than the date supplied by the annals (see n. 204). Columba's role in the inauguration of Áedán as king cannot be accepted without major qualifications, for the story too much reflects Adomnán's biblical approach to the subject of kingship (see n. 358), while Columba's designation of Áedán's successor may be wholly modelled on Samuel's choice of David to succeed Saul (see n. 85). These stories, together with that of Columba's prayers during the battle against the *Miathi* and the allusion to the royal lineage of Gabrán (II 22) tend to suggest that to Adomnán's Dalriadic audience Áedán was perceived as the major figure in the early history of the kingdom.

**85** Adomnán surely has in mind the scene in 1 Sam. 16:1–13 where Samuel passes over all Jesse's older sons, of whom only the first three are named, and then asks, 'Are here all thy children?' And Jesse answered, 'There remaineth yet the youngest', David, whom Samuel anoints as the future king of Israel at the Lord's direction. Adomnán's use of this Old Testament model in portraying Columba as one who chooses the future king is discussed in detail by Enright, *Iona, Tara, and Soissons*, pp. 15–19, and is important evidence that Adomnán was putting forward a biblical view of kingship; see Introduction, pp. 61–3. Significantly, the choosing of David is used in the *Hibernensis* to prove that a younger son may become king in preference to elder brothers; the passage (quoted by Enright, p. 27) appears only in the still unpublished B text of the canon collection and may be thought to contribute to the case for associating the collection with Adomnán (see n. 359).

**86** DOMNALL MAC ÁEDO, KING OF IRELAND Domnall mac Áedo was a kinsman of St Columba (see genealogical table, pp. xvi–xvii), and king of Cenél Conaill. He became high king about 628 and died in AU 642. If Domnall was in fosterage at the time of the meeting at Druim Cett, and if the annal date of 575 is accepted for this, he was already over sixty and still fighting for supreme power in 628–9 (see n. 206), and he would have been at least seventy-five years old at the time of his death, an exceptional age. Both these considerations lend support to my redating that meeting to *c.* 590 (see n. 204).

The inclusion of this story in the Life may well have had a political meaning for the Columban community. Domnall's important victory at Dún Cethirn is also mentioned by Adomnán (I 49), in connection with a prophecy made at the time of the meeting at Druim Cett. Finally, the extract, which is all that remains from Cumméne's book, singles out the attack on Domnall mac Áedo by the Dalriadic king Domnall Brecc as a breach of loyalty to Columba and his Irish kindred; this may have ended the relationship agreed at Druim Cett. It seems that when Cumméne was writing in the 630s or 640s Domnall was already a person of historical significance to the community in Iona.

In 642 the annals record 'Death of Domnall mac Áedo, king of Ireland, at the end of January'. No king had previously been given this title, and it can be compared with a mention of the death of 'Domnall, king of the Irish' in a Latin poem datable to the year 645 (Ó Cróinín, *Peritia* 2 (1983), 80–81). Leading up to this, the annals have chronicled his career in unusual detail from his defeat by Suibne Menn in 628 (see n. 206), through his success in Leinster in the same year, to his victories at Dún Cethirn in 629 and Mag Roth in 637. The annals also record that 'Domnall mac Áedo camped at Druim Nao' in 641, though the significance of this is not known, and in 639, exceptionally, the death of his wife, Duinsech. It seems probable that he achieved a greater importance and prestige in Ireland than previous Uí Néill overlords. Abbot Ségéne and his nephew Cumméne were keen to associate St Columba with these successes of his later kinsman, no doubt to the benefit of their community.

**87** See Introduction, pp. 27–8, and nn. 88, 204.

**88** The opening words of the chapter, 'At the same time and in the same place', take us back to the previous chapter, where the setting is the meeting of the kings at Druim Cett. Adomnán is the earliest witness to the business of this meeting, which was primarily concerned with the relationship between the king of Dál Riata, both in Ireland and Scotland, and the Uí Néill overlord, Áed mac Ainmirech (see n. 204). The story in I 10 of St Columba blessing Áed's son Domnall describes a minor incident that occurred during the meeting. At II 6 reference is made to various healings on that occasion. This chapter is presented as another such trifling incident.

Scandlán mac Colmáin, apparently a child at the time of the meeting, was evidently the son of a ruler and was held as hostage by King Áed mac Ainmirech for the good behaviour of his father. It is perhaps surprising that a royal child-hostage should be kept in irons, and that he should remain in the king's entourage on a visit of this kind. The young Scandlán appears to have been on public view. His father was probably Colmán, king of Osraige, who died in AT 607. Colmán's successor was called Cenn Fáelad, and we may infer that during his reign Scandlán was in exile from Osraige. When Scandlán gained the kingdom is not known, but (on the basis of the prophecy) it was not later than 613; for he died in AT 644 as king of Osraige, and would then have been well over seventy years old if reckoned from the annal date of 575. The annals call him Scandlán Mór.

There are several Middle Irish accounts of the meeting at Druim Cett (see n. 204). These make Scandlán Mór the *son* of Cenn Fáelad; the *freeing* of Scandlán from his hostageship is treated as one of three reasons for the convention, although Adomnán clearly indicates that Scandlán would not be released for some time; one of these accounts, among the *Liber Hymnorum* prefaces to *Amrae Coluimb Chille*, claims that in gratitude for his release Scandlán made a gift to St Columba of 160 plough-oxen, which was regularly paid by the Osraige to the *familia* of Iona, and that in return the coarbs of St Columba were 'soul friends' to the rulers of Osraige; see *Liber Hymnorum*, I 163, II 54. These later accounts are probably extrapolation from Adomnán's story of the saint's prophecy, but they show less acquaintance with or interest in the history of Osraige in the late sixth and early seventh centuries.

89 Báetán, son of Muirchertach Mac Ercae, was the brother of Domnall and Forcus, kings of Cenél nÉogain, who enjoyed great success in the early 560s (see n. 80). Eochaid mac Domnaill was his nephew, the son of Domnall mac Maic Ercae. Their ancestor Muiredach was the father of Muirchertach Mac Ercae. Coming from the lineage of Cenél nÉogain, Báetán and Eochaid were able to take over the leadership of the Northern Uí Néill on the death of Ainmire mac Sétna in 569. They were defeated and killed together in 572, as described in the annals: 'The killing of two descendants of Muiredach, namely Báetán mac Muirchertaig and Eochaid mac Domnaill in the third year of their reign. Crónán mac Tigernaig, king of the Ciannachta of Glenn Geimin, killed them.' It may be inferred, therefore, that Columba was in Ardnamurchan in that year.

90 Ardnamurchan, the westernmost promontory of mainland Britain, is indeed rough and rocky. It is named three times by Adomnán, here, and II 10, 22.

91 ST LASRÉN, THIRD ABBOT OF IONA Lasrén mac Feradaig's position as companion is distinguished from Diarmait's as servant. Lasrén's father, Feradach mac Ninnedo, was Columba's first cousin; his uncle, Báetán mac Ninnedo, was high king from 572 to 586. Columba and

Lasrén were therefore socially on the same level. Lasrén's career in the family of Iona may be pieced together from brief references. At this stage, in 572, Lasrén is the saint's companion while travelling on whatever business in Ardnamurchan. He had perhaps entered the community as a youth, in view of the family connection. Later, I 29, Adomnán tells a story about him when he was in charge of work on the great house at Durrow. If one could be sure of the date of founding of Durrow (see n. 59), this could be dated more precisely; it is almost certainly later in Lasrén's career, perhaps in the 580s or 590s. It would appear that Lasrén had been appointed prior of Durrow much as Baithéne – another cousin, but nearer in age to Columba – was made prior in Tiree. About 600 Lasrén succeeded Baithéne as abbot of Iona and died in that office in AU 605; he was commemorated on 16 September, MTall.

**92** ST COLUMBA'S SERVANT DIARMAIT Diarmait, Columba's personal servant, figures often in the Life as the confidant of many of the saint's prophecies. It is perhaps safe to assume that Diarmait played an important part in perpetuating the memory of these stories, some of which could hardly otherwise have been known – unless, the sceptic may say, Diarmait is merely a literary prop to add verisimilitude to the stories. In view of the attention to detail with which Adomnán introduces many minor characters, a high proportion of them unimportant members of the monastic community, this interpretation is unlikely. Taking Adomnán at his word, therefore, this may be the earliest datable mention of Diarmait, in 572. He is, however, mentioned as one of the saint's original companions in the list of these (see n. 356), and was the person to whom St Columba disclosed the death of St Brendan of Birr (III 11; see n. 374). The date of the latter event is uncertain but may be as early as AU 565. Diarmait remained a lifelong companion, and was with St Columba in his last hours (III 23). It would appear, therefore, that he served the saint for at least the thirty-four years of his pilgrimage, and had perhaps joined his household before 563. His loyalty to and love of St Columba emerge constantly from the stories told, and were reciprocated: at one point, when Diarmait was gravely ill, the saint prayed the Lord that he would not take Diarmait's soul before his own (II 30). The prayer was granted, and Adomnán adds that Diarmait survived the saint by many years. It is possible, but not demonstrable, that he lived long enough to participate in the collection of testimonies to the saint's powers.

93 This name is given in a mixture of Irish and Latin, *Muirbolc Paradisi*. *Muirbolc* 'sea bag' means a bay; the term also occurs in *Muirbolc Már* on Hinba (see n. 194) and in northern Ireland (Annals of Ulster, 731). Reeves, p. 41n., equated *muirbolc* with 'murlough', i.e., *muirloch* 'sea loch', a different word; Skene, p. 325, then identified the place with 'Port-na-Murloch' in Lismore, while Fowler, p. 47n., further noted that Lismore (*lios mór*) could be rendered 'great garden' and so inferred a link with *Paradisus*. Watson, *Celtic Place-names*, p. 79, squashed this flat; *Port nam Murlach* in Lismore, properly rendered, is 'harbour of the dogfish'. The context in Adomnán, as Watson realized, suggests that Paradise Bay is in Ardnamurchan, where the obvious candidate is the beautiful, enclosed Kentra Bay: its shape, and the fact that at low tide it is almost empty of water, make it fit the term *muirbolc*; it is not clear what *Paradisus* would imply in a place-name. The reference to arrivals here by sea from Ireland was taken to signify 'traders' by Skene, p. 325. It would be wild guessing to conjecture a trading post in Ardnamurchan; the reference may rather indicate the ubiquitous sea-links between Ireland and Scottish Dalriada.

94 Oengus mac Áedo Commain, alias Oengus Bronbachal, became king of Cenél Coirpri, and died in AU 649. A young man at the time of the prophecy, he must indeed have been an old man when he died, fifty-two years after the saint's death. Cenél Coirpri Gabra was a minor kingdom, with its centre at Granard, Co. Longford, from the mid-sixth century a part of the overkingdom of the Southern Uí Néill. Reeves, p. 41n., noted that the annals and Adomnán were in harmony, and that Adomnán also agreed with the genealogy in Mac Firbhisigh's Genealogies, p. 167, which made Oengus Bronbachal son of Áed son of Comman son of Tuathal Máelgarb. 'Such harmony', Reeves remarked, 'in three independent records is a remarkable attestation of their accuracy.' The genealogy demonstrates that Oengus belonged to the line of Coirpre mac Néill, from whom Tuathal Máelgarb was counted third in descent; Tuathal died in AU 544, a victim of Diarmait mac Cerbaill, who followed him as high king (Byrne, *Irish Kings*, pp. 90–92). Reeves mistakenly associated Oengus with Cenél Coirpri Droma Cliab of north Sligo.

It is not without interest to note that Iona was already in the saint's lifetime a refuge for rulers, or their heirs, temporarily displaced in the political strife of Ireland. In the seventh century it would serve the same role for exiled Northumbrian royalty.

95 Áed Sláine, son of Diarmait mac Cerbaill, belonged to the ruling lineage of the Southern Uí Néill. Diarmait had been high king for twenty years before his murder in 565 (see n. 157), but for more than thirty-five years thereafter this position passed to the Northern Uí Néill. In 598, following the death in battle of Áed mac Ainmirech, St Columba's Cenél Conaill cousin, overking of the Northern Uí Néill and high king (on whom see n. 204), Áed Sláine, then king of Brega, became high king, simultaneously with Colmán Rímid. Adomnán's use of this title here, and of Diarmait in I 36, is noteworthy. In 600 Áed was responsible for the killing of his nephew, Suibne, son of Colmán Mór mac Diarmata, who was the head of Cland Cholmáin (another prominent lineage of the Southern Uí Néill) and king of Meath. This was the first act in a long feud between the two principal lineages of the Southern Uí Néill, the kings of Brega and the kings of Meath. Suibne was presumably a rival to Áed's power in the midlands, and was disposed of so that Áed could concentrate on securing his position *vis-à-vis* Colmán Rímid. This Colmán Rímid, son of Báetán, was a nephew of Domnall and Forcus (on whom see n. 80), and belonged to the Northern Uí Néill lineage of Cenél nÉogain. He and Áed Sláine both died in AU 604, under different circumstances; the annalist adds that 'they held the kingship of Tara at the same time with equal power'. When Adomnán says that Áed 'held power over only part of the kingdom granted him', he presumably implies that Colmán Rímid was in fact able to exercise greater powers of overlordship than Áed. The period of four years and three months would seem to be the time from Suibne's murder in 600 to Áed's own death in 604.

Adomnán, however, does not mention that Áed's own death was a vengeance killing, instigated by Suibne's son, Conall (AU 604), but carried out – according to the Annals of Tigernach – by Conall's foster-brother Áed Guastan and Báegal Bile. On the political implications of this vendetta between the two lineages of the Southern Uí Néill, see Byrne, *Irish Kings*, p. 154; Charles-Edwards and Kelly, *Bechbretha*, pp. 128–9.

96 Adomnán's *parricidali . . . peccato* renders Irish *fingal* 'a killing within the *fine* or kin-group', for which parricide would be an appropriate translation.

97 Rhydderch ap Tudwal (usually known in Welsh sources as Rhydderch *Hael* 'the Generous') was king of the British territory of Strathclyde, which included the Clyde Valley and Ayrshire. His royal seat, at

the rock of Dumbarton, was situated on the north bank of the Clyde, but we do not know whether his kingdom extended further north into the highlands. He was one of four North British rulers who fought together against the English ruler of Bernicia about 585–90 according to the ninth-century *Historia Brittonum*.

In the sixth and seventh centuries the British kingdoms (speaking a language closely akin to Welsh) remained powerful, occupying a considerable area from the northern part of Cumbria across Galloway to Dumbarton. They were, however, steadily losing territory to the English of Northumbria, and for a time in the seventh century their kings were subject to the Northumbrian kings, Oswald, Oswiu and Ecgfrith. On the other hand, good relations generally prevailed between the British and their northern neighbours, the Picts and the Scots of Dalriada. Áedán mac Gabráin, however, may have been involved in hostilities against the British territory of Manaw in 582–3 (see n. 81). The Welsh triads hint that in Rhydderch's time Áedán may have attacked Dumbarton (see Bromwich, *Trioedd Ynys Prydain*, pp. 147, 504–5) – this in spite of what Adomnán portrays as a close relationship between both kings and St Columba.

**98** See n. 133.

**99** The two laymen, named as Meldán and Glasderc, are unidentifiable, even though neither name is a common one.

**100** THE BURIAL GROUND OF IONA The fame of Iona as a burial place, especially for rulers, whose bodies were sometimes carried long distances to be interred there, cannot with confidence be traced back to the age of St Columba. Even so, this story shows that burial for laymen as well as for the monks was accepted at Iona. Since Meldán's son died there, his burial on the island is perhaps not surprising. When Ernán mac Glasderc eventually died, his body was presumably brought to Iona. One of the Scottish regnal lists shows that most kings of Scotland from Kenneth mac Alpin (d. 858) to Malcolm Canmore (d. 1093) were buried in Iona (Anderson, *Kings*, pp. 266–8, 273–6). The kings previous to Kenneth in list D were Pictish kings; but it seems likely that the custom, far from being invented by Kenneth, continued the practice of Dalriadic kings. If in Adomnán's time a king might be expected to come to Iona for his 'ordination', the connection between Iona and the Dalriadic kings could easily have extended to burial custom.

There is also some later, retrospective evidence. It appears from verses in the tenth-century Life of St Adomnán that Bridei f. Bili, king of the Picts (d. 692), may have been carried to Iona in his coffin. If so, his burial was during Adomnán's abbacy. About 1100 the English historian Simeon of Durham says that King Ecgfrith, killed in battle in Pictland in 685 (see n. 350), was buried in Iona, again while Adomnán was abbot. We do not know the basis for his statement, but Simeon was presumably aware that in his own time Iona had provided a royal burial place for centuries.

How early the name Reilig Odrain came to be attached to the burial ground is not known. It may underlie the story told of St Odran in the Middle Irish homily but, if so, the connection is not made explicit until Manus O'Donnell's account in 1532 (see n. 365). The personal name Máel Odrain (I 20 and n. 113) shows that it could go back much earlier. The three royal tombs described by Monro in 1549 are not mentioned in independent sources and have left no trace. In his time tradition had it that forty-eight Scottish kings, besides others, were buried here. By the nineteenth century a line of late medieval grave-slabs was called 'The Ridge of Kings'. Although this name is previously recorded in the eighteenth century, we know that the slabs were rearranged and enclosed by rails as recently as 1868. None of this bears witness to an actual royal grave.

The numerous early grave-markers from the Reilig Odrain are mostly simple, cross-marked stones. Of those bearing inscriptions, none commemorates a king; see Introduction, pp. 71–2.

**101** Colgu mac Áedo Draigniche is mentioned again at III 20. His name is found in the Genealogies of the Saints, § 90, as 'Colgu of Cell Colgan at Áth Cluana Medraige, and Fáeliu his sister [*soror*], son of Áed Draignig son of Lugaid' etc. Reeves, p. 45n., knew this from the version in the Great Book of Lecan, fol. 41ve, which names his church as Cluain Colgan and turns 'Fáeliu his sister' into two brothers Fáel and Sorar. In the list of saints' mothers (*CGSH*, pp. 169–81), § 69, the sister's name is given as Fáelinni, and their mother as Cullend.

**102** Healed, that is, of her sin; compare I 50. On the language of healing in connection with absolution, see the note by MacCarthy, pp. 29–30. Compare n. 132.

**103** The word for 'head' here is *primarius*, a word that Adomnán generally uses in a secular context (I 33, 35). The term is used of an abbot by Gildas in his letter to Uinniau (now only known from quotations), § 6; this is quoted in two Irish collections of canons, Cambridge, Corpus Christi College, MS 279, C[1], p. 57 (in manuscript; this mid-seventh-century collection is unpublished) and *Hib.*, 37. 31. The sense in which Colgu was 'head' of a church is not clear to me: the fact that he had a 'butler' who was apparently a layman, not sharing the communal life of the clergy, may suggest that Colgu was not in holy orders but was rather the proprietor of a private church.

**104** The word *hauritorium* has many meanings in Latin, bucket, ladle, jug – in short, anything in which water or the like may be drawn or drunk. The translation here is inevitably a guess based on the man's role as *pincerna* 'butler' (equivalent to OIr. *deogbaire*, the person who served the drink). Other guesses vary: 'ladle' (Reeves), 'tap' ('probably a leather tube', MacCarthy, p. 30), 'bottle' (Fowler, p. 31n.), 'jug' (Huyshe), 'pitcher' (Anderson and Anderson).

**105** Trénán moccu Runtir is an obscure figure, perhaps to be identified with the hypocoristic name, Mothrianóc, one of the seven sons of Oengus in the Genealogies of the Saints, §§ 209, 701.2, who was commemorated on 20 August (MTall.). Reeves, p. 47n., equates his lineage of moccu Runtir with *genus Runtir*, mentioned by Tírechán, § 8; the Tripartite Life translates this as Dál Ruintir and locates them in Clonkeen, Co. Louth. This appears acceptable.

**106** Lasrén moccu Moie is mentioned only in this story. He was presumably the keeper of the monastic garden, and may therefore have been responsible for its medicinal herbs (see n. 132). His people seem to have lived near Derry (see n. 53).

**107** Sailing to Tiree is portrayed as an almost daily event in the life of the community. The journey took half a day (II 15). In this story, an otherwise unknown monk, Berach, and the prior, Baithéne, were both intending to make the voyage separately on the same day. The usual practice was evidently to sail directly across the Sea of the Hebrides. The detour via the Treshnish Isles, with their many reefs, can hardly have been an attractive alternative.

MONASTERIES OF TIREE Tiree was an important monastic centre in Columba's time, being the site not only of a dependency of Iona but of other monasteries also. The Columban house at Mag Luinge is mentioned many times (see n. 182). Another monastery at *Artchain* is named at I 36. At III 8 Adomnán mentions 'the other monasteries of Tiree', suggesting that there were several. 'These may have included *Bledach*, attributed to St Brendan of Clonfert in the medieval Life of that saint, and an abortive foundation of St Comgall, established respectively some years before and about the same time as Columba's arrival at Iona' (RCAHMS, *Mull, Tiree, Coll*, pp. 27–8). There is no precise evidence to help identify any sites. Reeves collected all the information he could find, pp. 308–17.

**108** Báetán is described by Adomnán as *gente nepos Niath Taloirc. Nepos* generally represents Irish *ua* 'grandson, descendant'; this is a dynastic designation, therefore, and not a tribal one like the names in *moccu*. I have failed to identify the lineage. *Nia Taloirc* means 'Talorc's champion'. Talorc, however, is not an Irish name but a Pictish one. Perhaps Báetán was a Dalriadic Scot whose family had intermarried with a Pictish family, or whose ancestor had served as warrior to a Pictish ruler.

**109** Báetán and his companions, like Cormac Ua Liatháin (I 6, II 42), were engaged in a favoured ascetic pusuit, seeking retreat (*eremus*) in the ocean. What he hoped to find, no doubt, was an offshore island suitable for a small hermitage – a place such as Skellig Michael in Co. Kerry or Eileach an Naoimh in the Garvelloch Islands near Oban. The number of remote settlements still known suggests that such retreats were found by a fair number of ascetics, but in the course of time the search was treated as an end in itself, the theme of a number of saintly voyage-tales, of which we have already a foretaste in the Life (II 42).

By the time Adomnán was writing it is likely that the successors of Báetán and Cormac had reached the Shetlands, and for most of the eighth century there were Irish clergy living in the Faroes. We know this from an Irish writer, Dícuil, writing in Latin about 825, who was himself familiar with the Western and Northern Isles of Scotland, saying: 'Among these I have lived in some and have visited others, some I have only glimpsed, while others I have read about' (*De mensura orbis terrae*, VII 6). In his own book he mentions a group of islands, two days' fair sailing from the Northern Isles, referring apparently to the Faroes; here, he writes, 'For nearly a hundred years hermits sailing from our country, Ireland, have lived; but just as they were always deserted from the beginning of the world, so now because of the Northmen pirates they are emptied of anchorites and filled with countless sheep and very many different kinds of seabirds' (ibid., VII 15). Dícuil also mentions that by the 790s these Irish clerics would go further north to Iceland for the spring and summer. Writing of the Norse settlement of Iceland in the ninth century, the medieval Icelandic writer Ari says: 'There lived there Christians whom the Northmen called *papa*, but then they departed because they wished not to live with heathens, and they left behind Irish books and bells and crosiers, from which one could know that they were Irishmen.'

**110** I cannot identify Adomnán's *Lathreg inden*. The second word is presumably the lenited form of Finden, with the silent *fh* unwritten (as often later). *Lathreg* would therefore be the feminine noun, *láthrach* or *láithrech* 'house-site' rather than the masculine *lathrach* 'muddy place'. (For a similar name, compare Láithrech Briúin, now Laraghbrine, Co. Kildare; Hogan, *Onomasticon*, p. 475). Does the fact that Báetán was buried at Derry perhaps indicate that his little church was near there? Professor Ó Riain has suggested to me that Báetán was perhaps Buadán, patron of the parish of Culdaff in Inishowen, just north of Derry; his holy well, known as Tuaras Buadáin, was still remembered in the 1930s (Ó Muirgheasa, 'Holy wells of Donegal', pp. 159–60).

**111** The Andersons translated this: 'After some seasons in the oakwood of Calcach [Derry] he died and was buried there' (p. 249). Adomnán's word order is against this; he does not say that he became a resident of Derry, merely that he was buried there. Mrs Anderson's second edition has corrected this (p. 47).

**112** Where Adomnán says 'church' here, it is not clear whether he means that the people sought refuge within the church building or whether they and their livestock simply retreated within the vallum, into the area under the protection of the church. The latter is the more likely.

**113** Here again, with conscientious detail, Adomnán indicates the route by which information came to him. Báetán was a contemporary of Columba. Máel Odrain witnessed the fulfilment of the prophecy shortly after Báetán's death, and was alive to pass the story on to Adomnán, perhaps half a century later. He was presumably a member of the community and may have resided at both Iona and Derry.

The name Máel Odrain is noteworthy. It is of a common type and means 'tonsured one (devotee) of Odran'; Odran should be a saint's name. Now the graveyard of Iona and its chapel are dedicated to St Odran, who, according to a story first recorded in the Middle Irish homily, arrived in Iona with St Columba's original companions and was the first to die on the island (see n. 365). There is no mention of Odran in Adomnán, but here, no more than a generation or two after St Columba came to Iona, we find someone apparently named after a saint of that name.

**114** On the identification of *Hinba*, see n. 194.

**115** Adomnán provides the main evidence for the existence of penitential communities, where those performing a long period of penance lived together under a strict discipline. From this passage we learn that there were penitents in *Hinba*, and from I 30; II 39, p. 189, that there was a similar penitential community at Mag Luinge in Tiree, where Librán was appointed to do penance for seven years. Penitents often had a specially meagre diet and were required to say a greater number of prayers and psalms than other religious; it must have been a convenience, especially for those serving long periods of penance, to be able to do so communally. The practice of doing penance for months or years, so often mentioned in the Irish penitentials, did not preclude the immediacy of personal penitence and forgiveness; compare the experience of Fiachnae in I 30, who repents and is assured of forgiveness before being sent to Mag Luinge, presumably to join those living in penance.

**116** See I 26 and n. 130 on the relaxation of a day's fast and the sinfulness of refusing it.

**117** The association of Baithéne with the abbot, Columba himself, in granting this relaxation, suggests that Baithéne at this stage had charge of the monastery on *Hinba* (see n. 194) and of the penitents living there.

**118** The prohibition on eating mare's flesh is also found in a (?) seventh-century text *De disputatione Hibernensis sinodi*, § 13 (Bieler, *The Irish Penitentials*, p. 160): 'the penance for eating horseflesh, four years on bread and water'. Although the canons attributed to Adomnán (Bieler, *The Irish Penitentials*, pp. 176–81) are concerned chiefly with prohibited or contaminated foods, there is no mention of horseflesh, which is not prohibited by the Old Testament codes. The Irish law-tract *Bretha Crólige*, § 25, suggests that horseflesh was eaten in early medieval Ireland. Parts of several horse carcasses were found in excavations at Iona, but this need not indicate that their meat was consumed in the monastery; Barber, 'Excavations', p. 315.

**119** For a commentary on social and legal aspects of this story, see Charles-Edwards, 'Irish *peregrinatio*', pp. 50–51.

**120** Lugaid in this story is perhaps the same mentioned in II 5, 38, as Lugaid Láitir or Lugaid the strong, on whom see n. 224.

**121** Fasting (Irish *troscad*) was a recognized method of coercing a person of privileged status, such as a cleric, to deal with one's case. The modern hunger strike continues the notion, which is found in many parts of the world.

**122** As Dr Charles-Edwards has pointed out (see n. 119), pilgrimage or religious exile outside Ireland was in this period considered a greater form of self-abnegation than taking to the religious life in one's own district or elsewhere in Ireland. For an Irishman to become a monk in a British monastery was probably not unusual in this period, and in III 6 we hear of a Briton who died in Iona. Throughout the sixth century relations between the British and Irish churches remained very close. The spread of Christianity in Ireland owed much to British influence, though St Patrick is the only British *missionary* known to us by name. In the next generation or two, Britons such as Mochta and Uinniau were founding monasteries in Ireland; Uinniau wrote the earliest Irish penitential text and sought advice from Gildas. Even as late as 600 St Columbanus could link the British and Irish together as 'the western churches' (Letters 1.5, 1.9, 2.5, 2.9). With the more rapid abandonment of the Celtic method of calculating the date of Easter among the Irish than the British, it is possible that the second half of the seventh century saw a weakening or breaking of ties between the churches of Britain and Ireland. By the eighth century one has the impression that the church in Wales was very much in isolation, but this may be a false interpretation of the evidence for British conservatism. Adomnán, even with his interest in the Roman Easter, gives no hint that he would disapprove of sending someone to join a monastery among the Britons.

**123** The two peoples of Fir Lí and Uí Thuirtri were neighbours in the plain to the west of the River Bann. The lands of Fir Lí were north of

Lough Neagh, around the modern town of Castle Dawson, Co. Londonderry. The territory of Uí Thuirtri lay further south, on the west side of Lough Neagh. Both groups belonged to the larger collection of peoples known as the Airgialla. An association between Uí Thuirtri and Derry is perhaps indicated by the verses inserted in the annals at AU 669, referring to their king who 'was taken in his shroud to Derry' for burial.

**124** Reeves, p. 53n., refers to a story in which this letter of the alphabet is found as a sign that St Columba should go to Iona, that is, to Ì. For this story, see n. 354.

**125** THE COPYING OF BOOKS IN IONA This request provides a valuable insight into part of the process of book production; presumably every copy was checked against its parent by one monk reading from the one while another followed in the other. At the end of the Life Adomnán imposes on those who copy his work the request so to check the new copy and to pass on the injunction.

The copying of texts, especially liturgical texts, was an important occupation in Iona in Columba's day (and thereafter); Adomnán provides a good deal of information about it. For Columba himself it was an almost daily occupation according to the second preface, p. 106, and we several times see him disturbed while so engaged (I 25, II 16, 29, III 15). At the end of his life he was working on copying the Psalter (III 23, p. 228). Books written by the saint's hand were known in Ireland (II 8–9), and some were kept reverently in Iona (II 44–5). The text most often mentioned is the Psalter, but on one occasion it was a book of hymns (II 9). Books were also used for study (I 24), and Baithéne was expected to record in writing the saint's exposition of the Bible (III 18). Adomnán suggests that, in his expectation, literacy was a part of everyday life for the brethren, who might make notes on waxed tablets of things that seem of moment at the time (I 35); the fact that a date is noted in that story reminds one that Iona was an early centre of annal-keeping.

Books believed to have been written by Columba were kept for centuries. In the case of the early seventh-century Gospel Book of Durrow, the colophon attributing the writing to St Columba is a later (? tenth-century) forgery. The *Cathach* of St Columba is a much less spectacular book, but its claim *may* be genuine: the *Cathach* now consists of an incomplete Psalter on small parchment leaves, written in an Irish centre about 600; it was enclosed in a box and later in a reliquary, and was treated as a relic of the saint. Indeed, the book itself was only rediscovered when the reliquary was opened in 1813. The belief that this was one of the books copied by St Columba is at least a thousand years old; while it is not possible to be certain, the fact that the handwriting is judged to date from the late sixth to the early seventh century makes the tradition very plausible. Further, small crosses that decorate initials in the manuscript can be paralleled in the style of crosses incised on stones in Argyll. It is not impossible that this was in fact one of the books used to invoke the saint's help when Adomnán was abbot (II 44–5).

**126** Shouting is mentioned several times as the means by which an arrival at the west end of the Ross attracted the attention of the monastic boatman (here, and I 26, 27, 32, 43). The distance is nearly a mile; on still days, especially in the early morning or the evening, the voice would carry easily, but there must have been many days when the noise of wind and waves would have defeated the ears of the most attentive boatman. The system, however, must have worked satisfactorily, or it would have been changed. Visual signs – hoisting a flag or turning a coloured board – are more reliable (in daylight), and require less effort. In the nineteenth century, according to Reeves, p. 55n., the visitor set fire to a bundle of heather to raise a smoke-signal; 'as each owner of a boat has a particular signal spot, it is at once known on the island whose services are required'. More recently there has been a regular ferry, with the boat based at Fionnphort on Mull.

The proportion of visitors to St Columba's monastery who arrived across Mull rather than by sea is not apparent. Travellers from Ireland arrived by both routes.

**127** The Latin description of this hut, *in tegoriolo tabulis subfulto* 'in the hut supported on planks', is open to more than one interpretation. It could refer to a wooden hut with a wooden floor resting on joists, but Reeves, p. 360n., drew attention to Adomnán's mention of huts in the Nile delta, *in domibus transuersis trabibus suffultis aquas supra inhabitant* 'they live in houses supported on transverse beams above the waters' (*De Locis Sanctis*, II 30). Here he clearly means houses raised on stilts. In another reference to Columba's writing hut Adomnán says that it was *in eminentiore loco fabricatum* 'carpentered in a raised up place' (III 22). Here the simple meaning is that it was sited on raised ground. Taken together, however, the two passages suggest that Adomnán might refer to the one distinctive feature of the hut, that it was artificially raised up on wooden beams; Reeves went so far as to guess that it was 'probably two stories high'.

On the strength of the second passage, it was suggested by Fowler and Fowler ('Excavations') that this hut was sited on the rocky knoll in front of the abbey, Tòrr Ab. There are traces of stone revetments creating a small platform on the knoll. In this area their excavations revealed the stone base of a small hut, undated but almost certainly pre-medieval. This was abandoned, the site was levelled to make a sort of cobbled platform, and eventually a plinth was set up supporting a cross. The use of mortar showed that this base was late medieval, and it was reported to Reeves in the 1850s and seen by Sir Henry Dryden in the 1870s. The hut, uncovered in 1956–7 and now consolidated so that it is still visible, was interpreted as containing stone fittings, forming the supports for a seat or table. It is certainly 'in a raised up place' and appears to be a plausible situation for the abbot's hut, but a hut on wooden joists would hardly leave remains such as those excavated.

I am inclined to think that the most probable meaning of Adomnán's words is a hut resting on joists in a naturally elevated position. If that were a site like Tòrr Ab, the beams might have been meant to create a platform, enlarging the usable space; but that is sheer guesswork. What is clear is that the Life refers to two distinct buildings used by Columba: the hut in which he wrote and his lodging (III 21, 23), 'where at night instead of straw he had bare rock and a stone for a pillow'. This, which *might* have better matched the findings on Tòrr Ab, is not the hut described as 'in a raised up place'.

**128** This prophecy is expressed as two quatrains in the Middle Irish homily § 59:

> There is a fellow in the harbour,
> his staff in his hand;
> he will approach my little ink-horn
> and will spill my ink.
>
> He will bend down
> to seek to kiss me
> and will strike against my little ink-horn
> and leave it empty.

(tr. Herbert, *Iona, Kells, and Derry*, p. 262.)

The word *bachlach*, translated 'fellow' by Dr Herbert, is derived from the word *bachall* 'staff' in the second line; it may here rather mean 'pilgrim' or even 'monk', though it has also the derisive sense (see n. 241). The kiss of peace was a Christian greeting in the sixth and seventh centuries, and the modern Irish word for 'kiss', *póg*, is borrowed from Latin *pacem* '(kiss of) peace'. In the sixteenth century, when the story was incorporated in Manus O'Donnell's *Life*, § 211, it was changed to add that the visitor wished to kiss the saint's feet.

**129** It was common practice in the Middle Ages to fast on both Wednesday and Friday, when there would be no meal until after Nones, when the main meal was ordinarily taken (II 13). In Irish Thursday was sometimes called *dé dardóin* 'day between two fasts'.

**130** Compare above, I 21, where the arrival of St Columba leads to a relaxation of the penitential régime on *Hinba*.

An Irish canon attributed to St Patrick but more probably of sixth- or early seventh-century date argues that one should not take too rigorous a view of fasting: 'Concerning fasting without break. They decide that the coming of Christ the bridegroom shall find none of our laws of fasting. What else is the difference between a Novatian heretic and a Christian but that the Novatian fasts unceasingly, the Christian at a fixed time, so that place and time and person be observed in all things?' (*Synodus Patricii*, § 14; Bieler, *The Irish Penitentials*, pp. 188–90). The canon is repeated in *Hib.* 12.15 after a story from the Greek historian Eusebius to illustrate that virtue lies sometimes in not fasting on bread and water. In the same chapter *Hib.* cites an Irish synod: 'It is better when brethren arrive to show virtue for the sake of kindness and love, and to relax the rule of abstinence and the strictness of the daily fast, for the fast is still pleasing to the Lord when it is ended with the fruits of charity.'

This principle is illustrated elsewhere by a story in the first Life of St Brigit, § 54: 'St Ibar rejoiced with great gladness at the arrival of St Brigit, but he had no food for the arrival of the guest but dry bread and the flesh of a pig. So Bishop Ibar and St Brigit ate bread and bacon during the Lenten fast before Easter' (ed. Colgan, *Trias*, p. 532).

Two of St Brigit's nuns would not eat meat during the fast, and their portions were changed into snakes as a sign of the sinfulness of their rigorous attitude.

**131** Áedán mac Fergnai cannot be identified in MTall., the saints' genealogies, nor in the Life of St Brendan. The efforts of Colgan, *Trias*,

p. 377, n. 72, to pin him down among the twenty-three Áedáns in his martyrology are inconclusive; Reeves, p. 55n., appears to have recognized this, but none the less passed on Colgan's conclusion. I leave it to the curious to follow Colgan's discussion.

Brendan moccu Altae is the famous St Brendan of Clonfert, the Navigator (to be distinguished from St Brendan of Birr, on whom see n. 354). His only actual appearance in the *Life* is at III 17 in the company of other saints, including St Cormac Ua Liatháin, another navigator (II 42). All the recorded traditions concerning St Brendan tell how he was born in Co. Kerry. His principal church, however, at Clonfert, lies close to the west bank of the River Shannon on the edge of Connacht. This was founded according to the Annals of Ulster in 559 or 564, and the same annals date St Brendan's death to 577 or 583. He was commemorated on 16 May (MTall.).

**132** Medicines for the body are often compared with penance as the medicine for the soul in texts from early medieval Ireland. The preface to the second part of the Penitential of St Columbanus provides a good example: 'Diversity of offences causes diversity of penances. For doctors of the body also compound their medicines in diverse kinds; thus they heal wounds in one manner, sickness in another, boils in another . . . So also should spiritual doctors treat with diverse kinds of cures the wounds of souls, their sicknesses, pains . . .' (Bieler, *The Irish Penitentials*, p. 99). St Columbanus, however, is following the Pastoral Rule of St Gregory the Great, at the time a recent work.

The medicines sought were almost certainly special herbs, grown in the monastic garden (see n. 106). *Bretha Crólige*, § 27, mentions that the reason for making a herb garden was to care for the sick. As Reeves, p. 56n., observes, it is interesting to learn that lay people came to the monastery for medical attention. The physician (Irish *liaig*) would normally charge a fee for his services, but perhaps churches with a qualified person in the community may have seen this service as part of the ministry.

**133** Luigbe moccu Min is mentioned three times in the *Life* (I 15, 24, 28); in the first of these stories he is the saint's messenger to King Rhydderch at Dumbarton, and here he is sent to the royal seat of Dalriada, probably at Dunadd or Dunollie (see n. 136). A person with the very similar name Luigne moccu Min is mentioned below, II 18, 27, in each case as a youth, on whom see n. 249. Adomnán seems to be clear that Luigbe, who takes on responsibilities, and the youthful

Luigne are separate individuals from the same tribal group. A third member of the same group, Mosinu moccu Min, was a famous scholar and abbot of Bangor who died in AU 610. They presumably belonged in the north or north-east of Ireland.

Elsewhere in the Life we meet another pair of similar names. At I 43 a monk called Luigbe moccu Blai was the confidant to whom the saint spoke a prophecy and an explanation as to the manner of his clairvoyance. At III 15 and III 22 a monk called Luigne moccu Blai is mentioned as attending the saint in Iona. This would appear, then, to be a second pair of kinsmen called Luigbe and Luigne – perhaps too much of a coincidence?

Professor Ó Riain, 'Cainnech *alias* Colum Cille', p. 30, has argued that all these names represent not four individuals, not two individuals whose family names have become muddled, but one person. He suggests that Adomnán collected the stories by word of mouth and that different informants used different but similar names. In support of this he notes that the present story is followed (I 29) by one concerning the building of a great house at Durrow, and that at III 15 Luigne moccu Blai is with the saint when a second incident relating to that work is told. Second, that the story there follows an incident which happened by Loch Ness, while at II 27 in another story on Loch Ness the saint's companion was Luigne moccu Min. Since the adjacent stories essential to Ó Riain's argument (I 29 and III 14) do not involve any Luigbe or Luigne I am inclined to doubt his deduction.

134 In the Martyrology of Notker, written in the 890s at St Gallen in Switzerland – a monastery with strong Irish connections – the long entry for St Columba (based on Adomnán) offers an identification of the city that suffered in this way: 'He saw also in a sudden trance the destruction of the city in Italy which is now called "New" by an earthquake, nay by the glance of heaven's anger' (*PL*, 131.1102D). Since the seventeenth century scholars have identified this as Città Nuova on the Istrian coast (now in Croatia and called Novigrad). There is nothing in Notker's text to justify this, still less in Adomnán's; I doubt whether Notker would have considered this to be in Italy, but Cittanova in Calabria would simply be another guess. It seems to me more probable that Notker has brought his general knowledge to bear on the text of Adomnán and has inferred that an eruption of Mount Vesuvius was meant; he knew that the city close to the volcano was *Neapolis* 'New city', now Naples. Notker was no better placed than anyone since to know what Adomnán intended.

135 This incidental reference to trade between Dalriada and Gaul is one of the very few important items of written evidence for this trade, without which the interpretation of the archaeological evidence would be much less secure.

Where texts refer to foreign goods (OIr. *allmuire sét*), the implication is always that they were luxury goods, including wine and fine cloth. *Tecosca Cormaic*, § 1, lists 'ships putting into port' with such goods as one of the signs that a king's rule is successful. The church was an importer as much as were kings and nobles: Bishop Conláed's *transmarina uestimenta* in Cogitosus's Life of St Brigit were doubtless imported silks. Archaeological evidence for trade is on a humbler level. The commodity most often found in western Britain is pottery, imported from the western coast of France. Quantities have been found at more southerly sites, especially in Cornwall, where pottery from the Mediterranean area has also been found. Small amounts of 'D-ware' (from around Bordeaux) have been found at Dunadd, while the coarse 'E-ware' (also western France) has been found at more than a dozen sites in Scotland. These include Dunadd (see n. 136), Craig Phadrig (see n. 294), Dumbarton (see n. 97), Dunollie (see n. 342), and lesser sites on the west coast between Kintyre and Skye. A fragment of 'E-ware' has also been found in Iona. The vessels represented 'a robust kitchenware', including cooking-pots, cups and jugs of various sizes. Of all the Scottish sites Dunadd has yielded the greatest quantity, comparable with the amount from the Irish royal seat at Clogher (see n. 223). These finds are listed by Thomas, *Imported Pottery*, pp. 20–24.

Archaeologists have sometimes been led to speculate from the greater quantity at Dunadd than at other Scottish sites that Dunadd served as the centre for importing and distributing foreign goods. This simplistic inference has no doubt been encouraged by this reference in Adomnán to a ship from Gaul at a site that is most likely to be Dunadd. The parallel with Clogher, however, makes it extremely doubtful. Dunadd and Clogher were both royal sites, but Clogher is a good many miles from the coast. The quantity of finds there does not depend on its being a port for the importing of such wares. These two sites have been intensively excavated, whereas other sites have not all been subjected to such investigation; more pottery may await discovery.

Iona has been excavated over many years. The much smaller quantity of imported pottery may indeed suggest that the monks made less use of it than did royal households. It is impossible to know whether this means they imported less of other goods or made less use of wine or silks. Finds from Iona include a few exotic objects, such as the rim of a large bowl, identifiable as African red slipware of the late sixth century such as has been found at very few British sites (Thomas, *Imported Pottery*, pp. 8–9). Another commodity was needed by the monks: the yellow colouring orpiment from the Mediterranean area was used in manuscript decoration, and a piece of this has been found at Dunadd (Campbell, 'A cross-marked quern', p. 67).

While the ports and distribution centres in Ireland and Scotland are still unknown, at the other end of the trade route we know from Jonah's Life of St Columbanus, I 23, that Nantes was a port used by ships trading with the Irish. We may guess that the same is true of Bordeaux, since its ancient name, Burdigalia, was borrowed into Irish as *bordgal*, a word used to mean 'trading centre, emporium'.

**136** *Caput regionis* must, as the Andersons observed, mean 'the capital of the district'. *Caput* is used in this sense by Adomnán's contemporary, Muirchú, who describes Tara as *caput Scottorum* 'capital of the Irish' (Bieler, *Patrician Texts*, p. 74). *Regio* is often a difficult word to interpret, but I should take it here to mean the whole region of Scottish Dalriada.

Where was the capital of Scottish Dalriada? Since the middle of the last century it has been supposed that Dunadd in North Knapdale was the capital – a theory championed by Skene, *Celtic Scotland*, I, 229, though some of the literary evidence used by him refers to another site, the unidentified Dun Monaidh (Watson, *Celtic Place-names*, pp. 394–5). None the less, Dunadd was an important site, especially in the seventh to ninth centuries. The archaeological evidence is now summed up by RCAHMS, *Mid Argyll and Cowal*, I, 149–59. Written evidence amounts to no more than two entries in the annals, AU 683 and 736. In the present state of our knowledge it remains the site with the strongest claim to have been the principal seat of the rulers of Cenél nGabráin, and (under their rule, at least) the capital of Dalriada. This does not amount to proof, and views may have to be modified in the event of further archaeological discovery at other sites mentioned in the annals, such as Dunollie near Oban, probably the principal centre of Cenél Loairn (see n. 342).

In 1582 George Buchanan took the phrase to represent Irish *cenn tíre* 'head of the land', i.e., the headland of Kintyre. This was picked up by the Bollandist editor in 1698, and from there by Reeves, p. 57n. It was accepted by Watson, *Celtic Place-names*, p. 92, who went on to suggest where in Kintyre the ship might have called, Campbeltown Loch. *Regio*, however, unlike Irish *tír* or Latin *terra*, does not distinguish land from water but one territory from another.

137 On Lasrén mac Feradaig, see n. 91.

138 The great house, or *tech mór*, of Durrow is mentioned in III 15 (see n. 383), but here Adomnán uses an indefinite *cuiusdam maioris domus*. Although almost all students of the Life have assumed that this chapter and III 15 refer to incidents in the erection of the same building, Anderson and Anderson, p. 265n., sound a note of caution. Their caution is linguistically justified, and we do not know enough about the monastic buildings of Durrow to guess whether 'the great house' and 'a rather big house' are the same or different.

139 Fiachnae is described as *sapiens* 'the wise'. This term is regularly used in the annals as a personal epithet, indicating a noted scholar or teacher. In the list of chapters his nickname is given as *binc*, probably an error for *biuc* 'little' (see n. 23).

140 There is no obvious hill overlooking the site of the monastery, but the various knolls on Cnoc nan Carnan within the monastic vallum hardly suit the words 'at the top' (*in cacumine*). Cnoc Mór, somewhat further south behind the modern school, is probably the place intended, as Reeves, p. 58n., thought. That this was traditionally so is suggested by Boswell: 'There is, *near the village*, a hill upon which St Columbus took his seat and meditated and surveyed the sea' (*Journal . . . from the original manuscript*, p. 338; my emphasis).

141 Ps. 50:19 (AV 51:17). The reading of MS A, *cor contritum et humiliatum Deus non spernit*, is very close to the Vulgate's version of the Psalms *iuxta LXX*, which differs only in one word (*spernet*). The B MSS have different word order, *Deus contritum non spernit et humiliatum cor* (B2 differs in reading *aspernit*). Anderson and Anderson, p. 268n., rightly point out that this phrasing is in the style of Adomnán, and suggest that the reading of A may have been assimilated to the Vulgate. Although the scribe Dorbbéne would have known the Psalms by heart, we should not suppose that he would have thought it necessary or even desirable to 'correct' Adomnán's paraphrase. It is perhaps more likely that the B text shows Adomnán revising the wording to his more mannered style.

142 Mag Luinge ('plain of a ship') is here given as the name of the monastery in Tiree, on which see n. 182.

**143** Here we have another reference to a daughter-house of Iona in Dalriada, established under close supervision from St Columba. *Cella Diuni* in Latin presumably represents an Irish name, *Cell Diúin* (assuming *Diún* to be an o-stem name). Diún may have been its first incumbent, perhaps even its founder, but clearly here his brother Cailtan is a monk of St Columba, delegated to leave the mother-house and take charge of *Cella Diuni*. His title, *praepositus*, is twice used by Adomnán (I 41, II 18) to mean prior of a subordinate monastery. Here Anderson and Anderson take it in the same way and translate *cella* as monastery; this may overstate the scale of *Cella Diuni*. As *praepositus*, Cailtan may have had charge of the church, but the word does not require that he should have monks in his charge as well. It is interesting that Adomnán indicates that *Cella Diuni* still existed at the time of writing; if it was a very minor church, it had still managed to survive a hundred years. Its location 'by the loch of the River Awe' has never been established.

**144** The pilgrims expected to be able to attach themselves to the community for a year without taking the monk's vow, and the attitude of the brethren present suggests that their expectation was normal. St Columba's answer to these pilgrims, then, is particular: he is not saying that this custom was not followed at Iona, but that he has inner knowledge that these pilgrims are chosen by God to be monks. Similarly, their immediate profession of the monastic vow in the church may reflect the special circumstances and does not suggest that instant profession without a period of instruction and probation was usual.

**145** Adomnán's *uiuam Deo se ipsos exhibentes hostiam* paraphrases part of Rom. 12:1, *ut exhibetis corpora uestra hostiam uiuentem Deo placentem*.

**146** I interpret Adomnán's phrase *longa in breui christianae tempora militiae complentes* to mean that their one month as monks would be for them as good as years, with the contrast of *longa in breui* emphatically placed at the head of the clause. This is suggested by the very similar phrase, *consummatus in breui expleuit tempora multa*, in the Vulgate text of Wisd. 4:13, which I suspect Adomnán had in mind; the whole passage there argues that untimely death may be God's reward for the virtuous.

**147** Two stories are told of St Columba spending a few days in Skye, this and II 26. In neither are local inhabitants mentioned, so that it is not possible to guess at St Columba's business there. It is probable that most or all of Skye was Pictish territory in the sixth and seventh centuries; three Pictish symbol-stones still survive from the island.

**148** The conversion of Artbranan is one of very few stories mentioning the baptism of a Pict. The moral outline of the episode is of a common type: a person of natural goodness comes to the holy man to fulfil his life by accepting Christ in his last hours and dies soon after baptism. What actually lies behind the story's particulars is less clear. It is not certain that Adomnán's audience would know who Artbranan was or where he came from (see next note); it may be of real significance that he was a military leader, but without an intelligible context, would the audience make sense of that? The most tangible detail is the place-name 'Water of Artbranan', but, if this is merely a local name, why should Adomnán explain its origin? He does not, for example, add that a holy well or a church was established there. Macdonald, 'Iona's style of government', p. 176, suggests that 'we have here what is essentially the foundation legend of a Columban monastery in what was probably the Pictish territory of Skye', but if so, the account is oddly uninformative.

**149** The Latin, *primarius Geonae cohortis*, has been explained by Dumville, '*Primarius cohortis*', pp. 130–31. Reeves, p. 62n., had dismissed Colgan's supposition that Geona was the name of an island, and suggested that 'the Geona cohort was probably a Pictish corps, deriving its name from the district to which it belonged'. Watson, *Celtic Place-names*, pp. 74–5, could not locate it, although he rightly brushed aside a suggestion from Sir John Rhys that we read 'Genonae' ('Genunia', in the Greek writer Pausanias, referred to a part of England). Dumville, however, takes *Geonus* as an adjective derived from the place-name *Cé*, the name of a Pictish province thought to extend over what is now Banffshire and Aberdeenshire (Watson, *Celtic Place-names*, pp. 108–9, 114, 515; Wainwright, 'The Picts and the problem', pp. 46–7). If this is right, we must think of Artbranan as having travelled a considerable distance. That Artbranan was a Pict is supported by the fact that an interpreter was needed for him to understand the saint's preaching (compare II 32 and n. 286).

**150** This manner of burial seems, on the face of it, more appropriate to heathen custom than for a newly baptized Christian. Cairn burials have been discovered in Pictland, but there is also literary evidence from Ireland for Christian burial in this manner. Compare, for example, Tírechán, § 38: 'There Patrick buried his driver [*or* attendant], Totmáel, and gathered stones for his burial place and said, "Let him be like this for ever, and he will be visited by me in the last days"' (Bieler, *Patrician Texts*, pp. 152–3). A Christian gravestone dating from about AD 500 at Penmachno in North Wales has the cross and the inscription: 'Carausius lies here in this heap of stones' (Nash-Williams, *Early Christian Monuments*, p. 92).

**151** Adomnán seems to speak from direct acquaintance with this part of Skye.

**152** See n. 283 on St Columba's journey across Druim Alban.

**153** The list of chapter headings above, p. 108, identifies the loch as Loch Lochy. On St Columba's route by boat through the Great Glen, see below n. 297. The name of Loch Lochy occurs also in the Annals of Ulster in 729, in what is almost certainly an Iona entry concerning two battles in which the Pictish king Onuist f. Urguist defeated his rivals Naiton and Drust (but compare Watson, *Celtic Place-names*, p. 50).

**154** Gallán mac Fachtnai is otherwise unknown. The terms in which he is described demand a little explanation; the saint calls him *primarium de tuae praepositis dioeceseos*, a leader among the chief men of Colgu's 'diocese'. All three key words, *primarius*, *praepositus*, and *dioecesis*, may have an ecclesiastical meaning. On the strength of this, Colgan, *Acta*, p. 381, took Colgu for a bishop; Lanigan, *Ecclesiastical History*, II, 328, suggested that they merely came from the same diocese, retaining an ecclesiastical sense for this word, though not for *primarius* or *praepositus*. Reeves, p. 65n., goes into a discussion (now outdated) of the nature of ecclesiastical jurisdiction in sixth-century Ireland. All, however, have missed the point that *dioecesis* is nowhere used in early Latin writers from Ireland with a specialized ecclesiastical meaning; Adomnán uses the word in its non-specialized Late Latin sense 'district', and in the present chapter *regio* is used as a synonym. Gallán, therefore, need hold no church office, and *praepositus* is used in its secular sense.

It appears that Colgu mac Cellaig is of lesser status than Gallán. He was a monk of Iona, and figures as a companion of the saint there in III 15 as well as here. The circumstances of his return home, presumably a visit, are not made clear, but the return itself is obviously necessary to the story. It is not certain whether he is the same Colgu mac Cellaig whose death is recorded in AU 622.

**155** Waxed tablets were used for writing-practice or for notes or drafts that would in due course be copied on to parchment. The impression made by the stylus in the wax could be erased by placing the tablet in an oven for a short time. By chance, several such tablets, with their text still legible, were found at Springmount Bog in Ireland, and are now in the National Museum in Dublin; they have been dated to around AD 600. For illustrations, see Schaumann, 'Early Irish manuscripts'.

**156** Findchán mentioned here cannot be identified with any of the saints of that name in the Irish martyrologies; he may, however, have been the patron of the church of Kilfinichen on the isle of Mull. Nothing is known of him beyond this story.

**157** DIARMAIT MAC CERBAILL, KING OF IRELAND Adomnán is the earliest source to describe Diarmait mac Cerbaill as king of Ireland. The legend accepted by the annalist was that he succeeded Tuathal Máelgarb as Uí Néill overlord in 544 (see n. 94), and that both belonged to different lineages of the Southern Uí Néill. At this early date these lineages had barely emerged: the two dominant dynasties of the Southern Uí Néill in the historic period both claimed descent from Diarmait, so that it may be realistic to regard him as the earliest major ruler from the east midland dynasties claiming descent from Niall. 'Diarmait's immediate origins are obscure and may arouse some suspicion', writes Byrne, *Irish Kings*, p. 90. None the less, he enjoyed considerable fame in later times; Adomnán's words may reflect his late seventh-century reputation rather than sixth-century reality. Little can be said of his actual career, on which the annals are surprisingly reticent. He was defeated at the battle of Cúl Drebene in 561, and in 565 was supplanted by kings from the Northern Uí Néill (see n. 80).

Perhaps the most notable point that the annals make about King Diarmait is that in 560 he celebrated the Feast of Tara, *Feis Temro*, the pagan ritual marriage of the king and the goddess of sovereignty. (The word *feis* 'feast' is in fact the verbal noun of *foaid* 'sleeps (with)', indicating the sexual symbolism of the ritual.) The Annals of Tigernach specifically say that Diarmait was the last king to do this.

In the light of this fact Adomnán's words are most extraordinary. 'Ordained by God's will' is for this period a remarkable phrase to use of a king and reflects Adomnán's thinking on kingship (see Introduction, p. 61). That it should be used in conjunction with the title 'king of all Ireland' provides a still more remarkable clue to Adomnán's attitude, and that of his contemporaries, to the so-called 'high kingship', to which he refers again in his prophecy to Diarmait's son Áed Sláine (I 14). When one recognizes that Adomnán has changed the nature of the king's inauguration from an ancient pagan ritual to a Christian idea that must have been recent even in Adomnán's time, then one realizes that he is going out of his way to elevate the Uí Néill king and further to denigrate his killer. Indeed, since the killing of kings was commonplace in early medieval Ireland, the strong words later in this chapter, that Áed 'deserved such an end to life long ago for having killed the king of all Ireland', are no doubt a further reflection of Adomnán's biblical view. Old Testament kings were the Lord's anointed, and to kill such a king was sacrilege.

The question of Adomnán's political interests *vis-à-vis* the Uí Néill and the rulers of Dalriada is discussed in the Introduction, p. 63.

**158** Many points of interest emerge from this story. First, on Áed Dub's personal history: he is first mentioned in the Annals of Ulster as Áed Dub mac Suibne, the killer of Diarmait mac Cerbaill, high king, in 565 (see previous note); this comes as an interlinear note, but the Annals of Tigernach more fully state that Diarmait was killed at Ráith Becc in Mag Line by Áed Dub mac Suibne, king of the Ulaid, and his head was taken to Cluain and his body was buried at Connor. Adomnán does not mention that Áed Dub was king, but he does say that he came from the royal lineage of the race of Cruithin. From this we may place him in the ruling dynasty of Dál nAraide, from what is now Co. Antrim, though his exact genealogical connection is not known. King Diarmait was in Áed's territory when he was killed, and his burial place, Connor, was its principal church. Áed himself died in AU 588 as king of Dál nAraide and overking of Ulster. The Annals of Ulster describe his death as a *iugulatio*, suggesting that it was violent, and the annotator adds that it took place 'on a ship', a pale reflection of the story here.

The story of how Áed Dub killed Diarmait mac Cerbaill formed the subject of a popular tale, which survives in a medieval version, *Aidhed Dhiarmada* 'The death-tale of Diarmait' (O'Grady, *Silva Gadelica*, I, 72–82; tr., II, 76–88). According to the tale, Diarmait had killed Áed's father, Suibne, and then taken the son into fosterage. When it was prophesied that Áed would kill Diarmait, he was exiled to Britain, that is, before 565. Adomnán's story, however, concerns a period after the killing of Diarmait.

Áed had presumably exiled himself from Dál nAraide during a period of reverse in his struggle for the kingship, and had assumed the clerical habit. The account here of his ordination is remarkable (Reeves, p. 69n., quotes an indignant comment on it from the eighteenth-century Scottish Catholic historian, Fr Thomas Innes). On the political side, it suggests that an ambitious member of a royal lineage might seek to take holy orders without expecting to renounce the world. Earlier in the sixth century King Maelgwn of North Wales had entered monastic life, but returned to the world and his throne, provoking the indignation of Gildas. Ecclesiastically, our story illustrates the roles of the abbot and the bishop in relation to the ordination of a priest. It would be still more interesting to know from where the bishop was summoned; without that knowledge, one can hardly guess whether the bishop came to exercise his role as ordinary, or whether he was called to perform the pontifical sacrament of ordination with no implication for any jurisdictional role.

Áed's death, as picturesquely described here, conforms to the folktale motif of the threefold death – here by spearing, falling and drowning. Anderson and Anderson, p. 22, infer that the story was known as a popular tale before it was set down by Adomnán. The lake in whose waters Áed drowned was probably, as Reeves observed, p. 71n., Lough Neagh in Ulster.

**159** Reeves, p. 70n., gives a note on putrefying right hands in early saints' Lives.

**160** *Ommon* cannot be identified.

**161** Reeves, p. 71n., assumes that the route followed by the monks took the line of the old road, now a farm track that leaves the modern metalled road east of Cnoc Órain, past Maol Farm, and reaches the village road near the medieval nunnery. The place-name Bol-leithne mentioned by him is marked on the OS 1:10000 map higher up the hill than Maol Farm, though Reeves locates it nearer to Cnoc Órain; I doubt whether it is relevant to the location of *Cúl Eilne*.

I have wondered whether the monks may not rather have taken the higher but more direct route, leaving the Machair via Gleann Cùil bhùirg, then from the head of the glen striking down directly toward the abbey. This possibility is mooted in RCAHMS, *Iona*, p. 35.

**162** Adomnán says that at this period Baithéne was *dispensator operum* 'distributor of tasks'. Clearly Baithéne was in charge of the harvest work, but the phrase may mean more than that. It is possible that he had an official position that involved the daily allocation of manual work among the brethren.

**163** In the early churches of Britain and Ireland it was normal to pray standing with arms outstretched and raised. Figures are depicted in this position on some carved crosses. See also II 12, 31. The kneeling position was also in common use, and even a prostrate position (III 13).

**164** Reeves compares an anecdote in the Middle Irish homily on St Columba in which the young saint and his foster-father, Cruithnechán, were walking when Cruithnechán stumbled, fell and expired; the young saint remained with his foster-father and proceeded to recite his lessons, which could be heard a mile and a half away, so that it was said:

> The sound of Columb Cille's voice,
> great was its sweetness above every choir;
> for the extent of fifteen hundred paces –
> a great distance – it was clear
>
> (tr. Herbert, *Iona, Kells, and Derry*, p. 254).

The quatrain is quoted also among the *Liber Hymnorum* prefaces to the *Amrae*; *Liber Hymnorum*, I 165, II 57.

**165** Adomnán has brought this story out of the context of the saint's visit to King Bridei and his wizards (II 33–5) and inserted it here because of the voice element in the account.

**166** That is, Ps. 45 in the Authorized Version.

**167** A two-wheeled vehicle, drawn by two horses, was the conventional means (for those of sufficient wealth) of travelling quickly and lightly laden. A detailed description, based chiefly on heroic tales, is given by Greene, 'The chariot'. It was used by clerics as well as warriors, and seems to have been an efficient means of travelling. To facilitate travel, roads were made and maintained over the plains and rafted causeways through the bogs; it would be a mistake to imagine the chariot driven over open country.

**168** The plain of Brega, heartland of the Southern Uí Néill, lay north and south of the River Boyne in Co. Meath.

169 *Homo diues et honoratus in plebe*. By *honoratus*, Adomnán surely means that he was a man of high legal status or 'honour-price'; rank was in part, at least, a function of wealth, which was measured principally in cattle. A person's legal status was valid only within his own *tuath* 'people', so that Adomnán's phrase could be rendered in more specialized terms, 'of high honour-price in the *tuath*'. *Tuath* in Irish law, however, refers to the laity, and Lugaid is described here as a cleric, a point that is not integrated into the story. Reeves, p. 75n., observes: 'It seems that self-denial was not an invariable ingredient, even at this early period, in the clerical character.' But the point is probably that clerical orders were merely an adjunct to a man of high secular status.

170 The word *praetersoria* is not known from any other text. Colgan, *Trias*, p. 379, n. 83, guessed at the meaning from the context, and has been followed by Du Cange's *Glossarium* and by all students of the Life.

171 The word *maceria* means a stone wall or enclosure; it occurs in other texts as a rendering of Irish *caisel* 'cashel' (from Latin *castellum*), a stone-built ring-fort.

172 The word 'whore' here and in I 39, Latin *meretrix* reflects Adomnán's attitude to loose liaisons in a polygamous (and sometimes promiscuous) society; it does not suggest a commercial relationship.

173 Irish society in this period, judging by the frequency with which Adomnán refers to the murder of individuals – not necessarily political contenders – by their enemies, appears to have been violent, insecure and dangerous, notwithstanding elaborate laws regulating most social exchanges.

174 *Cainle*, which Adomnán mentions as both a district and a mountain, cannot be located. Hogan, *Onomasticon*, enters Adomnán's *regio Cainle* (here) s.v. *crích Cainle*, and his *mons Cainle* (II 17) s.v. *sliab Cainle*; for the former he offers no location, and for the latter only that suggested for the former (!) by Reeves, p. 75n., viz. 'in the neighbourhood of Trevet', Co. Meath, on the strength of the next chapter, I 40, which is irrelevant. Assuming that the mountain and the district are in the same position, there is nothing in either context to determine whether *Cainle* is in Ireland or Scotland. It would be mildly surprising for a district name to be unrecorded elsewhere if it were in Ireland, but this is not sufficient reason for supposing it was in Scotland; Watson made no attempt to

identify the place as a Scottish location. Further, Neman here and Silnán in II 17 have Irish names. A location in Ireland is perhaps more likely than in Scottish Dalriada.

**175** The practice of taking home the severed heads of defeated enemies appears frequently in Old Irish literature; it occurs also in the annals (see n. 158), and from time to time in the Lives of saints. For example, in the first Life of St Brigit, § 67, King Conall's army had achieved a victory, slaughtering and decapitating their enemies. On the way home, they camped in a convenient cashel. Stalked by survivors of the defeated enemy force, they were spied on in the cashel, but – thanks to St Brigit – the spies saw only a crowd of clerics, each with his book open in front of him: 'For so the army had placed the heads of the slain, and each man had a head placed in front of him.' The spies withdrew, and the defeated sent envoys to the victors to request the return of the severed heads.

**176** Trevet, Co. Meath, is not mentioned in any earlier source. It may have been still a little monastery in Adomnán's time, but it did not always remain small. It is first referred to in the Annals of Ulster in 739, recording the death of Cuanu Ua Bessáin, scribe of Trevet. Over the next three hundred years the annal collections intermittently record the deaths of abbots and bishops of Trevet.

**177** It is a moot point whether the monks of Trevet could choose a priest from perhaps several among their own number, or whether they had to choose one of those who served the needs of the local lay population because the monastery did not have its own priest. It is not even clear from Adomnán's wording whether their choice applied to this one Sunday (and another choice would be made another time), or whether they had chosen him as a permanent chaplain to the community. At no point does Adomnán indicate that the sinful priest was actually a monk belonging to the community. To my mind, the way in which Adomnán refers to the monks' choice, and the reason for it, does not accord with the minor choice – which of their in-house priests was on duty for the day – but the more significant choice: none of the monks in this little community was in priest's orders, and it was therefore necessary that they select from the neighbourhood a priest to act as chaplain and to celebrate mass in the monastery on Sundays. The implication here is that a small monastery was simply a group of religious, living together under a monastic vow, having their own chapel but without a resident priest.

If this state of affairs prevailed in many or most small monasteries, it must have significant implications for the assumption, among students of Irish church history from Todd to Hughes and beyond, that the organization of the church's mission depended on monasteries.

**178** Adomnán says that the man lived *in Coloso insula*, and at II 22 he refers to a party of raiders who sailed from Ardnamurchan and were sunk by a squall *inter Maleam et Colosum* 'between Mull and Coll'. Older commentators, including Reeves, Skene, and Fowler, took *Colosus* to be Colonsay, but the latter passage makes this geographically unlikely, as Watson, *Celtic Place-names*, p. 84, pointed out. One might add that the last paragraph of the present story suggests that Mag Luinge (in Tiree) was closer to *Colosus* than was Iona, another geographical reason for supposing that this is Coll, not Colonsay. Further, Watson gives linguistic reasons why *Colosus* should be Coll, and could not be Colonsay: it represents *Col-* with a Latin suffix, *-osus*, because in Old Irish intervocalic *s* would have been lost; Colonsay, on the other hand, appears to be a Scandinavian name, *Kolbeins ey* 'Kolbein's island', which can scarcely go back before the ninth century. The correct identification was first made, without arguing the case, by Stokes and Strachan, *Thesaurus Palaeohibernicus*, II, 276n.

These two references are the only mentions of Coll in written sources until a much later date, but the present passage indicates that the island was the normal dwelling place of the thief. His name shows that the island's inhabitants were probably speakers of Irish.

**179** Luigbe here may be either Luigbe moccu Min or Luigbe moccu Blai (see n. 133) or another of the same name.

Silnán is given his patronymic, mac Nemaidon, and his tribal name, moccu Sogin (II 4). Nothing else is known of him or his people. He lived at least until 623, giving testimony of St Columba's miracle in the presence of Abbot Ségéne (II 4).

**180** It evokes no surprise from Adomnán that a man should sail alone in a small boat from Coll to this western extremity of the Ross of Mull, just one of the many indications in this text of the ease with which the sea was used for communication and travel.

**181** It is known from the first Latin Life of St Brigit, § 74, that in seventh-century Ireland seals were hunted by boat using a spear attached to a line (called *murga* 'sea-spear' or *róngai* 'seal-spear' in a Middle Irish translation, edited by Stokes, *Lives of Saints*, p. 49). Remains from the carcasses of very young seals were found in excavations at the monastery in Iona (Reece, 'Recent work', p. 44; Barber, 'Excavations, 1979', p. 317). Their meat was eaten, and it appears from the Life of St Brigit that seal-meat might be offered to guests. Reeves, p. 78n., cites Martin Martin (*c.* 1700) to the effect that seals were eaten by the poorer people of the Isles at that date. Sealskin and seal-oil are likely to have been as important as the meat. (A copy of the Irish Life of St Columba by Manus O'Donnell, handwritten in Donegal in 1532, still survives bound in boards covered with sealskin; Oxford, Bodleian Library, MS Rawl. B. 514.)

**182** The monastic house in Mag Luinge 'the field or plain of a ship' was a dependency of Iona, and a house for penitents (I 30, II 39). Baithéne was its prior for a number of years, as is mentioned here and elsewhere (I 30, III 8), but after Columba's death and Baithéne's election to the abbacy, and probably for a considerable number of years (see II 39, p. 193), penitents from Iona continued to reside there. It may perhaps be inferred from the present passage that Tiree's favourable agricultural conditions helped to supply the needs of Iona (Reeves, pp. 78–9n.); on the other hand, Tiree is close to Coll, and this may simply have saved on transport.

Adomnán often tells us that it was situated in Tiree, and at II 15 he mentions its harbour. Reeves, p. 59n., attempted to identify this as Port na Luinge near Balemartine (compare Watson, *Celtic Place-names*, p. 92), and suggested that the monastic site was at Soroby, the site of a medieval chapel. There is no evidence to support this. RCAHMS, *Mull, Tiree, Coll*, p. 167, describes two medieval church-sites, at Kirkapoll (no. 310) and Soroby (no. 327), both dedicated to St Columba. There is slight evidence of activity in the early Christian period at Kirkapoll, and the report records two incised crosses from Soroby. Two entries in the annals are likely to refer to this place, recording a fire there in 673 and the death of Conall of Mag Luinge in 775.

There is no reason to associate the obscure St Brigit of Mag Luinge (mentioned in Irish saint-lists) with Tiree, as Reeves and Watson do on the strength of there being a chapel called Kilbride in the island. The place-name Mag Luinge is found elsewhere in Ireland.

**183** Little is known of the funeral rites of a layman. From this passage, it is evident that there was a funeral feast. A. C. Thomas, *And shall these mute stones speak?*, pp. 170–71, 205–6, discusses archaeological examples of graveside open-air hearths, presumably used to prepare the funeral feast.

**184** Lough Key, in the north of Co. Roscommon, lies west of the River Shannon in the province of Connacht. The River Boyle enters the lough at its south-west corner. The area was known in the Middle Ages as Mag Luirc. These lands, 'the fertile plain of Mag Luirg into which the Uí Briúin Aí were to expand, were crowded with small tribes' (Byrne, *Irish Kings*, p. 233). It is not obvious what business brought Columba and his companions to this spot, but a second story from this visit is told at II 19. On another occasion the saint is mentioned as visiting Cell Mór Díthruib a little further south (I 50). These places may perhaps lie on a route between Derry and Durrow.

**185** The poet (OIr. *fili*) occupied a position of high privilege in Irish society as part of a professional learned class, custodians of law, genealogy and other traditionally important learning.

**186** The word translated 'ruler', *tigern[i]us*, is a rare case of an Irish word with a Latin termination. OIr. *tigerna* means 'lord, chief', but its exact political significance at this date is hard to determine.

**187** See n. 133.

**188** Between this paragraph and the details given a few lines below, Adomnán provides several indications as to where this incident took place and who were the parties involved. The fight was between members of two rival branches of the Airgialla. It is not clear, however, whether the event was at all significant in the local political struggles or whether these were merely two more inconsequential violent deaths.

The Mugdorna, one of the group of tribes known collectively as the Airgialla, lived in south-west Ulster. The territory of Mugdorna was in what is now Co. Monaghan (where the barony of Cremorne represents the Irish *crích Mugdorna*). Cell Rois ('church of *ros* or headland') is identified by Reeves, p. 81n., with Carrickmacross in Co. Monaghan; this was presumably the principal church of the district of Fir Rois ('men of *ros*') on the southern edge of Airgialla territory; Máenach, prior of Fir Rois, is mentioned in AU 827. In Adomnán's time this area was evidently under the Mugdorna. On the basis of this passage, Byrne has written, 'We know from the testimony of Adomnán that the Mugdorna were powerful in the archaic period' (*Irish Kings*, p. 116), by which I take it he means the sixth and seventh centuries. (He also observes, p. 117, that the rise of Fir Rois as 'an independent sub-kingdom within Airgialla' during the ninth century divided the area of Mugdorna into two.)

Colmán Cú mac Ailéni, one of the two killed, belonged to the ruling dynasty of Mugdorna. His brother Máel Dúin mac Ailéni died in AU 611 as king of Mugdorna. The latter's son, Máel Bresail mac Máele Dúin, died in AU 665; an eighth-century poem describes him as 'king of Ráith Commair', adding 'he does not refuse any contest' (O Daly, 'A poem on the Airgialla', stanza 47). The place-name Ráith Commair, if it has been rightly identified as lying near Clonard in Co. Meath, suggests a considerable southern extension of territory.

The Airthir were another tribe within the group of Airgialla, living to the east and south of Armagh. It would appear that Rónán mac Áedo was killed during his father's lifetime; Áed mac Colgen, king of Airthir, died in AU 609, when the Annals of Tigernach describe him as 'king of Airgialla and the Airthir', adding that he died on pilgrimage at Clonmacnoise.

**189** At I 1, p. 112 Adomnán has already referred to this experience. On both occasions the explanation offered comes from St Benedict's words to Germanus, as told in Gregory the Great's Dialogues II 35 (and referred to again, IV 8). Gregory's book, a late-sixth-century account of the miracles of local saints in Italy, including a Life of St Benedict, was almost certainly not known in Iona until after St Columba's death. The explanation, therefore, did not derive from the saint's own words, nor probably from Luigbe's testimony 'in the presence of other saints'. The words and the explanation come from Adomnán's reading, a point that must cast doubt on the impression he tries to give that his statements depend on sworn witness; see Introduction, p. 59.

**190** Acts 9:15.

**191** 2 Cor. 12:2. Compare Bede's Life of St Cuthbert, § 7:

He was also wont to add in all humility something about any spiritual gift which the heavenly grace had bestowed on himself; sometimes he would do so openly, but sometimes he would be at pains to do so in a veiled manner, as though it had happened to another person. Nevertheless those who heard understood that he was speaking of himself after the example of the apostle of the gentiles, who now recounts openly his own virtues and now speaks under the guise of another person, saying: 'I knew a man in Christ about fourteen years ago, such an one caught up even to the third heaven', and so on (Colgrave, *Two Lives*, pp. 178–9).

**192** Reeves, p. 85n., recalls that the Council of Arles in 314 had laid down that 'opportunity of celebrating mass should be given to a visiting bishop', and that in 619 the second Council of Seville prohibited priests from celebrating in the presence of a bishop, even though the normal usage elsewhere in the West was for bishops and priests to concelebrate.

Warren, *Liturgy and Ritual*, p. 128, on the basis of this passage erected a theory that 'a very singular custom existed in Iona of two or more priests being ordinarily united in the Eucharistic prayer and act of consecration; to consecrate singly being the prerogative of a bishop, or of individual priests specifically selected and empowered to consecrate on account of their sanctity or eminence'; for the last point he refers to this Life, III 17. I think he is wrong on all counts: normally one priest would celebrate, therefore in III 17 one of the four saints is chosen to celebrate; in the present story, however, St Columba proposes to concelebrate in order to do honour to the guest as a fellow priest. When the visitor is perceived to be a bishop, status demands that the host give place to the guest of superior grade; but if the bishop were the host, he would surely invite a visiting priest or bishop to join him in the celebration. Thus the unusual custom, which Warren treats as peculiar to Iona (p. 128) but later as 'peculiar to the Celtic rite' (p. 129) will be found to have no existence at all.

**193** Ernán is described in the body of this chapter as St Columba's uncle; the same is said of him in the list of the saint's disciples (see n. 356). The genealogies of Cenél Conaill do not name him among the six brothers of St Columba's father (O'Brien, *Corpus*, p. 163), so that one must suppose that he was the saint's maternal uncle. He cannot be identified in the martyrologies or the Genealogies of the Saints. The dedication to St Ernán of the church at Creich near Fionnphort in the Ross of Mull is modern.

**194** THE MONASTERY OF *HINBA* *Hinba* is the name of an island where St Columba had established a dependency of Iona, which he himself from time to time visited (I 21, II 24) and where he sometimes resided (III 5, 17, 18). It appears from III 5 that the saint was staying on *Hinba* in 574, the year of the royal ordination of Áedán mac Gabráin (see

n. 358). *Hinba* must have been founded therefore between 563 and 574. It has been suggested that it was founded before Iona, but there is no positive evidence to support this (see Introduction, p. 18). The name is used as though there was only one monastery on the island, whereas on Tiree the monastery at Mag Luinge is specified because there were others on the island. We know however from III 23, p. 230, that there was a hermitage on *Hinba* at a place called *Muirbolc Már* (see n. 415). We also know that there were penitents living among the monks of *Hinba* (I 21), and that the church at the monastery was very small (III 17 and see n. 387). Baithéne (I 21) and Ernán (I 45) were at different times prior of *Hinba*.

Attempts to locate *Hinba* have generally proved inconclusive. The name itself does not survive; many of the smaller Hebridean isles now have names dating only from the period of Scandinavian settlement. We have only one certain datum: *Muirbolc Már* 'great sea-bag' or 'great bay' should be an identifiable physical feature. One story refers to visitors from Ireland arriving at *Hinba* in search of St Columba (III 17); since it does not mention their first landing at Iona, it is possible that *Hinba* lay on the route from Ireland to Iona.

Guesses as to its location have ranged far and wide: Thomas Innes thought it was in Uist or the Long Island (Reeves, p. 87n.). Reeves himself is muddled: at p. 87n. he takes *Hinba* to be 'north of and not far distant from' Iona, and mentions the island of Canna; at p. 127n. and 135n. he wonders whether it may not be 'Elachnave' in the Garvellochs (though this is not north of Iona); at p. 197n. he comments that 'the identification of this island remains the great desideratum in Hebridean topogaphy'; at p. 222n. he deduces from III 17 that it 'might . . . be north' of Iona; at p. 294 he reports F. W. Clark's view that *Hinba* was the pre-Viking name of Colonsay or Colonsay and Oronsay together; and at p. 366n. Fergnae's retreat to the great bay (III 17) makes him think again of the beehive cells on 'Eilean-na-Naomh'. MacCarthy (p. 34) and Hogan (*Onomasticon*, p. 456) both abstracted from this that Reeves thought *Hinba* was either 'Elachnave' or Oronsay. Skene set out a more detailed case for Eileach an Naoimh (pp. 318–24); he was followed by Huyshe (p. 44n.), but Fowler, though admitting Skene's 'good reasons', remained judiciously uncertain (p. 34n.). Watson reviewed the case for what he insists should be called 'na h-Eileacha naomha' 'the holy islets' (perhaps meaning the Garvellochs collectively), which he says offer no suitable *Muirbolc Már*. In this he is surely right. (On the possibility that this was Adomnán's *Elen*, see n. 250.) Seeking somewhere lying on route from Ireland to Iona with an inlet large enough to deserve this term, he sees the question as a choice between Colonsay/Oronsay and Jura. He favours Jura, finding his *Muirbolc Már* in Loch Tarbert, and Fergnae's hermitage in a local cave; he also derives *Hinba* from Irish *inbe* 'incision', which to him 'suggests the deeply indented isle of Jura' (*Celtic Place-names*, pp. 81–4), a speculative proposition.

In recent years W. D. Lamont has argued for the island of Gunna, between Tiree and Coll, but this was based on the premises that Ioan mac Conaill was on his way *home* to Coll when his boat foundered (II 22), though this is not what Adomnán says, and that his presence at *Hinba* (II 24) necessarily implies that this was close to Coll; both premises are mistaken. In reply W. R. MacKay held that *Hinba* had to be north of Mull. Against this background Dr J. L. Campbell has proposed his own island of Canna; this at least has a great *muirbolc* in the bay that divides Canna from Sanday, but it seems to me too far north to make good topographical sense.

My own view I advance only as a balance of probabilities; no decisive argument seems available. The island of Colonsay lies in a situation that makes sense in all the contexts where *Hinba* is mentioned. It lies on the sea-route from Ireland to Iona. Between Colonsay and Oronsay there is a substantial dry anchorage; in another passage I have suggested that the emptying out of the sea at low tide may be the characteristic of a *muirbolc* (see n. 93), and so I suggest that here is Adomnán's *Muirbolc Már*. On the island of Oronsay is a medieval priory; does this perhaps continue the site of the Columban foundation?

**195** The Late Latin word *canaba* 'hut, shed' is exceedingly rare; there are few texts in which Adomnán might have met it, though it is found in later texts from Ireland.

Reeves, pp. 88n. and 440, rightly saw that in two Latin Lives of Irish saints it was used more specifically of a building for drying and threshing corn. Corn-kilns were in common use in early medieval Ireland, and were still used in the Hebrides until the nineteenth century. Skene, 'Notes on the early establishments', pp. 330–49, sought to identify this site in Adomnán with the remains of a stone kiln seen on Iona in 1772 by Thomas Pennant. For this there is no basis, and it helped mislead Skene into locating the early monastery somewhat north of the present abbey – in fact, outside the northern part of the vallum that forms the enclosure.

Perhaps in reaction to Skene, the Andersons translate *canaba* as 'shed'

(p. 307), and in discussion (p. 115) argue that Reeves's examples merely imply that 'a *canaba* (shed) or *zabulum* (barn) could be used as a drying-house for grain, by lighting a fire under a wicker wheel, upon which the ears of grain were laid'. There is common sense here, but they overlook vernacular evidence that directly associates the word *canaba* with OIr. *áith* 'drying-kiln (for grain)'. First, there is the Life of St Cainnech, to which Reeves pointed. Here, in § 35, we are told that the saint's household 'had no craftsmen or labourers who could build a *canaba* for drying and threshing the ears of corn, but instead they threshed in the field on a space of ground packed down hard and smooth'. I have proposed that this text was written in the eighth century by someone who had read Adomnán's Life. Although *canaba* can here be translated 'shed' (and later in the passage we are told they worked *sine domo* 'without a building'), none the less, a more specialized sense seems to be understood; and in the manuscript a later hand (late-fourteenth-century) has glossed *canaba* as Irish *áith* 'kiln'. In the Life of St Ciarán (which survives in a Latin text of the early thirteenth century, based on an older source, and an Irish text perhaps datable to about 1100) the wheel arrangement for drying the ears is described in the Latin text. Again 'shed' makes sense in translating the Latin (Macalister so translates *canaba* in *Lives of St Ciaran*, p. 22), but in the Irish Life the word used is *áith* 'kiln' (so translated by Macalister, p. 86). It seems to me, therefore, that we should accept that in Hiberno-Latin *canaba* was used in a specialized sense, the building that housed the equipment for drying corn before threshing; we can probably infer that, like a mill, this building had just the one function.

**196** A cross set up in St Columba's time would not have been a free-standing cross with arms (such as we are now accustomed to), but a plain pillar stone with a cross incised on its surface. The incised cross may have been quite elaborate in design; several from Ireland are illustrated in Hughes and Hamlin, *The Modern Traveller*, p. 85.

Adomnán is as good a witness as we shall find for the purpose of erecting such crosses, in or near the monastic enclosure, or elsewhere. Nor is he alone in saying that such crosses were erected in commemoration of events at particular places; compare III 23, p. 227. Muirchú, Life of St Patrick, I 12, says that in his day a cross marked the place from where St Patrick, returning as a missionary bishop, first saw again the place of his earlier captivity. Probable eighth-century examples will be found in several saints' Lives: the Life of St Molua, § 3; the Life of St

Cainnech, § 24; the Life of St Fintan or Munnu, § 19; and the Life of St Áed, § 43.

**197** Various identifications have been proposed for this; several contenders in Mull and on the mainland nearby are listed by Reeves, p. 88n. The only guidance comes from the next place-name, *Cruach Rannoch*, whose location is in any case uncertain. Watson, *Celtic Place-names*, p. 94, favoured Salachan in Morvern (across the Sound of Mull from Aros); this settlement (at OD NM 613474) is now a few ruins, having been largely abandoned in the late eighteenth or early nineteenth century (see Gaskell, *Morvern Transformed*, p. 152). Skene, pp. 33, 264, and Anderson and Anderson, p. 87, prefer Corry on the west side of Loch Linnhe (OD NM 835525), below Sgurr Shalachain (but I note that Coire Shalachain occurs as the name of a high corrie to the west of that peak – an unlikely spot). These are nothing more than shots.

The second element is a diminutive of OIr. *sail*, *sailech* 'willow tree', and is common in place-names. The first element is Irish *coire* 'cauldron', common now in Scottish place-names as 'a more or less circular hollow in the hills, with only one outlet' (Watson, *Celtic Place-names*, p. 94); *if* that is what it means in this name, it is by far the earliest recorded example of corrie.

**198** This place-name *stagnum Crog reth* 'the lake of *Crog reth*' is not securely located. *Crog* is apparently an old Brittonic cognate of Irish *cruach* 'hill'; *reth* may be similarly related to Irish *raith* 'fern'; the name has no obvious modern reflex. Nor is it possible to derive from the context any sense of where one should be looking. Colgan thought it was in Ireland; Hogan, *Onomasticon*, p. 497, merely says 'in Scotland or Ireland'; Reeves, p. 88n., had no idea, but sensibly took it to be in Scotland. Skene, pp. 33, 328, guessed Loch Creran in Appin, but this is linguistically impossible. Watson, *Celtic Place-names*, p. 78, followed by Anderson and Anderson, pp. 159, 308n., noted that *raith* is the stem of the name Rannoch, and guessed that 'Cruach Rannoch' might apply to the range of hills west of Loch Rannoch. A more cautious translation would be: 'I live in the district by the shores of the loch of *Crog reth*.'

**199** This man is not mentioned elsewhere. His name is Irish. The folktale elements in this story have been discussed by Picard, 'The strange death of Guaire mac Áedáin'.

**200** Instead of the usual form Dal Reti, Adomnán here uses Korku

Reti, but in Irish tribal names *dál* and *corco* are used in exactly the same way. I therefore follow the Andersons, pp. 35, 309n., in associating Guaire with Dalriada. Reeves, p. 89n., looked instead to Corco Roíde, now Corkaree, Co. Westmeath, and was followed by Skene and Fowler. Adomnán, however, would not have written 'Reti' for 'Roíde' (a form found below, III 23, p. 230, and in Tírechán, § 16). In any case, as Reeves realized, this story has a coastal setting and Westmeath is far inland.

**201** This phrase is far from clear in its meaning: *cristiliam de astili eradebat* 'he was shaving away the *cristilia* from a spear-shaft'. The word *cristilia* occurs nowhere else; Colgan guessed that it meant the point of a spear, Reeves (p. 442) focused on *eradebat* and decided that *cristilia* meant the surface that had to be scraped off, 'rust' or 'bark'. Editors have followed one or the other. Picard, 'Strange death', p. 367, translates 'scraping the barbed point of a spear', and gives his reasons, pp. 371, 375. No explanation of the word or its meaning has been quite satisfactory from the linguistic point of view. Guaire may have been sharpening a stick by shaving off slivers at one end or he may have been stripping off the surface all along; in either case the stick is unlikely to have been already fitted with a (metal) spearhead.

**202** The phrase here, *post nonam diei horam* 'after the ninth hour of the day', appears only to signify the time of day, reckoned from sunrise to sunset. This usage is found below, 'after the tenth hour of the fourteenth day' (II 42). When the prophecy is fulfilled, however, the phrase is simply *post horam nonam*, which could mean 'after Nones', the office sung at the ninth hour in the middle of the afternoon (see n. 238).

**203** The Latin word here strictly means 'crane'. According to Gerald of Wales, describing Ireland about 1186, these birds were very numerous, sometimes in flocks of a hundred or more; *Topographia Hibernie*, I 14. Their bones have been found in archaeological deposits. (Cranes were also common in the English Fenland until the sixteenth century; by the eighteenth century they had become rare and accidental visitors.) It is, however, impossible to be sure that Adomnán's ornithology would have distinguished a crane from a heron; where Latin distinguishes between *grus* 'crane' and *ardea* 'heron', Irish *corr* applies to both these large waders. It seems to me that 'heron' may be the more appropriate translation for *grus*, here and elsewhere in Hiberno-Latin texts.

In one of the Middle Irish accounts of the meeting of the kings at Druim Cett (see n. 204), Columba is addressed as 'crane-cleric' (Irish *corrcléirech*), which he regarded as an affront. Dr Herbert translates the expression as 'stooping cleric', following B. MacCarthy's translation of the phrase *mac in chléirigh cuirr* in AU 1175.

I do not see in this passage any evidence that the heron or crane was the totem of St Columba's family in the pre-Christian period, as Finlay, *Columba*, pp. 23–4, supposes. Many birds and animals may have had totem functions in Celtic paganism, but that should not prevent their being mentioned by Christian authors without reference to pagan connotations.

**204** THE MEETING OF THE KINGS AT DRUIM CETT Adomnán refers three times to the conference of the kings (*condictum regum*) at Druim Cett (I 49, 50, II 6) and on two other occasions tells of minor events when he was at Druim Cett (I 10, 11). I take all of these references to signify a single occasion, the event that the Annals of Ulster describe thus: *Magna con[uen]tio Droma Ceta, in qua erant Colum Cille ocus Áedh mc Ainmirech* 'the great meeting of Druim Cett, at which were present Columb Cille and Áed mac Ainmirech'. (Editors of the annals have chosen to read *con[uen]tio* 'coming together, meeting'. The manuscript actually reads *contio* 'public assembly'. If one chooses to expand, one could equally read *con[dic]tio* 'talking together, conference', the word closest to Adomnán's *condictum*.)

There is general agreement that the location of the meeting-place is to be identified as the Mullagh, also known as Daisy Hill, less than a mile south of Limavady, between Derry and Coleraine; Reeves, p. 37n. In the early seventeenth century the place was the scene of an annual commemoration of the meeting, held on All Saints' Day each year, according to Colgan, *Acta*, p. 204 n. 13. Whether or not the site was precisely remembered, this locality conforms with Adomnán's evidence, which indicates that Columba passed through Coleraine on his way home after the conference. It lies on the borders of the territories ruled by the king of Cenél nÉogain and those of the Cruithin in the plain of Eilne. While the Annals of Ulster mention the presence of Áed mac Ainmirech and the saint, close kinsmen, it is clear from Adomnán that the conference was essentially between Áed and Áedán mac Gabráin, king of Dál Riata in both Scotland and Ireland. The meeting-place lay not far to the west of his Irish territory. We know that Áed's entourage included his son Domnall (I 10) and at least one royal hostage (I 11). One may guess that Áedán too was attended by his retinue, and that

Columba was present as close kin to Áed and as the leading holy man of Dalriada. St Comgall's presence may be inferred from this chapter; he was perhaps there as the chief holy man of the Ulaid. One can get this far merely from Adomnán's words and some attempted political geography.

Anything we may infer beyond this is highly doubtful. The first major problem is the date of the event. The Annals of Ulster assign a date of 575, one year after Áedán's ordination as king. Most historians have not demurred in accepting this, including Dr M. O. Anderson, Dr Bannerman, and Dr Smyth. Professor Byrne, however, acutely pointed out that in 575 Áed mac Ainmirech had not yet become king; *Irish Kings*, pp. 110–11 (though at pp. 13 and 106 he accepts the date 575). In fact, if we follow the annals, Áed had not even become king of Cenél Conaill, and it was more than ten years later that he became overking of the Northern Uí Néill and high king. Byrne goes on to say that the earliest known list of kings of Ireland does not include Áed, and that our knowledge of the high kingship from the death of Diarmait mac Cerbaill in 565 to the consolidation of Áed's position in the 590s is extremely uncertain. Within the framework of annal dates, however, it is clear that Báetán mac Ninnedo (d. 586), Áed's cousin, was king of Cenél Conaill and of the Northern Uí Néill until his death. Áed's first victory is given at two dates, 587 or 593. It would appear therefore that the conference at Druim Cett was entered retrospectively at the wrong date, and that we should rather date it to somewhere between 586 and Columba's death in 597. Comgall and Áedán were alive right through this period. A further clue that 575 is too early may be inferred from Adomnán: he mentions two boys present at the meeting, and in both cases their dates of death suggest a lifespan of nearly eighty years, which would be unusual at this date if not actually remarkable (see nn. 86, 88). If the date of the conference at Druim Cett is moved to *c.* 590, their ages at death would be unexceptional.

The business of the meeting is not mentioned by Adomnán nor by the Annals of Ulster. One may reasonably infer from the identity of the principal participants that the main business was to agree on relations between the Northern Uí Néill and the Dál Riata of Ulster and Scottish Dalriada. What they agreed is less easy to infer; any treaty between kings in early Ireland did not bind their successors, so that inference from later historical events is dangerous.

A good deal of speculation has been devoted to the agenda set out by the preface to the *Amrae Coluimb Chille*. This preface was written, as Dr Herbert has shown, in 1007, when Ferdomnach, abbot of Kells and coarb of Columb Cille, was installed at a great assembly under the patronage of Máel Sechnaill, overlord of the Southern Uí Néill and king of Tara. This was a revival of the Fair of Tailtiu, which had not been held since 927 (see n. 355). The preface seems to offer the meeting at Druim Cett as an ancient antecedent for the occasion. It associates the meeting with the writing of the *Amrae* and includes in the business Columba's protection of the poets of Ireland, a reflection of this aspect of his role in Middle Irish tradition.

**205** ST COMGALL OF BANGOR St Comgall was abbot of Bangor on the south side of Belfast Lough, a monastery that he founded, according to the Annals of Ulster, in 555 or 559. Adomnán refers to him as a founder of monasteries (III 17) and tells how St Columba clairvoyantly witnessed the drowning of certain monks of St Comgall while they were sailing on Belfast Lough (III 13). Comgall's death is recorded at AU 601 and 602, when he was credited with a great age: his birth was entered retrospectively in the annals for 516 and 520, making him at least eighty years old. His death was commemorated on 10 May, and the Martyrology of Tallaght unusually adds that he was then in his ninety-first year and had been abbot for 50 years 3 months and 10 days, a precise reckoning that was later repeated by the Annals of Tigernach.

The Martyrology of Notker, compiled at St Gallen in the 890s, contains a notice of St Columba, which refers to St Comgall as 'the sole heir of St Columba's virtues and merits'. The wording led Zimmer to believe that this was written between Columba's death in 597 and Comgall's in 601–2; if he were correct (which is doubtful), this would be an important contemporary witness to the high esteem in which St Comgall was held. What Notker says is that St Columba 'had very many pupils or comrades his equal in sanctity, but one, like Isaac, was the sole heir of his virtues and merits. This was Comgall, distinguished by the Latin name Faustus, teacher of St Columbanus, who was in turn the master of our learned father Gallus' (*PL* 131. 1103B). Comgall is mentioned as the link between Columba and Notker's own monastery of St Gallen.

Comgall's monastery at Bangor soon flourished, and Columbanus was a monk and student there in Comgall's lifetime. A seventh-century hymn-book known as the Antiphonary of Bangor still survives.

The Life of St Comgall, as we know it today, is an early thirteenth-century reworking of an older Life of uncertain date. (The older text is mentioned by Jocelin of Furness in the twelfth century.) It includes a story that appears to be an elaboration of the account by Adomnán of how Columba first entered the fortress of the Pictish king (II 35 and n. 299).

**206** The battle of Dún Cethirn is recorded in AU 629: 'the battle of Dún Cethirn, in which Congal Cáech fled and Domnall mac Áedo was victor, in which fell Guaire mac Forinnáin'. Its background is quite complex.

Domnall mac Áedo (see n. 86), the son of Áed mac Ainmirech, was blessed as a child at Druim Cett by his kinsman Columba. After Áed's death in 598 the high kingship was taken over by two rivals, Áed Sláine, king of Brega, from the Southern Uí Néill, and Colmán Rímid from the Northern Uí Néill lineage of Cenél nÉogain (see n. 95). After their deaths in 604 the kingship remained with Cenél nÉogain until 612, when it was taken by Máel Cobo, an elder son of Áed mac Ainmirech, who was king until his death in 615. During the next twelve years the two main branches of the Northern Uí Néill were at odds with one another, and the two branches of the Southern Uí Néill were likewise locked in a feud. This seems to have created opportunities for others. Máel Cobo was killed by Suibne Mend, who belonged to a minor lineage of the Cenél nÉogain: his becoming king of Cenél nÉogain was itself an achievement, and he appears to have been Northern Uí Néill overking and high king from 615 until 628. In that year he was able to defeat Domnall mac Áedo in the battle of Both. This is the first we hear of Domnall's efforts to seize the kingship, though we must presume he was already king of Cenél Conaill. Soon after the battle of Both, Suibne Mend was murdered by Congal Cáech, a king from an obscure branch of the Cruithin, who for ten years was to play a major part in the highest levels of Irish political warfare.

This complicated background sets the scene for two battles referred to in the Life, Dún Cethirn here and Mag Roth. The story is discussed in detail by Charles-Edwards and Kelly, *Bechbretha*, pp. 123–31. In this battle, in 629, Congal was defeated by Domnall mac Áedo. The exact location of the battle is uncertain, but it seems to have been between Limavady and Coleraine, and therefore very much on the borders of the Ulaid and the Northern Uí Néill, over whom Domnall was by now overking. Congal may have attacked in the hope of seeing off a powerful rival. It seems likely that success in this battle left Domnall without a serious rival for the high kingship. According to the mid- or late-seventh-century law tract *Bechbretha*, Congal Cáech was king of Ireland until he lost the sight of one eye through a bee-sting: this is the only early evidence that Congal held the kingship, but his tenure seems to have been brief, between the murder of Suibne Mend in 628 and this defeat in 629. He remained a threat to Domnall mac Áedo, however, and in 637 attacked Domnall's territory in alliance with Domnall Brecc, king of Dalriada. Domnall's victory on that occasion in the battle of Mag Roth was the subject of another prophecy by St Columba (see III 5 and n. 362).

**207** Fínán, who cannot be identified in the martyrologies, appears to have been a holy man not formally attached to the *familia* of St Columba nor to that of St Comgall. His presence as an anchorite 'beside [*iuxta*] the monastery of Durrow', but not belonging to it, provides an insight into a form of devotional life that was essentially solitary but did not seek a deserted location.

If Fínán was twenty at the time of the battle of Dún Cethirn, he was seventy when Adomnán became abbot. This is one of only two occasions when Adomnán mentions himself as the recipient of a testimony relating to the saint. He also explains how the miracle came to be recognized: the old men at Camus knew the prophecy; the young man brought the news, which they perceived as its validation, and it was he who lived on to testify to that. The other occasion is in III 19.

Camus, Co. Derry, is situated on the west bank of the River Bann three miles or so south of Coleraine. It was anciently called Cambus Comgaill, from which it would seem to have been a dependency of Bangor. Reeves, p. 97n., reports that the ancient cemetery preserved an early sculptured cross until it was overturned in 1760.

**208** Coleraine, on the east bank of the River Bann, lay in Mag nEilni 'the plain of Eilne', the area of plain between the rivers Bann and Bush, occupied by a branch of Dál nAraide. It is described as a *monasterium* here, yet has a bishop and clearly serves as the principal church for the people of Eilne. Tírechán also mentions the place, saying that Patrick (approaching from the south-west) 'crossed the River Bann and blessed the place where there is the small church of Coleraine in Eilne, where there was [*Bieler suggests we read* is] a bishop, and he founded many other churches in Eilne'; Patrick then moved on east across the River Bush to Dunseverick on the Antrim coast, but afterwards 'he returned to Mag nEilni and built many churches which now belong to Connor' (Bieler, *Patrician Texts*, p. 161). Connor was the principal church of Dál nAraide as a whole, but it seems that Coleraine was another, if less important, episcopal see in their territory. It does not feature in the annals until 731.

The offerings (*xenia*) referred to consist of food, as did those sent by St Columba to the reformed Erc in I 41, where the same word is used. It seems they are given as a mark of respect to the visiting saint and would be perhaps consumed at a feast held during the visit. Compare the offerings brought to Cell Mór Díthruib 'for his arrival', which are mentioned later in the chapter. They do not represent any formal tribute, and do not indicate that Columba was able to exercise powers of visitation at Coleraine.

**209** John O'Donovan in the 1830s identified Cell Mór Díthruib with the church of Kilmore, Co. Roscommon, on the west side of the River Shannon, three miles south of Jamestown (near Carrick on Shannon). Reeves, p. 99n., adds some corroboration. Nothing is known for certain about the early history of this place. Since OIr. *díthrub* means 'place without habitation, wilderness', it was presumably in origin an eremitical foundation.

The eighth-century Life of St Fintan or Munnu, § 5, has this to say: 'After this St Munnu came to the school of St Columb Cille at Cell Mór Díthruib, and there studied the sacred scripture with the saint.' St Columba, after singing the words taught by the Holy Spirit, prophesied to Baithéne that Munnu would himself be a spiritual teacher. Munnu next spent nineteen years at Devenish on Lough Erne, and then went to Iona, where he arrived shortly after St Columba's death. From this Anderson and Anderson, p. 70, calculated that the episode at Cell Mór Díthruib happened in 578. Adomnán, however, provides no evidence to support the possibility that Columba and Baithéne had established a school here; rather, Columba appears to be a visitor. Anderson and Anderson suggest that Cell Mór is near enough to Lough Key (see I 42, II 19) for this to belong to the same visit to Co. Roscommon.

**210** ST UINNIAU Here, and in I I, p. 110, Adomnán mentions St *Finnbar*, the bishop with whom St Columba studied as a young deacon in Ireland. Later in this chapter he calls him St *Uinniau*, and at III 4 St *Finnio*. The context makes it clear that all three forms of the name refer to the same person, but it is not so easy to identify him. The spellings *Uinniau* and *Finnio* are respectively British and Irish forms of the same name, made up of the word 'white' (Brit. *uuin*, later Welsh *gwyn*; Irish *finn*) and a hypocoristic suffix. *Finnbarr* means 'white crest', so that it would seem that this is the full form of the bishop's name; the other forms are diminutives.

St Finnbarr is the name of the patron saint of Cork, but one cannot assume that he is meant. The name *Finnian* is another diminutive, and there are two famous saints, St Finnian of Moville and St Finnian of Clonard. According to the annals, the former died in 549, the latter in 579, while St Finnbarr has no obit. Each saint was commemorated on a different day in the calendar, and when saints' genealogies came to be assembled each was given a different family tree. It is one of the fundamental canons of hagiography that the date of a saint's commemoration is conscientiously adhered to; two saints of the same name celebrated in different places on the same date may be different manifestations of the cult of the same saint. While these three saints have all the same name (in different forms), they are in all other respects distinct, and therefore ought to be separate historical individuals. Professor Ó Riain ('St Finnbarr'), however, has proposed to reject the so-called 'hagiographical coordinates' of place and feast day when dealing with Irish saints. He argues that the cult of a single saint has subdivided at a later date than the writing of this Life. If he is right, one cannot identify Uinniau with any one of the three later saintly cults: he is all of them. Even if Ó Riain is not right, it is none the less better to regard Uinniau as an unlocated sixth-century holy man, known to us from early sources, than to confuse the issue by seeking an identification with any one of the three distinct cults, of whose history in the sixth century nothing is known. For this reason I have always used the form *Uinniau* to avoid prejudging the issue and implying an equation with Finnbarr or one of the Finnians.

**211** This phrase is influenced by John 2:11. Christ's first miracle was imitated by a number of Irish saints, as noted by Reeves, p. 104n.

**212** On the agricultural year, see n. 335.

**213** Withies were commonly used as building material. Reeves, p. 106n., provides evidence from other saints' Lives and Fowler, p. 72n., cites place-name evidence for churches made of hurdles. Most of the monastery at Iona was probably built this way. This story refers to the lesser building materials, and another (II 45) mentions the import of large timbers for a house. Together they suggest that all building materials had to be shipped to Iona.

**214** The unidentified place *Delcros* (*delc* 'thorn' + *ros* 'headland') is obviously not far from Iona – indeed Findchán and his neighbours appear to be the local lay community, perhaps on the Ross of Mull.

The Middle Irish homily, § 33, treats the story as a local one, but has changed the setting from Iona to Derry.

**215** Adomnán names the hill in Latin, *munitio magna* 'the great fort', which in Irish is *dún mór*. Old Irish *dún* (like Scottish Gaelic *dùn*) means both 'fort' and 'hill'; Dùn Ì, the largest hill in Iona, was presumably called *Dún Mór* in the seventh century. There is no fort on the hill, but I do not think this has any significance. Reeves, p. 107n., preferred to seek traces of fortification on Dùn Bhùirg, on the north-west coast of the island.

**216** See n. 179 on Silnán mac Nemaidon.

**217** Retrospective medical diagnosis is never safe, since one does not know what reliance may be placed on the description of the symptoms. A fatal disease, spreading as an epidemic, characterized by pustules, and afflicting cattle as well as humans, would seem to be *variola* (smallpox, cowpox). The symptoms of this disease, and the epidemiology of an outbreak, were probably well known in the Middle Ages and could have been recognized by Adomnán's audience.

**218** Compare II 34. The two-word phrase *uita comite* from Gen. 18:10, 14, was a cliché of Christian Latin. (It was in fact a bad translation of a Hebrew phrase meaning 'about this time of year'; compare 2 Kings 4:16.)

**219** This use of bread can be paralleled in Bede's Life of St Cuthbert, c. 31. Reeves did not comment on the use of bread, but (p. 110n.) on the dipping in water of objects with holy associations to effect cures, which we see here and in II 5 and 33. While here the terms are specific, in II 5 Adomnán refers to a 'blessing' kept in a box and used in the same way, its substance not specified; then in II 17 a block of salt that had been blessed is likewise called a 'blessing', using two Latin words *benedictio* and the Greek-derived *eulogia*. The latter term is used specifically in liturgical Latin for the bread presented to the priest at the offertory, blessed by his prayers, from which the bread for the Eucharist was taken. The remainder was distributed or, as we see below in II 13, consumed at the monastic meal. On that passage, Reeves, p. 122n., gives a characteristically learned note, comparing the practice of Iona with other ecclesiastical sources. The Roman Catholic bishop MacCarthy, p. 82n., was keen to link Adomnán's account here with the reverent use of the *eulogia*, a connection that the Anglican Reeves had not made. In II 5 MacCarthy was confident that the 'blessing' in Mogain's box was a piece of bread, the *eulogia*.

**220** The territory of Árd Ciannachta is generally considered to have been the barony of Ferrard, in Co. Louth, roughly between Ardee and Drogheda on the modern map. This does not lie within the area indicated by Adomnán as between the River Delvin (which reaches the sea near Gormanston, south of Drogheda) and Dublin. We should probably infer that Árd Ciannachta occupied a more extensive area in the seventh century than later.

**221** The words *cum salubri pane* here mean simply 'with the bread that brings health'; I do not see an allusion to the sacrament as the bread that brings salvation.

**222** On the collection of testimonies, see n. 15 and Introduction, p. 56.

**223** Clochar Macc nDaiméni 'the stony place of the sons of Daiméne' is now Clogher, Co. Tyrone. Daiméne's death is recorded in AU 565, and his son Conall's in AU 609; according to the genealogies, there were eight or nine sons (O'Brien, *Corpus*, pp. 139, 140). The kindred of Daiméne (Síl nDaiméni) belonged to the Uí Chremthainn, one of the tribes of the Airgialla; from the sixth to the ninth century, the descendants of Daiméne were the principal lineage providing the rulers of Uí Chremthainn. The site of Clochar Macc nDaiméni (though not yet so named) was probably already in St Columba's time a royal seat, for Daiméne's father, Coirpre, is recorded as king of Airgialla at his death in AU 514.

The site has been studied by Richard Warner. He suggests that the 'stony place' took its name from a prehistoric walled enclosure, which by the fifth century was 'a ruin amid extensive stone rubble'. A new palisaded enclosure was built in the fifth century, and around 600 this was replaced by 'a very strong, though univallate, ringfort, whose occupation lasted to about AD 800 and whose occupants continued to import luxury goods . . . from Gaul and England'. He associates this rebuilding with the success of the sons of Daiméne in establishing control over their tribe.

The church at Clogher was founded on a site about half a mile north of the royal cashel; the date of its foundation is unknown.

An interesting but unanswerable question is whether the virgin

Mogain's 'house' was associated with the church or was part of her brothers' establishment.

**224** The name Lugaid was common in early medieval Ireland, so the nickname *láitir* 'strong' (here and at II 38) may be intended to distinguish him from another monk called Lugaid. Here Columba sends him as his representative to Clogher, and at II 38 Lugaid Láitir again figures in the same capacity, though there is no indication that the two stories relate to the same occasion. The name Lugaid also occurs without the nickname in I 22; in that story he was returning from Ireland, so we may perhaps infer that the same person is meant, and that he habitually travelled between Iona and Ireland on the saint's business. This was certainly inferred by MacCarthy, p. 36n., who describes him as 'the carrier of the monastery'. Among St Columba's original disciples (see n. 356) was Lugaid moccu Temnae, but one cannot tell whether he is the same or another.

**225** In Gregory's Dialogues, I 15, someone's hip is broken in two, and is miraculously healed with water blessed by Fortunatus. If Adomnán has borrowed from this story, he has taken only the most basic words, 'hip', 'broken in two', 'blessed', 'water'. The lively setting, the element of the pinewood box, and the saint's prophecy give the episode a circumstantial character.

**226** The 'blessing' in the box was an object that the saint had blessed; compare II 7, 33.

**227** Some words are missing from MS A here: *coram* 'in the presence of' is left open, with no one specified, but one must assume *te* 'you'; *describo* 'I write' is found only in the B MSS.

**228** The phrase *petra salis* 'a stone of salt' has been taken to mean a piece of rock-salt by all editors since Fowler, p. 77n. This is doubtful. A common Old Irish term for salt is *murluaithe* 'sea-ashes', indicating the coastal production of sea-salt, which would be moulded into cakes or bricks. Scott, 'Some conflicts', p. 115, writes: 'So far no trace of the briquetage associated with early salt moulding has been identified here [in Ireland]. However, since it is unlikely that rock-salt was mined in Ireland before the 19th century, we might identify the two "stones" of salt (*dá cloich tsailenn*) sent by St Senan to St Brigit as moulded salt blocks.' Cormac's Glossary actually derives *salann* 'salt' as *sáil* + *onn* 'sea + stone', 'stone of the sea'. The story indicates the method of storing salt.

**229** Some medieval book-satchels from Ireland survive; see Waterer, 'Irish book-satchels'.

**230** For Columba as a scribe, see n. 125.

**231** From this we learn that a weekly cycle of hymns was used in the church at Iona. What those hymns were, we can hardly begin to guess; no volume now survives that matches this description, and most of the hymns known from Irish manuscripts seem more suited to special occasions.

**232** Éoganán is an Irish name, not recorded in Pictland until the ninth century, when King Éoganán was the son of an Irish father. Yet Adomnán says this man was 'of Pictish origin'. Anderson and Anderson, p. 344n., suggest that a priest, living in Ireland but born in Pictland, and who possessed a book supposedly in St Columba's own handwriting, 'had very probably gone to Ireland from Iona, and may have been educated there'. He may have adopted an Irish name on the way, or at least put an Irish dress on his Pictish name.

Reeves, p. 117n., on the other hand, followed a now outdated approach of equating Picts with the Irish Cruithin, and tried to find a group of Cruithin near Leinster. Irish Picts, popularized by the eminent historian Eóin MacNeill and satirized by Sellar and Yeatman in *1066 and All That*, have had their day. 'The Irish Cruithin are never called *Picti*, and it is a serious error to speak, as MacNeill does, of "Picts" in Ireland' (O'Rahilly, *Early Irish History*, p. 342).

**233** Adomnán clearly indicates that he knew a holy well in Ardnamurchan dedicated to St Columba. Stories of this kind are common in Irish and Welsh saints' Lives; they are meant to explain the virtues of particular wells. Few such wells are remembered in the west highlands, but they remain common in Celtic areas where the Reformation did not weaken local superstitions to such a degree, especially in Ireland, Cornwall and Brittany. In Donegal today there are still many wells dedicated to St Columba. The next chapter (and note) shows the pagan origin of this cult of wells.

**234** While the worship of the well is condemned here, both this story and the previous one demonstrate that Adomnán approved the continuing reverence for miraculous holy wells. Pagan well-worship was easily transmuted into Christian practice, which survived widely until the beginning of this century, and still continues at places in Ireland and Brittany. Wells and springs have been places of religious devotion for many cultures. In Iron Age Britain it was an area where Roman and Celtic paganism harmonized easily; Ross, *Pagan Celtic Britain*, pp. 46–59.

**235** Several stories are told by Adomnán about the defeat or discomfiture of Pictish wizards (I 37; II 17, 32, 33, 34).

**236** I read *exinanire* in the Latin; this word is written as *ex in ani ré* in MS A, which the Andersons emend to *ex inani re* 'to no purpose, vainly'. They translate the sentence: 'Hearing this, he ceased to pour out vainly bitter water into the green wave [?] and began to pour out sweet and fervent paryers to the Lord.' Here they have had to translate *fundere* 'to pour' twice. The reading of the B MSS which I follow makes this unnecessary; *exinanire* 'to empty' provides a verb in the first part of the sentence. Their suggestion that pouring water into the sea was an Irish proverb of futility cannot be proven, and is not obviously relevant unless their reading is followed. The sentence includes an Irish phrase *hininglas* [i.e. *hi n-in glas* 'into the grey-green (sea)'].

**237** On St Cainnech, see n. 68. His monastery at Aghaboe is in Co. Laois, Ireland. The Life of St Cainnech, § 54, contains a shortened version of this story.

**238** THE MONASTIC OFFICE IN IONA The round of daily services was sung in Iona as in other monasteries, but the Latin words can be difficult to interpret. Most offices were known simply by the time of day when they were sung, 'the third hour', 'the sixth hour', 'the ninth hour'. In one instance it appears that these words mean no more than at a particular time of day (I 48 and n. 202). In most cases, however, I have interpreted such phrases as referring to the canonical hours when services were sung, distinguished by the names Terce, Sext and Nones.

The services for a particular day began in the evening with vespers (I 37, where Columba and his monks sang the service while staying in Pictland; III 23, p. 228). On Saturday night at least there was a midnight office (*media nocte*) followed by matins, perhaps at first light, when 'the morning hymns' were sung (III 23, p. 231). It is possible that the office of Prime was sung at the first hour (*prima hora*), but the one reference to this time of day makes no mention of a service (II 5). The offices of Terce and Sext are mentioned on St Columba's feast day (II 45), but the reference to 'the third hour' in II 15 is less clearly a service. Nones is mentioned twice (II 13, 38), apparently on ordinary days.

**239** The word is *eulogia*, on which see n. 219. This would be the main meal of the day.

**240** On shoes of this period, see n. 376.

**241** The saint's staff (Latin *baculum*, Irish *bachall*), like a bishop's crook, was not so much for support as a symbol of his saintly role. In his own Life, probably written in the eighth century, St Cainnech is referred to, sometimes contemptuously, as *baculatus* 'the man with a staff'. The taking of a staff came to signify entering monastic life: thus in 782 the Annals of Ulster mention 'the [taking of the] staff by Artgal mac Cathail, king of Connacht, and his pilgrimage the following year to Iona'; he was not a visiting pilgrim, for the term 'pilgrimage' also signifies the monastic life, and he died at Iona in 791. Saints' staffs were often preserved as relics. The *bachall* of St Patrick survived hundreds of years preserved as a relic, and the *bachall* of St Moluag of Lismore is even today in the care of its hereditary keeper, the Baron of Bachall, in the island of Lismore near Oban.

**242** The island is called *Oidecha insula* and *terrulae Aithche* in MS A; the two forms would be nominative and genitive of an Irish noun Aídech, gen. Aíthche (compare OIr. *adaig*, gen. *aithche* 'night'). In the B MSS the form is Ouidetha/Ouidecha (the letters c and t were easily confused). The name has not been explained linguistically.

Reeves, p. 123n., citing *Senchus Fer nAlban*, took *Oidech*, the form used in that text, to be an alternative name for Islay, and in particular guessed that it was the form underlying the Oa, that is, the southern part of the island. Bishop Forbes, Skene's translator, p. 47, thought Oidech was not Islay but 'near Isla, probably Texa'. (Skene himself, p. 325, noted from a fifteenth-century source that there was a 'cell of monks' on Texa in the later Middle Ages.) Although Adomnán elsewhere uses *Ilea insula* for Islay, I am persuaded by Bannerman, *Studies*, p. 107, that *Oidech* is a district of Islay in *Senchus Fer nAlban*. I do not see the need to suppose that Adomnán's meaning is different here because he uses *insula* 'island', even though this led Bannerman, p. 115, to follow Skene.

**243** An account has been given elsewhere for both Baithéne (n. 55) and Colmán (n. 70).

**244** On Mag Luinge, see n. 182.

**245** Mark 9:23.

**246** Colmán Ua Briúin is not identifiable. For another Ua Briúin, see n. 279.

**247** The place-name *Cainle* is discussed at n. 174. The story may take place in Ireland or possibly Scottish Dalriada but not in Pictland. Both Foirtgern or Foirtchern and Silnán are Irish names. The latter is an alternative to Sillán as the diminutive of Sinell (compare Silnán mac Nemaidon, I 41, II 4, and n. 179).

The word *maleficus* I have translated 'sorcerer', following previous translators. He appears as a person of little status, and so was not a native pagan priest or *druí*, which Adomnán would probably have rendered *magus*. Rather, he represents a continuing, superstitious belief in witchcraft, which St Columba seeks to discredit. The sorcerer's powers are not denied, but are attributed to the devil.

**248** This sentence tantalizes by alluding to a potentially extremely interesting set of circumstances, in which the saint acts as mediator and judge, but the story is never told.

**249** Luigne moccu Min is mentioned here and at II 27, and on both occasions he appears to be a young man. In this story it is not clear that he is actually a member of the community, but at II 27 he is called 'fellow soldier', and we should probably presume that he was. If he was an old man when he became prior of the monastery of *Elen* (see next note), this was presumably some time after St Columba's death.

On Luigbe moccu Min and the possibility that the two names refer to one person, see n. 133.

**250** *Elena insula* remains unidentified, and all attempts are mere guesses. Reeves, p. 127n., thought that 'if number and age of monastic ruins demand a preference, none [of the islands] bids fairer to be the spot in question (unless indeed this be the *Hinba* of Adamnan) than Elachnave or Eileann naoimh'. He goes on to describe the ruins of the ancient eremitical monastery on Eileach an Naoimh in the Garvelloch Isles (on which see now RCAHMS, *Islay and Jura*, pp. 170–82), and concludes: 'Query, is this Hinba?' It is, I think, more likely to be *Elen* than *Hinba* (on which, see n. 194). Another view identifies Eileach an Naoimh with *Ailech*, an island church associated with St Brendan of Clonfert. This does not advance our search for *Elen*. Even so, there are many other islands where there could have been an ancient monastery. On Canna, for example, there are the remains of one (RCAHMS, *Outer Hebrides*, p. 217; Dunbar and Fisher, 'Sgor nam Ban-naomha', pp. 71–5). Skene, who was committed to the theory that Eileach an Naiomh was *Hinba*, had to find an alternative location for *Elen*. He suggests (pp. 324–5) that *Elen* was Nave Island off the coast of Islay. In my translation I have assumed that *Elen* is a small island, and that Adomnán refers to *the* monastery there and not *a* monastery among several.

**251** Adomnán uses the name *Sale* here and at II 45. In the second instance it clearly refers to somewhere in Scotland, but here the location of the next story on Lough Key has aroused the suspicion that this *Sale* is different, and in Ireland. Reeves, p. 128n., proposed *either* the River Blackwater, Co. Meath, which is named *Sele* by Adomnán's contemporary, Tírechán, § 9; *or* the River Shiel, which flows into Loch Moidart, north of Ardnamurchan, in Scotland. The latter identification is denied by Reeves, p. 177n., for the Scottish *Sale* of II 45 on grounds of wind-direction (see n. 340). It seems to me, however, that Adomnán probably refers to the same river on both occasions, and that the river is the Shiel, as determined by Watson, *Celtic Place-names*, p. 76, in spite of Reeves. The association of the present story with a similar one on Lough Key is determined only by their fishing element.

The Andersons translate the words *praedicabilis uiri sociales strenui piscatores* as 'the memorable man's companions, active fishers', and at p. 70 refer to 'the fishing expedition that Columba ... shared with friends who were keen fishermen'. On the basis of this strong interpretation of *sociales*, they suggest that the story belongs to the saint's youth in Ireland and so favour Reeves's suggestion, the Blackwater, Co. Meath.

**252** The salmon of wonderful size is a cliché of many saints' Lives, among them Gregory, Dialogues, III 10.

**253** For Columba's visit to Lough Key, see I 42 and n. 184.

**254** I have here, after some hesitation, followed a suggestion made by Anderson and Anderson, p. 366n. The words 'for which St Columba and his companions gave hearty thanks to God', in all the manuscripts, come at the end of the next paragraph, where 'which' would refer to *duabus memoratis piscationibus*. This is possible: 'In these two catches of fish, which we have described, and for which St Columba and his companions gave . . .'. It seems to me to make better sense, however, as I have translated it; the displacement of the words may have resulted from their being written in the margin of Adomnán's draft.

**255** In early Irish society cattle were the basic form of wealth, and a person's status in law depended in part on wealth. This dramatic increase in his livestock would go a long way to providing Nesán with the property-qualification for a much higher status in law. Change of legal status, however, was not accomplished purely on the basis of property. One might move up the grades of commoner but not change class, even if one had the wealth to support clients and become a lord. To progress from commoner into the noble grades would take until the third generation; Kelly, *Early Irish Law*, p. 12.

**256** This story is introduced from the B MSS, from where it was first printed by Pinkerton. That additions in B may be the work of Adomnán himself is proven by the first-person note at the beginning of II 44 (see n. 332). The present paragraph is wholly in keeping with Adomnán's style – Bieler, [review], p. 179, pointed to the resemblance of one sentence to *De Locis Sanctis* I 9. 6 – and is the longest such addition. Whether or not by Adomnán himself, however, we may be sure that this story was added in B (rather than omitted by A) because in II 21 Adomnán refers to Nesán 'in the previous story'. The B text did not alter this to take account of the addition; the priority of A over B is thus assured.

**257** Colmán appears again in the next chapter, where we learn that he lived in Ardnamurchan.

**258** Ioan, son of Conall mac Domnaill appears again at II 24, on the latter occasion along with his brothers. The terms used are significant. Here Adomnán calls him *quidam malefactor homo bonorum persecutor* 'a certain man who does evil, a persecutor of the good'; in II 24 the brothers were excommunicated as persecutors of churches and as *malefactoribus sociis*. In that episode one of them, at the devil's prompting, attempted to kill the saint. All this suggests that the brothers formed a band of 'men of evil', OIr. *díbergaig* (see n. 45).

Reeves, p. 132n., observed a difficulty in the indication of Ioan's descent. In St Columba's time Áedán mac Gabráin (d. 609) was the head of the lineage of Cenél nGabráin, which took its name from his father. Ioan is specifically said to belong to this royal lineage. How, Reeves wondered, could Ioan son of Conall son of Domnall *son of Gabrán* have also been a contemporary of the saint? But Adomnán does not say that Ioan's grandfather Domnall mac Gabráin was Áedán's brother (although we know that he had a brother of that name). Reeves has drawn that inference from the fact that Ioan belonged to Cenél nGabráin. Is it possible that Ioan is a cousin of Áedán, and that his grandfather Gabrán is an otherwise unrecorded collateral, a generation or two earlier than Gabrán the eponym of the kindred? The term itself is probably used anachronistically by Adomnán – surely such a term would not come into use until more than one generation had elapsed since the eponym.

**259** Compare Evagrius's Life of St Antony, c. 62: 'Our Saviour Jesus Christ glorifies those who glorify him.'

**260** On St Columba's presence in Ardnamurchan, see I 12. The geographical indications suggest that 'Sharp Bay' (*Aithchambas Artmuirchol*) should be near the western end of the peninsula, perhaps Sanna Bay. Watson, *Celtic Place-names*, p. 94, took *áith* 'sharp' to mean 'narrowing to a point at the inner end', but there is no bay in Ardnamurchan that meets this description, and which would also permit the driving of Colmán's cattle to a beached boat.

**261** The number of exiled royalty who spent some time in Iona is not insignificant, and the list began in the saint's lifetime with Oengus *bronbachal* (see I 13 and n. 94). Here, however, Adomnán reveals that lay exiles, using St Columba's protection as a refuge, were not necessarily lodged in Iona (where the guest-house was perhaps unsuitable for such use; see n. 69), but were rehoused in an appropriate secular household.

**262** The extent of oakwoods in Islay is now very limited and confined to the south-east, between Laphroaig and Ardtalla. Adomnán elsewhere refers to oak forest on Skye (II 26) and by Loch Shiel (II 45). In his time there was an extensive belt of oak forest extending along the mainland coast of Scotland; see map in Darling and Boyd, *Highlands and Islands*, p. 135.

**263** Adomnán names the man *Lám Dess* later in the chapter, but here translates the name into Latin. O'Brien, *Corpus*, p. 671, records other personal names of similar form, *Lámfhind* 'white hand', *Lám feola* 'hand of flesh', *Lám fri éc* 'hand against death'.

**264** On Ioan, see II 22 and n. 258.

**265** This name is given in Latin (*insula . . . quae Latine longa uocitari potest*), and may represent the modern Gaelic name for the long line of the Outer Hebrides, *An tEilean Fada* 'the Long Island'. Reeves, p. 137n., thought this 'much too far north for the application in the text', and suggested Lunga or Luing, islands off the coast of Lorn. As Watson, *Celtic Place-names*, p. 91, pointed out, these names bear only a superficial resemblance; Lunga is etymologically Lingay 'heather island', a Norse name, while Luing means 'ship'. (This latter term derives ultimately from Latin *nauis longa* 'long ship' (as at II 45), but Adomnán would surely not have Latinized it merely as *longa*.) Watson, however, agreed with Reeves that Adomnán was unlikely to refer to the Outer Hebrides. I can see no justification for this view. If Ioan could range from *Hinba* to Ardnamurchan and Coll (II 22), his associates could have reached the Outer Hebrides; and distance was no object to St Columba's clairvoyance.

**266** While the express reason for the inclusion of this story is its illustration of the saint's vengeance, mentioned at the end of the chapter, this heading is striking for another reason. Adomnán himself in 697 'gave the Law of Innocents to the peoples' – a law framed to protect non-combatants from violence; see Introduction, p. 51.

**267** On early schools in Leinster, see Introduction, p. 11.

**268** 'Dishonour' (*dehonoratio*) renders OIr. *sárugud* 'violation of the protection provided by a person of high honour-price'. This was an offence in law, as MacCarthy, p. 104n., alone among previous editors, pointed out.

**269** Compare Acts 5:5.

**270** Wild boar were found in the oakwoods of the west coast of Scotland until the later Middle Ages; Darling and Boyd, *Highlands and Islands*, p. 63.

**271** See n. 283 on St Columba in Pictland.

**272** This is the oldest story of the Loch Ness Monster. Believers in that creature point to this tale to prove that Nessie or her kind have lived in the loch for over a thousand years. Unbelievers say that here is a typical early medieval water-beast story (a type of folk-tale for which there are scores of parallels), which twentieth-century story-mongers have latched on to as the starting point of a modern sequel, supposedly justifying their claim that a beast exists. Certainly, other water-beast stories in the Lives of Irish saints have not led to claimed sightings. A rational explanation is proposed by Thomas, 'The "monster" episode', to wit, that a walrus or some such creature had got a little way up river.

**273** On Luigne moccu Min, see n. 249.

**274** Swimming was common in early Ireland. According to a medieval legal commentary, riding, marksmanship, swimming and boardgames were among the things that a foster-father was to teach his foster-children if they were the sons of nobles. Commoners' sons learnt agricultural skills, so that it seems we have here only military and recreational pursuits; Kelly, *Early Irish Law*, pp. 87, 91. Swimming and diving as recreation are mentioned in the Irish tale of the Battle of Ventry (ed. C. O'Rahilly, line 494) and in Manus O'Donnell's Life of St Columba, § 149.

**275** When Adomnán says this, does he mean that they were converted? He uses a similar expression at II 32, 'the God of the Christians was glorified', but on neither occasion does he say that the Picts believed or were baptized.

**276** The wording of the title, 'in *this* island', shows that Adomnán was writing in Iona. The story itself belongs in the narrative of St Columba's last days (III 23), where it is alluded to. The reason for its transference to this point in the book is that it is treated as a miracle involving animals. The absence of snakes, and in particular of poisonous snakes, is often attributed to a saint's blessing. In Gregory's Dialogues, III 15, Florentius's prayers cause the snakes in his area to die, and a further prayer leads to the removal of their corpses by birds, so that 'the place of his habitation was altogether free from snakes'. Usually the means of removing the snakes is not made clear, but permanent freedom from them is attributed to the influence of several saints, most notably St Patrick in Ireland. Reeves, p. 142n., maintained that the absence of snakes from Iona continued in his day, though adders were not uncommon on the Ross of Mull.

**277** The monks 'were engaged in dry-stone work in the little western plain', according to the most literal rendering of the Latin. Reeves, p. 142, suggested taking *opus materiale* (which should mean 'timber work') as *opus maceriale* 'dry-stone work'; he was followed by Forbes and Fowler. MacCarthy and Huyshe translated it merely as 'manual work'.

In *De Locis Sanctis* I 19 Adomnán mentions *hunc agellulum . . . lapidum maceriam habentem* 'this small plot . . . which has an enclosing wall of stones'. The Andersons, p. 391, therefore translate, 'who were engaged upon building stone enclosures in the little western plain'; my translation is neither more nor less accurate, but I have assumed that a single enclosing wall (to keep livestock out of the fields) would be more to the point than a series of enclosures.

**278** As St Antony's death drew near, he went out 'to visit the brethren who were on the outer hill', and addressed them in similar words: 'My children, hear your father's last words, for I think you will not see me again in this world.' Adomnán seems to have taken this from Evagrius's Life of St Antony, c. 56, but to have adapted it considerably, giving a specific setting of his own.

**279** Nothing is known of Molua Ua Briúin. The dynastic name is not uncommon, though the best known group of this name was centred in northern Connacht and Breifne. One cannot assume that Molua belonged to this group. Colmán Ua Briúin (II 16) may or may not be related.

**280** What this story does not tell is St Columba's attitude to the eating of meat. Secular society was certainly carnivorous, but monks and nuns valued vegetarianism; their ordinary diet (if we are to believe saints' Lives) included meat only on an occasional basis. The implication here that animals should not be slaughtered is hardly borne out by I 41, where St Columba has some sheep slaughtered to give to a layman. Bones from the early levels of archaeological excavation in Iona indicate 'a strong preference for prime cuts of beef', with haunches of venison next in popularity (Reece, 'Recent work', p. 44).

**281** Parts of the boundary bank, or vallum, of Iona remain distinct on the ground even today, and detailed archaeological study has shown the course of much more. This is well exhibited in an aerial photograph and accompanying plan in RCAHMS, *Iona*, pp. 32–3. The boundary runs in an arc around the abbey at a distance of about three hundred feet. It is most easily seen on the north side, and especially at the north-west corner, between Burnside Cottage and Clachanach. Pennant observed it in 1772, noting that 'the whole of their religious buildings were covered on the north side by dikes, as a protection from the northern invaders'. On the west side the vallum runs along the rocky knolls of Cnoc nan Carnan, and on the east side the site seems to have been unenclosed, falling away to the shore. To the south-west and south it remains indistinct; geophysical surveys and limited excavation have revealed several possible banks, and it seems likely that they date from different periods. Any assessment of the enclosed area is difficult. Between the north end of the St Columba Hotel and the visible vallum north of the abbey, the boundary probably enclosed about twenty acres of useful land.

**282** A blacksmith, like other craftsmen, had a special status in secular society as one of the *áes dána* 'people of special skill'. Adomnán here provides evidence that the monastic craftsmen were themselves monks.

Fowler, p. 97n., raised a problem that we too readily overlook. Iron becomes liquid only at a very high temperature, and until the blast furnace was developed all iron-working was done with metal in the solid state. Knowing that Irish bells were made of iron beaten into a sheet and folded, then dipped in bronze, Fowler conjectured that the knife was bronze, which could easily be melted. But Adomnán's word *ferrum* must mean 'iron'. A possible explanation may be got from the Irish term *iarn aithlegtha* 'iron twice-melted, carburized iron'. B. G. Scott, *Early Irish Ironworking*, p. 183, has suggested that the terminology of *melting* was transferred from bronze-working to iron-working, but in the latter case meant softening by reheating, preparatory to reworking. See also *Ériu* 32 (1982), 154–6.

**283** Adomnán recounts a number of stories that have their setting 'when St Columba was journeying at the other side of Druim Alban' (I 34, II 31, III 14). Druim Alban, the principal chain of the Scottish mountains, was perceived by Adomnán (II 46 and n. 347) as providing a boundary between the Scots on the west and the Picts to the east of the mountains. St Columba's journey across Druim Alban was therefore to Pictland. Elsewhere Adomnán refers to events 'when St Columba stayed for some days in the province of the Picts' (II 11, 27, 32–5, and the forward reference in I 1, p. 109).

Dr Isabel Henderson, *The Picts*, pp. 74–5, suggests that the former group of stories, which are 'incidents . . . of an individual and unstereo-typed character', reflect Adomnán's knowledge of stories relating to the saint's travels among the Picts, while the latter group, centred around St Columba's visit to King Bridei near the River Ness, may have been drawn from a narrative of that visit. It certainly seems possible, even likely, that II 27, 32–5 derive from some such account; but I 34 from the other group is set on the route through the Great Glen – though not necessarily on the journey to King Bridei. Further, II 42 has a setting that merges the two formulae, 'when St Columba stayed for a time at the other side of Druim Alban'; on that occasion he commended Cormac Ua Laitháin to King Bridei.

It seems to me that the stories set on the saint's journey to and sojourn near the court of King Bridei, while perhaps deriving from a narrative source, are not actually distinguished from other Pictish stories by tidy formulae. Adomnán's use of two ways to introduce stories set in Pictland will not permit us to conjecture whether Columba visited the Picts east of Druim Alban once only or on several occasions.

**284** The name *Kailli au inde* is puzzling. First, the letter K is not generally used in Irish, but it is used also at I 49 *korkureti* for Corco Réti in the A text. Second, the last word is presumed to be *fhinde*; *fh* is silent in Irish, and often left unwritten (as in *Lathreg inden*, I 20 and n. 110). The middle word was regarded as *aui* (a very early spelling for *uí*, genitive of *aue*, later *úa*) by Watson, *Celtic Place-names*, p. 93, who takes the name as *Caill aui fhinde* 'of the wood of the descendant of Findia', treating *kailli* as genitive singular. Skene, p. 328, and Watson, p. 279, suggest that this was in Morvern, for no better reason than that they associated Fintan of the story with the patron of Killundine (*Cell Fhionntain*), Morvern. (The site has, however, now yielded two early medieval cross-marked stones; RCAHMS, *Mull, Tiree, Coll*, p. 149.) The Andersons, p. 395n., regard *Kailli* as nominative plural, and take the middle word as *au* 'ear', 'the woods of the white-eared' or even 'the woods of the white-eared goddess'. Neither suggestion is convincing.

**285** See n. 283 on St Columba in Pictland.

**286** It is worth noting that Irish was not understood by the ordinary Pictish laity. An interpreter was also mentioned at I 33.

**287** I have used 'wizard' as the translation of *magus* in deliberate avoidance of 'druid' (used by previous translators); the latter word has precise but different meanings in Iron-Age Gaul and Britain, pagan Ireland (and subsequently), and modern Wales or England, all of them inappropriate to Pictland. We know little of Pictish religion or superstition before the conversion: we may gather from this passage that it was polytheistic, and from II 11 that wells were worshipped. Neither of these facts justifies the use of an Irish term, even though *magus* may translate Irish *druí* in Ireland. The Latin word had international currency in portraying pagan priests as magicians, shamans, witchdoctors. The Andersons favour 'magician'.

**288** In Latin, *in quo hospitiolo* 'in which little lodging'. The question may ask, 'In which of the several buildings forming the homestead . . .?' or 'in which chamber partitioned off a larger hall . . .?'

**289** The last four words quote Acts 26:16.

**290** As Fowler, p. 100n., remarks, this paragraph reads like the end of a homily. It adds nothing to the narrative, which seems appropriately to end 'the God of the Christians was glorified'. What we have here, therefore, may be a glimpse of Adomnán the preacher, though Sulpicius too uses such homiletic perorations about St Martin. One should perhaps compare it also with the biblical exposition with which Adomnán rounds off I 43.

**291** We learn later in the chapter that Broichan had been the king's foster-father, and it is evident that he continues to enjoy a senior position in the royal household. Is it perhaps going too far to see here the king's wizard?

I can see no reason to accept the Andersons' equation of Broichan with an Irish druid, Froichan, whom the Annals of Tigernach associate with Diarmait mac Cerbaill in the battle of Cúl Drebene. That story is part of the legend that grew up around the battle, and can surely have no connection with Adomnán's account of Columba's doings in Pictland. Compare Anderson and Anderson, pp. 84–5.

**292** Slavery was widespread in Ireland in this period. Those held in slavery were often captives, and their release was one of the good works encouraged by the church and practised by the saints. In this case the Irish girl was presumably captured during a Pictish raid – perhaps one in which King Bridei played a part – against Scottish Dalriada.

**293** In Latin *peregrina captiua* 'captive exile'; in Irish Latin usage *peregrinus* primarily denotes separation from one's homeland rather than pilgrimage. There is no justification, therefore, for the suggestion that the wording 'may imply that she had been living as a nun in Britain' (Anderson and Anderson, p. 588).

**294** King Bridei's fortress (I 37, II 33, 35) above the River Ness was identified by Reeves, p. 151n., with Craig Phadrig, a site first described by John Williams in 1777. This timber-laced stone fort stands on the ridge west of Inverness, commanding views over the Beauly Firth, the plain around Inverness, and the valley of the River Ness. It is two miles or so from the river, but is most easily approached from that side, though the ascent is steep for about two hundred and fifty feet. Excavation in 1971 and the analysis of finds suggest that the fort was built in the fourth century BC. It was still occupied in the sixth century AD, but the fortifications were by that date long neglected. The excavators therefore doubted whether this could be King Bridei's fort; Small and Cottam, *Craig Phadrig*, p. 48. However, the find of a mould for use in making hanging-bowls indicates that the Dark Age occupation was not merely domestic, that it was still the home of someone of importance, and that there was contact with Irish culture; R. B. K. Stevenson in Small and Cottam, p. 51. Skene, *Celtic Scotland*, II, 105n., preferred Torvean as the site of Bridei's fortress.

**295** Whereas Adomnán usually refers to Columba as St Columba or by a periphrasis, the wizard simply uses his name.

**296** On this biblical phrase, see n. 218.

**297** A boat on Loch Ness would undoubtedly have made easier the route through the Great Glen, which was probably thickly wooded. The series of lochs – Loch Linnhe, Loch Lochy, Loch Oich and Loch Ness – seems to have made it possible to sail from Iona to King Bridei's fortress. In I 34 St Columba and his companions were following this route when they camped on the shore of Loch Lochy, but had to move their boat (*nauicula*) to safety. Here at II 34 the boat (*cimba*, *cimbula*) used on Loch Ness seems to have been quite large, manned by sailors, and square-rigged. Anderson and Anderson, p. 82, deduce that St Columba took his own boat north through the Glen and returned the same way; portage would have been necessary between Loch Lochy and Loch Oich, and again between Loch Oich and Loch Ness. Yet it appears from II 27 that there were local small boats on the River Ness (and that Columba did not have his own to hand). It seems to me possible, therefore, that there was enough local boat traffic on the loch for a small party to have got a passage without having to carry their own boat.

In Ireland in the early Middle Ages there is ample evidence to show that 'the Shannon and its lakes teemed with all sorts of vessels, engaged in activities which range from stealing pigs . . . to large scale military and naval encounters. In the inland waters, the dugout canoe (*coite*), of all sizes and dimensions, was in general use. . . . Large timber-built boats, equipped with a helm, were also in use in the inland waters and details of the construction are given in the law tracts' (Ó Corráin, *Ireland before the Normans*, pp. 68–9).

**298** Adomnán refers to an episode in the Life of St Germanus of Auxerre, c. 13, written about 480 by Constantius of Lyons; his account is much briefer than that in Constantius, but retains a number of phrases from the source. Elsewhere in the chapter Adomnán's vocabulary seems to have been influenced by the passage in Constantius; for example, the unusual word *cimba* 'boat' is used in both. (Bede, I 17, has the whole story of St Germanus's stormy crossing lifted straight from Constantius.)

**299** A different version of this story is given in the later Life of St Comgall. There St Comgall causes the gates of the fort to open, St Columba does the same for the doors of the king's house within the fort, and St Cainnech stops the king in his attempt to kill the saints with his sword by making the king's hand seize up.

**300** The Latin literally means 'on the first wearying of his journey to King Bridei'. That this is his *first* visit is integral to the story, but it does not necessarily mean that St Columba travelled more than once from Iona to visit the king's fortress. The use of messengers between the saint and Broichan in II 33 suggests that St Columba lodged a little distance away, from where he more than once made the tiring ascent to the fortress. The interpretation here adopted was proposed by Anderson and Anderson, pp. 81–2.

**301** Adomnán uses the word *senatus* twice. Here King Bridei is accompanied by his council; in I 1, p. 111, King Oswald called his *senatus* to gather round to be told of his vision. In both cases it probably means the nobles who, with their own war-bands, adhere to and support the king. The same usage is found in Muirchú's Life of St Patrick, I 21. In no case is it likely to mean a more formal royal council as a governmental institution.

**302** Terryglass, Co. Tipperary, was an important monastery on the east side of Lough Derg in the River Shannon. (There is a detailed map showing its position relative to other midland churches, including Durrow, in Hughes and Hamlin, *The Modern Traveller*, p. 26.) The church was founded by St Columba of Terryglass, a distant connection of the royal lineage of Leinster, who died in AU 549. The founder of Terryglass seems to have been already dead when the monks of his church invited St Columba of Iona to visit: Adomnán has resisted any temptation to bring the homonymous saints into contact.

**303** Notwithstanding modern objections to the locking of church doors, this was the normal practice throughout the Middle Ages.

**304** The use of a stake-trap (Irish *bir airndil*) is referred to several times in Irish legal texts. A legal commentary mentions also a weir-stake (Irish *bir na corad*), which was presumably a sort of fish-trap.

**305** The penalty in Irish for an unlawful killing was in the first instance a payment to the victim's family, but where the killer could not or would not pay, he became a *cimbid* (see II 39 and n. 312), whom the victim's family could choose to have killed or enslaved; Kelly, *Early Irish Law*, pp. 215–16. This story here is the only evidence that the penalty might extend to the killer's dependants.

**306** First identified by Anderson and Anderson, pp. 142, 414n. The Latin *nigra dea* 'black goddess' represents OIr. *lóchdae*.

**307** On Lugaid Láitir, monk of Iona, see II 5 and n. 224.

308 It is curious to learn that, instead of merely taking fresh water on board, the boat also carried milk, and that it was carried in a skin vessel rather than a wooden one.

309 The Latin words for ebb-tide (*salacia*) and flood-tide (*uenilia*) are extremely rare in written texts. If the seafaring monks of Iona spoke Latin in everyday life, the words may have been quite familiar. If, however, Adomnán had met them in his reading, the likely sources are St Augustine's City of God, VII 22, or perhaps the commentary on Virgil's *Aeneid* by Servius Donatus at Aeneid X 76.

310 On the connections between exile from one's homeland as punishment and penitential pilgrimage, see Charles-Edwards, 'Irish *peregrinatio*'.

311 'All his sins' seem not to have included the broken oath and its surrounding circumstances, only disclosed to St Columba after this confession. Perhaps we must excuse Adomnán this slight flaw in the logic of his narrative.

312 The details given in this story are extremely interesting as showing aspects of Irish law in action. The chapter deserves a detailed commentary by an expert in Irish law: I can offer only some brief notes.

A person who committed a serious offence (such as an unlawful killing or injury) was expected to redeem the offence by a payment to the victim (if alive) or his kin. Until the offence was redeemed the culprit became a *cimbid* 'prisoner, condemned person' (in Latin texts translated by *uinctus*), who was held in chains or fetters, and whom the victim or his kin had the right to kill or enslave (Kelly, *Early Irish Law*, pp. 97–8). The freeing of such persons is mentioned in a number of saints' Lives, where it may be done by persuasion and payment or by miraculous intervention. In this case the payment was made by a wealthy relative of the *cimbid*, though a non-kinsman might also do this. It was held that a person so delivered would feel a special gratitude and loyalty to the person who saved him. For this reason the law-tract *Crith Gablach* recommends that a king should include among his personal bodyguard someone whose life he had saved in this way.

In Librán's case he is said to have sworn an oath to his wealthy relative who delivered him, an oath that amounted to voluntary slavery. He wore the belt as a mark of this servile status (see n. 315), but absconded in order to become a monk. In legal terms he was now a runaway (Irish *élúdach*), a term that embraced those who absconded to avoid legal obligation, fugitives from justice, and runaway slaves. To extend legal protection to such a person was beyond even the power of a person of privilege such as a priest (Kelly, *Early Irish Law*, pp. 9–10). In receiving Librán Columba does not exonerate him.

313 On Mag Luinge as a place for penitents, see I 30 and n. 182.

314 Swords are commonly mentioned and sometimes described in the Old Irish heroic tales; see Mallory, 'The sword of the Ulster cycle', for a discussion of their forms, materials and decoration. The commonest term is *claideb*, though an older (and perhaps more specific) term *colg* is quite frequent. The *colg dét* is a sword with a hilt made of *dét* 'tooth'. Adomnán's words literally mean 'decorated with the teeth of sea beasts', but he almost certainly refers to some kind of walrus or whale ivory.

Reeves, p. 159n., and Fowler, p. 110n., cite as from the Roman author Solinus (early third century) a passage about how the Irish decorated their swords: 'Those who cultivate personal adornment decorate the hilts of their swords with the teeth of beasts which swim in the sea, for they are as white as ivory' (C. Iulius Solinus, *Collectanea rerum memorabilium*, ed. T. Mommsen, Berlin, 1895, p. 218). Anderson and Anderson, pp. 21, 424n., inferred that 'Columba's sword was a literary product of Adomnán's imagination'. Certainly Adomnán may have read Solinus, as had his English contemporaries Aldhelm and Bede. The passage in question, however, is not authentic Solinus, but one of numerous interpolations. It occurs only in three manuscripts, all dating from the tenth century (St Gallen MS 187; Engelberg MS 67; Paris, BN lat. 6810, originally from St Laumer at Blois). These manuscripts represent Class III of the transmission, a text-type attested earlier by quotations in Walahfrid Strabo, who worked at St Gallen in the early ninth century (Reynolds *et al.*, *Texts and Transmission*, p. 393). St Gallen attracted many Irish monks, and it is possible that this passage was added by an Irish copyist there about 800. On this basis, 'Solinus' becomes a parallel authority rather than a potential source for Adomnán.

Swords for honorific or ceremonial purposes are mentioned elsewhere. For example, in the first Life of St Brigit, § 90, the saint's father sent her to the king of Leinster to ask him to convert the temporary grant of a sword into a permanent gift. The grant of the sword was a symbol of the bond between the king and his man.

**315** The belt as a mark of slavery is not alluded to in any other text from early medieval Ireland, so far as I am aware. It is ordinarily said that slaves wore a special collar, but I have been unable to confirm this.

**316** The care of one's parents (a duty called in Old Irish *goire* 'warmth') was a legal obligation. Its avoidance placed the runaway in the same category as the fugitive from justice according to *Bechbretha*, § 39.

**317** Although the *familia* evidently maintained its own boats, with their sailors, for crossing between Derry and the mother-house at Iona and for the other voyages so often referred to in the Life, from this passage it appears that other boats used the harbour at Derry as a port of call when sailing between Ireland and Scotland. Were these sailors bringing goods for the monastery, or was the monastery of Derry already developing as an emporium?

**318** *Non in Britannia sed in Scotia resurges* 'You will rise again not in Britain but in Ireland.' It was assumed that where the body was buried, there the person would rise again on the last day. *Resurrectio*, therefore, is often used in Hiberno-Latin to mean 'place of burial'. It is a common motif in the Lives of Irish saints that in life they wander until they arrive at the place where it is meant by God that they should live out their lives and die; that place is the saint's *resurrectio*. Columba meant that Librán would die in Ireland. His reassurance, a few lines below, that he would die among the monks of the *familia* in Ireland and rise again with them may hint at the notion, later common in Ireland, that burial in certain cemeteries guaranteed the protection of the patron saint on the Day of Judgement.

**319** Reeds were used for thatching buildings (Bede, III 25: 'Fínán ... built a church in the isle of Lindisfarne suitable for an episcopal see, constructing it, however, not of stone, but of hewn oak thatched with reeds after the Irish manner'), and perhaps for other purposes. The reed-bed in Mag Luinge presumably supplied the needs of Iona. Its exact location in Tiree cannot be determined.

**320** Luigne's nickname was explained by the Andersons, p. 436n., as *tudicla*, a diminutive of Latin *tudes* 'hammer'; the diminutive *tudicula* is found in Classical Latin, but Adomnán elsewhere contracts *genicula* to *genucla*. Although Colgan had correctly printed *tudicla*, Reeves and those who followed him read *tudida*, which was never explained.

His occupation as a steersman (*guberneta* in A, *gubernator* in B) may mean that he was a specialist helmsman. The task of steering normally fell to the master of the ship, so that Luigne was perhaps a shipper, trading the coasts of Ireland and Scotland with his own boat. His dwelling in Rathlin Island (see n. 71) suggests that he plied between the two.

**321** In quoting Jesus (Matt. 19:5 or Mark 10:8, referring back to Gen. 2:24), St Columba is made by Adomnán to take sides on the Christian view of marriage, which was the subject of debate in the late seventh century. The Irish canon collection devotes a substantial section to the subject (*Hib.* 46. 1–38). The church set a high value on perpetual virginity as an element of the religious life, and saints are frequently held up as models for avoiding marriage. Here, however, the saint quotes scripture to the effect that this woman should not enter a monastery in order to avoid sexual relations; because she is married, sexual relations must follow. (Adomnán does not make clear whether the marriage had been consummated earlier and the present attitude was a change of heart, or whether she had refused sexual relations from the start.)

Other stories like this tell of saints providing help in maintaining the sexual side of a marriage. In the Life of St Brigit, for example, § 45: 'There came a married man asking St Brigit to bless some water which he might sprinkle on his wife, for she held him in hatred. So Brigit blessed water, and while his wife was out he sprinkled their house and food and drink and bed, and from that day his wife loved him greatly as long as she lived.'

Marriage was at this date a contract in law, and I know of no evidence from Ireland that it was ever solemnized by a priest. Irish law took a liberal view of both marriage and divorce, but a woman who left her husband without good cause was deprived of all legal rights. Kelly, *Early Irish Law*, pp. 73–5, summarizes the circumstances in which legal separation was accepted.

**322** Columba alludes to St Paul's statements on the legal aspect of marriage, Rom. 7:2–3 and 1 Cor. 7:39, and then paraphrases Matt. 19:6.

**323** Cormac Ua Liatháin's first voyage was mentioned by Adomnán at I 6, and he is again referred to at III 17 but there takes no part in the story. His pedigree occurs in the Genealogies of the Saints, § 227. At III 17 he is mentioned as a founder of monasteries but the only monastery with which he is associated is Durrow. In MTall. he is commemorated at 21 June as 'Cormac Ua Liatháin in Durrow'; later martyrologies make him bishop and anchorite there.

There is a valuable collection of poetry relating to St Columba, probably compiled by a scholar working for Manus O'Donnell, and now in Oxford, Bodleian Library, MS Laud misc. 615. This has preserved two interesting poems in Middle Irish, both dialogues between Columba and Cormac; they are printed (with O'Curry's translations) from a later copy by Reeves, pp. 264–75. In the first, *Dia do betha, a Chormaic cáin*, Columba receives Cormac after two years on the ocean, and foretells his resurrection at Durrow, which he praises. In the second, *Cormac hua Liatháin lí glán*, Cormac arrives at Durrow from Uí Liatháin and is directed by Columba to remain; in agreeing to do so, Cormac cuts off Columba's thumb, which would also remain in Durrow. The latter story is also referred to in the scholia on *Félire Oenguso*, p. 156, and in Manus O'Donnell's Life of St Columba, § 276, but in these two the little finger is substituted.

**324** The political position of Orkney in the late sixth century is obscure through want of information. It is apparent from this chapter that its ruler used the royal style as king (*regulus*) of Orkney, but that he was subordinate to King Bridei, who was king over all the provinces of the Picts. All the archaeological evidence points to the fact that Orkney was Pictish territory in the early Middle Ages; Ritchie, 'Orkney in the Pictish Kingdom'. An entry at 681 in the Annals of Ulster mentions the ravaging of Orkney by the Pictish king, Bridei f. Derelei, suggesting that he had sometimes to use force to maintain control over this subkingdom.

The Annals of Ulster record an expedition against Orkney by Áedán mac Gabráin, king of Dalriada, in the 580s. Dr Miller has noted that there is no mention of hostilities, and has speculated as to whether the Orcadians were more Scots than Picts, or even whether Áedán was assisting Bridei in defeating the local ruler. Such guesswork is free but unprofitable. The sense of the annal entry is that the king of Dalriada made a foray beyond his normal range of activity; the word *fecht* 'expedition' (cognate with English 'fight') shows that it was not a friendly visit to Irish-occupied territory. If King Bridei had been involved – whether as conqueror of Orkney with Dalriada or as defender against Dalriadic raiding – the annal might be expected to have said so.

325 According to the opening sentence of the chapter, Cormac was seeking a place of retreat, i.e., a hermitage. His arrival in Orkney some months off is prophesied; months pass and he arrives back in Iona, having successfully visited Orkney. The story, however, allows little or no time for him to live in Orkney. These islands, fertile and probably well populated, must be presumed to have offered no suitable retreat. Therefore he tried a third time.

326 Fowler, p. 117n., offered the suggestion that these creatures were a kind of jellyfish. They were thought by T. C. Lethbridge to be the fearsome mosquitoes of Greenland, clutching at straws for evidence that the Irish had reached that country!

327 There can be no doubt that some Irish monks did sail out into the unknown, trusting in God to bring them to a place of retreat where they could serve him in freedom from the pressures of society. Some such retreats are known: the classic example is Skellig Michael, visible on a clear day off the coast of Kerry; near to Iona the monastic settlement on Eileach an Naoimh probably falls into this category. In such cases one may well doubt whether the monks in retreat were self-sufficient or whether they depended in part on occasional support from monks in more fruitful locations. When Iceland was first settled from Scandinavia in the early ninth century, it is said that holy men from Ireland were already living there (see n. 109), and it has even been conjectured that such Irish voyagers had actually landed in America. A curious but well-documented case involves three Irishmen, Dubslane, Mac Bethu and Máelinmum, who set out in a boat without means of steering, trusting to God to bring them where he wanted. Their fate is known to us because in 891 they were brought up on the English coast and were taken to King Alfred, a memorable event recorded in the Alfredian text of the Anglo-Saxon chronicles.

Adomnán's accounts of Cormac (I 6 and here) provide the earliest evidence for such voyaging. Voyages and accounts of them were sufficiently popular with churchmen that there grew up a whole class of literature, *immrama* 'voyage tales'. The earliest ones to survive date from the late eighth century, but it is possible that such tales were already popular when Adomnán included this story in his Life of St Columba. The most famous of these tales is in Latin, the Voyage of St Brendan, but most were written in Irish; a good example is *Immram curaig Maile Dúin* 'Voyage of the coracle of Máel Dúin'. See Dillon, *Early Irish Literature*, pp. 101–30; Dumville, '*Echtrae* and *immram*', pp. 73–94.

**328** According to the Genealogies of Saints, § 160, Colmán mac Echdach was one of five saintly brothers:

Fintan mac Echdach, and Colmán – i.e., Columb of fair Ros Glanda, who was at Slanore and Midísel – and Nannid of Cell Tómma and Lugaid of Tír dá chráeb and Muiredach of Cell Alaid – i.e., the name of a spring – belonged to the Uí hAmalngada. These are the five sons of Eochaid. Aglend daughter of Lenin [i.e., sister of Colmán of Cluain Uama] was the mother of Fintan and Columb and Lugaid. Ligach Bregmuinech, however, was the mother of Nannid and Muiredach.

*CGSH* § 690.3 mentions a sister, Comaig, daughter of Eochaid by Aglend, 'who was at Slanore in the same church as her brother, Colmán mac Echdach, near the loughs of Erne'.

Slanore (Snám Luthir) was identified by Reeves as a townland near Kilmore, Co. Cavan, close to the upper loughs of the River Erne, Lough Oughter, etc. In the sixth century this lay in the territory of Coirpre Gabra (on which see n. 94), and it appears from a story told in the Life of St Ruadán (§ 5) that it might have been a principal church of that territory.

**329** Compare the similar story in the first Life of St Brigit, § 51:

When the bishop's driver had hitched up the chariot, he had forgotten to fit the linchpins against the wheels. He and the chariot travelled at speed over the plain. After a considerable time, when the bishop looked down at the chariot, he saw it had no linchpins. Then he leapt from the chariot, and, landing on the ground, he thanked God and blessed St Brigit, for he recalled that she had blessed the chariot.

The terms used by Adomnán (*obex*) and the Life of St Brigit (*rosetus*) are different, but the wheel and axle arrangement seems to be the same in both. The Irish word *tairnge* 'peg, nail' is used for this item in the heroic tales.

**330** Posthumous miracles, like those which now follow, are a common feature of saints' Lives from England and the Continent but are very rare in texts from Ireland. The only obvious parallel in early texts is in Cogitosus's Life of St Brigit, c. 31; here the workmen have cut a millstone in situ on the mountain side, but cannot move it, so the head of the church of Kildare bids them simply to tip it over 'in the name and power of St Brigit', with the result that it makes its own way undamaged down the mountain and through the bog to level ground. Thereafter that millstone showed miraculous properties.

331 Adomnán was personally involved in this story (and the next two). Even so, Brüning, 'Adamnans Vita Columbae', p. 251, pointed out a number of expressions indicating that the writing of this chapter was influenced by the similar story told in Gregory's Dialogues, III 15. There the people of Nursia 'hold aloft the tunic' and the rain 'was able to quench the ground'. It is possible that Gregory's account not only inspired the chapter but actually determined the action of the abbot and elders in the period of drought. Yet if they decided to imitate the citizens, would they necessarily have had St Columba's tunic with which to do so? I think we should assume that the monastery had both garments and books that they believed had been the saint's, for in the next chapter we learn that they were placed on the altar during a special service of intercession.

332 This sentence is not found in A, but I have introduced it here from B, where it is given as part of the chapter heading. Its obvious first-person immediacy shows that it is Adomnán's own addition in the B text, but it is out of line with the style of the chapter headings and makes better sense as the beginning of the chapter.

333 Lev. 26:19–20.

334 On the location of the Hill of Angels, see n. 385.

335 Adomnán here gives a useful indication of the agricultural calendar, since it appears that the fields had been ploughed and sown (*aratum et seminatum*) before the end of April. We learn from II 3 that the harvest was expected at the beginning of August. The growing season, therefore, was shorter and earlier in the year than the modern practice of sowing in May and harvesting in late September – an indication that in the sixth and seventh centuries climatic conditions were better than today.

The reference to ploughing possibly reflects the larger scale of monastic agriculture than modern crofting, which (until the nineteenth century) turned the land with the *caschrom*, or 'crooked spade'. On the other hand, the small farmer in II 3 is said to have ploughed his land.

336 In this and the following chapter I have translated Adomnán's authorial 'we' by the more personal 'I'. If the plural is taken as anything other than authorial style, it is unclear who is included. It seems most likely that Adomnán is here writing from his personal experience.

337 This and the next story both concern the harvesting of timber for use by the community. In the latter case we are told that the timber came from the mouth of the River Shiel on Loch Moidart – an area where there are still broad-leaved woods today.

338 Anderson and Anderson, p. 425n., show how a mistaken reading in Reeves's text led to the interpretation of this passage as meaning that a longship was dug out from a single tree-trunk. Dugouts were used on inland waters, but were unstable at sea, and therefore of little use to the monks of Iona.

339 Adomnán's Latin may here mean 'the beams of a great house' or 'the great beams of a house'; the former seems preferable. The 'great house' was almost certainly the principal communal building of the monastery (see nn. 377, 383), which – we learn from this passage – must have been rebuilt in Adomnán's time.

340 The identification of this site as the River Shiel and of the island called *Airthrago* as Eilean Shona (in Loch Moidart) were made by Watson, *Celtic Place-names*, pp. 75–7. Reeves, p. 177n., on the basis of Adomnán's names for winds, thought that the River *Sale* (on which see n. 251) could not be Shiel, but offered no alternative. Skene, pp. 326–7, took the island of *Airthrago* to be that now known by the Norse-derived name Kerrera, and the river name he associated with the Isle of Seil, an association demolished on linguistic grounds by Watson, p. 76.

341 There is no surprise in the fact that Adomnán should visit Ireland from time to time in order to attend a synod. As successor to St Columba he was one of the most important Irish ecclesiastics. To this he added the influence that his personal qualities earned him, with the result that at least once in his career he persuaded a synod to take significant decisions. This was in 697, at the synod held at Birr, a place close to the boundaries of three provinces, Munster, Leinster and the Uí Néill. Here, with the help of his kinsman Loingsech, who was then supreme Uí Néill overlord, he succeeded in getting his own Law adopted. Unusually, this appears to have been a national assembly, and there is no other occasion known that so well fits Adomnán's words, *post Euerniensis sinodi condictum*. It would seem, therefore, that this story may be dated to 8–9 June 697, the only datable point in Adomnán's narrative. It further follows that, just as the synod was in the hundredth year after Columba's death, so now Adomnán was returning home to keep the hundredth anniversary on the saint's feast day.

SYNODS IN THE IRISH CHURCH Synods, attended by bishops, abbots and other clergy, and at least sometimes also by kings and other secular rulers (compare n. 355), appear to have been important in the Irish church. Although we know the date and circumstances of only a few sixth- and seventh-century synods, non-specific references to a synod are quite numerous, and there is a substantial body of canon texts apparently enacted by Irish synods during this period. Only a few texts represent the results of individual synods, and all of these are difficult to date. There is a greater quantity of material broken up into single clauses and cited in the collection of canons known as the *Hibernensis*. The evidence of this collection, probably first assembled soon after the year 700, suggests that different synods may have adopted conflicting views on matters other than the Easter question. It is extremely uncertain to what extent synods had the authority to put into practice decisions taken, or over what sections of the community. It seems possible that, at least during much of the seventh century, synods in different areas or at which different churches were represented might take independent decisions. There is no evidence for an archbishop or a supreme synod with recognized authority to establish or impose cohesion among the various groups within the Irish church.

The decision known to have been achieved through Adomnán's influence stands as a rare example of cohesive action. The enactment of the Law of Adomnán was supported by representatives from most of Ireland and Scotland, including from the Picts. If we follow Bede in thinking that Adomnán persuaded the northern churches in Ireland to adopt the Roman calculation of Easter, this too may have been a synodal decision, which removed a major divisive problem. Neither decision, however, led to any increased unity between the individual churches of Ireland, and the number of synods known from the eighth century and later is fewer than for the seventh.

**342** Cenél Loairn ('the kindred of Loarn') were one of the three main dynastic groups in Scottish Dalriada. Their territory formed the northern part of Dalriada, and their name survives in the modern district of Lorn around the Firth of Lorn. Bannerman, *Studies*, pp. 113–14, suggests that Cenél Loairn occupied Ardnamurchan, Morvern, Lorn at least as far south as Dunollie, near Oban, and probably also the islands of Coll, Tiree and Mull. Evidence, it must be admitted, is scanty.

**343** *Sainea* was taken by Reeves, p. 181n., to be Shuna, a small island between the larger island of Luing and the mainland. He was followed by MacCarthy, Skene, and Fowler, 'but', noted Watson, *Celtic Place-names*, p. 91, 'Shuna is a Norse name, and apart from this fatal objection the phonetics are impossible.' One can only guess at its location from the geographical data. On this count also, Shuna appears to fail: an easterly wind would be needed for a swift voyage from Shuna to Iona, but Adomnán says that a southerly carried them there.

Adomnán was coming from Ireland, but contrary winds had prevented him from proceeding as fast as he would wish. He may or may not have been off course among the Cenél Loairn, since it is not known for certain which islands were settled or ruled by which of the *cenéla*. The two obvious candidates for *Sainea*, in terms of route, are Colonsay and Jura; the other of the two seems likely to be *Hinba* (see n. 194). Bannerman, *Studies*, pp. 111–12, accepted Watson's argument that *Hinba* is Jura, and so on the strength of II 24 assigned Jura to Cenél nGabráin. With Jura so disposed of, Bannerman takes *Sainea* to be Colonsay, which he therefore assigns to Cenél Loairn. I cannot regard either the identifications of the islands or their dynastic affiliations as established.

**344** So far as we can tell, it appears that mass was normally celebrated straight after the midday office of Sext (at the sixth hour) on Sundays (III 12, 23, p. 225) and on feast days (II 39, p. 189, here, III 11, 12). For mass the monks wore white (III 12), like the blessed in heaven and the angels (III 16, 23); indeed, since Columba died in his white tunic (II 44), it may be that white was worn all day. On such days there was a special meal (III 12), apparently eaten after mass and before Nones.

**345** On this biblical principle, see I 1, p. 112, and n. 47.

**346** The first of the two visitations of plague in Adomnán's time was that of 664–8, referred to several times in the Irish annals, which carried off many leading ecclesiastics and others. Its onset is recorded by the Annals of Tigernach in 664:

> An eclipse of the sun at the ninth hour on 1 May, and during that summer the sky was seen aflame. A great plague reached Ireland on 1 August, at Mag nItha in Leinster. There was an earthquake in Britain. The plague first erupted in Ireland in Mag nItha among the Fothairt. It was 203 years since St Patrick and 112 years since the first great plague.

The annalist is reckoning from the date of St Patrick's death as 461 (one of several dates given in the annals); the previous major plague had afflicted all Europe about 547–9. This account bears comparison with Bede, III 27:

In the same year of our Lord 664 an eclipse of the sun occurred about the tenth hour on 3 May; and a sudden plague, which first decimated the southern parts of Britain and later spread into the province of the Northumbrians, raged for a long time and brought widespread death to many people. . . . The plague was equally destructive in Ireland.

Bede goes on to tell the story of Ecgberht (*c.* 639–729), an Englishman, later a priest at Iona, who was delivered from the plague in 664 while staying at the monastery of Rath Melsigi (Clonmelsh, Co. Carlow) in Ireland. The discrepancy between the annals and Bede over the date of the eclipse suggests that the annal was contemporary, and that Bede has taken the date from an intermediary source with a mistake in the figures: astronomical calculation shows that the eclipse was total at 3.58 pm on 1 May. In early May the ninth hour would have begun before four o'clock and ended before five o'clock; 'hours' were longer in summer than winter, and the tenth hour would have lasted until after six o'clock.

The second of the two visitations had a less well defined onset but deaths from plague are recorded in England or Ireland for most years between 680 and 686.

347 Adomnán's treatment of Druim Alban, the spine of Britain, as the boundary between the Picts and the Irish may be misleading. The centres of Pictland certainly were east of the mountains, while the Irish occupied the western side at least as far north as Ardnamurchan. It is not certain, however, to what extent the north-west of Scotland, Skye and the Outer Hebrides were settled by the Irish at this stage.

In Adomnán's own time an Irish church was established at Applecross (AU 671, 673) opposite Skye, but in St Columba's day it is likely that Skye, Raasay and the Outer Hebrides were still largely Pictish territory. This is suggested by the survival of Pictish carved stones at several places in Skye, Raasay and Pabbay near Harris. The Dark Age settlement at the Udal, North Uist, consisted of houses similar to those excavated at Buckquoy in Orkney, which may be taken as Pictish. While the divide between the centres of Dalriada and Pictland can be thought of as following Druim Alban, there was probably a vaguer boundary zone in the western highlands and islands.

348 One could wish that Adomnán had named the monasteries that St Columba had founded in Pictland and Scottish Dalriada.

349 ALDFRITH, KING OF NORTHUMBRIA Aldfrith, the son of King Oswiu, was king of Northumbria from 685 until his death in 705. According to the annals, he also had an Irish name, Fland Fína; Middle Irish sources say that Fína was the name of his mother and that she was the daughter of Colmán Rimid (d. 604), high king and Northern Uí Néill overlord from the lineage of Cenél nÉogan. Oswiu was in exile between 617 and 633, and he may have spent this time among the Irish with his brother Oswald (see n. 41); he was probably aged about twenty-six or twenty-seven when his exile ended. Aldfrith's Irish name may be explained if Oswiu had married there and the child was named in the languages of both parents.

His career is obscure until he was chosen to succeed his younger half-brother, Ecgfrith, as king of Northumbria in 685. We know from the anonymous Life of St Cuthbert, III 6, that in the year before Ecgfrith's death he was in Iona; and Bede's Life, c. 24, adds that 'for some considerable time before this he had been pursuing his studies in the regions of the Irish, suffering a self-imposed exile to gratify his love of learning'. It is possible that he had been in Iona throughout the early years of Adomnán's abbacy. It is not known whether his friendship with Adomnán dated from this period or from an earlier time. One of the less reliable compilations of annals describes him as *dalta Adamnáin* 'Adomnán's pupil' (*Fragmentary annals of Ireland*, pp. 54–5). The future king had also studied in southern England with Aldhelm, apparently in the 660s, and, soon after Aldfrith's accession, Aldhelm dedicated to him his grammatical treatise, *Epistola ad Acircium*.

The story told in the Lives of St Cuthbert indicates that the succession after Ecgfrith was unclear, and it was not obvious that Aldfrith was a likely heir. His devotion to learning has given rise to speculation that he might have aspired to the priesthood, and in a rare misapprehension Plummer thought that Ecgfrith intended to make his brother a bishop, 'perhaps with the idea of excluding him from the succession to the crown' (*Baedae opera historica*, II, 263; the sources cited refer to Ecgfrith's desire to make Cuthbert a bishop). In the twelfth century William of Malmesbury inferred that Aldfrith had gone to Ireland soon after Ecgfrith's accession in 670, 'whether by force or out of indignation', because at that time he had been passed over for the succession, but there is no evidence that Ecgfrith regarded him as a threat. I find it difficult, therefore, to accept Dr Moisl's suggestion that the reason for the attack on Brega in 684 (see next note) was as a pre-emptive strike against Aldfrith's supporters ('The Bernician royal dynasty', p. 123) or Dr Smyth's that it was to punish the Southern Uí Néill king, Fínnechta Fledach, for allowing Aldfrith a refuge at Durrow. Nor do I accept Dr Smyth's inference that Bede could have known the name of Durrow only if Aldfrith had spent some of his exile there (*Celtic Leinster*, pp. 118–21). It is not impossible that Aldfrith did study there, perhaps with Adomnán, but there is no decisive evidence on the matter. It is certainly possible that Aldfrith spent a good many years among the Irish, as a child before his father returned to England in 633 and in later life.

Bede tells us that King Oswiu was fluent in Irish; his son is said to have composed in that language, and several surviving works are attributed to him in the manuscripts, under his Irish name Fland Fína mac Ossa. One of them, a poem in praise of Ireland, calls him 'the chief sage of knowledge in Ireland' (printed by P. Walsh, *Ériu*, 8 (1915–16), 64–74). He was also regarded as the author of a collection of proverbial sayings (edited by V. E. Hull, *Speculum*, 4 (1929), 95–102).

350 King Ecgfrith of Northumbria invaded Pictland in 685. He was defeated and killed on 20 May at the battle of *Nechtanes mere*, now Dunnichen Moss, near Forfar in Angus. The name Dunnichen represents *Dún Nechtain* 'Nechtan's fort'. Although the mere was drained in the last century, the battlefield can be confidently located. Its site has even been the scene of psychic perceptions.

The circumstances of Ecgfrith's battle are not wholly irrelevant to Adomnán's visit to King Aldfrith, Ecgfrith's half-brother and successor. Bede portrays Ecgfrith as rushing towards self-destruction, first in 684 with an unprovoked attack on Brega in Ireland, against the warnings of St Ecgberht, 'sparing neither churches nor monasteries from the ravages of war' (Bede, IV 26). Next, in 685, rashly and against the advice of St Cuthbert, Ecgfrith invaded Pictland: 'the enemy pretended to retreat and lured the king into narrow mountain passes where he was killed with the greater part of his forces' (ibid.). This defeat Bede sees as divine punishment for the attack on the Irish clergy by the commander of the Irish expedition, Berht.

The actual background to Ecgfrith's invasion of Pictland may be quite different. For some years the Pictish king, Bridei f. Derelei, appears to have been asserting his power, and he seems to have posed a serious problem to Ecgfrith as he strove to free Pictland from its tributary condition. Bridei's victory liberated the Picts (and the Irish of Dalriada) from nearly fifty years of Northumbrian overlordship.

Simeon of Durham, writing about 1100 and therefore not an authoritative source, makes the comment that after the battle Ecgfrith's body was taken to Iona for burial. This may have been a guess, based on his knowledge that until his own day kings of Scotland were buried in Iona. Yet if Simeon had any foundation for his comment, there are interesting implications. Now, we know that Ecgfrith's half-brother, Aldfrith, was staying in Iona in 684, perhaps for a period of years. The possibility is there that Aldfrith might still have been on the island. If so, Ecgfrith's men may have gone there primarily to greet Aldfrith as the new king. Iona was, of course, a suitable place for royal burial, but most unusual for an English king. Another possible factor may have been pressure from the victorious Picts. This would then be the immediate background to Adomnán's visit to his friend.

Bede (v 15, 21) also mentions that Adomnán 'was sent by his nation on a mission to Aldfrith, king of the English, and remained in his province for some time'. But it is from the Annals of Ulster that we learn the purpose of this embassy, for they record that in 686 'Adomnán brought back to Ireland sixty prisoners', that is, those captured by Berht in 684. His relationship with Aldfrith and the new king's different outlook no doubt meant that the mission was not a difficult one.

351 Adomnán's two visits to England can probably be dated to 685–6 and 686–7. On their circumstances, see Introduction, pp. 47–51.

352 On St Columba's early life, see Introduction, pp. 8–12. The priest Cruithnechán has the patronymic mac Cellacháin in the Middle Irish homily, § 21. His name may be commemorated in the name Kilcronaghan, a parish in Co. Derry.

353 The assembly is identified below as happening at Teltown (see n. 355).

354 St Brendan of Birr, also called St Brendan the elder (to distinguish him from St Brendan of Clonfert, the Navigator, on whom see n. 131), is historically very obscure. The annals give two dates for his death, 565 and 572. His lineage is found in the Genealogies of the Saints § 124, and he is commemorated on 9 May, MTall., and 9 November in *Félire Oenguso* and other martyrologies. (November is missing from MTall.)

A story quoted by Ussher from a lost Life of St Brendan of Birr illustrates the name Ì:

Columba, when he wished to set out overseas from Ireland into exile, sent a messenger to St Brendan the elder, abbot of Birr, . . . asking that he should point out to him where he should choose to settle in exile. Then Brendan looked to heaven silently for a moment and as one rapt in thought ordered that the ground be dug up where St Columba's messenger was standing. Under his feet they found a stone, which Brendan picked up and studied closely. On it he found the shape of the letter I. Turning to the messenger, Columba's servant, he said: 'Report this to your master. I, that is, Go into the island of Ì, where you shall find increase of virtue, and from where many souls will go to heaven, and the place will have great honour' (Ussher, *Whole Works*, VI, 240).

The fourfold pun involves the Latin command, *i* 'go', the Irish preposition *i* 'in, into', the noun *ì* 'island', and *Ì*, being the name of the island in Irish. The text of this Life came from the collections of Henry FitzSimon, S.J., and may have been written or abridged in the late thirteenth century; see Sharpe, *Medieval Irish Saints' Lives*, p. 378.

355 Teltown, Co. Meath, was famous in the early Middle Ages as the site of *Oenach Tailtenn* 'the Fair of Tailtiu', held annually at the beginning of August until the late ninth century, from which time it became irregular, falling into abeyance from 927. Binchy has shown that the Fair was an assembly of peoples under the rule of the Southern Uí Néill ('The Fair of Tailtiu and the Feast of Tara', pp. 115–27). He refers to Adomnán's story, suggesting that by about 560 the clergy from the Uí Néill territories may have begun to attend this regional assembly, even though the kingship was not fully Christianized. 'Hence,' he suggests, 'the "synod" – which, needless to say, has grown in later legend into a vast gathering of the saints of Ireland – may well have been a meeting of ecclesiastical and secular dignitaries from the kingdoms of the Southern Uí Néill held during the fair.' As to the offences with which St Columba was charged, see Introduction, p. 13.

356 In all the manuscripts this sentence is written at the end of III 4, after a story from Columba's youth. It does not make sense there, for we know that Columba was already forty-one when he left Ireland. The confusion was in some measure compounded by Reeves, p. 196n., who cited a later abridgement of the Life (now known as Pseudo-Cumméne), in which this sentence comes between the story of III 4 and another story involving Uinniau, II 1; Pseudo-Cumméne clearly understood this passage as referring to Columba's younger days, and the problem is

repeated by Skene, Fowler, and Huyshe. Anderson and Anderson, p. 472n., proposed transferring the sentence to the end of III 3, where I give it in square brackets. Its displacement in the manuscripts may have arisen from its being added in the margin of the author's original and not properly keyed to its intended place. One implication of this transposition to the end of III 3 is that it produces an association between Columba's excommunication and his leaving Ireland on pilgrimage. The inference of an actual connection has often been made; see Introduction, pp. 13–15.

THE LIST OF ST COLUMBA'S COMPANIONS After the Life in the B manuscripts there is a short text listing people closely associated with St Columba. The spelling of the names in Irish in this list exhibits a number of early features and is quite compatible with that used for names in the B text of the Life. On linguistic grounds, therefore, I should say that this list dates from Adomnán's time or very soon after, and that it is contemporary with the archetype of B. It begins by naming the twelve disciples with whom Columba founded the monastery of Iona:

These are the names of the twelve men who sailed with St Columba when he first came to Britain from Ireland: two sons of Brendan, [1] Baithéne (also called Conin), who succeeded St Columba, and his brother [2] Cobthach; [3] Ernán, uncle of St Columba; [4] Diarmait his servant; [5] Rus and [6] Fiachnae, two sons of Ruadán; [7] Scandal mac Bresail maic Énda maic Néill; [8] Lugaid moccu Temnae; [9] Eochaid; [10] Tochannu moccu Fir Chete; [11] Carnán mac Branduib maic Meilgi; [12] Grillán.

This is followed by two short genealogical notes:

St Columba's parents were Fedelmid mac Ferguso, his father; Eithne, his mother, daughter of Mac Naue. Eogan was his younger brother. Also his three sisters, [1] Cuimne, mother of the sons of Dícuil, who are called Mernóc and Caschéne, [2] Meldal, and [3] Bran (who is buried in Derry);

St Columba's cousins: Mincholeth, mother of the sons of Énán, one of whom was called Colmán; Sínech, mother of the men of moccu Céin of Cúl Uisci, whose names are Áedán the monk (who is buried at Cúl Uisci) and Cróní moccu Céin (who is buried at Durrow); and she was the grandmother of Tocummi moccu Céin, who ended this present life, worn out with old age, as a priest at Iona. Amen. Thanks be to God.

The first, Baithéne, has been mentioned often in the Life. His father, Brendan, was the brother of St Columba's father. Neither the alternative name Conin nor the brother Cobthach are mentioned elsewhere; perhaps these details were introduced, even fabricated, for the sake of the parallel with Matt. 10:2, 'Simon, who is called Peter, and Andrew his brother'. Similarly, the sons of Ruadán may be intended to parallel the sons of Zebedee. Ernán is mentioned in the Life and Diarmait is often referred to. The other names are not found in other sources, though Scandal is given an Uí Néill pedigree; his grandfather Énda mac Néill was the eponym of Cenél nÉnda, one of the lesser dynasties of the Northern Uí Néill.

The names in the second and third lists reinforce the association between Columba's relatives and his churches, noting kinsmen related through the female line who were buried at Derry or Durrow, and another who became priest at Iona.

357 On St Uinniau, see n. 210.

358 THE ROYAL ORDINATION OF ÁEDÁN The story told here hints at a remarkable innovation in the idea of kingship. Instead of being inaugurated by a pagan ritual, as Diarmait mac Cerbaill had been at the feast of Tara (see n. 157), Áedán is presented as being made king of Dalriada through 'ordination' by the local holy man, Columba. Áedán became king in 574, less than ten years after Diarmait's death. One may wonder whether it is credible that Columba brought about so great a change in a land that was by no means wholly Christian. As told, it appears that Áedán was readier to go to Iona than Columba, who had to be compelled by three nights of angelic commands. The innovation is the Lord's, not Columba's. It has often been accepted as a historical event, but there is surely room for doubt.

Dr Michael Enright (*Iona, Tara, and Soissons*, pp. 5–78) has argued that the story should be seen as part of Adomnán's exposition of his biblical theory of kingship. The story of Columba's choosing Eochaid Buide as Áedán's heir (I 9) was modelled on Samuel's choosing David to replace King Saul. This story, though the parallel is less complete, may be seen as reflecting Samuel's original anointing of Saul. Although the word *ordinatio* does not necessarily imply anointing, Dr Enright compares its use in the *Hibernensis* in this precise sense to introduce quotations from the first book of Samuel, which provides the Old Testament model. Taken with Adomnán's allusion to the inviolability of Diarmait mac Cerbaill as ordained by God (I 36 and n. 157), these stories strongly suggest that Adomnán held a view of anointed kingship formed by his reading of 1 Samuel. Enright further argues that the compilers of the *Hibernensis*, Ruben of Dairinis (d. 725) and Cú Chuimne of Iona (d. 747), framed their chapter *De regno* on the basis of Adomnán's views, following him in his interpretation of 1 Samuel. Through the transmission of the *Hibernensis* in Francia, Adomnán's thinking lay behind the anointing of Pippin as king of the Franks in 751, an event that stands at the head of all subsequent coronation rituals. He thus defends the Irish hypothesis for the origin of royal anointing against the rival hypothesis, that the practice began in Visigothic Spain with King Wamba in 672 and his immediate successors. In either case, 1 Samuel lies in the background, as it lies behind the reference to the anointing of kings in Gildas, *De Excidio Britanniae*, c. 21. Much scholarship has been devoted over the years to the history of royal anointing, and, although Adomnán's evidence is recognized as important, not all scholars agree that he is the innovator ultimately responsible for the medieval practice.

There is, moreover, nothing in the evidence nor in Dr Enright's argument to prove that any Irish king was actually anointed until 793, when the annals mention 'the ordination of Artri mac Cathail to the kingship of Munster'. This closely follows the anointing of King Offa's heir in England in 787; both events should be viewed in the context of Frankish anointing rituals in this period.

Nor is it entirely clear that even the theoretical case can be attributed solely to Adomnán and his followers. The story as told here is completed only by the quotation from Cumméne's book, giving the saint's prophecy, which Adomnán had omitted. It seems almost certain that Cumméne had told a story, therefore, that involved Columba in Áedán's royal inauguration. Again, Dr Enright argues from Adomnán's description of Diarmait mac Cerbaill as *ordinatus* that the new theory of kingship should be linked with the desire to make the king of Ireland different in quality from other kings. But there is evidence that this title, at least, was used in the 640s (see n. 86). It seems probable that the political concerns underlying this episode had their place in Cumméne's work, but it is possible that the language of ordination was contributed by Adomnán. Certainly the case for Adomnán's biblical perspective is compelling, and this may be sufficient to explain the story of Eochaid Buide. The quotation from Cumméne, however, forces us to leave open the question of when and in what way the abbot of Iona became involved in the Dalriadic royal inauguration. It is beyond our knowing whether there was any important involvement when Áedán became king in 574.

**359** Enright, 'Royal succession', pp. 89–90, has suggested that the writer intends an allusion to the book mentioned in 1 Sam. 10:25. Here Saul has been anointed by Samuel and hailed as king by the people: 'Then Samuel told the people the manner of the kingdom (*legem regni*) and wrote it in a book and laid it up before the Lord.' Enright goes on to speculate that an actual book, kept at Iona in Adomnán's time, was understood to be the one shown to Columba by the angel; this suggestion, first made by Levison, seems to me unlikely. Adomnán does not say that the angel gave the book to Columba; and if he thought it worth mentioning that the scar dealt him in the vision remained with him, surely he would have made it clear if he thought that the book was preserved. I take it that the glass book belongs in the vision, and guesswork as to whether its description implies that it was bound in crystal or enamelwork or whatever seems to me misdirected.

360 CUMMÉNE'S BOOK The passage printed within square brackets is very significant. It is written in Dorbbéne's manuscript in a script rather smaller than his usual hand; there is nothing otherwise to suggest that this passage was entered in a space on the page, and it appears that the text was written consecutively. The passage is also found in the ninth-century Metz MS and in the shorter recension of the Life, but it is missing from the three B MSS. It is not possible to know whether Adomnán intended its inclusion, or whether it was an unauthorized addition by Dorbbéne that entered the tradition of the A text.

The great importance of the passage lies principally in the fact that it permits a glimpse at the written sources available to Adomnán. Cumméne was the seventh abbot of Iona, nephew of Ségéne, fifth abbot (623–52), and great-nephew of Lasrén, third abbot (600–605). It is very likely that he entered the community as a youth, and he was probably a member during Ségéne's abbacy. He was so closely linked with the community that his authorship of a book about St Columba's miraculous powers was as much an act of family piety as of monastic devotion.

It is generally assumed that Adomnán made extensive use of Cumméne's book, and that its authority underpins the *Life*. There is no way actually to test this, except by considering Adomnán's treatment of this passage. All we may say is that Adomnán knew that Columba 'prophesied the future of Áedán's sons and grandsons and great-grandsons' and that Cumméne quoted the prophecy. This may imply that the extract from Cumméne's book is meant to remedy Adomnán's omission, with the implication that the rest of the story came from Cumméne's book. This argument is important in two ways. At a general level, it would mean that where Adomnán had Cumméne's book as a source, he used it thoroughly, without omitting other significant passages. With specific reference to the story of the king's ordination, it would mean that this story was already in Cumméne's work.

Alas, we do not know how much Adomnán used this source, what it contained nor when it was written. Dr Herbert has plausibly suggested that Cumméne was responsible for recording the testimonies that were collected during Ségéne's abbacy, and that much of the Iona material in the Life, material rich in circumstantial detail, derived from that record; attractive though this theory is, there are problems (see n. 15). Cumméne's book was not completed until after 637, for the passage quoted refers to the Battle of Mag Roth (see n. 362); how much later one can only guess.

The basis for such guesswork must be the prophecy, which says 'from that day to this the family of Áedán is held in subjection'. Dr Marjorie Anderson has suggested that after the battle Domnall Brecc not only lost control of Dál Riata in Ireland but had also to share rule in Scottish Dalriada with Ferchar, the son of his old rival Connad Cerr, who did not descend from Gabrán; *Kings*, pp. 152–5. Domnall himself was killed fighting the British in December 642 (AU), but Ferchar's death is not mentioned in the Annals of Ulster until 693. This seems impossibly late, and does not help us determine how long Áedán's descendants were 'held in subjection'. In 673, however, the Annals of Ulster mention the death of Domnall Brecc's son Domangart, king of Dalriada. He seems to have been undisputed king from 660. His immediate predecessor was Domnall's brother Conall, who was probably without a rival after 654. By this date, therefore, it was no longer true to write that 'the family of Áedán is held in subjection'. This line of argument suggests that Cumméne's book was written before he became abbot in 657. It may most likely have been written for Ségéne between 637 and 652.

Other arguments, however, would permit a dating that is later still: the Northumbrian kings Oswald, Oswiu and Ecgfrith all enjoyed some form of overlordship over the kings of Dalriada; if this were the subjection alluded to, as Dr Anderson has recently suggested, it did not end until 685, long after Cumméne's death.

In Adomnán's time, the descendants of Áedán were not 'held in subjection' but were still ruling as kings of Dalriada, although from the 690s they had opposition to cope with. He perhaps dropped Cumméne's account of the prophecy as an embarrassment; its apparent fulfilment was no longer valid and it was perhaps also by now politically inconvenient.

Why the passage was reinstated in this way will doubtless remain a mystery. Whoever was responsible perhaps did not wish to allow the actual words of St Columba's prophecy to be left out of the Life. Alternatively, one might hazard that the latter's words were revived at a time when the descendants of Áedán were once more subject to an outsider – perhaps Ferchar Fota and his sons of the Cenél Loairn or Fiannamail Ua Dunchada, *c.* 698–700: could there be an implied criticism of a king from the line of Áedán who had offended Adomnán, Columba's successor?

**361** With the words *sceptrum regni huius* Cumméne may have meant no more than 'dominion over this kingdom', using *sceptrum* in its figurative sense, as commonly in Classical and Late Latin. I know of no evidence to suggest what form a king's regalia took in sixth- or seventh-century Ireland, and so cannot guess whether the use of the term had any concrete significance. The kingdom must be Scottish Dalriada and not Irish Dál Riata, as Anderson and Anderson once argued (see n. 71).

**362** The battle of Mag Roth took place in 637; since this was 'in our own time', this comment must be part of the extract from Cumméne's book and not an observation added by Dorbbéne (who was probably born after 637). Cumméne's words are in a sense misleading because Domnall Brecc, the invader, suffered defeat at the hands of Domnall mac Áedo, here called 'grandson of Ainmire', who was the son of Áed mac Ainmirech. The Annals of Tigernach record the battle more fully than the Annals of Ulster: 'The battle of Mag Roth was won by Domnall mac Áedo and by the sons of Áed Sláine. Domnall was king of Tara at the time of the battle, in which fell Congal Cáech, king of the Ulaid, Fáelchú together with many nobles, and Suibne mac Colmáin Cuair.'

The circumstances of the battle are complicated. Much of the background has been set out at n. 206. Domnall mac Áedo of the Northern Uí Néill had for ten years been an enemy of Congal Cáech, a king of the Cruithin, who had become overking of the Ulaid. Congal, it seems, persuaded Domnall Brecc to support him in an attack against Domnall mac Áedo, who was at this date king of Ireland. How much of his territory was ravaged by this alliance we do not know, nor do we know where: this aspect of events is mentioned only by Cumméne. Domnall mac Áedo, in alliance with the sons of Áed Sláine, rulers of Brega, defeated Domnall Brecc at Mag Roth in Co. Down. It would seem that his invasion of Uí Néill lands had been turned back and that Domnall

Brecc and Congal Cáech were driven homewards into Ulaid territory before their crushing defeat in this battle. Victory seems to have consolidated Domnall mac Áedo's position, and he died from natural causes in January 642. His peaceful end had been foretold by St Columba (I 10).

In the same year Domnall Brecc was defeated and killed by the Britons of Strathclyde. Cumméne's version of the prophecy recognizes that his reign ended in failure, but it is not clear in what sense the descendants of Áedán mac Gabráin were held in subjection (see n. 360).

**363** On the contacts of Iona and the Irish churches with the British, see n. 122.

**364** In Hebrew law a priest was contaminated if he was present at the time of death (Lev. 21:10–11). The Christian church as a whole took a different view, but it appears that the Irish, who drew much of their canon law from the Old Testament rather than from councils or papal decrees, may have observed the Mosaic custom at this date.

**365** Adomnán here cuts right across the well-known but much later story of how St Odran voluntarily died and was the first person to be buried in Iona.

THE BURIAL OF ST ODRAN The date at which this story began to take shape remains uncertain. The possibility of an early origin is admitted by the mention of a monk in Iona called Máel Odrain, 'devotee of St Odran' (see n. 113). The oldest version of the story now known dates from the twelfth century, and it is retold in different ways at different dates. Since the story continues to be alluded to in many popular books, I have judged it appropriate to show here the degree to which the story has changed.

The twelfth-century form of the story is told in the Middle Irish homily, at the point where St Columba has chosen to settle in Iona:

> Columb Cille said to his company: 'It would benefit us if our roots were put down into the ground here', and he said to them: 'Someone among you should go down into the soil of the island to consecrate it.' Then obedient Odran rose up and said: 'If I be taken, I am prepared for it', said he. 'Odran,' said Columb Cille, 'you will be rewarded for it. No one will be granted his request at my own grave, unless he first seek it of you.' Then Odran went to heaven. (tr. Herbert, *Iona, Kells, and Derry*, p. 261.)

Manus O'Donnell, nearly four hundred years later, has changed only a little, but he ties the event to the name of the graveyard:

Columb Cille said to his company: 'It would benefit us if our roots were put down into the ground here where we have come, and whatever holy man of our company is willing to die and be buried beneath the soil of this island, I shall give him the kingdom of God.' Then St Odran who was with Columb Cille said: 'I am willing to die under this covenant.' 'I shall give you the kingdom of God', said Columb Cille, 'and I shall give you this, that no one who makes a request at my tomb or my resting-place will be granted it unless he first seek it of you.' Odran then died according to the will of God and Columb Cille, and he was laid beneath the soil of the island. For this reason *Reilig Odrain* 'Grave of Odran' is the name of that place today. (*Life of St Columba*, §§ 205–6.)

Columba's strangely primitive request is unexplained, but so far there is no grotesque sequel. When we come to the next account, this side of the story has grown. The first modern version, derived from oral tradition, is given by William Sacheverell in 1698:

At the corner of this enclosure stands a decayed oratory, they call Oran's Chapel; the vulgar ascribe the building of it to Columbus, and tell a comical story on the subject, which, if true, shows that saints themselves are not always free from whimsies. The story thus:

Columbus dreamed a famine (which grievously afflicted the North parts of Britain) would never cease unless he buried a man alive. He acquainted his monks with it, and the veneration they had for the man made them take it as the decree of the Almighty, and seriously to consider of a person who ought to expiate for the sufferings of a whole nation. Amongst these one Oran offered Columbus to be the man, provided he would build a chapel to be called by his name. Columbus assented, and built the chapel, and put the man standing upright into the grave, with a promise it should be opened again at the end of twenty-four hours; which was done accordingly, and Oran, still living, began to entertain Columbus and his company with so particular an account of the state of the dead, that the good man did not think it safe to trust him any longer among the living, but ordered the grave to be closed again upon him, and sent him to the other world, where he had already made so good an acquaintance. (p. 102)

Martin (*Western Isles*, p. 260) mentions 'St Ouran's church' and the Reilig but tells no tale. Pennant (*A Tour in Scotland*) is merely allusive, mentioning 'the chapel of St Oran . . . which legend reports to have been the first building attempted by St Columba'. A fuller version is given in *Iona in 1771* by an Irish Tourist, whose quoted lines of Gaelic must come directly from island tradition:

In the time of building St Columba received divine intimation to bury one of his companions alive, as a sacrifice necessary to the success of his undertaking. . . . It seems the lots doomed Oran to so dreadful a destiny. Three days afterwards Columba opened the grave to see what might be the fate of his friend. Oran raised his swimming eyes and said

*Cha'n bhuill am bàs na iongantas*
*Na iofroin mar a teistonas*

'There is no wonder in death, and hell is not as it is reported.' The saint was so shocked by such sentiments that he called out in a great hurry

*Ùir, ùir air sùil Òrain*
*Mar labhair è tuille còmhradh*

'Dust, dust over Oran's eye, that he may speak no more' (p. 22; I have made some typographical corrections in the Gaelic).

The two sayings are quoted in a slightly different form in *The Native Steam-Boat Companion* (Edinburgh, 1845), p. 114; presumably these two written versions draw independently on the oral form of the story. This is also the form of the story that has most influenced modern writers. Another version of the story was noted down in Eriskay towards the end of the nineteenth century by Fr Allan Macdonald. In this version the victim is said to be Columba's brother 'Dobhran'; the verse utterance is given as *Ùir, ùir, air sùil Dhobhrain, mu'n faic e'n corr dhe'n t-saoghal 's dhe'n pheacadh* 'Dust, dust, on Dobhran's eye, before he see any more of the world and of sin' (*Celtic Review* 5 (1908–9), 107–9).

For the sake of comparison I add here the similar story that is told in the Life of St Finnbarr, a text that may date originally from the late twelfth century, and which resembles the early version of Odran's story. Finnbarr and Bishop Mac Cuirb (the saint's confessor) had marked out the cemetery at the new foundation of Cork. In the Latin text (a thirteenth-century revision) Finnbarr then says, 'Everyone who is buried in the soil of this cemetery, hell shall not close over him on the Day of Judgement', at which Mac Cuirb asks to be the first to be buried there. He at once died and was buried. In the Irish text Mac Cuirb takes the initiative, saying to Finnbarr, 'If my body is the first to go under the ground here, and my soul goes to heaven, I will not allow anyone who dies within the circuit of Cork to go to hell' (Plummer, *Vitae Sanctorum Hiberniae*, I, 71; id., *Bethada Náem nÉrenn*, II, 17).

**366** On the Airthir who lived in Co. Armagh, see n. 188.

**367** In the complicated question of how the church spread in Ireland, it has often been assumed that this pattern was widespread, as personal devotion led to the establishment of personal monasteries. Kathleen Hughes, *The Church in Early Irish Society*, pp. 75–7, emphasized the importance of whole families deciding to enter the religious life, converting the family estate into the endowment of a monastery and thereby continuing to enjoy the fruits. The available evidence is too limited properly to judge the significance of either pattern, but past discussion has always tended to exaggerate the part of churches founded for the monastic life over those established for pastoral reasons.

**368** Skene, 'Notes on the history', p. 337, indulges in a specious argument leading to the conclusion that the place to which St Columba withdrew was the miscalled 'Culdee's Cell'. The remains of this small hut to the west of Dùn Ì hardly allow any archaeological interpretation; RCAHMS, *Iona*, pp. 256–7. It is first called the Culdee's Cell by Dugal Campbell in 1792, who gives the Gaelic as *Cathan* or *Cothan Cuildich*. This is now marked on maps as Cobhan Cuilteach. Skene writes: 'This is usually translated the Culdee's Cell, but allow me to say at once that there is no such word in the Gaelic language as Cuildeach, signifying a Culdee. It is a modern introduction into our Gaelic dictionaries, emanating from the nonsense about Culdees. . . . Cabhan Cuildeach [Skene's spelling] means simply the sequestered hollow.' On all counts Skene is quite right, though his point has been generally passed over. He goes on, however, to equate 'sequestered hollow' with Adomnán's *remotior locus* 'rather secluded place'.

**369** Compare Eph. 6:13–17.

**370** One wonders how many monasteries there were in Tiree (see n. 107) besides the Columban house at Mag Luinge, where Baithéne was prior (see n. 182).

**371** Perhaps Columb the Smith, commemorated on 7 June, MTall.

**372** The province of *Mide* (Meath) lay in the middle of Ireland, to the west of the modern Co. Meath and more in the area of Co. Westmeath. Adomnán uses a Latin phrase meaning 'in the midland part'.

**373** Two Englishmen are mentioned by Adomnán as belonging to the community of Iona in St Columba's time, Genereus Saxo here and Pilu Saxo (III 22). St Augustine's mission to the English began only a few months before St Columba's death in 597, and the evidence for Christianity in Kent before that date is all associated with Frankish connections. The mission from Iona to the English of Northumbria likewise did not begin until a generation after St Columba's death. How then is one to explain the presence of Englishmen as monks in Iona when the English at large remained pagan?

The Roman Catholic historian John Lanigan, writing in 1822, assumed an otherwise unknown Irish mission: 'It can scarcely be doubted that they [the Irish] were the instruments used by the Almighty for the conversion of those early Anglo-Saxon Christians in Columba's time; and that, with regard to a part of the nation, they got the start of the Roman missionaries in the blessed work of bringing them over to the Christian faith' (*Ecclesiastical History*, II, 174; quoted by Reeves, p. 209n.).

My suspicion however is this: far from the Irish having mounted an otherwise undocumented mission into pagan England, these two reflect the possibility that some English travelled abroad, in Ireland or North Britain, where they encountered Christianity. Where the contact was not military, it is possible that some may have settled and been converted. From among their number, these two have become monks. Iona was obviously well known to the English in the generation after St Columba's death. When Æthelfrith's sons, Oswald and Eanfrith, went into exile, neither they nor their countrymen were Christian, yet they came to Iona and were converted (see nn. 38, 41).

**374** On St Brendan of Birr, see n. 354. If the date of his death is taken as 565, this would have happened very soon after the settlement of Iona; on the other hand, his death may have been several years later.

Manuscripts of the shorter recension omit the chapter heading, and it may have been such a copy that misled the compiler of an extended Life of St Brendan of Clonfert in the late thirteenth century. He inserted a reference to this story, not realizing that it properly relates to St Brendan of Birr: 'Nor is this to be passed over which may be read in the Life of St Columba the abbot. Just as Christ announced to the apostles the death of Lazarus, so St Columba foretold in the Spirit to his disciples concerning St Brendan's death. For he had seen his soul carried to heaven by choirs of angels, and for that reason he ordered the brethren to celebrate a solemn mass in his honour' (Plummer, *Vitae*, I, 151).

**375** St Colmán moccu Loígse was commemorated on 15 May, MTall. He appears with his brother Senach as founder of two churches, Tulach macc nComgaill and Druim Togae, in the Genealogies of Saints §§ 145, 187. The second entry, § 187, omits the name of their father, Comgall, and identifies Druim Togae with the church of Oughaval, near Stradbally, Co. Laois (on which see Reeves, p. 212n.).

A story is told of St Colmán and St Columba in the Life of St Fintan of Clonenagh – not in the original version in *Codex Salmanticensis* but in the revised version D, probably compiled at Ferns, in Leinster, about 1225:

There was a young man called Colmán, a religious cleric, born in the province of Leinster, of the people called the Loígse. For the sake of prayer and pilgrimage, he travelled to St Columba in Iona and remained for a time with him. When he wished to return to Ireland, he said to St Columba: 'O holy man of God, how am I to live in my home district and still confess my sins to you?' St Columba said: 'Go to that holy man whom I see every Saturday night standing among the angels before Christ's tribunal.' The blessed youth said: 'Who is that saint, and what manner of man is he?' St Columba answered: 'He is a holy and beautiful man of your race, ruddy of face with bright eyes, little hair and that white.' The youth said: 'I know no such man in my province save St Fintan.' . . . Then St Colmán received the licence and blessing of St Columba and returned cheerfully to Ireland.

This story was known to Manus O'Donnell (who, I think, knew the whole Dublin collection of saints' Lives; Sharpe, 'Maghnus Ó Domhnaill's source', pp. 604–7); he incorporated it into his Life of St Columba (§ 249), but changed the identity of St Colmán moccu Loígse into the more familiar St Colmán Elo (on whom see n. 70).

**376** A mass of evidence for leather shoes was unearthed in excavations at Iona; it is described by Barber, 'Excavations', pp. 318–28. Radiocarbon analysis has dated the ditch from which this material came to the late sixth or seventh century, pp. 310–11. The types of shoes included some like those worn by the man depicted at the front of St Matthew's Gospel in the Book of Durrow, a type also known from Ireland. There is an older and more general discussion by Lucas, 'Footwear in Ireland'.

**377** THE MONASTIC BUILDING IN IONA Macdonald, 'Monastery and monastic life', pp. 287–8, has pointed out that this indicates that the ordinary monks slept in one large building. At III 19 the title mentions 'chambers', leading Macdonald to suggest that the monastic *domus* 'was partitioned internally into divided *cubicula* giving on to an open floor-space'. The popular picture of individual beehive huts is not supported. Compare n. 383 below on the monastic house at Durrow, which was circular in plan. Excavations at Iona disclosed two concentric arcs of postholes in the area of the modern cemetery just north of Reilig Odran; Barber, 'Excavations', pp. 299–303. These *might* be from such a circular building, but the complete outline was not recovered. To judge from the arcs, the building would have had a total diameter of nearly sixty-five feet, including what may have been a verandah of about ten feet around it. Barber, p. 358, is cautious not to leap to these conclusions.

**378** This additional meal was probably eaten in the early afternoon, after the midday service comprising Sext and mass. There would ordinarily have been no midday meal until the main meal in the refectory after Nones (II 13).

**379** This allusion to the particular and permanent position of St Martin's name in the liturgy at Iona indicates his very prominent place in the community's devotions. What the prayer was that distinctively mentioned him is not known, but it was apparently used on all major feasts. It would appear to have been a prayer for departed saints, perhaps headed by St Martin; the name of St Colmán the bishop was presumably added to a list rather than substituted for the name of Martin.

The importance of St Martin of Tours in the Irish church is well established, though most of the evidence comes from after Adomnán's time. But already, the degree to which Sulpicius's Life of St Martin influenced Adomnán's work proves that Martin provided one of the most widely recognized models of sanctity. Jonah, in his Life of St Columbanus, I 22, mentions that when the saint travelled from Ireland to France – near enough to 590 and, in any case, when Columba was still alive – he made a point of visiting St Martin's tomb at Tours. There are two early Latin hymns from Ireland in his honour, one in the *Liber hymnorum* and the other recently uncovered by Professor Michael Lapidge (*Celtica*, 21 (1990), 240–51). For detailed studies of the later manifestations of devotion to St Martin in Ireland, see P. Grosjean, *Analecta Bollandiana*, 55 (1937), 300–348. Among these later traditions is one found at Derry in the twelfth century that St Columba brought from Tours to Derry the gospel book that had lain on St Martin's body (Middle Irish homily, § 35); this book is mentioned as one of the relics kept by the coarb of St Columba at Derry until it was carried off by the Anglo-Normans (AU 1166, 1182).

**380** Adomnán's Latin *stagnum uituli* 'the calf's lough' translates the Old Irish name for Belfast Lough, Loch Láig, which is used in the scholia on the *Félire* of Oengus.

**381** The name *Airchartdan* has been generally equated with Glen Urquhart, and has been explained by Watson, *Celtic Place-names*, p. 95, as representing British/Welsh *ar* 'on' or in place-names 'next, against' and *cardden* 'copse'; compare Anderson and Anderson, pp. 157–8. 'British' is probably an inappropriate term so far north, but the evidence for the Pictish language presents several Brittonic features.

St Columba's route on this occasion was evidently overland along the northern side of the Great Glen. When he left the province of the Picts, he did so by boat, sailing up the River Ness and southwards along the loch (II 34 and n. 297).

**382** On Colgu mac Cellaig, see n. 154, and on Luigne moccu Blai, see n. 133.

**383** The building is called in the title *rotundum monasterium* and in the text *magna domus*. Reeves, pp. 215–16nn, following Petrie, 'Round Towers', pp. 282–3, was misled into thinking that a high, round building *must* be a round tower (such as remains at Glendalough or Clonmacnoise), and that they were used 'as monastic abodes'. Petrie believed that the domestic buildings were all 'small and detached cells', so that the great house could not be domestic, nor could it be a church since the known church buildings are all rectangular: what remained was what he was looking for, the round tower. We now know, however, that round towers belong to a later period of Irish monastic architecture.

Bullough, 'Columba', p. 120n., thought that the great house was the monastic church; for its round shape he compared Adomnán's account of the round Church of the Holy Sepulchre in *De Locis Sanctis* I 2. But Macdonald has argued persuasively that *monasterium* is chiefly used of the principal domestic building in which much of the communal life took place and where most of the monks slept (see n. 377). He suggests that this is what is meant here, and that at Durrow it was – perhaps unusually – circular in plan; see Macdonald, 'Monastery and monastic life', pp. 284–5.

384 The words *cum grandi protestatione* do not make it clear whether his affirmation belongs in the category of formal testimonies (see nn. 15, 391) collected after the saint's death.

385 The 'knoll among the fields' where Columba held converse with angels was also the place where the saint's book and tunic were taken to induce rain to fall on the freshly sown fields (II 44). It has always been identified with the steep-sided hillock overlooking the machair near the gates of An Sithean farm. (The name *An Sithean* 'fairy mound' was the name applied to the hillock before interest in the saint revived; Reeves, p. 219n.) The modern name Cnoc nan Aingeal translates Adomnán's *colliculus Angelorum*; or, vice versa, Adomnán may prove the antiquity of the name. The earliest modern reference to 'Angel Hill' is by Pococke (*Tours*, p. 86), who visited in 1760. The Gaelic is first recorded by Pennant in 1772.

386 All four of these saints have been mentioned elsewhere in the *Life*; see nn. 68 (Cainnech), 131 (Brendan), 205 (Comgall), and 323 (Cormac). In this story, St Cormac is not given a role – perhaps indicating that some element in the tale has been lost. There are many other stories, more or less improbable, of a similar kind in which groups of saints are assembled together corroborating one another's holiness.

387 As Fowler, p. 147n., observed, this passage shows that the Gospel was read outside the church – 'to persons in the position of catechumens', he suggests. Warren, *Liturgy and Ritual*, p. 99, thought Adomnán referred to an additional Gospel reading immediately before the liturgy itself. I suspect it merely means there was no sermon between the Gospel and the commencement of the liturgy.

The celebration of the mass was, as the terms used for it indicate, a sacred mystery conducted by priest or bishop. This was so throughout Christendom: where churches were large buildings, a rood screen separated the celebrant from the people. In the Orthodox Church the celebration of mass remains a mystery, whereas in the West it has become progressively a more public action. The need for a screen was not present in the earliest churches: there the confirmed were admitted to the mystery, and catechumens not yet confirmed were excluded. As the Church grew to embrace the majority of the people, the screen came to divide the priest from the people as a whole, emphasizing the sacred mystery.

In many places, including Ireland and Scotland, it was convenient to build churches of very small size in which the priest could perform the liturgy while the faithful remained outside. Under such circumstances it appears that the early stages of the service took place outside, and that for the celebration itself the priest entered the building as he would otherwise enter the sanctuary.

Not all churches were built with this in mind. In Iona all the monks entered the church. We know from written sources that at Armagh and Kildare a large number of the faithful entered the church. In the case of Kildare, the evidence of Cogitosus's Life of St Brigit is specific that they used different doors from the ones used by the bishop and abbess, and were screened from the sanctuary, into which only the clergy and nuns entered. The great majority of churches in Ireland, Scotland and England, however, in the sixth and seventh centuries must have been like that on *Hinba*. Adomnán here provides the evidence for how the tiny churches known from archaeological evidence functioned; what is surprising is the implication that the brethren remained outside. This would have been less surprising if this were a church in a pastoral context with the laity remaining outside.

**388** THE CHURCH ON EIGG It is not certain from these words that there was a church on Eigg at this date. The earliest reference clearly implying a church is the annal for 617: 'the burning of Donnán of Eigg on 17 April with 150 martyrs' (Annals of Tigernach and additions to the Annals of Ulster; the number of martyrs conflicts with other sources). There was still a church there in 724, when the Annals of Ulster mention the death of Oan, *princeps Ego* 'erenach of Eigg', and in 752, when the Annals of Tigernach have the death of Cummíne Ua Becce, religious of *Eco* (presumably Eigg). The site of the monastery has been discussed by Macdonald, 'Two major early monasteries', pp. 57–64.

Two versions of the death of St Donnán are known, both printed with discussion by Reeves, pp. 303–9, but both now available in better editions. The Latin account in the Book of Leinster is probably the older, but its date is uncertain:

Eigg is the name of a spring in Aldasain. And there Donnán and his community suffered martyrdom. This is how it came about. A rich woman used to dwell there before the coming of Donnán and her flocks grazed there.

On account of the ill-feeling she had towards Donnán and his community, she persuaded a number of bandits to kill him. When these bandits arrived in Eigg, they found them chanting their psalms in the oratory and they could not kill them there. Donnán however said to his community:

'Let us go into the refectory so that these men may be able to kill us there where we do our living according to the demands of the body; since as long as we remain where we have done our all to please God, we cannot die, but where we have served the body, we may pay the price of the body.'

In this way, therefore, they were killed in their refectory on the eve of Easter. Fifty-four others died together alongside Donnán. (*Book of Leinster*, VI, 1688)

This story is repeated in the scholia of the earliest glossed copies of *Félire Oenguso*. The scholia in two late medieval copies instead relate in Irish how Donnán had approached Columba to be his soul-friend and Columba refused, saying: 'I will be soul-friend only to people of white martyrdom; that is, I will not be your soul-friend because you and all your community with you will suffer red martyrdom.'

**389** FERGNAE, FOURTH ABBOT OF IONA Fergnae seems to have joined the *familia* in St Columba's lifetime. He succeeded Lasrén as abbot in 605 and died in 623. He was commemorated on 2 March, MTall. During his abbacy the Annals of Tigernach record the destruction of a church on Tory Island in 617 and the (?re-)building of a church there in 621; the church here still belonged to the *familia* of Iona in AU 733.

Unlike his predecessors, Fergnae probably did not belong to the saint's kindred of Cenél Conaill, even though seventeenth-century scholars gave him a distant kinship (which Reeves incorporated in his Genealogical Table, p. 342). Early genealogical sources do not confirm this, while Middle Irish scholia refer to him as Fergnae *Brit* 'the Briton'. Herbert, *Iona, Kells, and Derry*, pp. 39–40, draws attention to his having *cognati* in Britain according to the late Life of St Baithéne (which exists only in a late-thirteenth-century version, very brief, and based in part on Adomnán); Reeves, p. 463, also referred to this, supposing the British connection to have been on his mother's side. This would be so if *cognatus* is used in its strict sense, 'relative by marriage'.

**390** The word *exedra* 'alcove, recess' (originally from Greek) has been much discussed, most recently by Macdonald, 'Monastery and monastic life', pp. 283–4. Its use in *De Locis Sanctis* I 7 is very like this passage, and in both the word means 'side-chapel'. Warren, *Liturgy and Ritual*, p. 92, supposed it served as a sacristy.

391 Adomnán uses strong, formal language here, that Commán told him the story *sub testificatione* 'in sworn witness'. He uses such words elsewhere, usually of statements made in the presence of his predecessors Fergnae or Ségéne, from which Dr Herbert inferred (see Introduction, p. 40) that formal testimonies were taken in the 620s or thereabouts. Adomnán himself was not then present: does he imply, therefore, that statements continued to be put on record under oath in his own time? Perhaps so. In I 49 he mentions that Fínán, anchorite of Durrow, *protestatus est* 'testified in public' concerning the fulfilment of a prophecy, and adds that the statement was made to him, Adomnán, in person. The language is not as formal as in the present case, but the two together may hint at the continuing collection of sworn depositions.

392 Mentioned above, I 17; see also n. 101.

393 I have translated *alumnus* as 'foster-son' rather than 'pupil' because this is more appropriate in the other contexts where the word occurs in the text; see n. 55. The boy, Mes loen, is said to be studying *sapientiam*, which usually means 'sacred learning'; yet it is clear that he was a lay youth rather than one intending to become a monk. The story indicates, therefore, that children might be fostered by churchmen and educated in sacred learning, even where there was no intention to pursue the religious life. The boy's disobedience, however, may have coloured the story: perhaps he was intended for the church but failed to live up to expectations. The saint's reference to his living *luxuriose* should be interpreted in the light of the common use of *luxuria* as one of the seven sins, lechery.

394 On Columba's hut, see n. 127.

395 Adomnán refers to the chronologically displaced story, II 28, in which the season is said to be 'early summer'. Linking this passage with the previous story, III 22, it seems that Columba 'began to live in pilgrimage in Britain' at this time of year. More precisely, he expected to die on the thirtieth anniversary of his beginning his pilgrimage in Britain, but he was left to live a further four years. Between the end of III 22 and the beginning of III 23, Adomnán is saying, not quite directly, that Columba's pilgrimage began on the same date as he died. Now, later tradition specifically gives the date of his landing in Iona as the eve of Whitsunday (Middle Irish homily, § 51); in 563 this day fell

on 12 May according to the orthodox Easter calculation, but using the Irish table (*Peritia* 6/7 (1987–8), 234–5, cyclic year 42) the date comes out as 9 June, the date of Columba's death. Could this be coincidence? Or may we accept that later tradition was correct, preserving the date in relation to the Church's calendar, whether or not anyone remembered that the movable feasts would have all changed along with Easter?

**396** The words *desiderio desideraui* 'with desire I have desired' are quoted from Luke 22:15.

**397** See II 28.

**398** Prov. 15:13. Adomnán's quotation, however, does not follow the Vulgate but the Greek text, the Septuagint. This indicates that the quotation is used at secondhand, since the passage is so translated from the Greek in Evagrius's Life of St Antony, c. 67.

**399** These words are largely a quotation from Evagrius's Life of St Antony, c. 18.

**400** This usage is borrowed from Evagrius's Life of St Antony, c. 15: 'The Lord entrusted our soul to us; let us keep the loan as we received it'. Compare 1 Tim. 6:20, 2 Tim. 1:12, 14.

**401** *Per parasticiam ecclesiae* is a puzzling phrase. The word *parasticia* occurs nowhere else. O'Donnell, translating the passage into Irish in 1532, took it to mean 'wall': 'And he said further that wondrous was the subtilty of angels, for he had seen the angel passing through the walls (*tria balla*) of the monastery outward and inward doing no hurt nor harm neither to himself nor to the walls' (§ 359). A medieval guess is found in the Life in *Codex Salmanticensis*, § 31, where the phrase is changed to *culmen ecclesie* 'through the roof of the church', which Reeves, p. 230n., accepted. The Andersons, p. 112n., follow, adding only that 'there was no vent in the church roof', and translating 'roof-courses' (p. 521). Since Reeves, only MacCarthy, p. 171n., has offered a further guess, rendering *para posticiam* 'by the back gate of the church' in his note and 'through the vestibule' in his text; he is not persuasive.

**402** The Lord's night means from dusk on Saturday night until dawn on Sunday; Sunday itself began with vespers on Saturday night. In what follows, 'Sabbath' refers to Saturday (as it still does to Jews), the seventh day when the Lord rested; the Lord's day, Sunday, was the start of the new week.

**403** There is a play on words: *sabbatizare* means 'to keep the Sabbath', but having explained the Hebrew sense, Columba means also 'when I shall rest after my labours'.

**404** Josh. 23:14, 1 Kings 2:2.

**405** Adomnán here quotes again from Evagrius's Life of St Antony, c. 58: 'Indeed, my dear ones, as scripture saith, I shall go the way of my fathers. For now my Lord invites me.' The words *patrum gradiar uiam* (*gradior* in Evagrius) are not a direct quotation from the Vulgate.

**406** On crosses, see n. 196. On the use of the millstone as a cross-base, Anderson and Anderson, p. 115, suggest that this was a wooden cross fixed in the hole on the upper side of a hand-quern. Many small quernstones were turned up in excavations at Dunadd in 1905; one of them bears an incised cross, which links it with crosses of Iona, as Ewen Campbell has shown, 'A cross-marked quern', pp. 60–64. In the face of this evidence for the use of hand-querns it seems needless to conjecture the early existence of a mill in Iona, but it should be said that such a hand-quern would not support even a wooden cross more than two or three feet tall. Table-mounted querns, both stones pierced by a spindle, are known from early medieval contexts, and these may be up to three feet in diameter. A stone of this kind could support a rather taller cross, held in the socket with wedges. Actual mills, powered by a horizontal water-wheel on a vertical axle, were in use in Ireland by the seventh century; these could be larger, but clear evidence is not available from the sixth century.

A late medieval example of an ordinary millstone, perhaps reused as the base of a wooden cross, was found beside the Street of the Dead (Barber, 'Excavations', p. 308 and plate 19a; RCAHMS, *Iona*, p. 239).

**407** The cows were milked in the *bocetum*, Irish *buaile* 'booley, cattle pen'; one should not think of a milking-parlour or dairy. The distance from the monastery may suggest that it was merely a pen in the field where they were grazed. Reeves, p. 231n., gives other references; two of these are to Lives probably written in the eighth century: the Life of St Lugidus, § 21, and the Life of St Ruadán, § 8, to which one may add another of similar date in the Life of St Fínán, § 32. One may also compare a similar word with the same meaning in two seventh-century Latin sources, *boellium* in Cogitosus's Life of St Brigit, c. 16, and *bovellum* in *Hib.* 53. 5.

**408** Mayer, 'Das mantische Pferd', p. 133, cites this story as the earliest in his collection of references to horses with prophetic or similar gifts. The closest parallel is in the Life of St Folcwin of Lobbes.

In 1906, when a piece of earthwork behind the house Clachanach was being cleared away to permit a building addition, the skeleton of a small horse was found firmly embedded six feet deep in the embankment. The ninth Duke of Argyll, reporting this in his book *Passages from the Past*, speculated as to whether this was Columba's friend. His description hardly gives an archaeological context. Apart from the evidence that horsemeat was eaten (see n. 118), I suspect that more than one horse has died in Iona during the past 1,400 years.

**409** See also I 30. The little hill is probably that now called Cnoc nan Carnan, across the metalled road from the gate to the Abbey. This knoll is within the vallum of the monastery.

**410** Ps. 34:10–11.

**411** ST COLUMBA'S BURIAL PLACE Although Adomnán speaks later of St Columba's burial in Iona, this is the only reference to his grave. It would appear that when Adomnán wrote, Columba lay in a simple grave marked with a stone, probably like many of the stones now in the Abbey Museum. The expression he uses for the memorial, *titulus monumenti*, is taken from the Bible, Gen. 35:20. About the middle of the eighth century, however, Columba's body was enshrined in an elaborate reliquary of precious metal. This reliquary was the object for which the Vikings killed the monk Blathmac in Iona in 825 – an event described in verse by Walahfrid Strabo about 840. The fate of the reliquary is uncertain, but relics of St Columba were venerated at more than one place, in both Ireland and Scotland, in the ninth century and after. In the early eighteenth century Fr Thomas Innes reports a local belief that the saint's corporeal relics were not removed from the island: 'It is the constant tradition and belief of the inhabitants of Ycolmkill and of the neighbourhood at this day that St Columba's body lies still in this island, being hidden by pious people at the time of the new Reformation, in some secure and private place in or about the church, as it used frequently to be in former times during the ravages of the infidel Danes' (*Civil and Ecclesiastical History*, p. 214; quoted as 'declamation' by Reeves, p. 316).

The location (or locations) of the original grave and of the eighth-century shrine are now irrecoverable. I know no reference to either between the account of Blathmac's death and the seventeenth century. In 1693 John Fraser of Tiree, describing Iona, mentions 'Columbus his buriall there in a litle Capell be himselfe'. In 1698 William Sacheverell refers, p. 101, to 'the monument of Columbus' at the west end of the church, adding, 'At the end of this monument stands a little chapel.' The configuration he meant is unclear, but about the same date Martin, *Western Isles*, p. 258, records: 'Near to the West-end of the Church in a little Cell lies Columbus his Tomb, but without inscription.' This corresponds to St Columba's Chapel, rebuilt in 1962, beside the west door of the abbey. The chapel, whose original parts are of the local Torridonian flagstone, is dated by the RCAHMS, *Iona*, p. 42, to the ninth or tenth century. Ian Fisher suggests there, p. 48, that this was 'St Columb Cille's little church' visited with reverence by King Magnus Barelegs of Norway in 1098, and argues that the first chapel on this site may have been built to mark the original grave at the time when the saint's remains were exhumed and enshrined in the main church.

While largely conjecture, this makes more sense than Reeves's presumption, p. 317n., that St Columba's grave was in the main Reilig Odrain, and much more sense than the arguments of Drummond, *PSAS* 10 (1872–4), 613, and Skene, ibid., 11 (1874–6), 330–49, that the original grave was at Cladh an Dìsirt, several hundred yards north of the abbey (and outside the vallum), which they thought was the site of the early monastery. It was their argument that gave the name St Columba's Pillow to the cross-marked rounded pebble found (by Mr MacArthur, tenant of Clachanach farm) at Cladh an Dìsirt about 1870, now in the Abbey Museum, no. 26 (RCAHMS, *Iona*, pp. 188–9). There are four other cross-marked pebbles from Iona (ibid., p. 16). The cross on St Columba's Pillow is of a later style than Columba's or perhaps even Adomnán's time. The name was obviously inspired by Adomnán's words here.

**412** Columba's last words, as the Andersons noted, p. 24, might have been remembered and retold by Diarmait, who alone could hear them. On the other hand, the words of Jesus echoed at the beginning of this speech remind one of the last words attributed by Bede to St Cuthbert. Columba's words are *inter uos motuam et non fictam habeatis caritatem cum* *pace*; Cuthbert's last words begin, *pacem, inquit, inter uos semper et caritatem custodite diuinam* 'always keep peace and divine charity among you' (Bede's Life of St Cuthbert, c. 39). Bede describes Cuthbert's last days in the words of Herefrith, priest of Lindisfarne, from whom he may indeed have learnt the account. His written source, the anonymous Lindisfarne Life, gives no last words. It is no less possible, however, that Bede has put words into Cuthbert's mouth; the speech goes on to express views of great importance to Bede on the unity of the Church and, in particular, the need to observe Easter at the proper time. Adomnán likewise may have expressed his own views through Columba's words; the Andersons suggest that he implies 'that dissension over the date of Easter was a sin greater than error in its date'; see above, n. 67.

Bede wrote twenty years after Adomnán but did not know this Life. He was, however, influenced by Evagrius's Life of St Antony, c. 58, which was also known to and quoted by Adomnán.

**413** Here again Adomnán quotes from Evagrius's Life of St Antony, c. 59.

**414** Not located. Colgan, *Trias*, p. 386, took it to be in Ulster, a probable inference from Adomnán but not a necessary one in the context. In his *Acta*, p. 453, he emended the reading to a different place-name. Hogan, *Onomasticon*, p. 263, seems to have overlooked Adomnán, but cites the Life of St Columba in *Codex Salmanticensis*; this Life is an abbreviation, which has taken this passage directly from Adomnán, yet Hogan none the less locates the place 'in or nr. Leix', a wild shot.

**415** Irish *muirbolc* ('sea bag') means 'bay', so this is 'the Great Bay'. Compare *Muirbolc Paradisi* (I 13 and n. 93). Since we are told that Fergnae 'spent the rest of his days on *Hinba*', the place of the anchorites at the Great Bay must be in that island. This fact has played its part in attempts to locate *Hinba* (see n. 194).

**416** Ernéne moccu Fir Roíde must have lived at least into the 640s if the young Adomnán (born in 628) had met him.

Druim Tuama, first mentioned here, appears to be a Columban foundation; it was certainly part of the *familia* in the seventh century. The name survives as Drumhome, south of Donegal, in the territory of Cenél Conaill, the kindred to which Adomnán belonged. It seems likely that this story takes us back to a period before Adomnán had left his native district to pursue his studies. In this context Ernéne's 'firmly attesting' (*cum grandi testificatione*) the truth of the story can hardly imply a formal deposition (see n. 15). Reeves, p. 238n., points out that the remains of the old (presumably late medieval) church stood in the ancient burial ground at Mullinacross near the coast (now briefly described by Lacy, *Archaeological Survey*, p. 284). It is next mentioned in AU 921: 'Cináed son of Domnaill, erenach of Derry and Druim Tuama, and chief counsellor of Cenél Conaill of the North died.' This shows that the church was still part of the *familia* and closely associated with Derry, and with Columba's kindred of Cenél Conaill, more than two hundred years after Adomnán's time. Reeves, p. xlin., cites from Hugh Ward's *Sancti Rumoldi Acta* (1631), p. 219, a contemporary story of a miracle at St Adomnán's holy well in the parish of Drumhome.

**417** The River Finn rises near Fintown, Co. Donegal, and flows eastward to join the River Mourne near Strabane; the river from the confluence to its outfall in Lough Foyle is now known as the River Foyle, which flows past the Columban monastery of Derry. The teams of fishermen presumably worked the lower reaches of the river.

**418** On St Columba's burial place, see n. 411.

**419** The formula *quantus et qualis* 'how great and how special' is used several times in the Life. The passage here nearly resembles *De Locis Sanctis* I 1: 'Thus one should carefully note how great and how special is the honour which this chosen and famous city has in the sight of the eternal Father.'

**420** 'This was the end of life for Antony, and the beginning of his rewards' (c. 60) is one source in the Life of St Antony. In what follows Adomnán has fused this with another passage, 'He was added to his fathers according to the order of the scriptures' (c. 59). This last phrase sets Adomnán off on a doxology that does not so much quote phrases from the Bible as reassemble words and ideas; he follows in part a similar passage of Sulpicius Severus in a letter about the death of St Martin (*Ep*. 2.8).

**421** The continuance of such manifestations at the grave of the saint is something not mentioned of other Irish saints. Adomnán, however, does not say that he had himself witnessed it, although he has said elsewhere (II 45–6) how he had other experiences that he regarded as posthumous miracles of St Columba.

**422** In describing the spread of St Columba's reputation, Adomnán's exaggeration is derived from Evagrius's Life of St Antony, c. 61.

**423** Adomnán has presented an example at I 23 of how, after a book had been transcribed, the copy should be compared with the original; this took two people, one to read the first text and another to follow in the second. That story in effect sets a bad example, inasmuch as Columba is represented as not needing to make this check. The injunction here, calling on later copyists to check their copies in this way, is similar to that found in several works of the Fathers. The earliest example of it so far pointed out was in a lost work by the second-century Greek Father, Irenaeus, *Peri ogdoados*, quoted by a later Greek writer, Eusebius, in his own *Historia Ecclesiastica* V 20. Reeves, p. 242n., and Fowler, p. 165n., quote the Greek. Eusebius was translated into Latin in the late fourth century by Rufinus, whose work was widely circulated and was probably known to Adomnán. It is, for example, quoted in the *Hibernensis*. The same passage of Irenaeus was quoted with a little variation by Jerome, *De uiris illustribus*, c. 35, where he also gives a Latin rendering. This work too was probably available to Adomnán. Brüning, p. 253, was convinced that Jerome was Adomnán's immediate model. To my mind, however, Adomnán has put the injunction so completely into his own words that he was not copying but adapting a well-known formula.

**424** On the scribe Dorbbéne, see above, pp. 75–6, 235–6. This form of invitation to the reader to pray for the copyist who wrote the manuscript is found, sometimes in similar words, in other manuscripts from Ireland. For example, a gospel book a century later than Dorbbéne's copy of Adomnán ends with these words: 'Whoever may read and understand this narrative, let him pray for Mac Regol who copied it.' Hence the book, now Oxford, Bodleian Library, MS Auct. D. 2. 19, is known as Mac Regol's Gospels.

At the end of his *De Locis Sanctis*, Adomnán, as the author, invited a prayer for himself, but first for Arculf, whose oral account he had set down. In its opening words, it resembles his injunction to copyists here (see previous note):

I beseech any who wish to read these brief books to implore divine mercy for the holy priest Arculf, who, being a frequenter of the holy places, most willingly dictated to us his experiences of them. And I have set them forth, albeit in a lowly style, though daily beset by laborious and almost insupportable business from every quarter. Thus I admonish the reader of these experiences that he neglect not to pray Christ the judge of generations on behalf of me, the writer, a pitiable sinner.

AMEN.

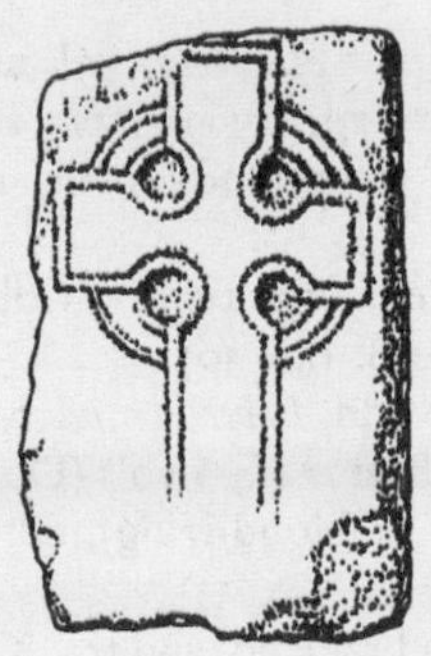

# Bibliography

*Medieval sources [to 1540]*

*Actus Siluestri*, ed. B. Mombritius, *Sanctuarium sue Vitae sanctorum* (Milan, 1480; new edn Solesme, 1910), II, 508–31.

Adomnán, *De Locis Sanctis*, ed. and trs. D. Meehan and L. Bieler, Scriptores Latini Hiberniae 3 (Dublin, 1958).

*Amrae Coluimb Chille* (Praise of Columb Cille), ed. and trs. W. Stokes, 'The Bodleian Amra Choluimb Chille', *Revue celtique*, 20 (1899), 30–55, 132–83, 248–89, 400–437, and 21 (1900), 133–6.

Annals of Tigernach, Third fragment (AD 489–766), ed. and trs. W. Stokes, *Revue celtique*, 17 (1896), 116–263.

Annals of Ulster, ed. and trs. S. Mac Airt and G. Mac Niocaill, *The Annals of Ulster (to AD 1131)* (Dublin, 1983)

*Apgitir Chrábaid* (Alphabet of Piety), ed. and trs. V. E. Hull, *Celtica*, 8 (1968), 44–89.

*Bechbretha* (Bee judgements), ed. and trs. T. M. Charles-Edwards and F. Kelly (Dublin, 1983).

Bede, *Historia ecclesiastica gentis Anglorum*, ed. and trs. B. Colgrave and R. A. B. Mynors (Oxford, 1969); trs. L. Sherley-Price, R. E. Latham, D. H. Farmer (Harmondsworth, 1955; 3rd edn, London, 1990).

—, Life of St Cuthbert, ed. and trs. B. Colgrave, *Two Lives of St Cuthbert* (Cambridge, 1940), 142–307.

Book of Armagh, ed. J. Gwynn, *Liber Ardmachanus* (Dublin, 1913).

Book of Leinster, ed. R. I. Best *et al.*, 6 vols (Dublin, 1954–83).

*Bretha Crólige* (Judgements of blood-lying), ed. and trs. D. A. Binchy, *Ériu*, 12 (1934–8), 1–77.

*Cáin Adomnáin* (Adomnán's Law), ed. and trs. K. Meyer (Oxford, 1905).

*Codex Salmanticensis*, ed. W. W. Heist, *Vitae Sanctorum Hiberniae e codice olim Salmanticensi* (Brussels, 1965).

Cogitosus, Life of St Brigit, ed. J. Bolland, *Acta Sanctorum*, Feb. I

(Antwerp, 1658), 135–41; trs. S. Connolly and J.-M. Picard, *Journal of the Royal Society of Antiquaries of Ireland*, 117 (1987), 5–27.

*Coibnes Uisci Thairidne* (Pedigree of conducted water), ed. and trs. D. A. Binchy, 'Irish law tracts re-edited', *Ériu*, 17 (1955), 52–85.

Columbanus, Letters, ed. and trs. G. S. M. Walker, *Sancti Columbani Opera*, Scriptores Latini Hiberniae 2 (Dublin, 1957), 2–56.

Columb Cille's address to Ireland, ed. and trs. E. O'Curry in W. Reeves, *The Life of Columba, Founder of Hy, written by Adamnan* (Dublin and Edinburgh, 1857), 285–9.

Constantius, Life of St Germanus, ed. W. Levison, MGH *Scriptores rerum Merovingicarum* (1884–1920), VII, 247–83.

Dícuil, *Liber de mensura orbis terrae*, ed. and trs. J. J. Tierney and L. Bieler, Scriptores Latini Hiberniae 6 (Dublin, 1967).

Eusebius, *Historia ecclesiastica*, ed. T. Mommsen (Berlin, 1903–9).

Evagrius (trs.), Life of St Antony, *PL* LXXIII, 125–70.

*Félire Oenguso* (Martyrology of Oengus), ed. and trs. W. Stokes, Henry Bradshaw Society 29 (London, 1905; rep. Dublin, 1984).

First Life of St Brigit, ed. J. Colgan, *Trias Thaumaturga* (Louvain, 1647), 527–42; trs. S. Connolly, *Journal of the Royal Society of Antiquaries of Ireland*, 119 (1989), 5–49.

Genealogies of Saints, ed. P. Ó Riain, *Corpus Genealogiarum Sanctorum Hiberniae* (Dublin, 1985).

Gerald of Wales, *Topographia Hiberniae*, ed. J. F. Dimock, Rolls Series 21 (London, 1861–91), V, 3–204; trs. J. J. O'Meara (Harmondsworth, 1982).

Gildas, *De Excidio Britanniae*, ed. and trs. M. Winterbottom (Chichester, 1978).

—, Fragments of lost letters, in *De Excidio Britanniae*, ed. and trs. M. Winterbottom (Chichester, 1978), 143–5.

Gregory the Great, Dialogues, ed. A. de Vogüé (Paris, 1978–80).

*Hibernensis, Collectio canonum*, ed. F. W. H. Wasserschleben, 2nd edn (Leipzig, 1885).

*Historia Brittonum*, ed. T. Mommsen, MGH *Auctores Antiquissimi* XIII (Berlin, 1892–8), 143–219.

*Liber Hymnorum*, ed. J. H. Bernard and R. Atkinson, *The Irish Liber Hymnorum*, 2 vols, Henry Bradshaw Society 13–14 (London, 1898).

Life of St Cainnech, ed. W. W. Heist, *Vitae Sanctorum Hiberniae e codice Salmanticensi* (Brussels, 1965), 182–98.

Life of St Colmán Elo, ed. W. W. Heist, *Vitae Sanctorum Hiberniae e codice Salmanticensi* (Brussels, 1965), 209–24.

Life of St Comgall, ed. C. Plummer, *Vitae Sanctorum Hiberniae* (Oxford, 1910), II, 3–21.

Life of St Cuthbert, ed. and trs. B. Colgrave, *Two Lives of St Cuthbert* (Cambridge, 1940), 60–139.

Life of St Fínán, ed. W. W. Heist, *Vitae Sanctorum Hiberniae e codice Salmanticensi* (Brussels, 1965), 153–60.

Life of St Fintan of Clonenagh, ed. W. W. Heist, *Vitae Sanctorum Hiberniae e codice Salmanticensi* (Brussels, 1965), 145–53; ed. C. Plummer, *Vitae Sanctorum Hiberniae* (Oxford, 1910), II, 96–106.

Life of St Fintan or Munnu, ed. W. W. Heist, *Vitae Sanctorum Hiberniae e codice Salmanticensi* (Brussels, 1965), 198–209.

Life of St Kentigern, ed. and trs. A. P. Forbes, *The Lives of Saint Ninian and St Kentigern* (Edinburgh, 1874).

Life of St Lugidus or Molua, ed. W. W. Heist, *Vitae Sanctorum Hiberniae e codice Salmanticensi* (Brussels, 1965), 131–45.

Life of St Molaisse, ed. C. Plummer, *Vitae Sanctorum Hiberniae* (Oxford, 1910), II, 131–40.

Life of St Ruadán, ed. W. W. Heist, *Vitae Sanctorum Hiberniae e codice Salmanticensi* (Brussels, 1965), 160–67.

Martyrology of Tallaght, ed. H. J. Lawlor and R. I. Best, Henry Bradshaw Society 68 (London, 1931).

Middle Irish homily on St Ciarán, ed. and trs. W. Stokes, *Lives of Saints from the Book of Lismore* (Oxford, 1890), 117–34, 262–80.

Middle Irish homily on St Columba, ed. and trs. M. Herbert, *Iona, Kells, and Derry* (Oxford, 1988), 211–86.

Muirchú, Life of St Patrick, ed. and trs. L. Bieler, *The Patrician Texts in the Book of Armagh*, Scriptores Latini Hiberniae 10 (Dublin, 1979), 62–122.

Notker, Martyrology, *PL* CXXXI, 1029–1164.

O'Donnell, Manus, *Beatha Coluimb Chille*, ed. and trs. A. O'Kelleher and G. Schoepperle (Urbana, Ill., 1918; rep. Dublin, 1994).

Reginald of Durham, Life of St Oswald (part), ed. T. Arnold, Rolls Series 75 (London, 1882–5), I, 326–85.

*Saltair Coluimb Chille* (Psalter of Columb Cille), MS Oxford, Bodleian Library, Laud misc. 615.

*Sanas Cormaic* (Cormac's Glossary), ed. K. Meyer, *Anecdota from Irish Manuscripts*, IV (Halle, 1912).

*Senchus Fer nAlban* ('Genealogy of the men of Scotland'), ed. and trs. J. W. M. Bannerman, *Studies in the History of Dalriada* (Edinburgh, 1974), 41–9.

Sulpicius Severus, Life of St Martin, ed. J. Fontaine, Sources chrétiennes

133 (Paris, 1967); trs. F. R. Hoare, *The Western Fathers* (London, 1954).

Tírechán, ed. and trs. L. Bieler, *The Patrician Texts in the Book of Armagh*, Scriptores Latini Hiberniae 10 (Dublin, 1979), 124–62.

Tripartite Life of St Patrick, ed. K. Mulchrone (Dublin, 1939); trs. W. Stokes, Rolls Series 88 (London, 1887).

Walahfrid Strabo, Life of Blathmac, ed. E. Dümmler, MGH *Poetae Latini Aevi Carolini*, II (1884), 297–301; (part) trs. A. O. Anderson, *Early Sources of Scottish History*, 2 vols (Edinburgh, 1922; rep. Stamford, 1990), I, 263–5.

*Later works [after 1540]*

Anderson, A. O., and M. O. Anderson, *Adomnan's Life of Columba* (Edinburgh, 1961; 2nd edn, Oxford, 1991).

Anderson, M. O., *Kings and Kingship in Early Scotland* (Edinburgh, 1974; 2nd edn, Edinburgh, 1980).

Argyll, [G. D. Campbell, 8th] Duke of, *Iona* (London, 1870) .

Bannerman, J. W. M., *Studies in the History of Dalriada* (Edinburgh, 1974).

Barber, J. W., 'Excavations on Iona, 1979', *Proceedings of the Society of Antiquaries of Scotland*, 111 (1981), 282–380.

Bieler, L., Review of Anderson and Anderson, *Irish Historical Studies*, 13 (1962–3), 175–84.

—, *The Irish Penitentials*, Scriptores Latini Hiberniae 5 (Dublin, 1963).

—, *The Patrician Texts in the Book of Armagh*, Scriptores Latini Hiberniae 10 (Dublin, 1979).

Binchy, D. A., Review of Anderson and Anderson, *Studia Hibernica*, 3 (1963), 193–5.

—, 'The Fair of Tailtiu and the Feast of Tara', *Ériu*, 18 (1958), 113–38.

Boswell, J., *Boswell's Journal of a Tour in the Hebrides with Samuel Johnson, Ll.D., now first published from the original manuscript*, ed. F. A. Pottle and C. H. Bennett (London, 1936).

Bourke, C., 'Early Irish hand-bells', *Journal of the Royal Society of Antiquaries of Ireland*, 110 (1980), 52–66.

—, 'Early Irish bells', *Seanchas Dhroim Mór*, 4 (1986), 27–38.

Branford, V. V., *St Columba: a study of social inheritance and spiritual development* (Edinburgh, 1912).

Bromwich, R., *Trioedd Ynys Prydain* (Cardiff, 1961; 2nd edn, 1978).

Brüning, G., 'Adamnans Vita Columbae und ihre Ableitungen', *Zeitschrift für celtische Philologie*, 11 (1915–17), 213–304.

Bullough, D. A., 'Columba, Adomnan, and the achievement of Iona', *Scottish Historical Review*, 43 (1963–4), 111–30, and 44 (1964–5), 17–33.

Bury, J. B., *The Life of St Patrick and his place in history* (London, 1905).

Byrne, F. J., 'The Ireland of St Columba', *Historical Studies*, 5 (1965), 37–58.

—, *Irish Kings and High Kings* (London, 1973).

Campbell, D., 'Parish of Kilfinichen and Kilvickeuen', in *The Statistical Account of Scotland*, ed. J. Sinclair, 21 vols (Edinburgh, 1791–9), XIV (1792), 170–211.

Campbell, E. N., 'A cross-marked quern from Dunadd and other evidence for relations between Dunadd and Iona', *Proceedings of the Society of Antiquaries of Scotland*, 117 (1987), 59–71.

Campbell, J. L., *Canna: the story of a Hebridean island* (Oxford, 1984).

Charles-Edwards, T. M., 'The social background to Irish *peregrinatio*', *Celtica*, 11 (1976), 43–59.

—, and F. Kelly, *Bechbretha* (Dublin, 1983).

Clark, F. W., 'United parish of Kilfinichen and Kilviceuen. Iona', *New Statistical Account of Scotland*, 15 vols (Edinburgh, 1845), VII.ii, 312–39.

Colgan, J., *Acta Sanctorum Hiberniae* (Louvain, 1645; rep. Dublin, 1947).

—, *Trias Thaumaturga* (Louvain, 1647).

Colgrave, B., *Two Lives of St Cuthbert* (Cambridge, 1940).

Darling, F. F., and J. M. Boyd, *The Highlands and Islands*, New Naturalist 6 (London, 1964; 2nd edn, London, 1969).

Dillon, M., *Early Irish Literature* (Chicago, 1948).

Doherty, C., 'The cult of St Patrick and the politics of Armagh in the seventh century', in J.-M. Picard (ed.), *Ireland and Northern France AD 600–850*, (Dublin, 1991), 53–94.

Dumville, D. N., '*Echtrae* and *immram*: some problems of definition', *Ériu*, 27 (1976), 73–94.

—, '*Primarius cohortis* in Adomnán's Life of Columba', *Scottish Gaelic Studies*, 13 (1978–81), 130–31.

Dunbar, J. G., and I. Fisher, 'Sgor nam Ban-naomha (Cliff of the Holy Women), Isle of Canna', *Scottish Archaeological Forum*, 5 (1973), 71–5.

Enright, M. J., *Iona, Tara, and Soissons: the origins of the royal anointing ritual*, Arbeiten für Frühmittelalterforschung 17 (Berlin, 1985).

—, 'Royal succession and abbatial prerogative in Adomnán's *Vita Columbae*', *Peritia*, 4 (1985) [1987], 83–103.

Feachem, R. W., 'Fortifications', in F. T. Wainwright (ed.), *The Problem of the Picts* (Edinburgh, 1955; rep. Perth, 1980), 66–86.

Finlay, W. I. R., *Columba* (London, 1979).

Forbes, A. P. (trs.), *Life of Saint Columba, founder of Hy, written by Adamnan*, ed. W. F. Skene, The Historians of Scotland 6 (Edinburgh, 1874).

Fowler, E., and P. J. Fowler, 'Excavations on Tòrr an Aba, Iona, Argyll', *Proceedings of the Society of Antiquaries of Scotland*, 118 (1988), 181–201.

Fowler, J. T., *Adamnani Vita S. Columbae* (Oxford, 1894).

—, *Prophecies, Miracles, and Visions of St Columba* [*Columcille*] (London, 1895).

Fraser, J., 'Brief answer to Mr Wodrow's queries' [1701], in J. Maidment (ed.), *Analecta Scotica* (Edinburgh, 1834–7), I, 117–20.

—, 'A short description of I or Iona 1693', in A. Mitchell and J. T. Clark (eds.), *Geographical Collections relating to Scotland, compiled by Walter MacFarlane*, 3 vols, Scottish History Society (Edinburgh, 1906–8), II, 216–17.

Gaskell, J. P. W., *Morvern Transformed* (Cambridge, 1968).

Greene, D., 'The chariot as described in Irish literature', in A. C. Thomas (ed.), *The Iron Age in the Irish Sea Province* (London, 1972), 59–73.

Harvey, A. J. R., 'Retrieving the pronunciation of early insular Celtic scribes', *Celtica* 21 (1990), 178–90 and 22 (1991), 48–63.

Henderson, I. B., *The Picts* (London, 1967).

Herbert, M., *Iona, Kells, and Derry: the history and hagiography of the monastic familia of Columba* (Oxford, 1988).

—, 'The preface to *Amra Coluim Cille*', in D. Ó Corráin *et al.* (eds.), *Sages, Saints and Storytellers*. (Maynooth, Ireland,1989), 67–75.

Hogan, E., *Onomasticon Goedelicum* (Dublin, 1910).

Hughes, K. W., *The Church in Early Irish Society* (London, 1966).

—, and A. Hamlin, *The Modern Traveller to the Early Irish Church* (London, 1977).

Huyshe, W., *The Life of St Columba* [*Columb-Kille*], *AD 521–597* (London, 1906).

Innes, T. *Civil and Eclestiastical History of Scotland* (1729), ed. G. Grub (Aberdeen, 1853).

*Iona in 1771. An account by A Tourist, translated from the Irish* (Oban, 1883).

Kelly, F., *A Guide to Early Irish Law* (Dublin, 1988).

Lacy, B., *Archaeological Survey of Donegal* (Lifford, 1983).

Lamont, W. D., 'Where is Adamnan's Hinba?', *Notes and Queries of the Society of West Highland and Island Historical Research*, 7 (1978), 3–6.

—, 'Hinba once more', *Notes and Queries of the Society of West Highland and Island Historical Research* 12 (1980), 10–15.

Lanigan, J., *Ecclesiastical History of Ireland*, 4 vols (Dublin, 1822).

Levison, W., 'Konstantinische Schenkung und Silvester-Legende', *Miscellanea Francisco Ehrle*, Studi e testi 37–8 (Rome, 1924), II, 159–247.

Lucas, A. T., 'Footwear in Ireland', *Journal of the Co. Louth Archaeological and Historical Society*, 13 (1956), 309–94.

Macalister, R. A. S., *The Latin and Irish Lives of Ciarán* (London, 1921).

[MacCarthy, B.,] Review of Fowler, *Irish Ecclesiastical Record*, 3rd S., 16 (1895), 472–7.

MacCarthy, D., *Life of St Columba or Columbkille* (Dublin, 1861).

Macdonald, A. D. S., 'Two major early monasteries', *Scottish Archaeological Forum*, 5 (1973), 57–64.

—, 'Aspects of the monastery and monastic life in Adomnán's Life of Columba', *Peritia*, 3 (1984) [1986], 271–302.

—, 'Iona's style of government: the toponomastic evidence', *Peritia*, 4 (1985) [1987], 174–86.

MacKay, W. R., 'Hinba again', *Notes and Queries of the Society of West Highland and Island Historical Research*, 9 (1979), 8–17.

M'Lauchlan, T., *The Early Scottish Church: the ecclesiastical history of Scotland from the first to the twelfth century* (Edinburgh, 1865).

Macleod, Fiona [*pseud.*], *Iona* (London, 1910; rep. Edinburgh, 1982).

Mallory, J. P., 'The sword of the Ulster cycle', in B. G. Scott (ed.), *Studies on Early Medieval Ireland: essays in honour of M. V. Duignan* (Belfast, [1981]), 121–8.

Martin, M., *A Description of the Western Isles of Scotland* (London, 1703; 2nd edn, London, 1716).

Mayer, A., 'Das mantische Pferd', in B. Bischoff and S. Brechter (eds.), *Liber Floridus Paul Lehmann* (St Ottilien, 1950), 131–51.

Merry, E. C., *Odrun: the rune of the depths, given in dramatic pictures* (London, 1928).

—, *The Flaming Door: a preliminary study of the mission of the Celtic folk-soul by means of legends and myths* (London, 1936; rep. Edinburgh, 1983).

Miller, M., '*Hiberni reuersuri*', *Proceedings of the Society of Antiquaries of Scotland*, 110 (1978–80), 305–27.

Moisl, H., 'The Bernician royal dynasty and the Irish in the seventh century', *Peritia*, 2 (1983), 103–26.

Monro, D., Description of the Western Isles (1549), ed. R. W. Munro, *Monro's Western Isles of Scotland* (Edinburgh, 1961).

Nagy, J. F., 'The herons of Druim Ceat revisiting, and revisited', *Celtica*, 21 (1990), 368–76.

Nash-Williams, V. E., *Early Christian Monuments of Wales* (Cardiff, 1950).

*Native Steamboat Companion* (Edinburgh, 1845).

O'Brien, M. A., *Corpus Genealogiarum Hiberniae*, I (Dublin, 1962; 2nd edn, Dublin, 1976).

Ó Corráin, D., *Ireland before the Normans* (Dublin, 1972).

ÓCróinín, D., 'Early Irish annals from Easter-tables: a case restated', *Peritia*, 2 (1983) [1984], 74–86.

O Daly, M., 'A poem on the Airgialla', *Ériu*, 16 (1952), 179–88.

O'Grady, S. H., *Silva Gadelica*, 2 vols (London, 1892).

Ó Muirgheasa, E., 'The holy wells of Donegal', *Béaloideas*, 6 (1936), 143–62.

Ó Néill, P. P., 'The date and authorship of *Apgitir Chrábaid*: some internal evidence', in P. Ní Chatháin and M. Richter (eds.), *Irland und die Christenheit. Bibelstudien und Mission* (Stuttgart, 1987), 203–15.

O'Rahilly, T. F., *Early Irish History and Mythology* (Dublin, 1946).

Ó Riain, P., 'St Finnbarr: a study in a cult', *Journal of the Cork Historical and Archaeological Society*, 82 (1977), 63–82.

—, 'Cainnech *alias* Colum Cille, patron of Ossory', in P. de Brún *et al.* (eds.), *Folia Gadelica* (Cork, 1983), 20–35.

Pennant, T., *A Tour in Scotland, and Voyage to the Hebrides* (Chester and London, 1774).

Petrie, G., 'The Ecclesiastical Architecture of Ireland, anterior to the Anglo-Norman invasion; comprising an essay on the Round Towers of Ireland', *Transactions of the Royal Irish Academy*, 200 (1845).

Picard, J.-M., 'The purpose of Adomnán's *Vita Columbae*', *Peritia*, 1 (1982) [1983], 160–77.

—, 'Bede, Adomnán, and the writing of history', *Peritia*, 2 (1983) [1984], 50–70.

—, 'Structural patterns in early Hiberno-Latin hagiography', *Peritia*, 4 (1985) [1987], 67–82.

—, 'The strange death of Guaire mac Áedáin', in D. Ó Corráin *et al.* (eds.), *Sages, Saints, and Storytellers* (Maynooth, 1989), 367–75.

Plummer, C., *Venerabilis Baedae opera historica*, 2 vols (Oxford, 1896).

—, *Vitae Sanctorum Hiberniae*, 2 vols (Oxford, 1910).

—, Bethada Náem nÉrenn (Oxford, 1922).

Pococke, R., *Tours in Scotland 1747, 1750, 1760*, ed. D. W. Kemp, Scottish History Society, 1st S., 1 (Edinburgh, 1887).

RCAHMS Royal Commission on the Ancient and Historical Monuments of Scotland, *Argyll* III *Mull, Tiree, Coll & North Argyll* (Edinburgh, 1980).

—, *Argyll* IV *Iona* (Edinburgh, 1982).

—, *Argyll* V *Islay and Jura* (Edinburgh, 1984).

—, *Argyll* VI, VII *Mid Argyll and Cowal* (Edinburgh, 1988– ).

—, *Outer Hebrides, Skye and the Small Isles* (Edinburgh, 1928).

Reece, R., 'Recent work on Iona', *Scottish Archaeological Forum*, 5 (1973), 36–46.

Reeves, W., *The Life of St Columba, Founder of Hy, written by Adamnan* (Dublin and Edinburgh, 1857).

Reynolds, L. D., *et al.*, *Texts and Transmission: a survey of the Latin classics* (Oxford, 1983).

Ritchie, A., 'Orkney in the Pictish Kingdom', in A. C. Renfrew (ed.), *The Prehistory of Orkney* (Edinburgh, 1985), 183–204.

Ross, A., *Pagan Celtic Britain. Studies in Iconography and Tradition* (London, 1967).

Ryan, J., 'The abbatial succession at Clonmacnois', in J. Ryan (ed.) *Féil-sgríbhinn Eóin mhic Néill* (Dublin, 1940), 490–507.

Sacheverell, William, *An Account of the Isle of Man, with a Voyage to I-Columb-Kill* (London, 1702).

Schaumann, B. T., 'Early Irish manuscripts', *Expedition*, 21/3 (Philadelphia, 1979), 33–47.

Scott, B. G., 'Some conflicts and correspondences of evidence in the study of Irish archaeology and language', in B. G. Scott (ed.), *Studies on Early Medieval Ireland. Essays in honour of M. V. Duignan* (Belfast, [1981]), 115–19.

—, *Early Irish Ironworking* (Belfast, 1991).

Sharpe, R., 'Hiberno-Latin *laicus*, Irish *láech*, and the Devil's men', *Ériu*, 30 (1979), 75–92.

—, 'Gildas as a Father of the Church', in M. Lapidge and D. N. Dumville (eds.), *Gildas: New Approaches*, Studies in Celtic History 5 (Woodbridge, 1984), 193–205.

—, 'Maghnus Ó Domhnaill's source for Adomnán's *Vita S. Columbae and other vitae*', *Celtica*, 21 (1990), 604–7.

—, 'Saint Mauchteus, *discipulus Patricii*', in A. Bammesberger and A. Wollmann (eds.), *Britain, 400–600: Language and History*, Anglistische Forschungen 205 (Heidelberg, 1990), 85–93.

—, *Medieval Irish Saints' Lives: an introduction to Vitae Sanctorum Hiberniae* (Oxford, 1991).

Skene, W. F., 'Notes on the history and probable situation of the early establishments at Iona', *Proceedings of the Society of Antiquaries of Scotland*, 11 (1874–6), 330–49.

—, *Celtic Scotland. A History of Ancient Alban*, 3 vols (Edinburgh, 1876–80).

—, ed., and A. P. Forbes, trs., *Life of Saint Columba, Founder of Hy, written by Adamnan*, The Historians of Scotland (Edinburgh, 1874).

Small, A, and M. B. Cottam, *Craig Phadrig* (Dundee, 1972).

Smyth, A. P., 'The earliest Irish annals', *Proceedings of the Royal Irish Academy*, 72 C (1972), 1–48.

—, *Celtic Leinster* (Dublin, 1982).

—, *Warlords and Holy Men: Scotland 80–1000* (London, 1984).

Stokes, W., *Lives of Saints from the Book of Lismore* (Oxford, 1890).

—, *Félire Oengusso. The Martyrology of Oengus the Culdee*, Henry Bradshaw Society 29 (London, 1905; rep. Dublin, 1984).

—, and J. Strachan, *Thesaurus Palaeohibernicus*, 2 vols and suppl. (Cambridge, 1901–10; rep. Dublin, 1975).

Thomas, A. C., *A Provisional List of Imported Pottery in post-Roman western Britain and Ireland* (Redruth, 1981).

—, 'The "monster" episode in Adomnán's Life of St Columba', *Cryptozoology*, 7 (Tucson, Ariz., 1988), 38–45.

—, '*Gallici nautae de Galliarum prouinciis*—A sixth/seventh century trade with Gaul reconsidered', *Medieval Archaeology*, 34 (1990), 1–26.

—, *And Shall These Mute Stones Speak? Post-Roman inscriptions in Western Britain* (Cardiff, 1994).

Todd, J. H., *St Patrick, Apostle of Ireland* (Dublin, 1864).

Ussher, J., *The Whole Works*, ed. C. Elrington, 17 vols (Dublin, 1844–64).

Wainwright, F. T., 'The Picts and the Problem', in F. T. Wainwright (ed.), *The Problem of the Picts* (Edinburgh, 1955; rep. Perth, 1980), 1–53.

Walker, John, 'Report on the Hebrides' (1764), ed. M. M. McKay (Edinburgh, 1980).

Ward, C., 'Preliminary remarks to a report by Irish missionaries on their labours in the Hebrides, *c.* 1625', in C. Giblin (ed.), *Irish Franciscan Mission to Scotland 1619–1646* (Dublin, 1964), 47–50.

Ward, H., *Sancti Rumoldi Acta* (Louvain, 1631).

Warner, R. B., 'Irish place-names and archaeology. iii. A case study: Clochar macc nDaimini', *Bulletin of the Ulster Place-name Society*, New S., 4 (1982), 27–31.

Warren, F. E., *Liturgy and Ritual of the Celtic Church* (Oxford, 1881); rep. with Introduction by J. Stevenson, Studies in Celtic History 9 (Woodbridge, 1987).

Waterer, J. W., 'Irish book-satchels or budgets', *Medieval Archaeology*, 12 (1968), 70–82.

Watson, W. J., *Celtic Place-names of Scotland* (Edinburgh, 1926).

# Index